EUROPE'S POPULATION IN THE 1990s

Europe's Population in the 1990s

Edited by

DAVID COLEMAN

OXFORD UNIVERSITY PRESS
1996

Oxford University Press, Walton Street, Oxford OX2 6DP

Oxford New York
Athens Auckland Bangkok Bombay
Calcutta Cape Town Dar es Salaam Delhi
Florence Hong Kong Istanbul Karachi
Kuala Lumpur Madras Madrid Melbourne
Mexico City Nairobi Paris Singapore
Taipei Tokyo Toronto
and associated companies in
Berlin Ibadan

Oxford is a trade mark of Oxford University Press

Published in the United States
by Oxford University Press Inc., New York

British Library Cataloguing in Publication Data
Data available

Library of Congress Cataloging in Publication Data
Europe's population in the 1990s / edited by David Coleman.
Includes bibliographical references.
1. Europe—Population. I. Coleman, D. A.
HB3581.E884 1995 95-23844
304.6'09'049—dc20
ISBN 0-19-828894-8 (pbk)
ISBN 0-19-828896-4

Typeset by Best-set Typesetter Ltd., Hong Kong
Printed in Great Britain
on acid-free paper by
Bookcraft (Bath)Ltd, Midsomer Norton, Avon

PREFACE

The State of Europe's Population

This book describes and analyses key aspects of Europe's population at a time of great ferment in European political and social change, when more attention than ever has been focused not just upon individual states but upon developments embracing many European countries. One of the most prominent of the latter was the creation of the European Union (EU) in 1993 by the Maastricht Treaty. At the time of writing most of the states of the European Free Trade Area (EFTA) have applied to join this Union, which is already linked with the EFTA through the European Economic Area set up in 1993 to facilitate trade and labour movement. The Maastricht treaty marked a further step in the powers of the various EU bodies to press for greater harmonization and common practice between member states in a wide variety of economic, social, and welfare arrangements, notably through the 'social chapter'. Much of this is predicated upon a belief that the economies and societies of member states have been converging and that such convergence should be encouraged further. Indeed many enthusiasts for European unity look forward to a time when a common European identity may replace national distinctions. Demographic indicators (except perhaps those of mortality) are not yet included in the targets for convergence and neither are they yet subject to Commission Directives. Nonetheless, on conventional socio-economic models of fertility and other demographic variables, a greater demographic similarity between member states would be expected to follow convergence in economic and welfare arrangements. The international comparisons in demographic behaviour presented in this book provide important indicators of the extent to which convergence in social behaviour is, or is not, already proceeding in contemporary Europe.

In Eastern Europe, by contrast, economic and military alliances in the form of COMECON and the Warsaw Pact, the political suzerainty of the Soviet Union which held them together, and that Union itself have been swept away and with them an earlier attempt to impose a common economic and social order on several European states. The East European and Soviet communist dictatorships, which had appeared so durable and threatening since the end of the Second World War, all collapsed between 1989 and 1991. That has increased the number of independent European countries by eight, to over forty. As a result of the disappearance of the Soviet Union, which spanned Europe and Asia, the United Nations has extended the notional boundaries of Eastern Europe to include the European former members of the Soviet Union and in doing so extended Europe's edge to the North Pacific Ocean, with an increase in population size to match (table P.1).

Under communism, the Eastern countries developed various features in common which contrasted with the Western post-war demographic experience in birth rates (Grasland 1990), death rates (Höhn and Pollard 1991, Guo 1993), marriage, and household formation, transcending such differences as had existed before the Second World War (Leasure 1992, Monnier 1991). Most Eastern European countries never shared the West European marriage pattern of late marriage, common lifetime celibacy, and households based on nuclear rather than extended families (Hajnal 1965, Ní Bhrolcháin 1993, Rychtarikova 1993), although some countries which found themselves on the wrong side of the Iron Curtain after 1945, such as the Baltic states, the Czech lands, and East Germany, had, before that time, a distinctly Western form of family demography. Compared with the open societies of the West, such international migration as took place was limited and strictly controlled, most emphatically by the wall and minefields set in place in 1962 in order to prevent emigration from East to West Germany. Now, amidst radical economic and political reconstruction and uncertainty, vital rates are changing rapidly in some of these countries and most are experiencing international migration, both in and out, on a large scale for the first time since the Second World War and its huge refugee movements (Kosinski 1970). It may be that in the medium term they will rejoin the European demographic 'mainstream' (Coale 1992). In the short run, they are certainly becoming less like each other than they were, as birth rates and survival have fallen markedly in some of the less

TABLE P.1. *New Europe and its population, 1993*

Northern Europe	population (millions)	Western Europe	population (millions)	Southern Europe	population (millions)	Eastern Europe	population (millions)
Estonia	1.6	Austria	7.9	Albania	3.4	Belarus	10.3
Finland	5.1	Belgium	10.1	Bosnia	4.6	Bulgaria	9.0
Iceland	0.3	Denmark	5.2	Croatia	4.8	Czech Rep.	10.3
Ireland	3.6	France	57.5	Greece	10.3	Hungary	10.3
Latvia	2.6	Germany	80.3	Italy	57.3	Poland	38.4
Lithuania	3.7	Luxemburg	0.4	Macedonia	2.2	Romania	22.8
Norway	4.3	Netherlands	15.2	Malta	0.4	Moldova	4.4
Sweden	8.7	Switzerland	6.9	Portugal	9.9	Russia	148.7
UK	58.0			Slovenia	2.0	Slovak Rep.	5.3
				Spain	39.1	Ukraine	52.1
				Yugoslavia	10.5		
Total	87.7		183.5		144.2		311.5

TABLE P.1. (*cont.*)

Grand total	**727.0**
'Traditional' Western Europe (i.e., non-communist but including former East Germany)	380.2
Pre-1989 'Traditional' Eastern Europe (Warsaw Pact: communist countries except FSU, Albania, former Yugoslavia, and excluding East Germany)	96.1
Albania and former Yugoslavia (3.4m. + 24.0m.)	27.4
Former Soviet Union (European Republics only)	223.3
Grand Total	**727.0**
EU countries (12 members as in 1993, and including former East Germany)	346.7
EFTA countries (6 members as in 1993)	33.1
European Economic Area (EU + EFTA − Switzerland)	372.9

Notes: Population totals at 1 January 1993 except:
Estonia, Germany, Greece, Albania, Russia, Belorussia, Ukraine, Bosnia, Croatia, Macedonia: 1992;
Micro-states Andorra, Liechtenstein, Monaco, San Marino, Vatican City, etc., are excluded;
Cyprus, population 0.73m., is formally considered to be part of Asia;
Germany includes former East Germany (from 3 October 1990), population 15.8m. in 1992;
In 1993 'Yugoslavia' included only Serbia and Montenegro (from 27 April 1992);
Former Yugoslavia included Bosnia, Croatia, Macedonia, Montenegro, Serbia, Slovenia (24.0m.);
Non-European FSU countries not counted here: Armenia, Azerbaijan, Georgia, Kazakhstan, Kirghizstan, Turkmenistan, Uzbekistan.
Source: Council of Europe 1994, Population Reference Bureau Inc. 1994.

developed Eastern countries (Romania, Bulgaria, Russia) and much less in others (Poland, former Czechoslovakia).

Europe's populations, especially those in the West, have also shown novel changes in behaviour, sometimes called the 'second demographic transition', which may owe little to the direct influence of economic or political events. In the first demographic transition, from the late nineteenth century to the mid-twentieth century, life expectancy was transformed from about 40 years to about 70 and average family size of five or six children ever born was transformed to about two. Indeed in most countries a two-child family norm was established by the 1930s (Coale and Watkins 1986), while mortality continued to decline further until it reached an apparently stable position by the 1960s. All Europe, indeed all the industrial world, then seemed to share a general pattern of convergence towards similar demographic patterns, reflecting a similar economic basis, standards of living, welfare systems, education, and lifestyles (Blayo 1987, Blum 1989, Coleman 1991). European populations, economies, and welfare systems are still accommodating to the demographic ageing process, and the slow-down in population growth, which the reduction in fertility of the first demographic transition inevitably created.

Since the 1960s, a further phase of radical change has begun in Europe's demography, reflecting and contributing to new developments in social organization, beliefs, and attitudes, in economic progress, and in scientific and medical knowledge. In Western Europe, the reduction in mortality which stalled in the 1960s has resumed, so that survival improves year by year at all ages of life except for young adulthood, and now adds for the first time to the demographic ageing process. International migration from outside Europe, which began on a large scale in the 1950s and 1960s, was in decline by the mid-1980s. Since then very rapid increases, especially in those seeking asylum and in illegal immigrants, have taken gross immigration flows to Europe to record levels (over two million per year) and have pushed immigration control and the assimilation of foreign populations to the top of many countries' political agenda (Salt, Singleton, and Hogarth 1993, King 1993, Widgren 1994). The fertility decline which followed the 'baby boom' of the 1960s had ceased or had even reversed in some Northern European countries by the late 1980s. Concomitant declines to low levels of fertility, hitherto unknown, are in progress at the time of writing in Southern and Eastern Europe. In some countries in both these regions the number of deaths each year already exceeds the number of births.

A decline of the indigenous population seems imminent in some European countries. Europe as a whole is set to become demographically marginalized as almost all the additional three billion people forecast to be added to the world's population by 2025 will live in the third world, notably in Africa. Population ageing, and the demographic burden of dependency set in train by the first demographic transition, will be accelerated by the new decline in fertility (Gauthier 1993). These trends, whose effects upon the age structure can readily be forecast (Lutz 1991), have already attracted much policy concern because of their tendency to undermine the solvency of pay-as-you-go state pension and other welfare schemes, and their implications for medical costs and the size of the future work-force (Davis, Bernstam, and Ricardo-Campbell 1986, International Labour Organization 1989, Johnson, Conrad, and Thomson 1989, Ermisch 1990).

The establishment of low fertility since the end of the 'baby boom' has been accompanied by radical changes in living arrangements, sexual habits, and the position of marriage. Since the 1960s, divorce and abortion have been legalized and in most cases made readily accessible in most European countries. Welfare and legal systems have generally reduced or abolished the distinction between legitimate and illegitimate birth. Sexual activity begins at younger ages and is nearly universal before marriage. Cohabitation before marriage is normal in many countries. The popularity of marriage falls as the mean age of marriage rises to levels not seen since before the war. It is these latter changes in particular, allegedly reflecting a new primacy of individual aspiration over traditional restraints and obligations to a wider society, which are thought to warrant the term 'second demographic transition' (Lesthaeghe and Meekers 1986, van de Kaa 1987). The widespread prevalence of such forms of behaviour is not in doubt, although their trends may not mark such a clear discontinuity with the past as has been claimed (Cliquet 1991). Neither are concepts based on the supremacy of individualistic needs easily compatible with recent increases in fertility in some Northern European countries. Certainly the rate at which different populations have adopted these patterns have differed greatly, thereby creating a renewed diversity in Europe's population in matters of sexual behaviour, living arrangements, and family forms, as well as in the birth rate.

These new patterns of family formation and living arrangement have important consequences, among them: increasing the number of households and reducing their average size; increasing the number of one-parent families and 'reconstituted families', and thereby raising the number of children who experience unconventional parenting to a quarter or more in some countries. These trends increase welfare burdens and housing demand, and more controversially are claimed to have effects upon the personal and psychological development of the children themselves. As this book will show, the causes of these radical changes are also much disputed, with arguments, not all compatible, variously favouring changes in ideas and values, in economic trends, and in welfare and legal developments as the underlying causes. The relationships between fertility and other aspects of social behaviour may themselves be changing. For example, it has long been established that married women who worked had fewer children than those who did not, irrespective of the exact mechanism or the direction of causality involved. Recently, however, in Norway and some other countries, women at work have been shown to be just as likely as those at home to have a third child (Kravdal 1992), possibly as a result of improvements in family and child support.

A conference on Europe's Population in the 1990s was held at the London School of Economics in April 1993 under the aegis of the British Society for Population Studies, in order to review some of these demographic developments in Europe. This book presents revised and updated versions of the papers presented there, together with two papers specially written for this book in order to make the coverage of topics more complete. A few publications have already appeared on comparative European population (see Noin and Woods 1993, Blum and Rallu 1993). Published annual demographic and other statistics on a pan-European basis are more complete than in the past (Eurostat 1993, Council of Europe 1994). This volume, however, can claim to be the first collection of demographic papers all written in English to cover all major parts of Europe.

The first chapter, written especially for the book, describes and compares fertility patterns and trends in European countries.

Europe's population as a whole has the lowest fertility of any major block of countries, on average well below the replacement rate (equivalent to about 2.1 children per woman). In most Western countries, fertility has been below this figure since the early 1970s. But recent trends are divergent, not convergent. In Eastern Europe and the European parts of the former Soviet Union, where birth rates were generally higher than in the West, fertility is now declining, markedly in some countries, following the upheavals after 1989. The renewed decline in the birth rate in Southern Europe, which began fairly abruptly around 1980, has given those countries the lowest national birth rates in the world (equivalent to an average family size of under 1.3 in Spain and Italy). By contrast, in north-west Europe, birth rates increased up to the early 1990s and in Sweden the rate was above replacement level in 1990.

Much of the fertility decline since the 1960s is accounted for by delays in the timing of births: in many Western countries, the mean age of mothers at first birth is now about 28. Childlessness is likely to become more common than it was, and on present trends some countries face really small completed family sizes; little more than one child on average. The proportion of births outside marriage now varies tenfold between different European countries, from over 50 per cent in Sweden to under 5 per cent in Greece, and it still remains generally lower in Eastern Europe. Birth rates in most European countries are becoming more homogeneous at the sub-national level, but more different from each other at national level in respect of fertility and of living arrangements. European values, attitudes, and behaviour in relation to fertility are not yet uniform or harmonized.

The second chapter, by Kath Kiernan, looks in more detail at partnership behaviour. Marriage rates have been falling throughout Western Europe since the 1970s, a trend now becoming apparent in the East as well. The general increase in cohabitation has been partly responsible for the general reduction of marriage rates and the increase in mean age at marriage. Cohabitation remains much less common in Eastern and Southern Europe. Countries in Eastern Europe traditionally had, and still have, younger marriage ages than those common in the West. Cohabitation had changed its characteristics. The very poor and the divorced are still particularly prone to cohabit, but there are now more 'nubile' cohabitations which resemble married couples. However, cohabitation still tends to be more fragile and less fertile than marital unions.

Because of high and increasing divorce rates and of births outside marriage, single-parent families now account for between 5 per cent and 17 per cent of all families in different countries. Many of these changes are associated with a much more central role of work in many women's lives, while men's place in the work-force has if anything declined, with corresponding revisions in the roles of men and women in the home and in the domestic economy.

The third chapter, by John Salt, documents the rise in immigration to Europe from the east and south, and the growth of the population of foreign origin. By 1992, there were over eighteen million foreigners legally resident in Western Europe. In the EC (as it then was)—which comprises most of Western Europe's population—35 per cent of foreigners were from other EC countries, 65 per cent were 'third country nationals'. The legally resident foreign population in Eastern Europe was about a third of a million, with many more present illegally. During the 1980s and 1990s populations of foreign origin have generally increased (with the main exception of France, because of its high rates of naturalization), by 3.4 million since 1988 alone. Germany was a net loser of foreign population in 1980 but is now a substantial net gainer. Since the late 1980s immigration to Europe, while increasing in all countries, has been predominantly a German problem as Germany has acquired about half Europe's 'regular' migrants and up to two-thirds of its asylum claimants.

Countries which were formerly sources of emigration (in the Mediterranean region, and Finland) have become important immigration centres. Some Eastern European countries have experienced particularly strong rises in the numbers of immigrants. Mass migration pressure from the more developed Eastern countries to the West is now unlikely, especially as they become part of the system of European border controls. But pressures to emigrate remain strong in Romania and the former Soviet Union. Pressures on Europe's southern frontier will be more persistent, because of the third world's rapid population growth, low incomes, and political instability, leading to an extended debate about the relationship between development assistance and migration.

During the 1960s, all the European countries underwent a slowing-down in the reduction of death rates. But after 1970, mortality trends in Eastern Europe and in the other countries showed a marked divergence. Chapter 4, by France Meslé, analyses these trends and shows that while progress resumed in Western countries the situation continued to worsen in the East, to varying degrees. For example, the former East Germany experienced the least acute mortality crisis, while mortality in Albania and Yugoslavia, which started from very unfavourable levels, improved considerably. In Bulgaria and Hungary, however, mortality trends have been particularly unfavourable during the last twenty years.

Detailed comparisons of these two countries with England and Wales, and with France, show that the mortality crisis was particularly severe among males of working age. Mortality for almost all the causes of death increased in the Eastern countries, especially cardio-vascular diseases, cerebro-vascular diseases, and cancer, while these causes of death mostly declined in the Western countries. Only deaths from infectious disease showed a downward trend. It is not easy to account for these marked contrasts in mortality. Poorly developed medical systems, a traditional fatty diet, and the increase in alcohol consumption and cigarette smoking in the East must all have contributed to some degree to their deteriorating mortality trends, whereas favourable changes were taking place in these factors in Western countries.

Trends in fertility and its economic environment have been complex, as John Ermisch shows in Chapter 5. Both the relative stability of the birth rate since the mid-1970s in Northern Europe and the steep falls in Southern Europe were accompanied by trends toward later marriage, more divorce, and a growing proportion of women in paid employment. Economic considerations play an important part in these family formation decisions, particularly women's earning opportunities relative to men's, the relative gains made by single, married, and cohabiting households, and the effect of welfare on fertility. Birth rates have been inversely related over time to average pay; and low fertility itself raises work-force participation. There has been a strong relationship between the increase in divorce rates and the percentage of married women in employment.

Economic models of household formation and fertility suggest that low birth rates, high divorce rates, and a high level of women's participation in paid work will continue. Indeed in some countries the continuation of work-force trends implies a further fall in the birth rate, even though subsidies for child care and other family benefits can have a slight positive effect upon family size.

A different and not entirely compatible view of the origins of the diversity of family arrangements is given by the analysis of the European Values Study by Ron Lesthaeghe and Guy Moors in Chapter 6. This shows marked differences in values between persons in different forms of living arrangements (such as living with parents, single, married, and cohabiting). The biggest differences in attitudes were observed between those cohabiting and those who were married, with married people being the more conservative group. Respondents with strong religious beliefs placed a higher value on marital fidelity, the importance of children, paying taxes, and opposing the misuse of drugs. Children brought up in an environment where religion was practised were less likely to choose unconventional living arrangements. In some surprising areas, especially religious attitudes which emphasized individuality, co-habitants gave the more affirmative responses.

A major problem in analysing the results of this study was to decide whether the relationship between values and living arrangements was primarily due to a selection process, whereby people with particular values favoured different living arrangements, or an affirmation process whereby people in different living arrangements acquired distinctive attitudes. In fact, these relationships between values and living arrangements were not dependent upon socio-economic status. People in more stable living arrangements (for example, marriage) claimed higher levels of life satisfaction than others.

Should projections of European population decline, implicit in the low fertility of many countries, be regarded as serious demography or a false alarm? In Chapter 7, Heather Joshi compares the simple United Nations projections for different parts of Europe with projections made by the EC and with scenarios developed by Eurostat, which allowed for immigration. Even with zero migration, the UN and EC projected only a minor population decline to 2020 with considerable differences between Northern Europe (hardly any decline) and Southern Europe (more substantial decline, especially in Spain and Italy, but also in Germany). The Eurostat scenarios forecast decline in population only when the 'pessimistic' migration, mortality, and fertility assumptions were chosen. The fertility assumptions were, as usual, the most important, and the effects of the age structure still give momentum to population growth.

Taking all these considerations together, it seems more likely that there will be population stagnation in the EC and in Europe as a whole, rather than drastic population decline. There is, however, no doubt about the further continuation of demographic ageing. There are contradictory views as to the implications of these projections among those who desire to increase the supply of 'home-grown' citizens to check depopulation. In the past, they criticized working mothers for putting their children second, but now they urge improved conditions for working mothers. In a response to this antithesis, the message of this chapter is to put the quality of life first; to take care of the people, and let 'population decline' take care of itself.

The ageing of Europe's population, as well as the threat of population decline, has captured much attention as a demographic challenge to the stability of economic and welfare arrangements, especially pensions, to the affordability of medical care, and to the ability of the future work-force to meet the demands placed upon it by a larger number of dependants. In Chapter 8, Emily Grundy demonstrates the demographic causes of the growth of the elderly population and compares the position in various countries of Europe. Since the beginning of the century European countries have experienced substantial absolute and relative increases in the elderly population. Over 15 per cent of the population is now aged 65 or over in many Western countries, although the proportion in some Eastern European countries is hardly yet 10 per cent. These proportions are due to increase rapidly early next century as the Western 'baby boom' cohorts move into retirement. This is primarily a consequence of the long-term fall in the birth rate, but increased survival is now making a bigger contribution to population ageing, at least in Western Europe.

The social and economic impact of these demographic trends, and therefore their effects on the state of the elderly themselves, is much affected by trends in work-force participation, marital status, the proportion of old people with living children, and the extent to which people in different generations habitually live together. These vary considerably between different European countries, in some of which older people are more likely to have living children and living spouses than in the past. Even though children are less likely to live with their parents, they still provide much of the help that they need. Longer-run prospects for such family support are less favourable, however.

In Chapter 9, Anne Gauthier analyses in detail an important question raised in several of the other chapters: namely, do higher levels of family benefits have a positive effect on fertility by encouraging parents to have more children, or do higher levels of benefits unintentionally undermine the family by encouraging marital breakdown and welfare dependency? A major problem in resolving this question is the contrary expectations arising from economic theory itself. Family welfare policies could increase fertility by reducing its costs. Alternatively, or possibly at the same time, they could tend to reduce fertility, or increase it in inappropriate ways, by encouraging divorce and single-parent status and by helping to create an 'underclass'. There are also serious methodological problems in the way of a satisfactory explanation of the demographic effects of welfare, either intended or unintended.

Such American and British studies as are available present contradictory findings, but, taken together, they suggest that higher levels of welfare benefits do have a small effect on families. Other determinants, however, such as education and income, are likely to have more effect. Any effective policies directed towards family support would need to address several such factors at once.

Note: in this volume the European Union is usually denoted 'EC' for pre-1993 data, 'EU' for 1993 and later.

REFERENCES

BLAYO, C. (1987), 'La fécondité en Europe depuis 1960: convergence ou divergence?', *European Population Conference 1987*, Jÿvaskÿla, Liège, International Union for the Scientific Study of Population, Plenaries, 47–111.

BLUM, A. (1989), 'Démographies de l'URSS et des pays de l'Est. Continuité ou rupture?', *Notes et Etudes Documentaires*, 4891–92: 11–39.

—— and RALLU, J.-L. (eds.) (1993), *European Population ii. Demographic Dynamics*, Paris: John Libbey Eurotext.

CLIQUET, R. L. (1991), *The Second Demographic Transition: Fact or Fiction?*, Strasburg: Council of Europe.

COALE, A. J. (1992), 'The Problems of Estimating Future Mortality in the former USSR', paper presented to the colloquium The Population of the Former Soviet Union in the 21st Century, Amsterdam, Royal Netherlands Academy of Arts and Sciences, September/October 1992.

—— and WATKINS, S. C. (1986), *The Decline of Fertility in Europe*, Princeton: Princeton University Press.

COLEMAN, D. A. (1992), 'European Demographic Systems of the future: convergence or diversification?', in Eurostat (ed.), *Human Resources at the Dawn of the 21st Century*, Luxemburg: Office for Official Publications of the European Communities: 137–79.

COUNCIL OF EUROPE (1994), *Recent Demographic Developments in Europe*, Strasburg: Council of Europe Press.

DAVIS, K., BERNSTAM, M. S., and RICARDO-CAMPBELL, R. (eds.) (1986), *Below-Replacement Fertility in Industrial Societies*, New York: Population Council.

ERMISCH, J. (1990), *Fewer Babies, Longer Lives*, York: Rowntree Foundation.

EUROSTAT (1993), *Demographic Statistics 1993*, Luxemburg: Office for Official Publications of the European Communities.

GAUTHIER, A. H. (1993), 'Towards Renewed Fears of Population and Family Decline?', *European Journal of Population*, 9(2): 143–68.

GRASLAND, C. (1990), 'Systèmes démographiques et systèmes supra-nationaux: La Fécondité européenne de 1952 à 1982', *European Journal of Population*, 6(2): 163–92.

GUO, G. (1993), 'Mortality Trends and Causes of Death: A Comparison between Eastern and Western Europe 1960s–1970s', *European Journal of Population*, 9(3): 287–312.

HAJNAL, J. (1965), 'European Marriage Patterns in Perspective', in D. V. Glass and D. E. C. Eversley (eds.), *Population in History*, London: Edward Arnold.

HÖHN, C., and POLLARD, J. (1991), 'Mortality in the two Germanies in 1986 and trends 1976–1986', *European Journal of Population*, 7(1): 1–28.

INTERNATIONAL LABOUR ORGANIZATION (1989), *From Pyramid to Pillar. Population Change and Social Security in Europe*, Geneva: International Labour Office.

JOHNSON, P., CONRAD, C., and THOMSON, D. (eds.) (1989), *Workers versus Pensioners: Intergenerational Justice in an Ageing World*, Manchester: Manchester University Press.

KING, R. (ed.) (1993), *Mass Migration in Europe: The Legacy and the Future*, London: Belhaven.

KOSINSKI, L. (1970), *The Population of Europe: A Geographical Perspective*, London: Longman.

KRAVDAL, Ø. (1992), 'The weak impact of female labour force participation on Norwegian third-birth rates', *European Journal of Population*, 8: 247–64.

LEASURE, J. W. (1992), 'The historical decline of fertility in Eastern Europe', *European Journal of Population*, 8(1): 47–76.

LESTHAEGHE, R., and MEEKERS, D. (1986), 'Value changes and the dimensions of familism in the European Community', *European Journal of Population*, 2: 225–68.

LUTZ, W. (ed.) (1991), *Future Demographic Trends in Europe and North America. What Can We Assume Today?*, London: Academic Press.

MONNIER, A. (1991), 'L'Europe de l'Est, différente et diverse', *Population*, 46(3): 443–61.

NÍ BHROLCHÁIN, M. (1993), 'East–West marriage contrasts old and new', in A. Blum and J.-L. Rallu (eds.), *European Population ii. Demographic Dynamics*, Paris: John Libbey Eurotext: 461–82.

NOIN, D., and WOODS, R. I. (eds.) (1993), *The Changing Population of Europe*, Oxford: Blackwell.

POPULATION REFERENCE BUREAU INC. (1994), *World Population Data Sheet 1994*, Washington DC: Population Reference Bureau Inc.

RYCHTARIKOVA, J. (1993), 'Nuptialité comparée en Europe de l'Est et en Europe de l'ouest', in A. Blum and J.-L. Rallu (eds.), *European Population ii. Demographic Dynamics*, Paris: John Libbey Eurotext: 191–210.

SALT, J., SINGLETON, A., and HOGARTH, J. (1993), *Europe's International Migrants. Data Sources, Patterns and trends*, London: HMSO.

VAN DE KAA, D. J. (1987), 'Europe's second demographic transition', *Population Bulletin*, 42(1).

WIDGREN, J. (1994), 'The key to Europe: a comparative analysis of entry and asylum policies in Western countries', Stockholm: Swedish Ministry of Culture.

CONTENTS

LIST OF FIGURES

LIST OF TABLES

LIST OF ABBREVIATIONS

AFDC	Aid to Families with Dependent Children
ASFR	age-specific fertility rates
BSPS	British Society for Population Studies
CBR	crude birth rate
CDR	crude death rate
CMEA	Council for Mutual Economic assistance, often known as COMECON (an economic and trade grouping of former Communist countries, now dissolved)
DDR	Deutsche Demokratische Republik, the former East Germany
EC	European Community (EU from 1993); for list of member states see figure 7.6
EEA	European Economic Area (since 1993; EC plus EFTA countries, but without Switzerland)
EFTA	European Free Trade Association (Austria, Finland, Iceland, Norway, Sweden, Switzerland)
EU	European Union (EC before 1993)
EUROSTAT	The Statistical Office of the European Communities (Luxemburg)
FGR	Federal German Republic, the former West Germany
FSU	Former Soviet Union
IIASA	International Institute for Applied Systems Analysis (Laxenburg, Austria)
INED	Institut National d'Études Demographiques (Paris)
IOM	International Organization for Migration (Geneva)
NIC	newly industrializing country
OMI	Office des Migrations Internationales (France)
OPCS	Office of Population Censuses and Surveys (London, for England and Wales)
PPR	parity progression ratio
SOPEMI	Système d'Observation Permanente des Migrations (an

	international network for reporting migration data organized by the OECD, Paris)
TFR	total fertility rate
TPFR	total period fertility rate
UN	United Nations (New York and Geneva)
UNDP	United Nations Development Programme
WHO	World Health Organization (Geneva)

LIST OF CONTRIBUTORS

DR D. A. COLEMAN, Lecturer in Demography, Department of Applied Social Studies and Social Research, Barnett House, Wellington Square, Oxford OX1 2ER

PROFESSOR J. ERMISCH FBA, Professor, ESRC Research Centre on Micro-Social Change, University of Essex, Wivenhoe Park, Colchester CO4 3SQ

DR ANNE HÉLÈNE GAUTHIER, Lecturer in European Social Policy, Department of Applied Social Studies and Social Research, Barnett House, Wellington Square, Oxford OX1 2ER

DR EMILY GRUNDY, Reader in Social Gerontology, Age Concern Institute of Gerontology, King's College, Cornwall House Annex, Waterloo Road, London SE1 8WA

PROFESSOR HEATHER JOSHI, Deputy Director, Social Statistics Research Unit, City University, Northampton Square, London EC1V 0HB

DR K. E. KIERNAN, Reader in Social Policy and Demography, Department of Social Policy and Administration, London School of Economics, Houghton Street, Aldwych, London WC2

PROFESSOR R. LESTHAEGHE, Professor of Demography, Steunpunt Demografie, Centrum voor Sociologie, Vrije Universiteit Brussel, Pleinlaan 2, B-1050 Brussels, Belgium

DR FRANCE MESLÉ, Senior Researcher, Institut National d'Études Demographiques (INED), 27 rue du Commandeur, 75675 Paris Cedex 14, France

DR GUY MOORS, Research and Teaching Assistant in Sociology, Steunpunt Demografie, Centrum voor Sociologie, Vrije Universiteit Brussel, Pleinlaan 2, B-1050 Brussels, Belgium

DR J. SALT, Senior Lecturer in Geography and Director, Migration Research Unit, Dept of Geography, University College London, 26 Bedford Way, London WC1H 0AP

1

New Patterns and Trends in European Fertility: International and Sub-National Comparisons

DAVID COLEMAN

1.1 Introduction

This chapter describes European fertility patterns and differences in the early 1990s, their recent trends, and some of their components in terms of timing, birth order, and births inside and outside marriage. Its aim is descriptive, not analytic; it does not attempt to explain the trends in terms of detailed changes in the broader economic or social environment. Demographic responses to economic or welfare arrangements, and to changing ideas and values, are dealt with in Chapters 5, 6, and 9. The new family patterns and domestic arrangements are considered in detail in Chapter 2, and some of the consequences of fertility trends for future population ageing, and for population size and distribution in Chapters 8 and 7 respectively. Low fertility also raises the question whether the 'missing' births reflect a welfare deficit or pose a demographic problem. The effects of family policies upon the birth rate are discussed in Chapter 9. The other components of demographic change, those of migration and mortality, are described in Chapters 3 and 4 respectively.

An overview of trends

The birth rate in 'Western' Europe, taken as the twelve EC countries plus the seven EFTA countries, was the lowest of any major bloc in the world at the beginning of the 1990s. The total fertility rate (TFR) was 1.6 in 1990. Compared with the other major components of the industrial world, Western Europe's low fertility was then matched only by that of Japan (TFR, 1.6). Natural increase (the excess of births over deaths) and the total fertility rate in Western Europe were both considerably lower than in the countries of European origin overseas, such as the United States and Australia (figure 1.1), where TFR averaged about 1.9. By 1992, however, political change and economic collapse in the Western parts of the former Soviet Union had brought the birth rate in the Russian Federation down to even lower levels (TFR, 1.5) than in the West. The birth rate continues to fall in some countries, notably in the east and south, but in others, mostly in Northern and Western Europe, the birth rate has been increasing since the mid-1980s after a period of stability. It can no longer be said that the countries of Europe are converging on a common pattern of fertility. Fertility differences within countries, however, continue to

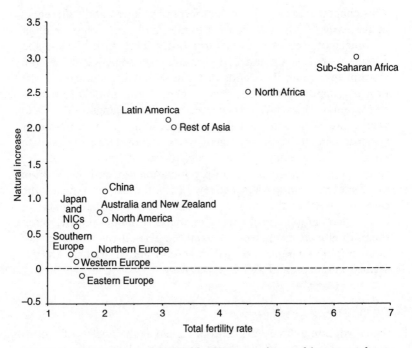

FIG. 1.1. *Major regions of the world, 1994: rate of natural increase and total fertility rate*

Source: Data modified from Population Reference Bureau Inc. 1994

diminish. Overall, these low birth rates, maintained now for two decades, are without precedent in history and their likely future development is causing increasing concern because they promise further population ageing and, in some countries population decline (see Chapter 8 and Chapter 7 in this volume).

Defining Europe

In the early 1990s Europe has experienced its biggest political upheavals since the Second World War. Communist regimes throughout Eastern and Southern Europe, and in the former Soviet Union itself, have collapsed and generated a large number of smaller successor states (table 1.1), formerly considered to be provinces of larger entities although some had previous histories as independent states. The new map has been recognized officially by a new United Nations statistical classification of the countries of the various regions of Europe. Thus Northern Europe has gained Estonia, Latvia, and Lithuania from the former Soviet Union, appropriately enough in view of their history and their position to the west of 'Hajnal's Line'. This divide, running approximately from St Petersburg to Trieste, and first established statistically by Hajnal (1965), separates the historical Western European marriage pattern of late and frequently avoided marriage and of households based on nuclear families from that of European Europe where marriage always tended to be earlier and nearly universal and where households were often complex. In Western Europe, although the Federal Republic of Germany retains the same name, it has acquired the population (of seventeen million) of the former East Germany, previously counted in Eastern Europe. In Southern Europe the break-up of Yugoslavia has created five successor states. Recent demographic data are not available for all of them. Eastern Europe has lost the former East Germany to the Federal Republic, but it has gained two new states comprising the territory and population of the former Czechoslovakia.

According to the new United Nations definitions, Eastern Europe has also gained the western parts of the former Soviet Union (Belarus, Moldova, Russia, and Ukraine) and thereby more than doubled in population size. This makes for a heterogeneous and over-large demographic grouping. Formerly the immense Soviet Union comprised a region by itself, as far as United Nations

TABLE 1.1. *New and old Europe: a classification, 1990 and 1994*

Northern Europe		Western Europe		Southern Europe		Eastern Europe		USSR		Western Asia		Central Asia	
1990	1994	1990	1994	1990	1994	1990	1994	1990	1994	1990	1994	1990	1994
	Estonia	Austria	Austria	Albania	Albania	Bulgaria	Belarus	Armenia	(none)		Armenia		Kazakhstan
Finland	Finland	Belgium	Belgium		Bosnia	Czechoslovakia	Bulgaria	Azerbaijan			Azerbaijan		Kirghizstan
Iceland	Iceland	Denmark	Denmark		Croatia		Czech Rep.	Belarus		Cyprus	Cyprus		Tadzhikistan
Ireland	Ireland	France	France	Greece	Greece	E. Germany		Estonia			Georgia		Turkmenistan
	Latvia	W. Germany	Germany	Italy	Italy	Hungary	Hungary	Georgia		Turkey	Turkey		Uzbekistan
	Lithuania				Macedonia	Poland	Poland	Kazakhstan					
Norway	Norway	Luxemburg	Luxemburg	Malta	Malta	Romania	Romania	Kirghizstan					
Sweden	Sweden	Netherlands	Netherlands	Portugal	Portugal		Moldova	Latvia					
UK	UK	Switzerland	Switzerland		Serbia & Montenegro		Russia	Lithuania					
					Slovenia		Slovak Rep.	Moldova					
				Spain	Spain		Ukraine	Russia					
				Yugoslavia				Tadzhikistan					
								Turkmenistan					
								Ukraine					
								Uzbekistan					

Source: United Nations.

classifications were concerned. Straddling Europe and Asia, it contained fifteen republics of both European and Asiatic culture and its demography was consequently difficult to classify in aggregate form. The two most 'European' of the Asiatic republics, Christian Armenia and Georgia, which are South of the Caucasus, have been assigned to Western Asia along with Muslim Azerbaijan; the rest of the former Soviet Asiatic republics are now considered to be part of Central Asia. The latter two groups will not be discussed further in this chapter. As a result of these boundary changes, the population of Europe is increased by 214 million and that of Asia by seventy million.

Measuring fertility

The following discussion uses relatively straightforward demographic indicators to summarize international demographic patterns and trends. Comparative studies are always reduced to the lowest common denominator of the statistics being compared. The simplest measure, the crude birth rate (CBR), is still useful because, in conjunction with the crude death rate (CDR), it gives the rate at which births exceed deaths in the population, and therefore, in the absence of net migration, the rate of population growth (or decline). But it is best avoided for comparisons between countries with different age structures, although the differences in short-run trends compared with other measures, or even the annual total of births, is not great (Murphy 1992a). The period total fertility rate (TFR), the number of babies the average woman would produce if she experienced current age-specific fertility rates throughout her own lifetime, is the rate most frequently used in this chapter. It eliminates the effects of age-structure differences when making comparisons between the fertility levels of different populations. The TFR only corresponds with the final completed family size of real cohorts of women if age-specific fertility rates remain constant over time. As the timing of fertility is constantly shifting by being delayed (as at present) or brought forward, the TFR tends to exaggerate (or at present, to underestimate) final completed fertility (see Cooper 1991). Therefore measures of the timing of births (mean age at first birth) are needed, as are data on the completed family size (CFS) of cohorts of women.

In recent years much interest has been shown in the 'distributional' aspects of family size (Lutz 1992), that is, the proportion of births which are first, second, and third order, etc., the distribution of families according to whether they comprise one, two, three, or more children, and the probability of a woman with one child progressing to a second, from a second birth to a third, and so on. The latter probabilities are known as 'parity progression ratios' and when summed add to the completed family size of cohorts. They are easy to calculate for cohorts of women who have completed their families, given simple data on completed family size according to number of children ever-born from censuses or surveys.

More attention is now being paid to period fertility rates based upon such parity progression ratios calculated not for cohorts of completed fertility but on a period (current) basis. In theory, this enables a form of the period total fertility rate that is free from the distorting effects of shifts forward or backward in the timing of births to be calculated. A calculation of period parity progression ratios needs data on birth intervals or on the current distributions of women according to the number of children they have had, as well as on births according to birth order, depending on the method adopted (Ní Bhrolcháin 1987, Feeney and Yu 1987, Feeney and Lutz 1991, Lutz 1992, Ní Bhrolcháin 1993, Murphy and Berrington 1993). Unfortunately the calculation of such rates demands data which are only routinely available for a few European countries: for example, time series of annual distributions of mothers by parity as well as of births by order (available for Hungary), or data on the duration of time since the previous birth (birth intervals, available for Sweden), depending on whether the method of Lutz or that of Feeney is being used. Often the total fertility rates calculated in this way are about 0.1 or 0.2 above the value of the conventional TFR for the same year, showing, it is believed, the extent to which the conventional TFR based upon age-specific rates is currently underestimating the 'real' current intensity of fertility. Such calculations have only been attempted for a few industrial countries: France (Rallu and Toulemon 1993a, 1993b, Calot _et al._ 1993), Italy, Great Britain (Murphy and Berrington 1993), Japan (Ogawa and Retherford 1993). In general, parity-progression-based measures give higher estimates of fertility than does the TFR over most of the period since the 1970s, when fertility has been declining, and lower estimates (where they are available) in the last few years, when fertility has been increasing. But this finding is not entirely consistent and in some cases the differences are trivial.

1.2 Current Period Fertility Levels

The current levels of period fertility in Europe in 1988 are summarized in figure 1.2, which maps the total fertility rate (TFR) by major region. Fertility in almost all European countries is below and in some cases well below the replacement rate of fertility (TFR, 2.1). At the time of writing, 1992 was the last year for which the TFR was available for almost all European countries. In that year, the average TFR for the EC was 1.58 and for Western Europe as a whole was 1.63. Britain's relatively high fertility (1.82) is shared by some of its neighbours in north-western Europe. All countries to the west (Ireland and Iceland) and most to the north (Sweden and Norway) have similar or higher fertility. But to the east and south all have lower fertility, some markedly so, with the exception of France. A 'fertility depression' centred upon Germany may be discerned, as well as a low-fertility belt affecting all the Mediterranean countries, a feature which has been present since at least 1981. In Eastern Europe, in some countries, recent fertility (Poland and the Czech Republic) has not declined much since the collapse of communism. But in the former East Germany, in Bulgaria, and in Romania it has fallen to low levels similar to those in Mediterranean Europe or even lower.

The high-fertility countries of Europe include Ireland, Iceland, Great Britain, France, Norway, and Sweden. Malta and Cyprus might be added to the list as small less-developed countries whose fertility transition is not quite complete. Ireland and Iceland have never experienced low fertility. Norway and Sweden experienced lower fertility than the others in this group in the early 1980s; their birth rates have now increased considerably. Partly as a consequence of this high fertility these countries still show a positive natural increase of 0.27 per cent (table 1.2) compared with 0.18 per cent for the EC. Only a few European countries have shown a natural decline (that is, an excess of deaths over births) in the early 1990s. These include Germany and (more recently) Romania and the Russian Federation. But many more are scheduled to do so in

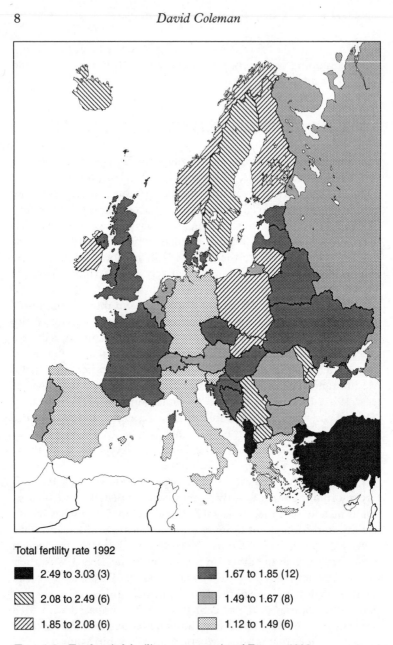

Total fertility rate 1992

▓	2.49 to 3.03 (3)	▓	1.67 to 1.85 (12)
▨	2.08 to 2.49 (6)	▒	1.49 to 1.67 (8)
▨	1.85 to 2.08 (6)	░	1.12 to 1.49 (6)

FIG. 1.2. *Total period fertility rate, countries of Europe, 1992*

Note: Latest data available for Albania, Bosnia-Herzegovina, Croatia, 1990.
Sources: Statistisches Bundesamt, Bevölkerung und Erwerbstätigreit Fachserie, Reihe, 1992;
Council of Europe, Recent Demographic Developments in Europe 1995; Russian
Federation State Committee on Statistics, The Demographic Yearbook of the
Russian Federation 1993; Eurostat, CUBX Database.

TABLE 1.2. Natural increase and fertility, Europe, 1992

Country	Births	Population 1 Jan. 1993 (000s)	CBR per 1000 (1992)	Rate of Natural Increase (%) (1992)	TFR 1992	Mean age at birth		% of TFR to mothers age ≥ 30	Mean age at first marriage		% of births illegitimate	CFS women born in 1955
						First	All		M.	F.		
Albania	77,361[a]	3,353.1[c]	25.20	1.810	3.03[b]	n/a	n/a	34.6[b]	n/a	n/a	n/a	n/a
Armenia	77,825[a]	3,645.1	21.50	1.520	2.84[b]	n/a	25.2[b]	19.4[b]	n/a	n/a	5.2[b]	1.78
Austria	88,759	7,909.6	12.10	0.150	1.51	26.0	27.3	27.7	27.6	25.7	25.2	
Belarus	127,971	10,280.8[c]	13.90	0.110	1.80[a]	22.3[a]	25.0[a]	16.3[a]		22.5[d]	8.5[b]	1.79
Belgium	120,550	10,068.2	12.40	0.200	1.59[d]	25.9	27.6	28.4[h]	26.4	24.7[a]	8.9	2.03
Bulgaria	89,134	8,956.1	10.50	-0.220	1.43	21.8	23.6	11.2[a]		21.9	18.5	n/a
Cyprus	11,710	725.0	20.00	1.110	2.68	24.7	27.5	29.0		24.0[a]	1.1	2.13
Czechoslovakia	196,345	15,630.2	12.60	0.210	1.92[a]	22.5[b]	24.9[b]	14.4[a]		20.9[d]	8.2[b]	2.06
Czech Rep.	121,705	10,322.3[c]	11.80	0.010	1.71	22.5[b]	24.8[b]			21.5[b]	10.7	1.84
Denmark	61,467	5,180.6	13.10	0.130	1.76	26.8[a]	28.5[a]	36.6[a]	29.8[a]	27.9[a]	46.5[a]	2.01
Estonia	19,320[a]	1,562.1[c]	12.30	-0.030	1.78[a]	22.9[a]	25.5[a]	19.5[a]		23.0[a]	31.1[a]	1.87
Finland	63,390	5,055.1	13.30	0.340	1.85	26.9[a]	29.2[a]	39.6	27.8[a]	26.6[a]	27.4[a]	2.03
France	765,473	57,526.6	12.90	0.380	1.73	27.2[ag]	28.4[af]	38.6[a]	27.5[a]	26.0[a]	27.5[a]	
Georgia		5,472.4[c]	16.30	0.540	2.10[b]	24.2	26.1[a]	20.9[b]		24.2[a]	18.7[a]	
Germany	720,794	80,274.6[c]	9.00					38.4[b]				
W. Germany	681,537	62,699.0	10.87	-0.100	1.48[b]	27.1[ae]	28.5[ae]	35.6	28.0[a]	26.5[a]	11.1[a]	1.58
E. Germany	88,289	15,789.8[c]	5.59	-0.590	0.75	24.9[a]	28.4[a]	15.7[d]		24.5[a]	41.7[a]	1.82
Greece	101,657	10,046.0	10.10	0.070	1.42[b]	25.0[a]	26.9[a]	29.3[a]	27.8[a]	24.1[a]	2.4[a]	1.93
Hungary	121,724	10,310.2	11.80	-0.260	1.77	22.6	25.2	19.4		21.6	15.6	1.90
Iceland	4,609	262.4	17.70	1.110	2.21	24.6	28.4	38.6		26.8[a]	57.0	2.54
Ireland	51,659	3,556.5	14.50	0.590	2.11	25.9	29.2	49.7	27.9[b]	25.9[b]	18.0	2.65
Italy	567,268	57,245.0	9.70	0.050	1.25	26.9[b]	28.9[b]	40.5[b]	28.0[b]	25.6[b]	6.7	1.74
Latvia	31,569	2,606.2	12.00	-0.150	1.73	22.5	25.2	20.0		22.4		n/a
Lithuania	53,617	3,736.5	14.30	0.320	1.89	22.6	25.2	20.2		n/a	7.9	1.65
Luxembourg	4,665	395.2	13.10	0.290	1.67	n/a	28.4	36.9	27.8	25.9	12.7	n/a
Malta	5,474	363.0	15.20	0.720	2.04	22.3[d]	n/a	37.4		n/a	1.7	
Moldova	69,654	4,347.8	16.00	0.580	2.26[a]		25.0[a]	17.9		22.3[d]	11.0[b]	
Netherlands	188,979	15,238.6	13.20	0.440	1.59	28.0[e]	29.6[c]	51.7	27.8[a]	26.6	12.5	1.87
Norway	59,200	4,299.2	14.00	0.360	1.88	25.9	28.3	36.4		26.4[a]	42.9	2.02

TABLE 1.2. (cont.)

Country	Births	Population 1 Jan. 1993 (000s)	CBR per 1000 (1992)	Rate of Natural Increase (%) (1992)	TFR 1992	Mean age at birth		% of TFR to mothers age ⩾ 30	Mean age at first marriage		% of births illegitimate	CFS women born in 1955
						First	All		M.	F.		
Poland	513,616	38,418.1	13.40	0.310	1.93	22.6	25.7	23.0		22.2	7.2	2.19
Portugal	118,560	9,859.6	12.02	0.140	1.55	25.0	27.4	31.6	26.1a	24.5	16.1	1.95
Romania	260,393	22,778.3	11.40	−0.020	1.50	22.3	24.4	16.7		22.0	15.0	2.34
Russia	1,988,858b	148,164.1c	10.70	−0.150	1.55	22.0d	25.7d	19.2b		22.5d	13.5d	n/a
Slovak Rep.	74,640	5,307.9	14.08	0.400	1.97			15.9				
Slovenia	19,982	1,994.2	10.00	0.030	1.34	24.2	26.4	20.5		24.1	27.7	1.91
Spain	404,564	39,114.3	9.80	0.100	1.23	26.5b	28.9b	40.0b	26.7b	25.3b	9.6b	1.95
Sweden	115,900	8,692.0	14.20	0.390	2.09	26.7	28.8	39.4		27.8a	49.5	1.95
Switzerland	81,180	6,904.6	12.60	0.360	1.60	28.0	29.2	45.5	29.2a	27.3	6.7	1.73
Ukraine	596,785	51,801.9c	12.10	−0.070	1.72	n/a	n/a	15.2		n/a	11.9a	
UK	798,600	57,960.0	13.78	0.260	1.84	25.4a	27.5g	33.4a	25.8		30.8	2.03
Great Britain	781,000	56,388.0c	13.50	0.250	1.84		27.5e	34.3	26.9	24.8	31.1	1.95
England & Wales	689,700	51,277.0c	13.50	0.250	1.84	25.4e	27.5e	29.1	26.8	25.1	31.2	1.79
Scotland	65,800	5,111.0c	12.90	0.090	1.67		27.2e				30.3	
N. Ireland	26,500	1,610.0c	16.46		2.26		28.0e				18.7	
EC	3,937,500	346,756.3	11.40	0.140	1.48	26.2	28.1	30.4	27.3	24.9	16.1	
EEA	4,287,300	373,004.3	11.49	0.150	1.49	24.5	27.1		26.9	24.0	19.1	1.97

Notes:
a 1991 data.
b 1990 data.
c Population data are 1992.
d 1989 data.
e Mean age at birth: Germany, Netherlands, and England and Wales all births. The remainder legitimate births only.
f France: data on mean age at birth refer to current marriages only.
g Data refer to England and Wales, not UK.
h 1988 data.

n/a = not available.

Fifteen ex-USSR republics separated 1991, Czechoslovakia divided late 1992, Germany unified 3 October 1990.
Sources: Austria, Finland, Norway, Sweden, Switzerland: Council of Europe 1994; EC countries: Eurostat (1993a, 1993b), Council of Europe 1994, Eurostat 1993c, EEA: Eurostat 1993c; Former Soviet Union and Eastern Europe: Council of Europe 1994 and Goskomstat (1994) UK: OPCS 1994.

the next decade or so according to current trends (see Joshi, Chapter 7 below).

1.3 Trends in Period and Cohort Fertility

Since the Second World War, all Western European countries have shared a number of fertility trends. A short post-war baby boom immediately followed the reunification of families after military demobilization. A period of lower fertility followed in the reconstruction years of the late 1940s and early 1950s, although even then the birth rate usually remained just above replacement level except in West Germany and Austria. An unexpected prolonged period of higher fertility characterized the late 1950s and 1960s, when most Western European economies were growing rather rapidly. This is the 'baby boom' proper, whose rise and fall alike took demographers by surprise. Then followed a decline to below-replacement fertility (not paralleled by concomitant economic decline), where most European countries still remain. Most Western European countries reached the peak of the baby boom within a year of 1964, a remarkable coincidence in timing. Most of these countries fell below replacement level fertility (2.1) in about 1972.

Within these general similarities, the trends of fertility shown in Figures 1.3 to 1.6 indicate that different regions of Europe have behaved in rather different ways since the Second World War (Grasland 1990). The European regions appear to divide on roughly geographical or linguistic grounds in respect of their fertility trends. Sweden and Finland never experienced very low fertility, Sweden had only a modest baby boom, while Finland scarcely exhibited a boom at all. Germany and Luxemburg maintained modest fertility throughout the period. With the exception of France, the German-speaking countries and other countries adjacent to Germany have had a TFR below 1.6 since around 1975, while all the other north-west European countries, including France, have hardly ever seen their TFR fall below 1.6 (figures 1.3 and 1.4). Popular commentaries often speak of 'Europe's falling birth rate'. This is wrong. While fertility in north-west Europe and Central Europe is relatively low, it has remained at its present level for about two decades. In a century of demo-

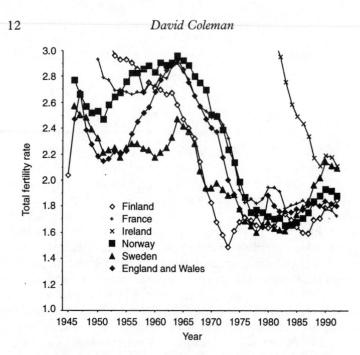

FIG. 1.3. *Total fertility rate trends in selected Northern and Western European countries, 1945–1992*

Sources: Council of Europe 1994 and previous issues, Eurostat 1993a and 1993b and previous issues, and national statistical yearbooks.

graphic turmoil, this is the longest period without radical change. Fertility in some Northern and Western European countries has risen substantially since the mid-1980s, notably in the case of sweden which reached replacement rate once again around 1990. As Figure 1.3 and Appendix table 1A.1 show, however, this advance in fertility appears to have levelled off or retreated somewhat in a number of countries since then.

Southern European countries have behaved differently (figure 1.5). Italy has not achieved high fertility since the late 1940s. The peak Italian postwar TFR was 2.70 in 1964, 0.24 less than the United Kingdom in the same year. Italy now vies with Spain for the lowest TFR in the world (1.3; see figure 1.4) and is closely followed by the other Mediterranean countries. The Italian fertility decline started a few years later than that of other countries but only ceased in 1985 when it had achieved the world's lowest period fertility. Greece likewise showed little 'baby boom' effect and its

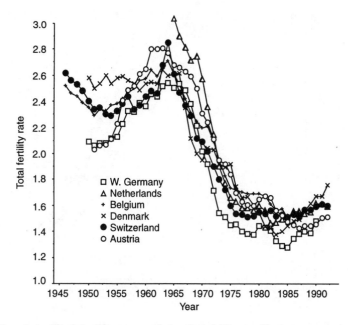

FIG. 1.4. *Total fertility rate trends in selected Western European countries,*
1945–1992

Sources: Council of Europe 1994 and previous issues, Eurostat 1993a and 1993b and
previous issues, and national statistical yearbooks.

birth rate was considerably below that of the United Kingdom
during the 1960s, although it did not decline much until 1980.
Spain and Portugal maintained consistently high birth rates during
the 1960s and 1970s, but around 1980 they joined Greece in a
rapid decline which has not yet (in the early 1990s) ended and
which may take their period rates below those of Italy.

Since the Second World War fertility in the USSR and Eastern
Europe has developed in somewhat divergent directions from
those in the West (figure 1.6; see also Blayo 1987, Blum 1989,
Vichnevsky *et al.* 1993). Despite some notable post-war upswings
in births, for example in Poland, the countries of Eastern Europe
and the Soviet Union show no baby boom in the 1950s and the
1960s on the Western model. Instead these decades were a period
of generally declining fertility. This is not surprising, given the
higher starting point of fertility in the more rural and less developed
economies of Eastern Europe, the earlier and more universal mar-

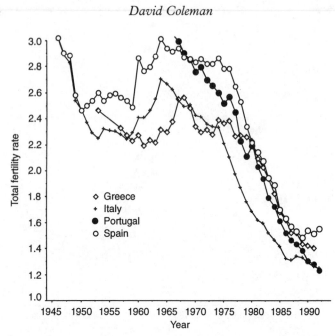

FIG. 1.5. *Total fertility rate trends in Southern European countries,*
1945–1992

Sources: Council of Europe 1994 and previous issues, Eurostat 1993a and 1993b and
previous issues, and national demographic yearbooks.

riage typical of countries east of 'Hajnal's Line' (Ní Bhrolcháin
1993). However, not all East European countries started the post-
war period at much higher levels of fertility than those found in the
West. For example, the completed family size of cohorts of Polish
and Yugoslav women born around 1930 was between 2.5 and
three, while that of Bulgarian women born in 1930 was already
little more than two and increased only slightly up to the cohorts
born in 1950 (Blayo 1987). The level of cohort fertility in Hungary
has remained below two for all cohorts of mothers born after 1935.
The Baltic States showed particularly low levels of fertility before
the Second World War (Katus 1994). Similarly modest but irregular trends, without much trace of a Western 'baby boom', are
evident in the birth rates of the more western Republics of the
former Soviet Union (figure 1.7; data are not available for every
year). These, responding to a common regime, show a much more
constrained pattern of fertility variation. As in the poorer parts of

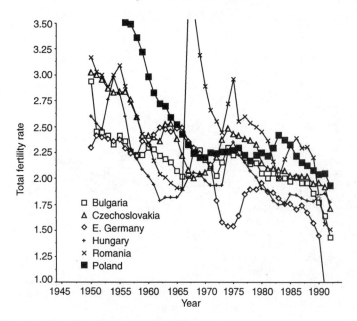

FIG. 1.6. *Total fertility rate trends in Eastern European countries,*
1952–1992
Sources: Council of Europe 1994 and national demographic yearbooks.

Eastern Europe, there have been marked falls in the birth rate since
1990.

In these countries the general transition to very low fertility, and
major fluctuations such as the 'baby boom', which might have
occurred under a post-war free market system, have been retarded
or suppressed by various aspects of the communist system. These
have included a political system which permitted only limited
personal autonomy and spending (Leasure 1992); few satisfactions
outside the family (Mozny 1992); welfare policies with interven-
tionist demographic as well as welfare aims (David 1982); and
limited access to contraception—deliberately engineered by some
governments and inherent in the economic situation of all of them.
Regulation of access to legal abortion, a front-line method of family
limitation in these countries, has been another major factor (Blayo
1991). Higher levels of married female work-force participation
and severe problems of housing also combined to depress the birth
rate (see Ermisch, Chapter 5 below).

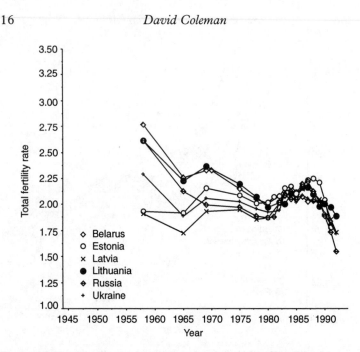

FIG. 1.7. *Total fertility rate trends in some former republics of the Soviet Union, 1958–1992*
Sources: Council of Europe 1994 and Goskomstat 1989.

Pro-natalist policies, which have traditionally been favoured by Communist governments, provided income and welfare incentives to encourage the birth rate so as to guarantee the growth of the future labour force while still enabling mothers to remain in the present one. In general in the industrial world it has proved difficult to show unequivocal positive effects of family or pro-natalist policies on birth rates (see Gauthier in this volume, Chapter 9). However, radical liberalization (as in East Germany in 1972) or near prohibition (as in Romania in 1966) of the availability of abortion were followed by marked short-term effects on birth rates. The latter comprised, from 1966 until 1990, the most harsh pro-natalist population policy in modern demographic history (Ghetzau 1991). The low points of fertility in Hungary and Romania in the 1960s occurred at the same time as the peak of the West's baby boom. Other changes include the development of patterns of near-universal and early marriage in, for example, what is now the Czech Republic which were somewhat different from the West European marriage pattern (Rychtarikova 1993, Ní Bhrolcháin 1993) which the inhabitants of the Czech lands had previously embraced.

Political events since 1989 have removed the underlying reasons for this partly artificial divergence in trend. The transitional period that has followed, in which command economies, with their guaranteed employment and subsidies, have been removed and only partially replaced by market forces, has been accompanied by considerable economic disruption (UN ECE 1992), rising unemployment, falling output and living standards, and in some cases (such as the Ukraine) hyperinflation. It is not surprising that birth rates have fallen substantially since 1989 in some Eastern and former Soviet countries. For example in Bulgaria, TFR fell from 1.96 in 1988 to 1.53 in 1992; that in Romania fell from 2.32 in 1988 to 1.51 in 1992 and to 1.44 in 1993. By 1992, the declining number of births in Romania and in the Russian Federation (where TFR fell to 1.35 in 1993) was less than the increasing number of deaths (Council of Europe 1994, Goskomstat 1994).

For completeness, data are also given for other non-European countries of the industrial world. The English-speaking countries abroad reached their (higher) fertility peaks somewhat earlier, between 1957 (United States) and 1961 (Australia and New Zealand). While all exhibited below-replacement fertility in the late 1970s, all have recently shown an upturn, to above-replacement rates in the case of the United States and New Zealand (figure 1.8), although this trend, like that in Sweden, appears to have peaked. Fertility in Japan has been relatively low since the 1960s, and has since resumed its decline. Birth rates in the newly industrialized countries (NICs)—Hong Kong, Singapore, Taiwan, and South Korea—have declined rapidly since the 1970s from previously very high levels (figure 1.9). The TFR data for all these graphs, together with some data for 1993, are given in Appendix Table 1A.1.

1.4 Completed Family Size

The TFR is based upon the synthetic cohort principle, as if the experiences of different women of different ages were combined into one real lifetime. Changes in the real completed family size of real cohorts of women by the time they reach the end of their

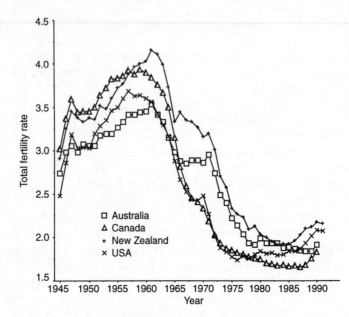

FIG. 1.8. *Total fertility rate trends in the Neo-Europes, 1945–1992*
Sources: National demographic yearbooks.

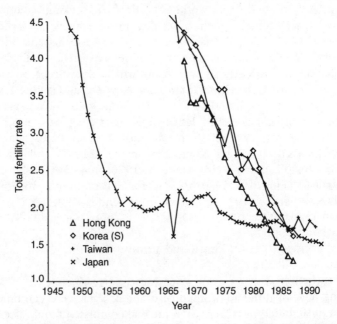

FIG. 1.9. *Total fertility rate trends in Japan and the NICs, 1945–1992*
Sources: National demographic yearbooks.

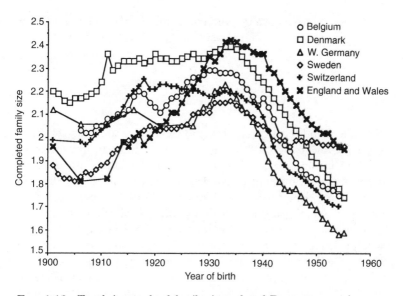

FIG. 1.10. *Trends in completed family size, selected European countries, women born 1900–1955*

Sources: Festy 1979: 300–1; Sardon 1990: table 5.

childbearing period are less volatile. For example, England and Wales ends up with about the same completed family size for women born in 1955 as for women born in 1900—just under 2.0 (figure 1.10). England and Wales achieved its demographic transition early (Coale and Watkins 1986). Women born in 1900, who had their babies in the 1920s and 1930s, had already achieved a family size of about two children (see Glass and Grebenik 1954, OPCS 1987a). Such low fertility was then matched only by that of Sweden. The baby boom did lead to a real increase in completed family size—to a peak of 2.42 in England and Wales for women born in 1934. At the beginning of the period shown in figure 1.10, mean completed family size of English cohorts was among the lowest in Europe. By its end, it was among the highest.

The latest figures for 'completed family sizes' in figure 1.10 refer to women born in 1955, who are still only 39 at the time of writing and have not quite completed their family building. For figure 1.10 family size has been estimated up to age 45 using current age-specific fertility rates. This is not a strong assumption.

In Britain, women born in 1945 had completed 96 per cent of their family size by age 35, 98 per cent by age 37, and 99.5 per cent by age 40.

1.5 Mean Age at Maternity

To understand fertility patterns and trends it is necessary to make a distinction between 'timing' effects relating to the start of childbearing and the spacing of births, and 'quantum' effects relating to the total number of children ever born. In theory the two components are separate and independent. The persistence of fecundity over the age of 40 makes it quite possible for a woman to have a family of three children (which is large by modern standards), starting at over age 30, while women could equally choose (especially through 'terminal' contraception by means of sterilization) to have one child at age 20 and then no more. Nevertheless, despite the availability of efficient contraception, women who start childbearing early still tend to have larger families than those starting later. This is probably because the desire for children affects marriage and its timing. It is not easy to distinguish the relative importance of the effects of timing and of quantum in determining the overall level of contemporary births in cohorts which have not yet completed their fertility (see Ryder 1980). Some timing effects can be compared by looking at the mean age at first birth, which has been increasing in all Western countries since the early 1970s (figure 1.11). This has had a depressing effect upon period measures of fertility, even if completed family size remains unchanged.

In the 1950s and 1960s, the reduction in the mean age at first birth was closely connected with the reduction in the mean age at marriage. At that time, almost all births occurred within marriage. Since the 1970s, mean age at marriage has indeed been in retreat; but the timing of marriage is now more loosely connected with the timing of first birth because of the popularity of cohabitation (see Kiernan, Chapter 2 below) and the growing number of first and later births which occur outside marriage. By 1992 the proportion of births outside marriage ranged from over 50 per cent in Sweden to less than 3 per cent in Greece (the figure for Great Britain being 31 per cent). The mean age at marriage for men and for women in

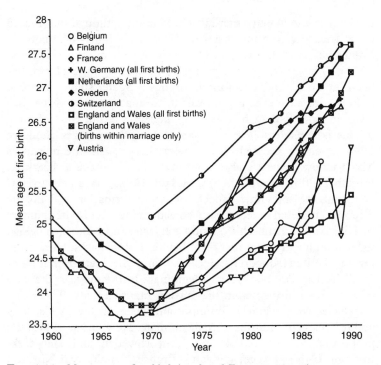

FIG. 1.11. *Mean age at first birth in selected European countries, 1960–1990*

Note: Except where indicated these data refer to marital births only. See text.
Sources: Council of Europe 1991, Eurostat 1991a, and OPCS 1987a, 1987b, 1987c, 1992a, and 1992b.

Britain was one of the youngest in Western Europe; about six months earlier than the overall average for both sexes.

Mean age at the beginning of the first cohabiting union is typically less than that at first marriage. Cohabitation preceded 58 per cent of all marriages in Great Britain in the late 1980s (Haskey and Kiernan 1989), 57 per cent of all marriages in France in the early 1980s (Leridon and Villeneuve-Gokalp 1988), and almost all marriages in Sweden (Nilsson 1985). In the 1980s current cohabitation was less frequent in Belgium, Italy, Ireland, and Switzerland (see Kiernan, Chapter 2 below: table 2.2), and much less so in Greece. No data are available for Eastern Europe. In France, up to 1980, the decline in the number of first marriages was fully compensated by the increase in extra-marital cohabitation, although that ceased to be true after the marriages of 1980. Two-thirds of unions in France begun in the years 1982–5 were outside marriage (Leridon 1990a). The greater part of the recent rise of illegitimate births has been in such 'stable informal unions'. Such 'stable informal unions' are not exactly equivalent to marriage, however (see Kiernan and Esthaugh 1993). In general, fertility in informal unions is considerably lower than in formal marriages (Lelièvre 1993). Neither are such unions very 'stable', and the marriages which follow them are also more likely than average to break up (Hoem 1990b, Leridon 1990b, Haskey 1992a). Age at marriage, cohabitation, and other aspects of union formation will not be discussed in detail here; they are considered further in the chapters by Kiernan (2), Ermisch (5), and Leshaeghe and Moors (6) below.

Data on mean age at first birth have two drawbacks. Only those for the United Kingdom, Germany, and the Netherlands refer to all births. The rest refer to legitimate births only; in the case of France, to births within the current marriage only. These discrepancies were relatively unimportant when, in the 1950s, only about 5 per cent of births were illegitimate. Now, in the 1990s, the proportion varies from 50 per cent (Sweden and Denmark) through 25–30 per cent (Finland, France, Britain, and Norway) down to 10 per cent (Germany). This variation affects statistics on the timing of first births as births outside marriage tend to be to younger women. For example, in England and Wales in 1992, mean age at first birth for all births, both inside and outside marriage, was 26.0 years. For births within marriage only it was 27.8 years. Mean age at birth for all orders of birth was 29.1 for births of all orders within marriage only and 25.2 for births of all orders outside marriage only (OPCS 1994). In England and Wales in 1990 the average mean age at first birth was over one year younger than the average for West Germany and two years younger than that for the Netherlands.

1.6 Younger and Older Mothers

These differences in timing of births between countries are emphasized by substantial differences in the proportions of births, or of the TFR, contributed by younger and by older mothers. Although sexual activity is becoming more common among teenagers in Western countries, teenage motherhood is relatively uncommon and, with the exception of England and Wales (Babb 1993), has generally become less common in Europe during the 1980s. Except for the United Kingdom, age-specific fertility rates (ASFR) for teenagers (age 15–19) in all Western countries in 1991 are below 24 births per thousand teenagers, and most rates are less than ten per thousand (table 1.3). In Eastern Europe, however, with a tradition of considerably earlier marriage and nearly universal marriage, almost all teenage age-specific fertility rates are over 32 (except Slovenia, 21, and former East Germany, 26). Some (Bulgaria) are double that. On that basis, the United Kingdom, with a teenage ASFR of 33, is demographically more akin to Eastern than to Western Europe. Almost all of these Western teenage births are illegitimate. A recent small-scale British study suggested that a high proportion of such births were unplanned and unwanted and the mothers are less likely than older mothers to be in a cohabiting or a marital sexual union (Family Planning Association 1994). In the United Kingdom these mothers are also more likely than average to be of unskilled manual social class origin, living in local authority accommodation, and of West Indian immigrant origin.

A later start to childbearing means that relatively more births occur to women aged over 30. In the Netherlands, where childbearing is particularly late, ASFRs at age 20–24 have almost halved between 1975 and 1991 while at ages 30–34 and 35–39 they have almost doubled (figure 1.12 and table 1.3). In England and Wales the changes have been more modest. ASFRs have increased for women aged 30–34 over the decade by 27 per cent and for those aged 35–39 by 44 per cent, although this has only brought them back to the levels of the late 1960s (Jones 1992).

This general move towards later maternity is accentuated by some specific factors. Remarried women restarting family building, who now account for about one birth in ten, naturally tend to have their additional births rather later in life than average. Women of foreign nationality (in the United Kingdom, overseas-born women), who also contribute about one in ten to all births in Europe, also contribute a higher than average proportion of all the

TABLE 1.3. *Age-specific fertility rates, selected European countries, 1991*

Country	Year	15–19	20–4	25–9	30–4	35–9	40–4	45–9	TFR	% TFR < age 20	% TFR ≥ age 30
Albania	1990	15.4	167.1	213.6	133.3	55.7	17.4	2.7	3.03	2.5	34.6
Armenia	1990	79.9	240.7	137.3	74.7	26.5	5.9	0.4	2.83	14.1	19.0
Austria	1991	22.7	88.9	106.3	60.0	21.9	3.5	0.2	1.52	7.5	28.2
Belarus	1991	45.2	168.0	88.1	39.5	14.4	3.2	0.2	1.79	12.6	16.0
Belgium	1988	11.7	81.9	134.1	65.5	18.7	3.1	0.3	1.58	3.7	27.8
Bulgaria	1991	69.1	142.9	66.7	24.4	8.2	1.7	0.1	1.57	22.1	11.0
Cyprus	1991	33.2	157.8	164.8	91.2	36.2	6.6	0.4	2.45	6.8	27.4
Czechoslovakia	1991	48.1	175.8	104.9	39.7	12.5	2.2	0.1	1.92	12.5	14.2
Denmark	1991	8.8	68.9	135.2	89.7	29.8	4.2	0.1	1.68	2.6	36.8
Estonia	1991	47.9	149.3	89.3	45.7	20.2	4.3	0.2	1.78	13.4	19.7
Finland	1991	11.8	73.6	137.9	100.6	38.8	7.8	0.5	1.86	3.2	39.8
France	1991	9.3	71.0	137.0	91.0	36.6	7.3	0.5	1.76	2.6	38.4
Georgia	1990	60.2	177.4	110.5	61.7	24.4	5.8	0.3	2.20	13.7	20.9
Germany, W.	1990	12.4	57.3	108.8	81.1	28.2	5.1	0.3	1.47	4.2	39.1
Germany, E.	1989	25.9	133.6	105.2	38.2	11.6	1.8	0.1	1.58	8.2	16.3
Greece	1991	19.9	82.1	96.1	57.0	20.5	4.0	0.4	1.40	7.1	29.3
Hungary	1991	38.1	146.1	117.4	49.7	16.8	3.2	0.1	1.86	10.3	18.8

Country	Year										
Iceland	1991	27.9	102.3	137.3	107.7	52.4	10.0	0.1	2.19	6.4	38.9
Ireland	1991	16.6	63.4	146.7	128.2	65.7	15.1	1.0	2.18	3.8	48.1
Italy	1990	8.9	53.7	94.5	71.7	29.0	5.4	0.2	1.32	3.4	40.4
Latvia	1991	51.1	151.1	94.3	49.3	20.9	4.9	0.2	1.86	13.7	20.3
Lithuania	1991	47.9	167.7	106.7	54.4	20.9	4.6	0.3	2.01	11.9	19.9
Luxemburg	1991	9.2	61.8	120.0	93.9	30.9	5.0	0.1	1.60	2.9	40.5
Malta	1990	11.2	83.8	163.3	99.0	39.9	12.8	0.7	2.05	2.7	37.1
Moldova	1991	62.4	202.6	106.3	53.0	21.2	5.4	0.2	2.26	13.8	17.7
Netherlands	1991	6.3	40.6	116.4	115.6	38.9	5.3	0.4	1.62	1.9	49.5
Norway	1991	16.7	89.7	140.3	98.3	34.3	5.1	0.2	1.92	4.3	35.9
Poland	1991	32.2	164.0	122.3	59.8	25.2	6.2	0.3	2.05	7.9	22.3
Portugal	1991	23.5	85.3	110.2	65.2	24.3	5.8	0.5	1.57	7.5	30.4
Romania	1991	49.8	131.1	78.6	34.2	13.9	4.0	0.3	1.56	16.0	16.8
Russia	1990	55.6	156.8	93.2	48.2	19.4	4.2	0.2	1.89	14.7	19.1
Slovenia	1991	21.0	112.2	95.0	39.8	13.5	3.1	0.1	1.42	7.4	19.8
Spain	1990	12.1	49.5	98.1	73.5	27.3	5.8	0.4	1.33	4.5	40.1
Sweden	1991	13.1	94.0	154.1	111.9	42.8	7.2	0.3	2.12	3.1	38.3
Switzerland	1991	5.5	50.3	120.5	99.6	34.6	5.6	0.2	1.58	1.7	44.3
Ukraine	1991	59.2	159.2	85.3	39.6	14.5	3.2	0.1	1.81	16.4	15.9
United Kingdom	1991	32.9	89.1	120.4	86.8	32.0	5.1	0.3	1.83	9.0	33.9

Source: Council of Europe 1994.

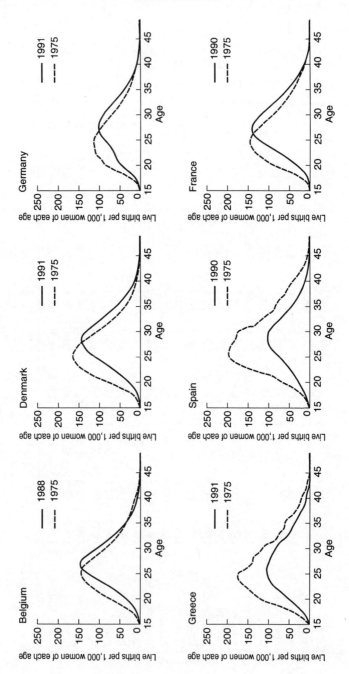

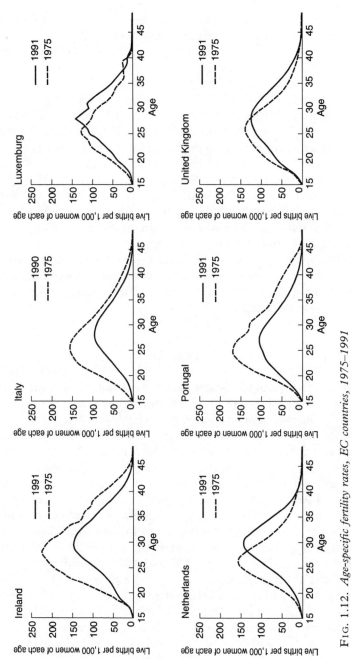

FIG. 1.12. *Age-specific fertility rates, EC countries, 1975–1991*

Source: Eurostat 1993b: fig. E-3, pp. 94–5. Reproduced by kind permission of Eurostat.

births to women aged 30 and over. Such women tend to have higher fertility which extends later into married life.

Around 1991 in Western Europe the proportion of the TFR contributed by women over the age of 30 was 34 per cent on average, ranging between 30 per cent (Portugal) and 49 per cent (Netherlands) (table 1.2). It is better to use the TFR for this measure rather than the simple percentage of births to women aged over 30, as the latter will also reflect differences in the age structure. In Eastern Europe, the proportion of the TFR contributed by such women was generally between 10 and 20 per cent. The proportion in England and Wales, 34 per cent, was one of the lowest. Only Greece, Portugal, Belgium, and Austria had lower proportions of births to older women. The most remarkable pattern of delayed childbearing is found in the Netherlands (49.5 per cent of TFR from births to women aged 30 or over, see Bosveld *et al.* 1991), closely followed by Ireland (48 per cent). In the latter case this follows not so much from a late distribution of all childbearing, but from childbearing being continued for longer than is normal in the rest of Europe.

1.7 Birth Order

The distribution of births according to birth order and to the parity of mothers is the key to understanding family planning strategies and the interpretation of current period birth rates (see Lutz 1992). 'Parity' refers to the status of women in respect of the number of children they have already borne; birth order refers to whether babies are first-born, second-born and so on. Thus a birth to a woman of parity zero is a first birth, a birth to a woman of parity one is a second birth, and so on. Simple data on the numbers of births by birth order are routinely available for most industrial countries, at least for married women. In Belgium, France, Germany, and Switzerland, birth order data are published for births only within marriage. Until 1983 and 1985 respectively, Austria and Norway also published data by parity for legitimate births only. Parity progression ratios, conventionally derived from the distribution of the numbers of births to cohorts of women who have completed their fertility, have already been described.

TABLE 1.4. *Births by birth order, industrial countries around 1990*

	Births by birth order (per 1,000 live births)				
	1st	2nd	3rd	4th+	Total
Australia (legit.)	416	337	168	79	1,000
Austria (all)	476	337	124	63	1,000
Belgium (legit.)	469	335	125	71	1,000
Bulgaria (all)	459	394	93	54	1,000
Canada	443	365	149	43	1,000
Cyprus (legit.)	381	376	183	60	1,000
Czechoslovakia (all)	440	367	133	60	1,000
DDR (legit.)	480	373	105	42	1,000
Denmark (all)	470	355	130	44	1,000
Estonia (all)	463	327	136	74	1,000
Finland (all)	391	361	166	82	1,000
France (legit.)	429	332	154	85	1,000
FRG (legit.)	474	353	121	52	1,000
Greece (all)	445	392	115	48	1,000
Hong Kong	451	353	139	57	1,000
Hungary (all)	439	374	122	65	1,000
Iceland (all)	373	325	199	103	1,000
Ireland (all)	313	258	185	244	1,000
Israel (Jews)	277	264	210	249	1,000
Italy (all)	465	364	121	50	1,000
Japan	423	389	159	29	1,000
Korea (S)	448	385	111	56	1,000
Latvia (all)	478	329	123	69	1,000
Lithuania (all)	479	362	108	51	1,000
Luxemburg (legit.)	460	371	133	36	1,000
Netherlands (all)	438	357	137	68	1,000
New Zealand	374	340	183	103	1,000
Norway (all)	443	344	155	58	1,000
Poland (all)	471	315	113	101	1,000
Portugal (all)	514	317	97	72	1,000
Romania (all)	390	318	142	150	1,000
Singapore	403	377	160	51	991
Spain (all)	451	319	137	93	1,000
Sweden (all)	418	348	168	66	1,000
Switzerland (legit.)	448	376	134	42	1,000
UK (legit.)	395	362	157	86	1,000

TABLE 1.4. (*cont.*)

| | Births by birth order (per 1,000 live births) | | | | |
	1st	2nd	3rd	4th+	Total
England & Wales (all, 1985)	414	337	155	94	1,000
USA	412	327	160	101	1,000
USSR	390	318	142	150	1,000
Yugoslavia	421	355	115	109	1,000
Unweighted mean	431	347	142	80	1,000
Maximum	514	394	210	249	
Minimum	277	258	93	29	
Range	237	136	117	220	
Coeff. of variation	11	9	19	59	

Sources: Eurostat 1991, Council of Europe 1991, and national demographic yearbooks.

In general in Europe around 1990, the relative proportions of second and of third births have remained relatively high compared with the numbers of first births (table 1.4), even though period measures of fertility based on age-specific rates indicate average family sizes of little more than one in some countries. Such birth-order data can be summarized by calculating the period TFR for first, second, third, and higher-order births separately, and thus the proportion of the TFR which can be attributed to first, second, and higher order births births (see OPCS 1987a, 1994). Such data are not widely available for most European countries.

In the industrial world as a whole around 1990, about 43 per cent of births were first births, 35 per cent were second births, 14 per cent were third births, and 8 per cent fourth and over. The proportion of births which are third or higher is the most variable, as might be expected; the proportion of births which are second births is the least variable. The coefficient of variation (standard deviation/mean $\times$ 100) of the data in table 1.4 is 9 for second births, 19 for third, and 59 for fourth and over. Even though these are period data (the second births recorded in a given year will not usually be to the same women who had first births in that year) it can be inferred that when women have one birth it seems they usually go on to have at least a second, even if subsequent preferences then differ more widely.

True birth order (the birth order of all births irrespective of legitimacy, see OPCS 1987b) does not radically change the pattern of birth order derived from marital births alone. For example, while a higher proportion of illegitimate births than legitimate births are first births (60 per cent and 39 per cent respectively in 1985 in England and Wales), about one-fifth of illegitimate births in 1985 were second illegitimate births and about as many again were illegitimate births of higher order. The incorporation of all births into birth-order calculations increases the average birth order of births within marriage, because many women who have a birth outside marriage then go on to marry and have further births within marriage. Altogether in 1985 in England and Wales, 41 per cent of all births were first births, 34 per cent second, and 25 per cent third . or higher order.

1.8 Childlessness

There is nothing new about childlessness in Europe. In the past, up to 20 per cent of cohorts remained unmarried and of these the majority had no children (see Glass and Grebenik 1954, Wrigley and Schofield 1983): these features were characteristic of what is termed the West European marriage pattern (Hajnal 1965). Childlessness reached an all-time low in Britain and other West European countries among the cohorts born just after the Second World War. These were the most heavily married cohorts in British history—about 95 per cent of the 1946 cohort were married by age 35 and only about 9 per cent remained childless (irrespective of marital status; see Kiernan 1989b). Since then, the proportion of women remaining childless at each age has progressively risen. Lifetime childlessness is now an important and growing component of low fertility in Europe, and usually occurs within cohabitation or marriage rather than in a celibate state as formerly. Ireland may be one of the few remaining examples of the old pattern of childlessness.

Final levels of childlessness of women who are still in their reproductive years (say up to age 40) cannot yet be stated with confidence. Although recent cohorts of women in some countries are reaching record levels of childlessness by the age of 25 or 30, much of this may be a consequence of the postponement, not the cancellation, of childbearing. Trends in childlessness in completed cohorts of older women are shown in table 1.5. In a number of European countries about 20 per cent of women or more have remained childless up to their mid-thirties: West Germany (20 per cent); Austria (20 per cent); Finland (19 per cent); the Netherlands (18 per cent); and Switzerland (21 per cent). In Britain 16 per cent of women (married and otherwise) were still childless at the age of 37 in 1992, about the West European average. The proportions of childless women vary more than twofold between Western European countries, even between neighbouring France and Germany. However, the level of childlessness (a cohort measure) bears little relation to current period fertility rates. In a comparison of fifteen European countries for which both data are available, there was no statistically significant correlation (r = 0.09) between the 1989 period TFR and the proportion of childless women in 1989 among women born in 1950.

About 3 per cent of married couples suffer from 'primary sterility' from the beginning of their marriage (Werner 1986, Bongaarts and Potter 1983). That is, as a couple, they are biologically incapable of having children even though they wish to do so and attempt to do so. Such biological infecundity is not thought to vary much between populations, at least within Europe. However, infecundity does increase with age, and as mean age at first childbearing rises, more women who were previously fecund will find themselves sterile by the time they want to start a family, the more so in populations where mean age at birth is later than in others. The new pressures faced by many Western women in balancing desires for children and career have been described in personal accounts (for example Fleming 1994) and in numberless magazine articles. However, the level of sterility, which increases with age, does not rise to serious levels until after the age of 35. What matters more in determining the prevalence of childlessness is the difference in preferences, not just in respect of definite views on preferring no children, but more generally in the spread of attitudes which tend to delay family building and give it a low priority.

TABLE 1.5. *Percentage of women childless by age 40, selected European countries, birth cohorts from 1930 (per thousand women)*

Birth cohort	England & Wales		Austria	Belgium		Den-mark	Fin-land	France		West Germany		Ire-land	Italy[a]		Nether-lands	Norway	Portugal[a]	Spain	Sweden[a]	Switzer-land	Birth cohort
	All	Legit.		All	Legit.	Legit.	Legit.	All	Legit.	All	Legit.							Legit.		Legit.	
1930	13.8	16.0	17.2	16.8				13.0	12.7												1930
1931	14.4	16.4	16.4	16.3				12.4	12.3												1931
1932	14.4	15.8	15.5	15.9				12.3	11.8												1932
1933	13.0	14.4	15.0	15.4				11.7	11.6						15.4				14.7	21.4	1933
1934	11.5	13.8	14.7	15.0	13.5			11.2	11.1						13.0			14.2	14.0	20.5	1934
1935	11.4	14.0	14.8	14.8	13.6		15.9	10.5	10.3	9.2	18.1		15.5		14.8	9.6			13.9	18.6	1935
1936	11.5	14.4	14.4	14.5	13.0		15.6	10.1	9.9	9.9	17.9		15.4		12.4	9.5			13.5	17.0	1936
1937	11.6	14.4	14.4	13.8	13.2		15.5	9.4	9.4	9.8	17.2		14.5		12.7	9.4			13.4	15.8	1937
1938	11.2	14.3	14.0	13.8	13.1		15.3	9.4	9.1	10.4	17.1		13.8		11.7	9.2		12.0	13.5	14.7	1938
1939	11.3	14.5	14.1	13.5	13.1		14.9	9.4	9.0	10.2	16.6		14.1		11.7	8.9		11.6	13.3	13.9	1939
1940	11.1	14.3	14.3	13.1	12.1		15.2	8.3	8.0	10.6	16.8	19.8	12.6	13.6	10.3	9.5			13.0	13.9	1940
1941	10.6	14.0	14.6	13.1	12.0		16.3	8.3	8.1	11.1	17.0	20.7	12.4	10.7	12.1	9.0			13.2	14.7	1941
1942	11.3	14.7	14.5	13.2	12.3		16.3	8.9	8.6	12.1	18.1	20.1	12.6	14.7	11.6	9.4			13.2	16.1	1942
1943	11.6	14.6	15.0	12.9	12.1	8.9	16.6	8.2	8.0	12.5	18.2	18.0	10.9	11.9	11.9	9.7		11.0	13.0	16.7	1943
1944	10.7	14.8	15.1	13.0	12.3	8.1	16.6	8.2	8.0	12.8	18.4	17.3	11.6	11.0	11.1	9.5			13.1	16.7	1944
1945	10.2	15.7	14.4	12.8	12.6	9.2	16.5	8.1	8.3	12.7	18.8	16.8	11.4	11.9	10.3	9.2		10.2	13.2	17.6	1945
1946	9.6	15.8	14.8	13.1	13.2	9.4	15.5	8.5	8.2	11.8	18.7	17.3	10.4	10.3	10.5	9.1			12.8	17.5	1946
1947	12.9	16.8	15.0	13.1	13.2	9.4	15.7	9.2	9.6	12.4	18.2	13.9	10.6	10.1	11.7	9.4			12.9	17.4	1947
1948	12.2	18.5	15.2	12.8	13.7	10.8	16.1	8.2	10.0	13.2	18.8	13.9	11.0	11.5	11.7	9.6		10.0	12.8	18.0	1948
1949	13.0	19.5	15.4	13.6	13.7	11.0	17.1	8.6	10.5	13.7	19.4	13.9	11.2	11.2	12.8	9.9		9.8	12.7	18.6	1949
1950	14.0	20.6	16.1	13.4	14.2	12.2	17.4	8.3	11.1	14.8	20.7	14.3	11.4	12.2	12.9	10.0	11.0		13.1	19.8	1950
1951	15.0		16.9	13.9	15.3	12.4	17.8	8.0		15.9	22.0	12.5	11.2	12.3	14.0	10.4	9.9		13.9	21.2	1951
1952	15.0		17.6	14.3	15.3	13.2	18.3	7.9		17.4	23.2	13.4	11.8	12.6	14.7	11.0	10.8		14.3		1952
1953	16.0		18.3	14.3	16.2	13.7	18.4	8.1		18.6	24.5	13.1	11.8	12.7	15.5	11.7	10.3	9.5	14.6		1953
1954	16.0		19.7	14.7	16.5	13.9	18.5	8.4		20.3	26.0	12.7	14.0	14.0	16.0	12.7	11.2	9.6	15.1		1954
1955	16.0			15.2	17.0	14.2	19.1	8.3		20.3	25.9	14.2	13.0	14.9	16.8	13.5	9.7		15.8		1955
1956	17.0				17.3	15.0	19.7	8.2		20.9		14.5			17.1		8.5		15.6		1956
1957	17.0						20.6	8.4		22.1					17.8		10.5		16.1		1957
1958	17.0						21.2	8.8		22.9					18.0		9.5		16.6		1958
1959	17.0							9.8							18.7				16.6		1959
1960	18.0							10.2							19.5				16.6		1960

Notes: The lifetime fertility of cohorts born after 1950 has been completed by assuming the continuation of current age-specific fertility rates.

Legit. = within marriage.

[a] Two sets of data for the same country derived from different sources. For details see reference.

Source: Prioux 1993.

1.9 Wanted and Unwanted Births,
Contraception and Abortion

In European countries about 70 per cent of couples of reproductive age currently use some form of contraception and over 90 per cent have done so at some time in their lives (United Nations 1989). These are about the maximum figures which could reasonably be expected, given that not all women are fecund, not all are in sexual unions, and, of course, some actually wish to become pregnant. With the exception of Ireland, such variation as exists between European countries with respect to reported levels of contraceptive usage and methods, and levels of legal abortion, do not correspond well with observed levels of fertility (see table 1.5). Thus Denmark, with the highest abortion ratio, none the less has average fertility; Sweden, with the third-highest abortion ratio, also has the second-highest TFR, while Italy, with the world's lowest birth rate, has a level of legal abortion about the same as those two countries and also has one of the highest levels of use of the rhythm method, well known to be unreliable. The general practice of contraception in European countries has meant that family size can be achieved, at least potentially, with unprecedented accuracy both with respect to the number of children and to the accuracy of their timing. This has been accompanied by a convergence on a two-child norm in desired family size, even if this is not currently being realized in many countries. Although an approximately two-child average has been a feature of European demography since the 1930s, there are today fewer families with one or with three or more children than there were. In Britain, it is only since the marriages of 1970 that as many as 50 per cent of families (at nine years' marriage duration) have actually been two-child families (Kiernan 1983).

The general use of contraception does not mean that all births today are planned or wanted. The favoured methods in use in different countries vary considerably. For example, in Greece and in Eastern Europe (not shown in table 1.6), traditional and less effective methods such as withdrawal are still widely used, with considerable dependence on abortion, and within some countries there is considerable variation in use according to social and educational status, especially among young people. The cost of contraception also varies between countries—it is free in some, not in others (IPPF 1994). The conventional wisdom has been that the

TABLE 1.6. *Contraceptive usage and abortion, selected European countries in the 1980s*

Country	TFR c.1989	Abortion ratio[a] c.1989	Contraception (married women) — Year of survey	Contraception (married women) — % using currently	% of current users using — Sterilization (either partner)	Pill	IUD	Condom	Rhythm	Withdrawal	Other
Austria	1.45	179	1982	71	1	56	12	6	12	8	5
Belgium[b]	1.58	0	1982	81	21	39	10	8	5	16	1
Denmark	1.62	360	1975	63		35	14	39	1	2	9
Finland	1.70	219	1977	80	6	14	36	40	1	3	0
France	1.81	212	1978	79	5	34	13	8	9	29	2
France	1.81	212	1984	79							
Germany	1.39	124	1985	78	16	43	19	7	5	5	5
Greece[c]	1.50	1.5		60							
Ireland[d]	2.11	0									
Italy	1.29	340	1984	78	0	18	3	17	11	46	5
Netherlands	1.55	97	1985	76	19	55	12	9	2	1	2
Norway	1.88	276	1977	71	9	18	39	23	4	5	2
Portugal	1.50	5	1980	66	1	29	5	8	6	39	12
Spain	1.39	332	1985	59	8	26	10	21	6	27	2
Sweden	2.01	5	1981	78	4	30	26	32	6		8
Switzerland	1.57	233	1980	71	22	39	15	12	1	2	4
UK (GB)	1.81	233	1983	83	30	36	11	19	5	5	−2
Mean	1.65	153		73	11	34	16	18	5	14	2

Note: An abortion ratio of '5' is a nominal figure reflecting severe restriction to medical cases.
[a] Abortion ratio is the number of legal abortions per 1,000 live births per year.
[b] Contraception data on Belgium refers to Flanders.
[c] These official figures on legal abortion for Greece may considerably understate the real incidence (Langford, pers. comm.).
[d] Abortion is illegal in the Republic of Ireland. The number of abortions performed in Great Britain on women resident in the Republic of Ireland suggested an abortion ratio of at least 59 in 1989.
For details of whether data refer to 'married' or 'first married', etc., see UN (1989).
Blank indicates no data separately available for that method.
Sources: TFR and abortion data: Eurostat 1991, Council of Europe 1991, and national demographic year books; data by method: United Nations 1989, table 3 and table 10.

rise and fall of new methods of contraception has not been a major factor behind post-war fertility trends, but this view has recently been challenged (Murphy 1993).

Estimates from different sources suggest that, even in recent years, a substantial proportion of births in Europe are not wanted, although different sources do not give the same picture. About 30 per cent of births in England and Wales are reported as being 'unplanned' in that the conception did not occur as a deliberate act, although the resultant births are by no means all 'unwanted', a proportion which has not declined from 1975 to 1989 (Feissig 1991). Many of these unplanned births arise from method or user failures in contraception or, especially with teenagers, no use at all. It has been estimated that in the UK about 10 per cent of marital fertility arises from contraceptive failure, in that if all users had used the most effective methods, the TFR would be about 1.7 instead of 1.8 and if non-users employed even the least effective methods then the abortion ratio would fall by 30 per cent (Westoff, Hammerslough, and Paul 1987). Questionnaire surveys of married women in England and Wales who had given birth in 1967–8 suggest that 15 per cent of married women regretted that their recent birth had happened at all, a proportion which had declined to 11 per cent by 1975 and just 3 per cent by 1984 (Cartwright 1987), a trend which is not consonant with Feissig's results. It seems reasonable to suppose that the widespread use of the contraceptive pill since the 1960s, and the rise of contraceptive steriliz- ation to become the single most important means of contraception, might have reduced the number of unwanted births (Murphy 1993). These methods were, after all, intended to help women to control their fertility more effectively. None the less, in England and Wales in 1991 one in five of all known pregnancies (inside and outside marriage) were legally terminated, and overall it is esti- mated that almost half of all conceptions in England around 1990 were unintended or unwanted in some sense (Department of Health 1991).

Other estimates give higher figures for unwanted births. For example, Calhoun (1991), using data from the 1970s World Fer- tility Surveys, attempts to adjust for the self-censoring of reported levels of unwanted births. Mothers who have already had un- wanted children will be reluctant to specify ideal family sizes that would imply that their own children were unwanted. Adjustment for this asymmetry gives very high proportions of unwanted births, particularly in the United Kingdom. Education on contraception and responsible parenthood in Britain still seems to be deficient, as it is in some other European countries (IPPF 1991). As was noted above, high proportions of young people still have intercourse without any contraceptive precaution (Family Planning Assocation 1994). Laws permitting legal abortion still vary considerably between European countries. In some countries it is not available (Ireland and Belgium); in others such as Spain abortion has been available (since 1985) only on limited grounds; in most others it is more widely available on social grounds (Britain, though not Northern Ireland, since 1967 and Italy since 1978); in others abortion is effectively on demand. The latter is the case in most countries in Eastern Europe and the former Soviet Union, where abortion was a front-line method of contraception, alongside minimal availability of modern contraception. In Romania abortion was suppressed from 1966 to 1989 in order to increase population growth. However, Roman Catholic and traditional opinion has succeeded in restricting the legal availability of abortion since the end of the communist dictatorship in Poland and has pressed to do so in former Czechoslovakia as well. In Greece the legalization of abortion in 1986 recognized that Greek women had more (illegal) abortions than they had live-born children. Within countries, access to abortion can still be uneven under the same law, judging from the marked regional differences in non-marital pregnancies terminated by abortion. Such terminations are particularly low in North-West England (IPPF 1991, 1993, Coleman and Salt 1992, Family Planning Association 1994). In Britain, the proportion of pregnancies outside marriage which terminated in abortion stopped increasing in 1976 (at just over 40 per cent) and has been falling slowly since 1981 to 34.3 per cent in 1992 (Coleman and Salt 1992, OPCS 1994). There are various reasons, including welfare and access to state housing, why some unmarried mothers, even without a cohabiting partner, might find fulfilment and advantage in having a child.

1.10 Desired Family Size

Average family size in Europe has been about two children for the last sixty years. Surveys have shown that this is still, on average, the family size desired—or claimed to be desired—by most women. In most countries, the proportion of women stating that they do not want any children at all is still relatively low and has not increased much in the 1980s (EC Commission 1990). It may be argued that in giving these responses, women are merely repeating what they believe to be accepted norms or their own statistically likely fate. Even if that is true, national differences and trends remain interesting. Motivations for childlessness appear to be varied, but childless couples in Britain in the 1980s did not report that they had 'forgotten' to have children or that they had postponed childbearing and then found themselves to be infecund (Campbell 1985, Kiernan 1989b).

Current forecasts in Britain, based upon the family intentions questions in the General Household Survey, suggest that as many as 17 per cent of women born in England and Wales in 1975 and later will remain childless, compared with 14 per cent of those born in 1950. These figures do not match the stated expectations of recent cohorts as collected in fertility surveys. While the average number of children expected by women born in 1965–9 (the most recent available data, from women aged 16–21) is 2.2, with only 5 per cent expecting to remain childless, these patterns and expectations are known to change as people age (Shaw 1989).

According to the 'Eurobarometer' surveys of opinion in EC countries, in Belgium each year from 1982 to 1986 only about 6 per cent of women aged between 18 and 37 years stated that they wanted no children, although the proportion 'unsure' had increased from 4 per cent to 8 per cent. The Belgian figure is in fact rather high, only exceeded by that of Germany (9 per cent and 7 per cent in the two years respectively). However it may be significant that the number preferring just one child has doubled in most EC countries in ten years and has increased from 2 per cent to 10 per cent even in Britain. The highest proportions wanting one child only were in Belgium (18 per cent), Spain (22 per cent), Luxemburg (21 per cent), and Portugal (21 per cent) (EC Commission 1990).

Less variation can be seen in desired family size and the distribution of ideal family sizes than in observed levels of fertility (table 1.7). For example in 1989, respondents to the same survey in the twelve EC countries reported ideal numbers of children in the family clustered closely around the EC average of 2.1. The lowest were Germany, Spain, and Luxemburg (1.94, 1.97, and 1.99); the

TABLE 1.7. Ideal or desired family size in the twelve countries of the EC, 1979 and 1989

Country	TFR 1979	TFR 1989	Ideal size 1979	Ideal size 1989	None 1979	None 1989	One 1979	One 1989	Two 1979	Two 1989	Three or more 1979	Three or more 1989	European Values Study 1981[a] Familism	Nonconformism	Religiosity	Materialism (Inglehart scale)	Country
Belgium	1.69	1.58	2.15	2.01	6	5	7	18	59	52	35	41	2.77	2.31	2.83	1.19	Belgium
Denmark	1.60	1.62	2.31	2.13	3	3	3	9	60	65	37	32	2.41	2.78	2.06	0.88	Denmark
France	1.86	1.81	2.46	2.13	3	3	3	19	44	47	53	50	2.61	2.81	2.06	1.15	France
Germany	1.38	1.39	1.95	1.97	9	7	11	14	59	58	32	31	2.75	2.35	2.54	1.09	Germany
Greece	2.26	1.50	n/a	2.42	n/a	2	n/a	13	n/a	33	n/a	58	n/a	n/a	n/a	n/a	Greece
Ireland	3.23	2.11	3.62	2.79	2	2	1	9	17	42	81	66	3.45	1.70	3.42	1.32	Ireland
Italy	1.76	1.29	2.11	2.20	3	3	11	9	63	61	34	28	2.89	2.38	2.90	1.39	Italy
Luxemburg	1.48	1.52	2.17	1.99	5	3	6	21	62	56	33	38	n/a	n/a	n/a	n/a	Luxemburg
Netherlands	1.56	1.55	2.29	2.23	3	3	2	5	66	65	31	33	2.73	2.26	2.66	1.05	Netherlands
Portugal	2.11	1.50	n/a	2.01	n/a	3	n/a	21	n/a	55	n/a	45	n/a	n/a	n/a	n/a	Portugal
Spain	2.34	1.39	n/a	1.94	n/a	4	n/a	22	n/a	55	n/a	45	2.94	2.31	2.82	1.41	Spain
UK	1.86	1.81	2.29	2.14	2	2	2	10	71	67	27	31	2.95	2.33	2.33	1.12	UK
EC unweighted	1.93	1.59	2.37	2.16	4	3	5	14	56	55	40	42	2.83	2.36	2.62	1.18	
EC weighted			2.21	2.1													
UK rank	5=	2=	4=	5	8=	9=	8=	8=	1	1	9	10=	2	5	7	5	

Note:
[a] The scales for the values are all direct; that is, the larger the scale value, the higher the level of formilism, nonconformity, etc.
Sources: EC Commission 1990, table B; European Values Study data from Lesthaeghe and Meekers 1986, appendix table A1.

highest Ireland, Greece, and Netherlands (2.79, 2.42, and 2.23). The UK reported 2.14. Some of these preferences are in line with actual current fertility (for example, Germany, Spain, and Ireland) but others are not (Netherlands, Italy, and Greece).

The overall average has changed little since a similar EC survey in 1979 when the mean was 2.2 (EC Commission 1990). Over the decade, the proportion of people in each country expressing a preference for two children remained rather steady in most countries except Ireland, where the proportion almost doubled. Proportions preferring three or more fell somewhat over the decade, especially in those countries where that family size had previously been popular (Denmark, France, and Ireland). However, in 1979 over a third of the EC sample (35 per cent) expressed a preference for the larger family and 28 per cent did so in 1989; only in Spain did the proportion fall below 20 per cent. 'Convergence' on a two-child family norm is still far from universal. There is more change over the decade in each country regarding the proportion favouring no children or only one child. In some countries the proportions of these two together has more than doubled over ten years, including the United Kingdom, whereas there has been no change of opinion in Germany which still has the highest proportion in each year believing that the ideal family has no children at all (9 per cent and 7 per cent respectively).

Explanations for this variation in performance and in desired family size will not be discussed here, in what is simply a descriptive chapter. Such factors as relative wages and women's workforce participation levels are believed to be important in the determination of fertility trends over time within any particular country. It is more difficult, however, to make sense of current differences in patterns and trends between countries on the basis of these or other socio-economic measures conventionally used in fertility analysis, such as national income, urbanization, proportion of the work-force engaged in agriculture, and so on. Such variables yield very low or zero correlations with period fertility measures between European national populations (Coleman 1993). Ideas and values, and the education, media, and literacy which foster them, may be more important than had been thought in explaining both the decline in fertility during the demographic transition (Cleland and Wilson 1987) and current low levels of fertility in Europe. The so-called 'second demographic transition' is a tendency observed since the 1960s to new, even lower levels of fertility, and to new, higher levels of illegitimacy, divorce, cohabitation, and other alternative family forms (van de Kaa 1987, Lesthaeghe and Meekers 1986, Simons 1986). Both rational-choice and ideational models, however, have difficulty in accounting for the recent upturn in births. Economic and ideational factors affecting family size and living arrangements are discussed in Chapter 5 by Ermisch and in Chapter 6 by Lesthaeghe and Moors, while family and welfare policies and their effects are considered by Gauthier in Chapter 9 and also by, for example, Murphy and Sullivan (1985), Murphy (1992b, 1993), Ermisch (1991), and Joshi (1989).

1.11 Sub-National Variation in Fertility

The emphasis given to cultural variables in the explanation of fertility patterns and change has focused attention upon subnational areas which are culturally more homogeneous than large national populations. Such regional linguistic, religious, and ethnic differences within some European countries led Coale and his colleagues (1986) to base their analysis of fertility decline in Europe from 1870 to 1960 upon 450 provinces rather than the seventeen countries which they comprised. Over that century there has been a marked convergence in fertility levels within many continental countries. Demographically homogeneous nations have arisen with much less internal variation in fertility than hitherto, so that in recent years more of the fertility variability within Europe is statistically accounted for by variation between nation states, not between regions or provinces of those states (Watkins 1991). Furthermore, international variability has been increasing since the 1980s, not declining, as 'convergence' theory would lead us to expect (Coleman 1992).

Statistics on trends in national and sub-national levels of fertility from selected European countries are given in table 1.8. The trends described by Watkins have continued, at least up to 1985. Here the measure used is the total fertility ratio, not the Princeton fertility indices. Lack of suitable time-series makes it necessary to use a more restricted set of examples (ninety-five provinces or republics in eight European countries). The mean squared deviation of the

TABLE 1.8. *Analysis of variance of provincial total fertility rates in eight countries and ninety-five provinces in 1970, 1975, and 1985*

	Degrees freedom	1970			1975			1985		
		Sum of squares	Mean square	F, p	Sum of squares	Mean square	F, p	Sum of squares	Mean square	F, p
Between countries	7	6.2	0.89	3.482 0.0025	8.9	1.27	7.771 0.0001	10.5	1.51	15.139 0.0001
Within countries	87	22.2	0.26		14.2	0.16		8.6	0.10	
Total	94	28.4			23.1			19.2		

Country	N	1970			1975			1985		
		Unw. mean	Stan. dev.	Coeff. var.	Unw. mean	Stan. dev.	Coeff. var.	Unw. mean	Stan. dev.	Coeff. var.
Czechoslovakia	2	2.162	0.329	15.2	2.498	0.088	3.5	2.103	0.212	10.1
France	22	2.651	0.271	10.2	1.968	0.181	9.2	1.844	0.194	10.5
FRG	11	1.909	0.262	13.7	1.406	0.114	8.1	1.248	0.100	8.0
Italy	20	2.402	0.416	17.3	2.166	0.379	17.5	1.389	0.294	21.2
Netherlands	12	2.777	0.380	13.7	1.774	0.228	12.9	1.567	0.154	9.8
UK	11	2.492	0.254	10.2	1.886	0.266	14.1	1.841	0.211	11.5
USSR	9	2.367	0.412	17.4	2.246	0.296	13.2	2.281	0.238	10.4
Yugoslavia	8	2.725	1.361	49.9	2.575	1.114	43.3	2.219	0.837	37.7

Notes:
N = number of provinces.
Unw. mean = unweighted mean.
Stan. dev. = Standard deviation.
Coeff. var. = Coefficient of variation (standard deviation/mean × 100).
F = ratios of the mean square of variation between countries and of variation within countries to the residual (unexplained) mean square.
p = statistical significance of the F statistic.
Sources: See Coleman 1992.

TFR between these countries rose from 0.887 in 1970 to 1.505 in 1985; that for provinces within countries declined from 0.255 to 0.099.

By the mid-1980s most industrial countries had become relatively homogeneous with respect to fertility levels, with low coefficients of variation between their regions or provinces. The coefficient of variation within Belgium, France, Germany, the Netherlands, and the United Kingdom was between 8.0 and 11.5 around 1985. The United Kingdom figure is inflated by the high fertility of Northern Ireland. That for England and Wales alone is about 5 (table 1.9). The figure for England and Wales is one of the lowest of any of the countries analysed, as it was in the nineteenth century (Teitelbaum 1984), only approached by coefficients of 6.2 in Switzerland in 1989 and, further afield, 6.7 for the forty-seven prefectures of Japan in 1988. Other countries were more heterogeneous in respect of fertility and other demographic variables (Italy, 21.2, and Yugoslavia, 37.7). The European republics of the former USSR, which had shown rather different fertility levels in the recent past, had by the mid-1980s acquired similar average fertility levels (coefficient 10.4).

Since the 1970s convergence between the provinces in some countries has come to an end, at a low level of variability. France and the United Kingdom have maintained similarly low levels of provincial fertility differences since 1970. But the substantial relative differences between northern Italy and the Mezzogiorno have, if anything, increased over the same period despite a general decline in the average. For example, in 1987 Campania and Calabria in the south had almost double (1.82) the TFR of Friuli-Venezia Giulia (0.94) and of Emilia Romana (0.93). Where further reduction in variation within countries has taken place in the 1980s (17 to 10 in the former USSR, 50 to 38 in former Yugoslavia), it has primarily been due to declining fertility in a minority of high-fertility provinces or republics such as Kosovo and Macedonia in Yugoslavia, Moldavia, Georgia, and Armenia in the European former USSR, and Northern Ireland in the United Kingdom. In Yugoslavia, for example, the scale of the variation was dominated by the high fertility of the Kosovo region of Serbia with its indigenous Albanian Muslim population. Fertility in Bosnia, however, which also has a substantial Muslim population but of non-Albanian ethnic origin, was no different from that of its neigh-

TABLE 1.9. *Summary statistics on the variability of period TFR between the provinces of eight selected Western European countries around 1985*

Country	Year	Statistic					Pop. ('000s)	
		Mean TFR	N	R	Stan. dev.	Coeff. var.	National	Mean of regions
England & Wales regions	1985	1.79	9	0.18	0.06	3.5	49,924	5,547
England & Wales counties	1985	1.76	46	0.38	0.09	5.18	49,924	1,085
Great Britain regions[a]	1985	1.78	10	0.18	0.06	3.59	55,060	5,506
United Kingdom regions[b]	1985	1.84	11	0.75	0.21	11.5	56,618	5,147
France	1982	1.84	22	0.86	0.19	10.5	55,063	2,503
Italy	1985	1.39	20	0.96	0.29	21.2	57,080	2,854
Switzerland	1989	1.75	26	0.54	0.13	7.16	6,456	248
Netherlands	1985	1.56	13	0.46	0.15	9.54	14,454	1,112
Belgium	1985	1.54	9	0.37	0.11	7.34	9,858	1,095
Germany	1985	1.25	11	1.41	0.10	8.01	61,049	5,550
Spain	1985	1.61	17	0.78	0.23	14.3	38,423	2,260

Notes:
Means are unweighted.
N = number of regions of provinces.
R = range.
Stan. dev = standard deviation.
Coeff. var. = coefficient of variation (standard deviation ×100/mean).
Regions[a]: Scotland counted as one 'region' for statistical purposes.
Regions[b]: Scotland and Northern Ireland counted as one 'region' each for statistical purposes.
Sources: National Statistical or Demographic Yearbooks; Armitage 1987, for county data; Council of Europe 1990, table A2, for national populations;
  OPCS 1987c, table 2, p. 39, for UK and sub-national populations.

bours (see Appendix table A1.1). Some of these provinces or republics were marked by long-established religious, ethnic, linguistic, and socio-economic differences which were at that time recognized by semi-autonomous status. Many still have substantial rural populations and are located in marginal or remote areas, and would be expected to have higher fertility on those grounds alone. The republics of the former USSR, of Czechoslovakia, and some of the republics of former Yugoslavia have now, of course, become independent states, although Kosovo remains within Serbia.

On a smaller scale, a similar convergence is apparent in Switzerland. The urban cantons such as Neuchatel, Vaud, Basel, Geneva, Bern, and Zurich have maintained low fertility since the 1970s (children per mother, not TFR, between 1.7 and 2.0). Fertility in the remote ur-Swiss rural areas such as Schwyz, Nidwalden, Appenzell, Uri, and Obwalden, once much higher (2.4 to 2.9), was still declining at the end of the 1980s. By 1989, the coefficient of variation for all 25 cantons of Switzerland (excluding Jura), with its four official languages and its religious diversity, had fallen to 6.2 and has possibly reached a minimum. Many of the small differences between cantons have now persisted unchanged over more than a decade. Swiss cantons have small populations. Many are entirely rural, others primarily urban. This makes their current homogeneity even more surprising.

Diversity in language or religion by itself, therefore, does not necessarily sustain high levels of provincial variation within Western countries. The Belgian coefficient of variation in 1985 was very low (7.95), having fallen from high levels as recently as 1980 (18.7), despite the deepening institutional segregation of the two linguistically distinct regions of Wallonia (French) and Flanders (Dutch). Two major republics of former Czechoslovakia showed a diminution in the absolute and relative differences in their TFR from 1950 to the 1970s, with no further narrowing of the (relatively small) differential up to the time of their separation into two independent republics in 1992.

England and Wales has the lowest variation of any large country in Western Europe with respect to fertility (table 1.9). The range in TFR between the highest and the lowest standard regions in England and Wales is only 0.18, half the lowest on the Continent and a quarter of that in France (0.86), Italy (0.96), and Spain (0.78). The coefficient of variation for the TFR in England and Wales, 3.5, is less than half that of the nearest continental country and only a quarter of many of them. Most continental countries, however, are subdivided into rather larger numbers of smaller provinces or regional subdivisions. Therefore variation in TFR in England is also analysed according to county, and metropolitan district areas, of which there are forty-four. In fact this smaller subdivision only increases the range to 0.38 and the coefficient of variation to 5.2, still the smallest of the countries shown in table 1.5. Regional variation in fertility in Britain is, therefore, conspicuously low. A low variation in fertility at the county level in England, from 1870 to 1960, was noted in Coale and Watkins's study (1986) and by others (Teitelbaum 1984, Brass and Kabir 1978).

In England the much-discussed 'North/South' divide is not obvious in fertility terms. No pair of regions in England are as sharply demographically contrasted as, for example, are Limousin and Nord in France (1982 TFR 1.53 and 2.22 respectively); Liguria and Campania in Italy in 1985 (0.99 and 1.95 respectively); and Asturias and Murcia in Spain (1.26 and 1.92 respectively). These are paralleled by many other statistical differences (see Eurostat 1993) and of course in some cases by considerable differences in language or dialect, culture, and level of economic development. For example, in Germany the Hamburg *Land* (province) has a TFR of 1.10 in contrast with another predominantly urban *Land*, Berlin, with a TFR of 1.41 (influenced by the fertility of Turkish and other immigrants). Overall the coefficient of variation for the TFR of the German *Länder* in 1985 was about double that of the English regions. Even in the Netherlands in 1985, Groningen (1.41) and Flevoland (1.84) showed a bigger fertility difference than can be found between any English counties.

Watkins accounts for this demographic convergence within countries by the rise of ethnically and linguistically more homogeneous nations in Europe, stimulated by universal education and a modern economy, which, through its communications, media, and personal mobility brings even the inhabitants of the most remote areas into contact with a national culture. Gellner (1983) emphasizes the role of industrialization and economic modernization on the rise of a national language and national communication. Despite the rise of ethnic self-consciousness in many of the nations of Europe, demographic homogeneity within countries may be reinforced by demographic responses to national economic patterns that are increasingly dominated by the welfare and taxation policies of modern governments, which have a pervasive effect within countries but remain distinct between them. Overall, government expenditure accounts for over 40 per cent of the national income in most modern industrial countries (OECD 1985), with substantial consequences for the individual domestic economy and expenditure decisions. But we are still a long way from an adequate explanation of fertility trends and patterns even within individual countries, let alone understanding the reasons behind the differences in fertility between countries and their regions.

1.12 Conclusions

The pattern of fertility in Europe at the beginning of the 1990s is diverse, and is becoming more so. Expectations of convergence have not yet been realized and may not be. Since the 1970s, most countries in Northern and Western Europe have enjoyed the longest period of relative stability in their birth rate this century. Any movement in period fertility since the 1980s in these countries has been upward rather than downward. Furthermore, the difference in fertility between Germany and its neighbours, and the higher fertility of the Northern European countries and France, have now persisted for well over a decade, prompting speculation about their bases in differences of culture and attitudes, rather than in socio-economic distinctions between the countries concerned.

Elsewhere in Europe, in the South, fertility is still declining to low levels or may have stabilized at low levels. In Southern Europe, what has been termed 'Catholic fertility' seems to be a thing of the past. Those countries now have the lowest fertility in Europe, although they have conspicuously not adopted unconventional living arrangements on any large scale. The partial replacement of marriage and of marital fertility by cohabitation, and by what might be called 'Protestant illegitimacy', are becoming more salient in the north and west. In the east the former Soviet Union has produced seven new independent successor states in the geographical area which we are considering, former Yugoslavia five, former Czechoslovakia two. Previously, their fertility patterns were regarded as examples of regional or provincial fertility differentials. From a somewhat higher starting point both the new and the old countries of Eastern Europe have experienced declining fertility since the collapse of their former Communist regimes. In view of the political uncertainty and serious economic disruption these countries have undergone, this is hardly surprising; the least developed areas, and those undergoing the most radical change, have shown the greatest decline.

The question arises whether fertility is likely to remain at this low level. If it continued so, it would certainly give rise to population decline in many European countries (see Joshi, Chapter 7 below). In a few countries, births already exceed deaths. Much of the decline in fertility can be attributed to the postponement of childbearing throughout Western Europe, although this postponement has not ceased in countries where the birth rate is again increasing. Parity-based period measures of fertility tend to give somewhat higher estimates of the completed family size implicit in current birth rates; none the less in many countries this is still substantially under two children. Birth rates in other countries around the world are approaching, or have already declined to below the low birth rates already current in Europe.

We are accustomed to thinking of population growth as the major population problem. For Europe in the 1990s, and in the longer run for the world, however, demography's most fundamental problem is to explain why adults in rich countries, who have choice in the matter, continue to choose to have any children at all, and in so far as they do, if there is any enduring reason over and above transient social pressures, why the average should be around two children rather than some other number, possibly a much smaller one. Other chapters in this book will throw some light on this issue. But we cannot yet provide an adequate answer to it.

APPENDIX

APPENDIX TABLE 1A.1. *TFR trends, industrial countries, 1945–1992*

Year	Australia	Austria	Belgium	Bulgaria	Canada	Cyprus	Czecho-slovakia	East Germany	Denmark	Finland	France	West Germany	Greece	Hungary	Iceland	Ireland	Italy	Japan	Luxem-burg
1945	2.74				3.02												3.01		2.77
1946	2.98		2.52		3.37												2.89	4.63	
1947	3.06		2.46		3.60												2.83	4.38	1.99
1948	2.98		2.44		3.44												2.54	4.29	
1949	3.07		2.39		3.46													4.29	
1950	3.06		2.35	2.94	3.46		3.02	2.30	2.58	3.16	2.93	2.09		2.60			2.47	3.65	
1951	3.06	2.03	2.29	2.45	3.50		3.00	2.41	2.50	3.01	2.79	2.06		2.53			2.37	3.25	
1952	3.18	2.06	2.34	2.44	3.64		2.95	2.40	2.54	3.06	2.77	2.08		2.47			2.29	2.97	2.07
1953	3.19	2.07	2.33	2.41	3.72		2.87	2.38	2.60	2.96	2.69	2.08	2.46	2.76			2.25	2.68	
1954	3.19	2.11	2.37	2.33	3.83		2.83	2.36	2.54	2.93	2.70	2.12		2.98			2.32	2.47	
1955	3.27	2.23	2.38	2.41	3.83		2.84	2.37	2.58	2.93	2.68	2.13		2.81			2.31	2.37	2.13
1956	3.33	2.41	2.42	2.36	3.86		2.84	2.29	2.59	2.91	2.66	2.23	2.33	2.60		3.40	2.30	2.22	2.08
1957	3.42	2.49	2.47	2.26	3.93		2.76	2.24	2.56	2.86	2.68	2.33	2.27	2.29		3.50	2.28	2.04	2.13
1958	3.42	2.52	2.50	2.23	3.89		2.59	2.22	2.54	2.68	2.67	2.32	2.23	2.19		3.49	2.24	2.11	2.13
1959	3.44	2.61	2.56	2.23	3.94		2.41	2.36	2.49	2.76	2.74	2.39	2.27	2.09		3.62	2.29	2.04	2.16
1960	3.45	2.65	2.58	2.30	3.90		2.41	2.33	2.54	2.71	2.73	2.37	2.19	2.02	4.17	3.76	2.41	2.01	2.28
1961	3.54	2.80	2.64	2.28	3.84		2.40	2.42	2.55	2.70	2.81	2.46	2.23	1.94		3.79	2.41	1.95	2.35
1962	3.42	2.80	2.59	2.22	3.76		2.36	2.49	2.54	2.66	2.78	2.44	2.23	1.79		3.92	2.46	1.96	2.29
1963	3.33	2.81	2.68	2.19	3.67		2.52	2.47	2.64	2.67	2.88	2.52	2.22	1.82		4.01	2.55	1.98	2.32
1964	3.15	2.77	2.71	2.16	3.50		2.53	2.45	2.60	2.58	2.90	2.54	2.31	1.82		4.07	2.70	2.03	2.34
1965	2.98	2.68	2.61	2.07	3.15		2.38	2.48	2.61	2.47	2.83	2.51	2.30	1.82	3.71	4.03	2.67	2.14	2.38
1966	2.88	2.66	2.53	2.02	2.81		2.22	2.49	2.62	2.40	2.78	2.53	2.38	1.89		3.95	2.63	1.60	2.34
1967	2.85	2.63	2.42	2.03	2.60		2.08	2.36	2.35	2.32	2.64	2.49	2.55	2.01		3.84	2.54	2.22	2.24
1968	2.89	2.59	2.31	2.28	2.45		2.00	2.30	2.12	2.14	2.57	2.38	2.56	2.06		3.78	2.49	2.10	2.12
1969	2.89	2.50	2.25	2.27	2.41		2.04	2.24	2.00	1.93	2.53	2.21	2.48	2.04		3.84	2.51	2.06	2.02
1970	2.86	2.31	2.20	2.18	2.33	2.54	2.06	2.19	1.95	1.83	2.48	2.02	2.34	1.98	2.81	3.87	2.43	2.13	1.97

APPENDIX TABLE 1A.1. (cont.)

Year	Australia	Austria	Belgium	Bulgaria	Canada	Cyprus	Czecho-slovakia	East Germany	Denmark	Finland	France	West Germany	Greece	Hungary	Iceland	Ireland	Italy	Japan	Luxem-burg
1971	2.95	2.24	2.21	2.10	2.19	2.44	2.12	2.13	2.04	1.68	2.51	1.92	2.30	1.93	2.92	3.98	2.41	2.15	1.92
1972	2.74	2.11	2.09	2.02	2.02	2.40	2.20	1.79	2.03	1.58	2.43	1.71	2.32	1.93	3.09	3.87	2.36	2.18	1.72
1973	2.49	1.95	1.95	2.14	1.93	2.38	2.37	1.58	1.92	1.49	2.32	1.54	2.28	1.93	2.95	3.74	2.34	2.09	1.52
1974	2.40	1.92	1.83	2.29	1.88	2.20	2.48	1.54	1.90	1.61	2.13	1.51	2.39	2.27	2.66	3.62	2.33	1.93	1.55
1975	2.22	1.84	1.74	2.22	1.85	1.98	2.43	1.54	1.92	1.68	1.93	1.45	2.37	2.35	2.65	3.40	2.21	1.91	1.63
1976	2.14	1.70	1.73	2.24	1.83	2.23	2.41	1.64	1.75	1.72	1.83	1.45	2.39	2.23	2.52	3.31	2.11	1.85	
1977	2.04	1.63	1.71	2.20	1.81	2.25	2.38	1.85	1.66	1.69	1.86	1.40	2.27	2.16	2.29	3.27	1.98	1.80	1.45
1978	1.93	1.60	1.69	2.14	1.78	2.30	2.37	1.90	1.67	1.65	1.82	1.38	2.27	2.07	2.35	3.24	1.87	1.79	1.49
1979	1.92	1.60	1.69	2.15	1.76	2.38	2.33	1.90	1.60	1.64	1.86	1.38	2.26	2.01	2.49	3.23	1.76	1.77	1.48
1980	1.99	1.65	1.69	2.05	1.75	2.46	2.15	1.95	1.55	1.63	1.95	1.44	2.23	1.90	2.48	3.23	1.69	1.75	1.50
1981	1.94	1.67	1.67	2.00	1.64	2.37	2.09	1.87	1.44	1.65	1.95	1.44	2.09	1.88	2.32	3.07	1.62	1.74	1.55
1982	1.94	1.66	1.61	2.01	1.63	2.50	2.10	1.86	1.43	1.72	1.91	1.41	2.02	1.79	2.26	2.96	1.59	1.77	1.49
1983	1.93	1.56	1.56	2.00	1.62	2.48	2.08	1.81	1.38	1.74	1.79	1.33	1.94	1.75	2.24	2.76	1.52	1.80	1.44
1984	1.88	1.52	1.57	2.00	1.63	2.48	2.07	1.76	1.40	1.70	1.81	1.29	1.82	1.76	2.08	2.59	1.46	1.81	1.43
1985	1.89	1.47	1.50	1.97	1.61	2.38	2.03	1.76	1.45	1.64	1.82	1.28	1.68	1.85	1.93	2.50	1.41	1.76	1.38
1986	1.87	1.45	1.54	2.01	1.59	2.40	2.02	1.70	1.48	1.60	1.84	1.35	1.62	1.84	1.85	2.44	1.32	1.72	1.44
1987	1.85	1.43	1.54	1.96	1.58	2.32	2.02	1.74	1.50	1.59	1.82	1.38	1.52	1.82	2.05	2.34	1.31	1.69	1.41
1988	1.86	1.44	1.57	1.96	1.61	2.41	2.02	1.67	1.56	1.70	1.82	1.40	1.52	1.79	2.27	2.17	1.34	1.61	1.51
1989	1.86	1.45	1.58	1.86	1.66	2.34	1.95	1.57	1.62	1.71	1.79	1.46	1.43	1.78	2.21	2.08	1.33	1.57	1.52
1990	1.89	1.45	1.62	1.73	1.71	2.42	1.96	1.40	1.67	1.78	1.78	1.45	1.42	1.84	2.31	2.12	1.29	1.54	1.62
1991	1.84	1.50	1.57	1.57	1.70	2.33	1.92	0.91	1.67	1.80	1.77	1.42	1.40	1.86	2.19	2.08	1.26	1.53	1.60
1992	1.87	1.49	1.56	1.53	1.69	2.49	1.92	0.83	1.76	1.85	1.73	1.40	1.39	1.77	2.21	2.02	1.25	1.50	1.67
1993	1.84	1.48		1.48	1.66	2.27	—	0.78	1.75	1.81	1.65	1.39	1.34	1.69	2.22	1.93			1.70

Year	1	2	3	4	5	6	7	8	9	10	11	12	13	14	15	16	17	18
1945	3.97	2.91											2.48				2.04	
1946	3.70	3.25	2.77					3.02	2.57	2.62			2.96				2.47	
1947	3.41	3.45	2.66					2.90	2.50	2.56			3.18				2.68	
1948	3.22	3.38	2.57					2.88	2.48	2.53			3.03				2.38	
1949	3.10	3.33	2.52					2.58	2.39	2.48			3.04				2.27	
1950	3.06	3.38	2.53	3.71		3.17		2.46	2.32	2.40			3.03		3.74		2.18	
1951	3.05	3.36	2.47	3.75		3.03		2.50	2.21	2.34			3.20		3.29		2.14	
1952	3.05	3.52	2.58	3.67		3.00		2.54	2.23	2.35			3.29	2.98	3.60		2.16	
1953	3.04	3.48	2.64	3.60		2.88		2.60	2.25	2.30			3.35	2.97	3.38		2.22	
1954	3.05	3.60	2.67	3.58		3.00		2.54	2.17	2.29			3.46	2.86	3.34	2.45	2.21	
1955	3.05	3.72	2.76	3.61		3.09		2.58	2.25	2.33			3.50	2.86	3.16	2.51	2.22	
1956	3.08	3.77	2.83	3.51		2.89		2.59	2.28	2.38			3.61	2.90	3.02	2.54	2.35	
1957	3.10	3.88	2.83	3.49		2.73	6.47	2.56	2.28	2.44			3.68	2.90	2.76	2.65	2.45	
1958	3.16	3.96	2.86	3.36		2.59		2.54	2.24	2.34			3.63	2.81	2.77	2.76	2.52	
1959	3.11	4.00	2.88	3.22		2.43	5.77	2.49	2.23	2.37			3.64	2.82	2.74	2.83	2.56	
1960	3.12	4.03	2.83	2.98	3.01	2.34		2.86	2.17	2.44	5.75	2.66	3.61	2.81	2.80	2.84	2.68	
1961	3.22	4.16	2.91	2.83	3.18	2.17		2.76	2.21	2.48	5.59	2.77	3.56	2.84	2.73	2.93	2.77	
1962	3.18	4.11	2.89	2.72	3.21	2.04		2.80	2.25	2.46	5.47	2.84	3.42	2.80	2.68	2.95	2.85	
1963	3.19	3.99	2.91	2.70	3.08	2.01		2.88	2.33	2.68	5.35	2.88	3.30	2.68	2.66	3.06	2.88	
1964	3.17	3.73	2.96	2.59	3.15	1.96	4.66	3.01	2.47	2.85	5.10	2.94	3.17	2.60	2.64	3.03	2.93	
1965	3.04	3.33	2.93	2.52	3.08	1.91		2.94	2.41	2.61	4.83	2.86	2.88	2.53	2.71	3.09	2.85	
1966	2.90	3.44	2.89	2.43	3.05	1.90		2.91	2.37	2.47	4.82	2.76	2.67	2.46	2.65	3.00	2.75	
1967	2.81	3.35	2.80	2.33	3.00	3.66		2.94	2.28	2.37	4.22	2.66	2.53	2.43	2.56	2.88	2.65	
1968	2.72	3.33	2.75	2.24	2.90	3.63		2.87	2.07	2.29	4.33	2.58	2.43	2.39	2.48	2.87	2.57	
1969	2.75	3.27	2.70	2.20	2.85	3.19	3.07	2.86	1.94	2.12	4.12	2.48	2.42	2.37	2.44	2.82	2.47	
1970	2.57	3.16	2.51	2.20	2.76	2.89		2.84	1.94	2.09	4.00	2.41	2.48	2.39	2.29	2.68	2.40	3.25
1971	2.36	3.19	2.50	2.25	2.80	2.66		2.86	1.98	2.02	3.71	2.38	2.27	2.39	2.37	2.57	2.37	3.13
1972	2.15	3.01	2.39	2.24	2.70	2.55		2.82	1.93	1.90	3.37	2.19	2.01	2.47	2.35	2.27	2.17	2.99
1973	1.90	2.70	2.24	2.26	2.66	2.44		2.82	1.88	1.80	3.21	2.02	1.88	2.41	2.31	2.13	2.00	2.96
1974	1.77	2.57	2.14	2.26	2.60	2.72	2.40	2.87	1.89	1.72	3.05	1.90	1.84	2.41	2.28	1.97	1.89	2.77

APPENDIX TABLE 1A.1. (cont.)

Year	Malta	Nether-lands	New Zealand	Norway	Poland	Portugal	Romania	Singa-pore	Spain	Sweden	Switzer-land	Taiwan	UK	USA	USSR	Yugo-slavia	England & Wales	Scotland	Northern Ireland
1975		1.66	2.33	1.99	2.27	2.52	2.96	2.07	2.79	1.78	1.60	2.83	1.79	1.77	2.41	2.26	1.78	1.90	2.67
1976		1.63	2.27	1.87	2.30	2.57	2.55		2.79	1.69	1.54	3.08	1.72	1.74	2.37	2.25	1.71	1.80	2.69
1977	2.30	1.58	2.23	1.75	2.23	2.45	2.60	1.86	2.65	1.65	1.53	2.70	1.69	1.79	2.37	2.18	1.66	1.70	2.58
1978	2.00	1.58	2.09	1.77	2.17	2.23	2.54	1.84	2.53	1.60	1.51	2.71	1.76	1.76	2.33	2.15	1.73	1.74	2.64
1979	2.30	1.56	2.13	1.75	2.23	2.11	2.50	1.84	2.34	1.66	1.52	2.66	1.86	1.81	2.28	2.11	1.64	1.84	2.80
1980	2.20	1.60	2.04	1.72	2.25	2.19	2.45	1.74	2.22	1.68	1.55	2.52	1.89	1.84	2.26	2.12	1.88	1.84	2.78
1981	2.10	1.56	2.00	1.70	2.22	2.14	2.37	1.72	2.03	1.63	1.54	2.46	1.81	1.82	2.29	2.07	1.80	1.84	2.58
1982	2.30	1.47	1.95	1.71	2.30	2.07	2.17	1.71	1.94	1.62	1.56	2.32	1.78	1.83	2.35	2.11	1.76	1.74	2.51
1983	2.20	1.47	1.92	1.66	2.42	1.95	2.00	1.59	1.79	1.61	1.52	2.16	1.77	1.80	2.41	2.07	1.76	1.70	2.49
1984	2.20	1.49	1.93	1.66	2.37	1.89	2.19	1.61	1.72	1.65	1.53	2.05	1.77	1.81	2.40	2.11	1.75	1.68	2.48
1985	1.99	1.51	1.93	1.68	2.33	1.70	2.26	1.62	1.61	1.73	1.51	1.89	1.80	1.84	2.46	2.04	1.78	1.70	2.43
1986	2.00	1.55	1.96	1.71	2.22	1.63	2.39	1.45	1.52	1.79	1.53	1.68	1.78	1.84	2.52	2.01	1.77	1.67	2.45
1987	1.98	1.56	2.02	1.75	2.15	1.57	2.42	1.64	1.46	1.84	1.51	1.70	1.82	1.87	2.53	2.00	1.81	1.67	2.39
1988	2.07	1.54	2.09	1.84	2.13	1.53	2.31	1.98	1.43	1.96	1.57	1.85	1.84	1.93	2.45	1.98	1.82	1.68	2.37
1989	2.11	1.55	2.12	1.88	2.08	1.48	2.19	1.79	1.38	2.02	1.57	1.68	1.79	2.01	2.34	1.88	1.80	1.61	2.21
1990	2.05	1.62	2.18	1.93	2.04	1.51	1.93	1.83	1.30	2.14	1.59	1.81	1.83	2.08	2.26	1.88	1.84	1.66	2.24
1991	2.00	1.67	2.16	1.92	2.05	1.57	1.56		1.28	2.11	1.58	1.72	1.82	2.07			1.82	1.69	2.17
1992	2.12	1.59	2.12	1.88	1.93	1.54	1.51		1.23	2.09	1.58	1.73	1.79	2.07			1.80	1.68	2.08
1993	2.10	1.57	—	1.86	1.85	1.52	1.44		1.26	2.00	1.51	1.76	1.79	2.07			1.76	1.61	2.00

APPENDIX TABLE 1A.1. (*cont.*)

Year	Baltic Republics			Former Soviet Union						Former Yugoslavia						Other
	Estonia	Latvia	Lithuania	Armenia	Belarus	Georgia	Moldova	Russia	Ukraine	Bosnia	Croatia	Macedonia	Montenegro	Serbia	Slovenia	Albania
1958	1.93	1.91	2.61	4.69	2.76	2.53	3.55	2.62	2.29	3.91	2.20	4.11	3.47	2.56	2.23	6.85
1960																
1965	1.92	1.72	2.22	3.90	2.26	2.55	2.66	2.12	1.89	3.51	2.19	3.66	3.13	2.51	2.43	
1969	2.16	1.93	2.36		2.33	2.65	2.58	1.99	2.06							
1970				3.24	2.33											
1975	2.09	1.95	2.19	2.79	2.15	2.54	2.52	1.97	2.03	2.67	1.80	2.95	2.61	2.27	2.10	5.16
1977										2.35	1.91	2.70	2.34	2.32	2.18	
1978	2.01	1.86	2.07	2.43	2.05	2.30	2.37	1.89	1.96	2.01					2.23	
1979										1.90					2.43	
1980	2.02	1.87	1.97	2.31	2.01	2.25	2.39	1.88	1.93	1.88	1.92	2.45	2.13	2.28	2.10	3.62
1981	2.07			2.34				1.88		2.01			2.20	2.14	2.18	3.46
1982	2.08	2.01	2.02	2.32	2.08	2.24	2.57	2.02	1.94	2.02	1.90	2.44	2.22	2.26	2.11	3.58
1983	2.16	2.13	2.00	2.42	2.08		2.62	2.09	2.11	2.01	1.88	2.39	2.16	2.24	1.93	3.28
1984	2.17	2.15	2.10	2.49	2.13		2.67	2.05	2.08	1.97	1.87	2.34	2.09	2.31	1.82	3.40
1985	2.12	2.09	2.10	2.55	2.07	2.33	2.71	2.05	2.02	1.89	1.82	2.31	2.11	2.23	1.75	3.26
1986	2.19	2.15	2.16	2.56	2.08	2.30	2.78	2.19	2.09	1.83	1.76	2.26	2.03	2.21	1.72	3.07
1987	2.23	2.16	2.17	2.54	2.03	2.26	2.73	2.22	2.06	1.81	1.74	2.27	2.03	2.22	1.69	3.16
1988	2.25	2.11	2.10	2.51	2.03	2.14	2.64	2.13	2.03	1.80	1.74	2.21	1.95	2.21	1.71	3.03
1989	2.21	2.05	1.98	2.61	2.03	2.21	2.50	2.02	2.03	1.70	1.67	2.09	1.84	2.09	1.66	2.96
1990	2.04	2.02	2.00	2.84	1.91		2.39	1.89	1.91	1.70	1.63	2.06	1.79	2.10	1.55	3.03
1991	1.77	1.86	1.97		1.80	—	2.26	1.73	1.18		1.53	2.30			1.46	
1992	1.69	1.73	1.89	—	—	—	2.21	1.55	1.72		1.48	2.18			1.34	—
1993	1.45	1.51	1.67	—	1.75		2.10	1.39	1.55		1.52	—			1.31	—
Year	Estonia	Latvia	Lithuania	Armenia	Belarus	Georgia	Moldova	Russia	Ukraine	Bosnia	Croatia	Macedonia	Montenegro	Serbia	Slovenia	Albania

Notes: Different sources differ slightly for recent years.
Years missing are those for which no data are available.
Sources: Eurostat 1993; Council of Europe 1994; National Statistical Yearbooks.

NOTE

Some of the material in this chapter is a modified version of an earlier paper by the author published in 1993 as 'Britain in Europe: international and regional comparisons of fertility levels and trends', in M. Ní Bhrolcháin (ed.), *New Perspectives on Fertility in Britain, Studies on Medical and Population Subjects*, No. 55, London: HMSO. Thanks are due to Miss Sara Beale for preparing Fig. 1.2 and locating data, to the Council of Europe for unpublished TFR data for 1993, and to Eurostat for Fig 1.12.

REFERENCES

ARMITAGE, R. I. (1987), 'English regional fertility and mortality patterns 1975–1985', *Population Trends*, 47: 16–23.

BABB, P. (1993), 'Teenage conceptions and fertility in England and Wales, 1971–1991', *Population Trends*, 74: 12–17.

BLAYO, C. (1987), 'La fécondité en Europe depuis 1960: convergence ou divergence?', *European Population Conference 1987*, Jyvaskyla, Plenaries, Liège, International Union for the Scientific Study of Population: 47–111.

BLAYO, C. (1991), 'Les modes de prévention des naissances en Europe de l'Est', *Population*, 46(3): 527–46.

BLUM, A. (1989), 'Démographies de l'URSS et des pays de l'Est. Continuité ou rupture?', *Notes et Études Documentaires*, 489–92: 11–39.

BONGAARTS, J., and POTTER, R. G. (1983), *Fertility, Biology and Behavior: An analysis of the Proximate determinants*, New York: Academic Press.

BOSVELD, W., WIJSEN, C., and KUIJSTEN, A. (1991), *The Growing Importance of Fertility at Higher Ages in the Netherlands*. Paper presented to the EAPS/IUSSP/INED European Population Conference, Paris, October 1991.

BRASS, W. (1989), 'Is Britain Facing the Twilight of Parenthood?', in H. Joshi (ed.), *The Changing Population of Britain*, Oxford: Basil Blackwell: 12–26.

—— and KABIR, M. (1978), 'Regional variation in fertility and child mortality during the demographic transition in England and Wales', in J. Hobcraft and P. Rees (eds.), *Regional Demographic Development*, London: Croom Helm: 71–88.

CALHOUN, C. (1991), 'Desired and excess fertility in Europe and the

United States: indirect estimates from World Fertility Survey data', *European Journal of Population*, 7: 29–57.

CALOT, G., and CHESNAIS, J.-C. (1983), 'L'efficacité des politiques incitatrices en matière de natalité', in *IUSSP colloquium*, Liège: IUSSP.

CALOT, G., SARDON, J.-P. *et al.* (1993), 'Les mesures de la fécondité transversale: Réflexions autour d'un article', *Population*, 48(2): 405–42.

CAMPBELL, E. (1985), *The Childless Marriage*, London: Tavistock.

CARTWRIGHT, A. (1987), 'Family intentions and the use of contraception among recent mothers 1967–84', *Population Trends*, 49: 31–4.

CLELAND, J., and WILSON, C. (1987), 'Demand theories of the fertility transition, an iconoclastic view', *Population Studies*, 41: 5–30.

CLIQUET, R.L. (1991), *The Second Demographic Transition: Fact or Fiction?*, Strasburg: Council of Europe.

COALE, A. J., and WATKINS, S. C. (1986), *The Decline of Fertility in Europe*, Princeton: Princeton University Press.

COLEMAN, D. A. (1992), *European Demographic Systems of the Furture: Convergence or Diversity?*, Proceedings of the Eurostat conference 'Human Resources in Europe at the Dawn of the 21st Century', Luxemburg: Office for Official Publications of the European Community: 141–79.

—— (1993), 'The demographic transition in Ireland in international context', in J. Goldthorpe and C. Whelan (eds.), *The Development of Industrial Society in Ireland*, Oxford: Oxford University Press: 53–77. Published as *Proceedings of the British Academy*, 79.

—— (1993), 'Britain in Europe: International and regional comparisons of fertility levels and trends', in Ní Bhrolcháin, M. (ed.), *New Perspectives on Fertility in Britain, Studies on Medical and Population Subjects*, No. 55, London: HMSO: 67–92.

—— (in press), 'The concentration of immigrant and ethnic minority populations and the demographic and socio-economic consequences', in J. Schoorl and S. Voets (eds.), *The Demographic Consequences of International Migration*, Wassenaar: Netherlands Institute for Advanced Study.

—— and SALT, J. (1992), *The British Population: Patterns, Trends and Processes*, Oxford: Oxford University Press.

COMPTON, P., and COWARD, J. (1989), *Fertility and Family Planning in Northern Ireland*, Aldershot: Avebury.

COOPER, J. (1991), 'The divergence between period and cohort measures of fertility', *Population Trends*, 63: 19–21.

COUNCIL OF EUROPE (1990), *Demographic Developments in the Member States of the Council of Europe 1990*, Strasburg: Council of Europe Press.

—— (1991), *Demographic Developments in Europe 1991*, Strasburg: Council of Europe Press.

—— (1994), *Recent Demographic Developments in Europe 1993*, Strasburg: Council of Europe Press.

CRAIG, J. (1992), 'Fertility trends within the United Kingdom', *Population Trends*, 67: 17–21.

DAVID, H. P. (1982), 'Eastern Europe: pronatalist policies and private behavior', *Population Bulletin*, 36.

DECROLY, J.-M., GRIMMEAU, J.-P., NOIN, D., ROELANDTS, M., VANDERMOTTEN, C., and VANLAER, J. (1991), *Atlas de la Population Européenne*, Brussels: Éditions de l'Université de Bruxelles.

DEPARTMENT OF HEALTH (1991), *On the State of the Public Health 1990. Report of the Chief Medical Officer*, London: HMSO.

EC COMMISSION (1990), *European Public Opinion on the Family and the Desire for Children*, Luxemburg: EC.

ERMISCH, J. (1991), *Lone Parenthood: an Economic Analysis*, Cambridge: Cambridge University Press.

EUROSTAT (1991a), *Demographic Statistics*, Luxemburg: Office for Official Publications of the European Communities.

—— (1991b), *Two Long-Term Population Scenarios for the European Community. Scenarios prepared for the International Conference 'Human Resources in Europe at the Dawn of the 21st century'*, Luxemburg: Eurostat.

—— (1993a), *Regions Statistical Yearbook 1993*. Vol. 1, Series A, Luxemburg: Office for Official Publications of the European Communities.

—— (1993b), *Demographic Statistics 1993*, Luxemburg: Office for Official Publications of the European Communities.

—— (1993c) *The Population of the European Economic Area in 1992*, Rapid Reports 1993/7, Luxemburg: Eurostat.

FAMILY PLANNING ASSOCIATION (1994), *Children who Have Children*, London: Family Planning Association.

FEENEY, G., and YU, J. (1987), 'Period parity progression ratio measures of fertility in China', *Population Studies*, 41: 77–102.

FEENEY, G., and LUTZ, W. (1991), 'Distributional Analysis of Period Fertility', in W. Lutz (ed.), *Future Demographic Trends in Europe and North America: What Can We Assume Today?*, London: Academic Press: 169–95.

FEISSIG, A. (1991), 'Unintended pregnancies and the use of contraception—changes 1984–89', *British Medical Journal*, 19 Jan. 1991: 147.

FESTY, P. (1979), *La Fécondité des pays occidentaux de 1870 à 1970. INED Travaux et Documents*, Cahier No. 85. Paris: Presses Universitaires de France.

FLEMING, A. T. (1994), *Motherhood Deferred: a Woman's Journey*, London: Putnam.

GAUTHIER, A. (1991), *Family Policies in Comparative Perspective*, Discussion Paper No. 5, Centre for European Studies, Nuffield College, Oxford.

GELLNER, E. (1983), *Nations and Nationalism*, Oxford: Basil Blackwell.

GHETZAU, V. (1991), *Politique Pronataliste Coercitive, Fecondité et Avortement en Roumanie*. Paper presented to European Demographic Congress, Paris, October 1991.

GLASS, D. V., and GREBENIK, E. (1954), *The Trend and Pattern of Fertility in Great Britain: a Report on the Family Census of 1946*, Papers of the Royal Commission on Population, Vol. VI, London: HMSO.

GOSKOMSTAT (Soviet State Committee on Statistics) (1989), *Naselenye 1988 (Population 1988)*. Moscow: Finansy i Statistika.

—— (Russian Federation State Committee on Statistics) (1994), *Demographic Yearbook of the Russian Federation*, Moscow: Goskomstat.

GRASLAND, C. (1990), 'Systèmes Demographiques et Systèmes Supranationaux: la Fecondité Europénne de 1952 à 1982', *European Journal of Population*, 6: 163–91.

HAJNAL, J. (1965), 'European Marriage Patterns in Perspective', in D. V. Glass and D. E. C. Eversley (eds.), *Population in History*, London, Edward Arnold.

HASKEY, J. (1990), 'Identical addresses at marriage and pre-marital cohabitation: results from linking marriage registration and census records', *Population Trends*, 59: 20–9.

—— (1992a), 'Pre-marital cohabitation and the probability of subsequent divorce: analyses using new data from the General Household Survey', *Population Trends*, 68: 10–19.

—— (1992), 'Patterns of marriage, divorce and cohabitation in the different countries of Europe', *Population Trends*, 69: 27–36.

—— and KIERNAN, K. (1989), 'Cohabitation in Great Britain—characteristics and estimated numbers of cohabiting partners', *Population Trends*, 58: 23–32.

HOEM, J. (1990a), 'Social policy and recent fertility change in Sweden', *Population and Development Review*, 16: 735–48.

—— (1990b), 'Cohabitation in Sweden', Seminar at Nuffield College, Oxford, 1990.

HOFFMAN-NOWOTNY, H.-J., and FUX, B. (1991), 'Present Demographic Trends in Europe', in *Seminar on Present Demographic Trends and Lifestyles in Europe: Proceedings*. Strasburg: Council of Europe: 31–98.

HÖHN, C. (1991), 'International transmission of population policy experience in Western Europe', in United Nations (ed.), *Expert Group Meeting on the International Transmission of Population Policy Experience*, New York: United Nations: 145–58.

IPPF (INTERNATIONAL PLANNED PARENTHOOD FEDERATION) (1991),

'Special feature: abortion and contraception', *Planned Parenthood in Europe*, 20: 2.

—— (1993), 'Population policy and family planning in Europe', *Planned Parenthood in Europe*, 22: 2.

—— (1994), 'The cost of family planning', *Planned Parenthood in Europe*, 23: 1.

JONES, C. (1992), 'Fertility of the over 30s', *Population Trends*, 67: 10–16.

JONES, E. (1986), *Teenage Pregnancy in Industrialised Countries*, New Haven: Yale University Press.

JOSHI, H. (1989), 'The changing form of women's economic dependency', in H. Joshi (ed.), *The Changing Population of Britain*, Oxford: Basil Blackwell: 157–76.

KATUS, K. (1994), 'Fertility transition in the Baltic States', in W. Lutz, S. Scherbov, and A. Volkov (eds.), *Demographic Trends and Patterns in the Soviet Union before 1991*, London: Routledge.

KIERNAN, K. (1983), 'The structure of families today: continuity or change?', *The Family*, OPCS Occasional Paper No. 31, London: HMSO.

—— (1989a), 'The family: formation and fission', in H. Joshi (ed.), *The Changing Population of Britain*, Oxford: Basil Blackwell: 27–41.

—— (1989b), 'Who remains childless?', *Journal of Biosocial Science*, 21: 387–98.

—— and ESTAUGH, V. (1993), *Cohabitation Extra-Marital Childbearing and Social Policy*, London: Family Policy Studies Centre, Occasional Paper No. 17.

KIRK, M. (1991), 'The problem of fertility, 1936–1986', in M. Murphy and J. Hobcraft (eds.), *Population Research in Britain: a Supplement to Population Studies vol. 45. 1991*, London: Population Investigation Committee: 31–48.

LEASURE, J. W. (1992), 'The historical decline of fertility in Eastern Europe', *European Journal of Population*, 8: 247–64.

LELIÈVRE, E. (1993), Extra-marital births occurring in cohabiting unions', in M. Ní Bhrolcháin (ed.), *New Perspectives on Fertility in Britain. Studies on Medical and Population Subjects*, No. 55, London: HMSO: 111–22.

LERIDON, H. (1990a), 'Extra-marital cohabitation and fertility', *Population Studies*, 44: 469–88.

—— (1990b), 'Cohabitation, marriage, separation: an analysis of life histories of French cohorts from 1968 to 1985', *Population Studies*, 44: 127–44.

—— and VILLENEUVE-GOKALP, C. (1988), 'Les nouveaux couples: nombre, caractéristiques et attitudes', *Population*, 43(2): 331–74.

LESTHAEGHE, R., and MEEKERS, D. (1986), 'Value changes and the dimensions of familism in the European Community', *European Journal of Population*, 2: 225–68.

LUTZ, W. (1992), *Distributional Aspects of Human Fertility: a Global Comparative Study*, London: Academic Press.

MOZNY, I. (1992), *The Czech Family in Transition from Social to Economic Capital*. Paper presented to the international workshop 'Social Responses to Political and Economic Transformations in East/Central Europe', Prague, May 1992.

MURPHY, M. (1993a), 'Time-series approaches to the analysis of fertility change', in M. Ní Bhrolcháin (ed.), *New Perspectives on Fertility in Britain, Studies on Medical and Population Subjects*, No. 55, London: HMSO: 51–66.

—— (1992), 'Economic Models of Fertility in Post-War Britain—A Conceptual and Statistical Re-interpretation', *Population Studies*, 46, 2: 235–58.

—— (1993b), 'The contraceptive pill and women's employment as factors in fertility change in Britain 1963–1980. A challenge to the conventional view', *Population Studies*, 47, 2: 221–44.

—— and BERRINGTON, A. (1993), 'The construction, validation and interpretation of period parity progression ratios from large scale developed society household structure data: an exploratory analysis', in M. Ní Bhrolcháin (ed.), *New Perspectives on Fertility in Britain, Studies on Medical and Population Subjects*, No. 55, London: HMSO.

—— and SULLIVAN, O. (1985), 'Housing tenure and family formation in contemporary Britain', *European Sociological Review*, 1: 230–43.

NATIONAL COMMISSION FOR STATISTICS, ROMANIA (1992a), 'Evolutia Principalelor Fenomene Demografice in Anul 1991', *Informatii Statistice Operative*, No. 2 (March 1992).

—— (1992b), 'Evolutia Principalelor Fenomene Demografice in Semestrul 1, 1992', *Informatii Statistice Operative* No. 3 (August 1992).

NEWELL, C. (1988), *Methods and Models in Demography*, London: Belhaven.

NÍ BHROLCHÁIN, M. (1987), 'Period parity progression ratios and birth intervals in England and Wales 1941–1971: a synthetic life table analysis', *Population Studies*, 41: 103–25.

—— (1993), 'East-West Marriage Contrasts, Old and New', in A. Blum and J.-L. Rallu (eds.), *European Population, vol. 2: Demographic Dynamics*, Paris: John Libbey Eurotext: 461–79.

NILSSON, T. (1985), 'Les ménages en Suède, 1960–1980', *Population*, 40, 2: 223–47.

OGAWA, N., and RETHERFORD, R. D. (1993), 'The resumption of fertility decline in Japan, 1973–92', *Population and Development Review*, 19, 4: 703–41.

OGDEN, P. E., and HUSS M. M. (1982), 'Demography and pronatalism in France in the 19th and 20th centuries', *Journal of Historical Geography*, 8: 283–98.

OECD (1985), *The Role of the Public Sector*, OECD Economic Studies 4, Paris: OECD.

OPCS (1987a), *Birth Statistics 1837–1983, England and Wales*, Series FM1, No. 13, London: HMSO.

—— (1987b), *Period and Cohort Birth Order Statistics*, London: HMSO.

—— (1987c), *Population Trends*, 49, London: HMSO.

—— (1991a), *Mid-1990 Population Estimates for England and Wales*, OPCS Monitor PP1 91/1, London: OPCS.

—— (1991b), *National Population Projections 1989-based*, Series PP2, No. 17, London: HMSO.

—— (1991c), *Population Trends*, 66. London: HMSO.

—— (1992a), *Birth Statistics England and Wales*, Series FM1, No. 19, London: HMSO.

—— (1992b), *Population Trends*, 67, London: HMSO.

—— (1994), *Birth Statistics 1992 England and Wales*, Series FM1, No. 21, London: HMSO.

POPULATION REFERENCE BUREAU INC. (1994), *World Population Data Sheet 1994*, Washington DC: Population Reference Bureau Inc.

PRIOUX, F. (1993), 'L'Infécondité en Europe', in A. Blum and J.-L. Rallu (eds.), *European Population*, Vol. 2: *Demographic Dynamics*, Paris: John Libbey Eurotext: 231–54.

RALLU, J.-L., and TOULEMAN, L. (1993a), 'Les mesures de la fécondité transversale. I—Construction des différants indices', *Population*, 48(1): 7–26.

—— (1993b), 'Les mesures de la fécondité transversale. II—Application à la France de 1946 à 1989', *Population*, 48(2): 369–404.

RYCHTARIKOVA, J. (1993), 'Nuptialité comparée en Europe de l'est et en Europe de l'ouest', in A. Blum and J.-L. Rallu (eds.), *European Population*, Vol. 2: *Demographic Dynamics*, Paris: John Libbey Eurotext: 191–210.

RYDER, N. B. (1980), 'Components of temporal variations in American fertility', in R. J. Hiorns (ed.), *Demographic Patterns in Developed Societies*, London: Taylor and Francis: 11–54.

SARDON, J.-P. (1990), 'Le remplacement des générations en Europe depuis le début du siècle', *Population*, 45(6): 947–68.

SHAW, C. (1989), 'Recent trends in family size and family building', *Population Trends*, 58: 19–22.

—— (1990), 'Fertility assumptions for 1989-based population projections for England and Wales', *Population Trends*, 61: 17–23.

SIMONS, J. (1982), 'Reproductive behaviour as religious practice', in C. Höhn and R. Mackensen (eds.), *Determinants of Fertility Trends: Theories Re-examined*, Liège: Ordina: 131–45.

—— (1986), 'How conservative are British attitudes to reproduction?', *Quarterly Journal of Social Affairs*, 2(1): 41–54.

TEITELBAUM, M. (1984), *The British Fertility Decline*, Princeton: Princeton University Press.

TOPF, R., MOHLER, P., and HEATH, A. (1989), 'Pride in one's country: Britain and West Germany', in R. Jowell, S. Witherspoon, and L. Brook (eds.), *British Social Attitudes: Special International Report*. Aldershot: Gower.

UNITED NATIONS (1989), *Levels and Trends of Contraceptive Use as Assessed in 1988*, New York: United Nations.

—— (1991), *World Population Prospects 1990*, New York: United Nations.

UNECE (United Nations Economic Commission for Europe) (1992), *Economic Survey of Europe in 1991–92*, New York: United Nations.

VAN DE KAA, D. J. (1987), 'Europe's Second Demographic Transition', *Population Bulletin*, 42(1).

VICHNEVSKY, A., OUSSOVA, I., and VICHNEVSKAIA, T. (1993), 'Les conséquences des changements intervenus à l'Est sur les comportements démographiques', in A. Blum and J.-L. Rallu (eds.), *European Population*, Vol. 2: *Demographic Dynamics*, Paris: John Libbey Eurotext: 49–75.

WATKINS, S. C. (1991), *From Provinces into Nations: Demographic Integration in Western Europe 1870–1960*, Princeton: Princeton University Press.

WERNER, B. (1986), 'Trends in first, second, third and later births', *Population Trends*, 45: 26–33.

WESTOFF, C. F., HAMMERSLOUGH, C. R., and PAUL, C. (1987), 'The potential impact of improvements in contraception and fertility in Western countries', *European Journal of Population*, 3: 7–32.

WHITEHEAD, F. (1988), 'Population policy in the United Kingdom', in *UN/IUSSP Expert Group Meeting on the International Transmission of Population Policy Experience*, New York: paper unpublished but available from OPCS.

WRIGLEY, E. A., and SCHOFIELD, R. S. (1983), 'English population history from family reconstructions. Summary results 1600–1799', *Population Studies*, 37: 157–84.

2
Partnership Behaviour in Europe: Recent Trends and Issues

KATHLEEN E. KIERNAN

2.1 Introduction

The golden age of marriage which was prominent across many European countries during the 1960s and the early part of the 1970s is over. The youthful marriage patterns and near universality of marriage of this era are unlikely to return in the near future. With the rise in cohabitation (more pronounced in some countries than others), later marriage, and increased divorce, partnerships have become more varied and fragile in recent decades. Another key and long-term trend which is having a fundamental effect on partnership behaviour is the marked increase in women's participation in the labour market, a factor also explored in the context of family formation in Chapter 5. In this chapter we examine the demographic developments and the changing roles of men and women both in the market-place and in the home.

2.2 Trends in First Marriage

We commence with an examination of marriage patterns across a range of European countries. Since the late 1960s and early 1970s marriage rates in most European countries have declined. Younger generations of Europeans have been marrying less and among those who marry the trend has been to do so at older ages and over a wider range of ages than was common amongst their recent predecessors. In broad outline, the decline in marriage rates began in Sweden and Denmark in the late 1960s, then spread through most of Western Europe in the early part of the 1970s, and became

TABLE 2.1. *Mean age at first marriage among women marrying in 1975 and in 1990, various countries of Europe*

Average age	Countries 1975	Countries 1990
27	—	Denmark, Sweden, Switzerland
26	—	Finland, Iceland, Norway
25	Sweden	Austria, France, West Germany, Ireland, Italy, Luxemburg, Netherlands
24	Ireland, Italy Switzerland	Belgium, Portugal, United Kingdom
23	Denmark, Finland, Luxemburg, Portugal, Spain	East Germany, Greece
22	Austria, West Germany, Greece, Iceland, Netherlands, Poland United Kingdom	Poland
21	Belgium, Bulgaria, East Germany	Bulgaria, Hungary
20	Czechoslovakia, Hungary	Czechoslovakia

Source: Council of Europe 1992.

evident in the Southern European countries (Spain, Italy, Portugal, and Greece) around the mid-1970s. During the 1980s, the decline in marriage rates continued in most European countries but at a slower pace and there are some slight signs of increases in marriage intensity across a range of countries in very recent years. Until very recently there was little change in marriage rates in Eastern Europe. Signs of declines in marriage rates are now evident in some countries (for example, the former East Germany, Hungary, and Poland).

To illustrate some of these changes we can compare the mean age at first marriage among women in 1975, which is generally close to the lowest average age observed in the twentieth century for many countries, with the most recently available data (table 2.1). Generally speaking, up to the first half of the 1970s, the mean age at first marriage in most European states fell from a figure of somewhat over 24 years in 1960 to one of just over 23 years in 1970. Since then the mean age at marriage has generally risen in most countries. It is noticeable that in many of the countries the average age at marriage has increased by between two and four years regardless of the starting position. There is less movement in the values for Southern European countries and Ireland where the movement to a later age pattern of marriage has been more recent. It is clear that there is a good deal of intra-European diversity in marriage ages. In 1990 the highest values were recorded in Sweden and Denmark (with an average age at marriage among women of 27.4 years) and Switzerland (a figure of 27.0 years). The lowest values were to be seen in Czechoslovakia (20.9) Hungary (21.5) East Germany (23.2), and Greece (23.8). Marriage patterns in the United Kingdom are still among the youngest of the Northern and Western states of Europe.

Given that average age at marriage tends to correlate closely with overall propensity to marry, the degree of diversity suggests that marriage is more salient in some countries than in others.

2.3 The Rise of Cohabitation

Some of the declines in marriage rates and the movement to a later age at marriage that we have seen in many European countries are related to the rise of cohabitation.

The phenomenon of men and women living together outside marriage is not new. Before the 1970s it was largely statistically invisible and probably socially invisible outside the individuals' local community or milieu. In some countries there were sub-groups that were probably more prone to cohabitation than others: the very poor; those whose marriages had broken up but who were unable to obtain a divorce because there was no relevant legislation, or the conditions of such legislation as did exist were more stringent than nowadays, or it was very expensive to obtain a divorce; certain groups of rural dwellers; and groups ideologically opposed to marriage. The form of cohabitation that came to the fore during the 1960s in Sweden and Denmark, and the 1970s in other Northern and Western European countries, is new, and could be aptly termed 'nubile cohabitation', whereby young people predominantly in their twenties and early thirties live together either as a prelude to, or as an alternative to, marriage. Additionally, with the growth in divorce, which we will discuss later, 'post-marital cohabitation' is also likely to have become more prevalent with the divorced cohabiting either in preference to, or as a prelude to, remarriage. In many data sources it is difficult to distinguish between 'nubile' and 'post-marital' cohabitation.

Data on cohabitation tend to be scarce and generally emanate from surveys. This makes comparative analyses problematic, as sample sizes, coverage, and definitions are likely to vary. With these caveats in mind let us examine what information is available, and try to assess the meaning of cohabitation in different countries.

Table 2.2 shows the proportions of women cohabiting out of all women in a union (a marriage or a cohabitation) in a particular age group. We recognize that these are relatively crude data but they represent the few comparable data that could be mustered for a range of countries. Ideally we would have preferred to compare rates across a range of *de facto* and *de jure* marital status categories.

In all the countries for which a time series of data is available it is clear that there has been a large increase in the proportions of women cohabiting, particularly those in their twenties. For example, the proportions of women cohabiting amongst those in a union increased from 57 per cent to 78 per cent in Sweden over the period 1975–85, went from 11 per cent to 49 per cent in France between 1975 and 1988, and in Britain the proportion increased from 11 per cent to 32 per cent between 1980 and 1989. The peak ages for cohabitation are the early twenties and it is a relatively common practice in the Nordic countries with seven in ten Swedish and Danish women and one in two Norwegian and Finnish women in unions, cohabiting at these ages. Among the Western European countries shown in this table, youthful cohabitation seems to be more common in the Netherlands and France and perhaps West Germany and less common in Great Britain and Austria. Cohabitation at older ages, particularly in the thirties, is less common. At these ages in most of the countries the proportions of unions that are cohabitations were less than 10 per cent, the exceptions being Sweden, Denmark, and, to a lesser extent, Finland. These data, which are far from adequate for providing an accurate portrait of cohabitation behaviour in these countries, seem to suggest that cohabitation is a relatively youthful practice

TABLE 2.2. *Proportions of women cohabiting of all women in unions (marriages and cohabitations), various countries of Europe*

Country	Year	Age-group					
		16–19	20–4	25–9	30–4	35–9	40+
Sweden	1975	88	57	23	10	6	4
	1985	93	78	48	28	17	12
	1989	90	78	50	28	21	—
Great	1980	13	11	6	2	3	2
Britain	1986	42	24	10	7	4	4
	1989	62	32	14	9	6	3
Denmark	1976	84	48	17	10	5	7
	1985	88	75	41	20	10	7
Finland	1980	67	37	14	10	8	7
	1985	75	50	25	12	7	7
Norway	1977	—	21	6	2	2	1
	1987	83	59	23	8	5	5
Netherlands	1980	n/a	21	8	4	2	2
	1986	59	37	16	7	4	3
Switzerland	1980	38	23	8	4	3	2
Austria	1981	31	14	6	4	3	3
	1989	45	21	8	4	3	2
West	1978[a]	20		4		1	
Germany	1988[a]	45		11		3	
France	1975	36	11	7	3	—	—
	1985	69	40	17	9	6	4
	1988	—	49	23	12	6	6

Note:
[a] 8–25, 26–35, and 36–55: figures are estimates.
Source: Kiernan 1993.

and marriage has not been rejected permanently on a wide scale, as even in Sweden and Denmark, where the practice is more long-standing, the majority of unions among women in their thirties are marital unions.

There is a good deal of variation between (and within) European countries in the extent and nature of cohabiting unions. The countries may be subdivided into three main groupings: those where cohabitation is well established, those where it is emerging as a significant form of living arrangement, and countries where it is still rare (or possibly undetected).

The countries where cohabitation is relatively well established are Sweden, Denmark, and Iceland. Before the 1960s cohabitation and out-of-wedlock childbearing was not unknown in parts of Scandinavia, but it became more prevalent and visible during the 1960s. Since then it has increased dramatically, to the extent that pre-marital cohabitation is virtually the norm and couples frequently have their first and even second child in cohabiting unions. There is evidence that marriage is losing its monopoly on partnerships, but as we have seen this is not necessarily an outright rejection of marriage, as marriage frequently occurs at later ages. In these countries around one in two children are born

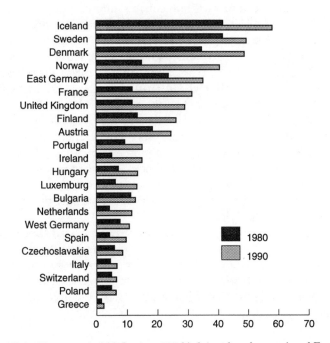

FIG. 2.1. *Extra-marital births (per 100 births), selected countries of Europe, 1980 and 1990*

Source: Council of Europe 1992.

outside marriage but the majority are born to cohabiting couples (see figure 2.1).

In Austria, Finland, France, Great Britain, the Netherlands, Norway, Switzerland, and West Germany cohabitation began to emerge during the 1970s primarily as a child-free, transitional phase preceding marriage. For example, whereas 30 per cent of French women marrying during the period 1974–6 had cohabited before marrying, by 1980–2 the proportion had risen to 65 per cent (Leridon 1990). A similar rise had occurred in Great Britain; whereas 34 per cent of those marrying in the period 1980–4 had cohabited, 50 per cent of women marrying in 1985–8 had done so (Haskey and Kiernan 1989). Cohabitation tends to be short-lived; for example, 50 per cent of cohabitants in the French sample had married within three years and it seems to be shorter still in Britain with 60 per cent of British men and women marrying within two years of starting to cohabit.

The group of countries where cohabitation came to the fore in the 1970s and escalated thereafter appear to fall into two distinct groups—those where extra-marital births are a significant minority of all births and those where extra-marital childbearing is still relatively rare. Figure 2.1 shows that the extent of extra-marital childbearing is relatively high in Austria, Finland, France, Great Britain, and Norway (more than 20 per cent), but in West Germany, the Netherlands, and Switzerland it is much less common (11 per cent or less). This suggests that in countries such as France, Britain, and Norway women may increasingly be having their children within cohabiting unions but that in the Netherlands, Switzerland, and the western part of Germany cohabitation is primarily a childless phase and marriage is still the pre-eminent context for having children.

In the Southern European countries of Greece, Italy, Spain, and Portugal and in Ireland and Eastern European countries cohabitation is seemingly rarer. There are few nationally representative sample surveys that have examined this topic but the clues that we have seem to suggest that it is rare, but may be emerging in large urban areas (Alabert *et al.* 1988, Lapinch 1991).

2.4 The Rise of Extra-Marital Childbearing

The rise in extra-marital childbearing that we see in figure 2.1 is probably intimately related to developments in cohabitation. In many Northern and Western European countries there has been a noticeable increase in the proportions of births outside marriage and in many of these countries extra-marital births are making a significant contribution to the Total Fertility Rate (TFR). The extent of extra-marital childbearing as measured by the proportion of all births that occur out of wedlock is very large: at one extreme are Iceland and Sweden, where over 50 per cent of children are born outside marriage. High ratios are evident in 1990 in Denmark (46 per cent), Norway (39 per cent), and East Germany (34 per cent). In East Germany the extent of extra-marital childbearing is probably not so strongly related to cohabitation as in the Northern European countries but more to policies relating to housing allocation and child-care which may have created a tendency for couples to marry after the birth of their first child (Höhn 1991). At the other extreme are countries like Greece with only 2 per cent of recorded births occurring outside marriage and Switzerland, Poland, and Italy with 6 per cent of extra-marital births in 1990.

Overall one is struck by the degree of intra-European variation in cohabitation and extra-marital childbearing. For example, both are most popular in the Nordic countries of Sweden and Denmark and relatively rare in, for example, Italy, Spain, and Ireland. In some countries there is a strong link between cohabitation and extra-marital childbearing, as in Britain and France, while in others, for example West Germany and Belgium, it is relatively weak.

Child-free, short-lived, pre-marital unions have become increasingly popular across a range of European countries. The extent to which children are born within cohabiting unions is more variable. As yet research on these topics is relatively scarce.

2.5 Who Cohabits?

We cannot directly answer this question for a range of European countries but provide some insights for Britain. Our analysis (Kiernan and Estaugh 1993) of General Household Survey data showed that British cohabitants tend to have a youthful profile: seven out of ten were under the age of 35. Teenage cohabitation and cohabitation beyond the age of 45 were relatively rare occurrences. Two out of three cohabitants have never been married and the one in three who have been previously married are in the main divorcees. Only a minority, 27 per cent, of the never-married cohabitants had ever had a child, whereas the majority, 84 per cent, of the separated and divorced cohabitants had had a child—most of these children were products of a prior marriage. Cohabitations still tend to be short-lived: by the time of interview one-third of couples had been living together for less than one year and only 16 per cent had lived with their partner for longer than five years.

2.6 Types of Cohabitants

Cohabitation is a complex affair encompassing a range of situations and living arrangements and different impetuses may well lie behind its various components. For example, our research on Britain identified three main groups. In order of size these were: young never-married childless couples; post-marital cohabitants; and never-married couples with children. The characteristics and circumstances of these groups were quite different.

Never-married childless unions tend to be short-lived. They either convert into marriages or break up. Four out of ten of the British public would advise young people to live together before marrying and this figure rises to two in three people of those aged under 45. The practice is becoming increasingly common and the trend may continue, so that it becomes the norm to live together before marrying, with pre-marital cohabitation becoming an institutionalized part of the mating process, in the same way that the period of engagement was in the recent past. This type of cohabitation is not confined to particular social groups: it seems to have been taken up by the young from working and middle-class families and those with differing levels of education. There were few observable differences between the socio-economic circumstances of these childless cohabitants and their childless married contemporaries. However, there was some evidence that cohabiting childless couples had more egalitarian attitudes and were more likely to share household tasks than their married counterparts. Lesthaeghe and Moors discuss differences in values in relation to living arrangements in Chapter 6.

Previously married cohabitants tended on average to be older and to have been cohabiting for longer. The majority had had children while married and many are in effect reconstituted families with all the attending complexities that such an arrangement entails. Fifty per cent of the post-marital cohabitants had dependent children. Across a range of socio-economic characteristics we found few differences between the remarried and these cohabiting families. The most noteworthy was that cohabiting women in step-family settings were more likely to be in receipt of maintenance than their remarried counterparts.

The third group were the never-married couples with children. Altogether only one in four of the never-married couples had had a child. But the findings in relation to these cohabiting families were the most striking. Compared with married-couple families these families were relatively disadvantaged. Cohabiting-couple families, on average, had significantly lower household incomes, were more likely to be in receipt of income support and housing benefit, were more likely to be in local authority accommodation, and the male partner was more likely to be unemployed or to be in semi-skilled and unskilled occupations than was the case in married-couple families.

Institutions, both public and private, will increasingly need to address the implications of rising levels of cohabitation, particularly if these unions become more long-standing and children are born and reared within them. How will they accommodate to the debate that in the simplest terms could be said to have two main points of view? One side argues that the legal distinction between marriage and cohabitation should be maintained as its removal would undermine the position of marriage. The other is reluctant to accord cohabitation full recognition on the grounds that it forces on unmarried couples a legal framework which, by the act of cohabiting, they may be trying to avoid. A similar debate raged in Sweden in the early 1970s and is still not fully resolved. Sweden is among the countries where cohabitation is most long-standing and prevalent, but even here there is a reluctance to accord the same rights to cohabitants and married couples.

2.7 The Rise of Divorce

The other major demographic development related to partnership behaviour is the rise of divorce. At the beginning of the 1970s the highest divorce rates were to be found in Denmark and Sweden in Northern Europe and in East Germany, Hungary, and Czechoslovakia in Eastern Europe. Divorce rates first began to rise in Eastern

Europe, where divorce laws were liberalized sooner than in most countries in the West (Rallu and Blum 1991).

Following the liberalization of divorce laws, divorce rates in many European countries continued their upward trend, frequently at a faster pace than in the years preceding legislative changes, and this pattern was followed by a period of stabilization in the mid- to late 1980s (see figure 2.2). At the end of the 1980s there was a good deal of variation in the level of divorce across European nations, with the highest rates occurring in Eastern European countries—the eastern part of Germany, Czechoslovakia, and Hungary, and in the Northern European countries—the United Kingdom, Denmark, and Finland. There were very low rates in the Southern European countries of Italy, Spain, Greece, and Portugal.

If recent divorce rates were to continue it is estimated that in

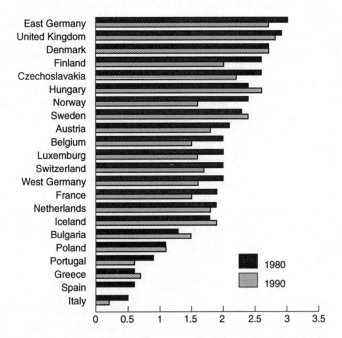

FIG. 2.2. *Crude divorce rates: divorces per 1,000 population, selected European countries, 1980 and 1990*

Source: Council of Europe 1992.

most countries in Europe the chances of couples divorcing would be around one in three: with Sweden, Denmark, and the United Kingdom highest at around two out of five (which is somewhat lower than the analogous rates for the United States of America and the former USSR with levels of one in two) and some of the Southern European countries lagging behind at one in ten or less (Hopflinger 1990, Haskey 1993).

With the rise of cohabitation the issue of the dissolution of unions is becoming ever more complex as the true number of separations is not captured. Divorce statistics are an underestimate of the totality of marital disruptions—both in times past and nowadays.

It is difficult to make general statements that apply to all countries but in those where divorce is more long-standing and more prevalent there has been a tendency for marriages to break up at an earlier stage in marriage than in other countries. If this pattern continues, as divorce becomes more common, more couples are likely to be childless and, among couples with children, the children are likely to be younger. As a consequence of marital disruption there has been a growth in lone-parent families, the residential separation of fathers from their children, remarried couples, and step-families.

2.8 Lone-Parent Families

A report for the European Commission (Roll 1992) provides estimates of the percentage of families with children under the age of 18 which were lone-parent families.

We see from table 2.3 that among the twelve EU countries the United Kingdom has the highest proportion of lone-parent families, at 17 per cent. The proportion may have increased still further since the time of this study. The estimate for 1991 for Great Britain from the General Household Survey was 19 per cent. At the other end of the scale are the Southern European countries such as Greece, Spain, and Italy with around 5 per cent of families being lone-parent families (including those arising from widowhood).

This report also highlighted the fact that the great majority of lone-parent families are headed by a woman (80–90 per cent). The largest group of lone parents were those who had experienced a

TABLE 2.3. *Lone-parent families as a proportion of all families with children under 18, late 1980s.*

	Estimates (%)
United Kingdom	17
Denmark	15
Belgium, Ireland	11–13
Luxemburg,	
Netherlands, Portugal	
Greece, Spain, Italy	5–6

Source: Roll 1992.

marital breakdown; the next-largest group comprised widows, while lone mothers who had never married were the smallest category.

The broad evidence suggests that over one-half of lone parents cease to be classed as lone parents within five years—through remarriage, children leaving home, or children attaining ages when they are no longer classified as children. Five years may seem a short time in the lives of adults, but for children this is a substantial part of childhood.

Remarriage rates, which rose in the years immediately after the enactment of more lenient divorce legislation in most European countries in recent decades, have taken a downturn. Some of this decline may be due to the fact that post-marital cohabitation has become more common or because people are cohabiting for longer periods of time or both. In countries where divorce is more prevalent and/or cohabitation is more rife formal remarriage rates would tend to be lower and the formation of *de jure* step-families less likely.

2.9 Economic Effects of Lone Parenthood

There is a good deal of evidence that lone mothers and their children are more likely to experience poverty or reduced economic circumstances than other types of families. The financial exigencies associated with marital breakdown arise from the precarious economic position of lone mothers, and the dis-economies of scale associated with the maintenance of two households, when fathers live apart from their children. The low incomes of lone-mother families are due to a combination of factors: low earnings from employment, lack of or low levels of child support from the natural father, meagre or inadequate state support.

Research using the Luxemburg Income Study has shown that the extent of financial deprivation in lone-mother families varies between countries. Sorensen's (Sorensen 1990) analysis of the well-being of lone mothers and married mothers in Germany, Sweden, and the United States of America showed that Sweden had come closest to solving the economic problems of lone-mother families. Swedish lone mothers tend to have lower incomes than their married counterparts, but few of them are defined as poor. In contrast, American and German lone mothers tended to have very low incomes and substantial proportions were poor.

Hauser and Fischer's (1990) analyses of the Luxemburg Income Study using data from six countries (Sweden, West Germany, the United Kingdom, Israel, Canada, and the United States) showed that the economic welfare position of lone-parent families in all six countries was worse than that of two-parent families. (They compared lone-parent families with minor children and married couples with minor children.) The relative welfare positions showed Sweden to be the most favourable, with the discrepancy between one- and two-parent families being rather small (13 per cent). The middle group consisted of West Germany, Israel, and the United Kingdom where there was a difference of around 20 per cent. In Canada the welfare position of one-parent families was on average about 34 per cent below that of two-parent families, and in the United States the difference was over 40 per cent.

Generous public benefits and the high labour-force participation of Swedish mothers account to a large extent for the relatively better position of Swedish lone mothers. The reasons for the intermediate position of West German lone mothers and British lone mothers are different. West German lone mothers have high labour-force participation rates (higher than those of married mothers in general), but there are less generous public transfers in favour of lone-parent families. In Britain lone mothers have lower labour-force participation rates (lower than those of married mothers) but there are relatively high public transfers compared with Germany and the USA.

2.10 Employment Trends

Alongside these demographic developments another trend which is having a fundamental effect on partnership behaviour is the marked increase in the level of women's participation in the labour market. The following discussion focuses on the EC countries, for which a range of comparable data are available.

Throughout the 1980s, women's share of total employment rose in all the Community states. Female activity rates in the ten EC countries stood at 31.0 in 1980 and 42.9 per cent in 1991 as compared with 54.4 and 67.5 per cent for men in the same years. (The figures for the twelve EC countries in 1991 were 43.8 per cent for women and 67.5 per cent for men.) This rise in female activity rates was largely due to the growth in part-time jobs in the service sector (EC Commission 1991). Levels of female participation in the labour market in the EC are still well below those observed in Eastern Europe (in recent times) and the United States of America.

Patterns of employment

Figure 2.3 shows that there are marked differences between the age patterns of employment of men and women, primarily arising from the advent of motherhood and its repercussions. These cross-sectional data do not provide us with direct information on the employment profiles of men and women as they move through life (for that we would need longitudinal information) but they provide insights into differences between the sexes and between countries.

The typical profile for men could be described as arch-shaped or as an inverted U-shape. Employment rates rise as young men complete their education and enter the labour force. Having entered, the majority of men remain in the labour force more or less continuously until they retire in their late fifties and early sixties. Differences in patterns of male employment across countries are small. Those that exist are largely confined to the two ends of the age spectrum, arising from variation in educational participation at the younger end and patterns of retirement at the other.

In contrast, the employment profiles of women are much more varied. At one extreme is Denmark, where the age pattern of employment is very similar to men's but at a slightly lower level. In France, the United Kingdom, and to a lesser extent West Germany, the curves for women are broadly similar to those observed for men but the rate of participation is lower, and lower than that seen among women in Denmark. The remainder of the countries exhibit somewhat similar profiles, in which participation tends to be high at young ages and then drops from the twenties onwards. The steepness of the decline and level of participation varies, with particularly sharp declines to be seen in Belgium, Ireland, Luxemburg, and Spain. These patterns are based on cross-sectional data and it is possible that as the more recent generations of young women age they may not leave the labour market to the same extent as earlier-born generations of women.

Part-time versus full-time work

Once men and women enter the labour market two major features distinguish their employment profiles: women are much less likely to have continuous occupational careers and they are more likely to work part-time. These differences are primarily a direct consequence of motherhood. The extent of part-time working is negligible among men and a significant, albeit minority, practice among women. For example, data from 1991 Labour Force Surveys (Eurostat 1993, table 34) show that overall in the twelve EC countries only 4 per cent of employed men were working part-time compared with 29 per cent of women. The extent of part-time working varies considerably across countries, as can be seen in table 2.4.

2.11 Earnings

It is notoriously difficult to compare the earnings of men and women directly because of the important structural differences that currently exist between the worlds of work of men and women. For example, there are differences in levels of training, qualifications, seniority, age structures, years in work, and variations across different occupational sectors and businesses of different sizes, in the extent of overtime and night-shift work and so on. But on average the earnings of women are less than those of men. For example, a

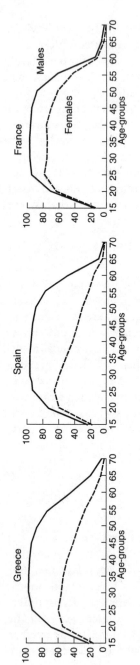

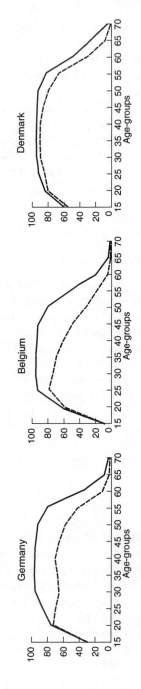

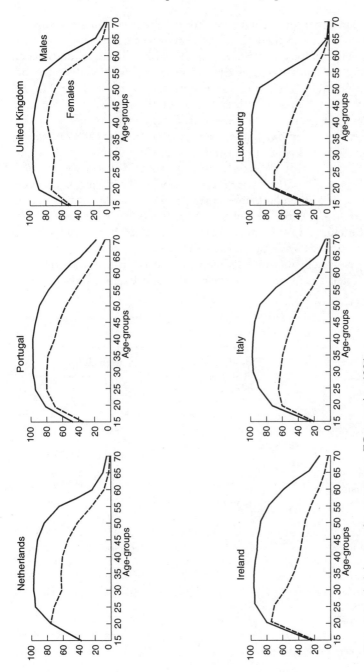

FIG. 2.3. *Activity rates by age-groups, EC countries, 1991*
Source: Eurostat 1993b: table 3.

comparison of the average gross hourly earnings of manual workers in industry across the EC countries in or around 1987 showed that in Denmark, Italy, and France female earnings were around 80 per cent of men's earnings, in Greece, Belgium, the Netherlands, and West Germany they were between 70 and 80 per cent, and in the United Kingdom, Ireland, and Luxemburg they were 70 per cent or less. The ratios were highest in Denmark at 86 per cent and lowest in Luxemburg at 65 per cent (Eurostat 1988: *Earnings, Industry and Services* (2), cited in EC Commission 1989: table 2.13). One reason frequently cited for women's lower wages is the time spent out of the labour market associated with having children and all the attendant consequences, such as the truncation of experience and the loss of seniority. If women increasingly have continuous employment histories then, other things being equal, wage differentials between men and women should shrink.

This growth in women's employment is probably altering the economic arrangements between men and women. Women may

TABLE 2.4. *Employees: percentage of men and women who work part-time and full-time in the twelve EC countries, 1991*

	Part-time		Full-time	
	Men (%)	Women (%)	Men (%)	Women (%)
12 EC countries	4	29	96	71
Belgium	2	30	98	69
Denmark	11	38	89	62
Germany	2	34	98	66
Greece	2	5	98	95
Spain	1	11	99	89
France	3	24	97	76
Ireland	4	17	96	83
Italy	3	10	97	90
Luxemburg	1	18	98	82
Netherlands	15	59	84	41
Portugal	2	6	98	93
United Kingdom	5	44	95	56

Source: Eurostat 1993, table 34.

increasingly be taking a greater share of the economic support of the household and men's prime responsibility is likely to have lessened. The proportion of women who depend on men and their degree of dependence may well decline further in the future, as women acquire more education, make more inroads into a wider range of occupations, progress up the occupational and political hierarchies, and take less time out of the labour market to care for young children.

2.12 Attitudes of Men and Women

Are attitudes concerning the roles of men and women changing? The available evidence does point to a clear change in sex-role attitudes over the last decade in most European countries, albeit from very different starting points. Men and women increasingly espouse what could be regarded as more egalitarian views. The following discussion largely draws on results from a series of Eurobarometer Surveys (1975, 1978, 1983, and 1987) carried out as part of the EC Commission research programme on changing attitudes of men and women.

The 1975 enquiry showed that one of the important issues that divided men and women was whether married women should work or not. In 1975, in the then nine EC countries, 33 per cent of married or cohabiting men stated that if they had the choice they would prefer their spouses to have paid work. By 1983 the proportion of men expressing the same preference had increased a little to 30 per cent. By 1987 the proportion had increased further to 47 per cent in the same nine countries and to 48 per cent in the now twelve EC countries. More detailed analysis of the 1987 data showed that the younger the men, the more educated the men, and the higher the family income, the more likely were the men to favour their wives working (EC Commission 1987). That men should express more favourable attitudes nowadays than was the case a decade or so ago to their wives being involved in paid work is not particularly surprising, given the upsurge of female participation in the labour market. However, men with working wives are not universally positive about the situation. In the 1987 survey, only 70 per cent of men with working wives were in favour of the situation. It would be interesting to know whether the analogous proportion for working women with working partners was similar or not.

The foregoing suggests a growing acceptance of female labour-force participation on the part of men. But perhaps the most interesting and illuminating insights are provided by the responses to a question posed on role distribution within the family. Respondents were asked which of the following three arrangements corresponded most closely to their idea of a family:

(*a*) a family in which both husband and wife have equally absorbing work, and in which the household tasks and looking after the children are shared equally between husband and wife (egalitarian option);

(*b*) a family in which the wife's work is less absorbing than the husband's, and in which she takes on more of the household tasks and looking after the children (middle option);

(*c*) a family in which the husband only works and the wife runs the home (home-maker/breadwinner option).

In 1987, in the twelve EC countries, support for the traditional roles of home-maker wife and breadwinner husband was least, with only 25 per cent of respondents stating that this arrangement corresponded most closely to their idea of a family. Forty-one per cent supported an egalitarian division of labour and 29 per cent supported the middle option. (The remaining 5 per cent supported none of the above or did not answer the question.)

The difference in the overall proportion of men and women favouring the 'egalitarian' model was small: 39 per cent of men as compared with 42 per cent of women. The younger the men or women the more likely they were to prefer this model. For example, 53 per cent of men aged 15 to 24 years and 47 per cent of those aged 25 to 39 years favoured equal roles as compared with 34 and 26 per cent of men aged 40 to 54 years and aged 55 and older respectively. The analogous proportions for women were 61, 49, 37, and 27 per cent respectively. The only difference between the sexes in the level of response is seen at the youngest ages where women were more likely to express a preference for the equal roles model (61 per cent) than were the men (53 per cent). Not surprisingly, men with working wives and women in the labour market were also more likely to favour this model.

There were substantial cross-national differences in the extent to which men and women favoured the different arrangements (figures 2.4 and 2.5). One extreme is represented by Denmark.

Danish men and women were the most likely of the EC citizens to prefer the 'egalitarian' model (51 per cent of men and 55 per cent of women) and the most likely to eschew the traditional model (12 per cent of men and 13 per cent of women); the responses of the

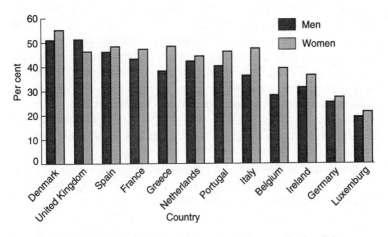

FIG. 2.4. *Desired family roles: proportions favouring equal roles, EC countries*
Source: EC Commission 1987.

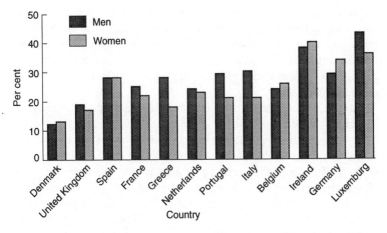

FIG. 2.5. *Desired family roles: proportions favouring traditional roles, EC countries*
Source: EC Commission.

two sexes were in accord. The other extreme is composed of a cluster of countries: West Germany, Ireland, and Luxemburg. In these three countries the proportions of men and women preferring the traditional home-maker/breadwinner model is greater than the proportion preferring the equal roles model. For example, 34 per cent of German women and 29 per cent of German men prefer the traditional model while 27 per cent of the women and 25 per cent of the men prefer the equal roles model. Traditional attitudes are also strong in Belgium. In the remainder of the countries, women express a preference for the 'egalitarian' model to a similar extent, with a range from 44 to 48 per cent. Men in this intermediate set of countries are less homogeneous than the women in their preference for the 'egalitarian' arrangement. The proportions range from 36 per cent of Italian men preferring this model to 51 per cent of British men.

In most countries the distribution of responses for men and women was broadly similar. The noticeable exceptions were Italian, Greek, and Belgian women, who were more likely than their male counterparts to prefer the equal roles arrangement, and in Greece, Italy, Portugal, and Luxemburg, the men were much more traditional than their female counterparts. Denmark is at the top of the twelve EC countries with regard to egalitarian attitudes and is also the EC country with the highest female labour participation rate. Let us take a closer look at some Danish data on changing attitudes to preferred family situations among mothers with small children. The Eurobarometer data discussed above related to couples regardless of their life-cycle stage, but families with young children are likely to experience more acute tensions between work and family life than childless couples or couples with older children.

Table 2.5 shows that there have been quite dramatic changes in responses between 1970 and 1985. In 1970, one in two of the mothers preferred the home-maker/breadwinner model of the father working full-time and the mother being a full-time housewife while in 1985 only one in six expressed a preference for this option. The most popular preference in 1985 was for a situation where both parents worked part-time while their children were small (presumably sharing economic and family responsibilities). The next most popular option was for the father to work full-time and the mother part-time, with around one-third of the women ex-

TABLE 2.5. *Attitudes to preferred family type among Danish mothers with small children in 1970, 1975, and 1985*

	1970 (%)	1975 (%)	1985 (%)
Father works full-time Mother housewife	53	32	17
Both work part-time while children are young	15	27	46
Father works full-time Mother works part-time	31	38	33
Both work full-time	1	2	3
Father stays at home Mother works	0	1	0
Total	100	100	99
Number in sample	1,759	1,840	1,034

Source: Christoffersen *et al*. 1987. Cited in Jorgensen 1991.

pressing a preference for this situation, a proportion that had remained steady over the period from 1970 to 1985. Both parents working full-time is a surprisingly unpopular option (3 per cent preferred this option) and preference for reversing the conventional roles is negligible. If both parents want to be involved in the world of work and the rearing of their small children then both parents working part-time may represent an ideal solution (still to be attained) but one parent working full-time and the other part-time is a pragmatic solution.

2.13 The Domestic Domain

It seems that espoused attitudes and preferences are becoming more equitable, but is behaviour in the domestic domain becoming more equal? To what extent do men and women share domestic responsibilities?

Questions posed in the 1990 Eurobarometer Survey No. 34 provide us with some insights (Kempeneers and Lelièvre 1992). Respondents in the twelve EC countries were asked: 'Who usually took care of the following tasks during your first child's pre-school

years, you or your partner?' Across all countries among men living
with a woman in a couple the only task that men were more likely
to take responsibility for was shopping (61 per cent); washing-up
was the next most likely activity (41 per cent), followed by taking
children to and from nursery school or child-minder (31 per cent);
and the least popular activities for men were dressing children (26
per cent), cooking (25 per cent), and cleaning (25 per cent). But
the picture is bleaker than it appears. These percentages refer to
men who undertook at least one of these activities, but it seems that
only 40 per cent of men fully took care of any one of these tasks.
Dutch and Danish men were most likely to be involved (one in
two) and Spanish men the least likely (one in five).

Denmark once again was among the leading countries in terms
of male participation in the domestic domain. Data from a Danish
Institute of Social Research Survey (see Jorgensen 1991) allow us
to take a closer look at the situation there. The Danish researchers
anticipated that fathers might be taking on an equal proportion of
the housework and were perhaps adopting a 'new responsibility' for
family life. However, they found rather 'conservative' sex roles in
families with dependent children. Men were mostly responsible for
traditional tasks such as indoor repair jobs. Women in about half of
the families were solely responsible for cooking and cleaning of the
house, and only in a third of the families did husbands and wives
share these tasks. Yet this is a society where the great majority of
women are economically active.

If wives are not employed or work part-time it would seem
logical in terms of maximizing household efficiency that the wife
should specialize more in domestic tasks. It also seems logical that
full-time housewives should perform more tasks than those women
who work part-time. However, in households where both partners
work full-time, one might expect the division of labour in the
household to be more equitable, unless one partner works much
longer hours than the other. Some data from Great Britain shown
in table 2.6 (Kiernan 1992b) allow us to examine how the division
of labour within the household varies according to employment
status of the wife. In 1991, respondents to the British Social
Attitudes Survey who were living with a partner were asked which
one was 'mainly responsible for general domestic duties' in
the household. The great majority, 75 per cent, stated that the
woman was responsible and 16 per cent said the duties were shared

TABLE 2.6. *Responsibility for domestic duties according to employment status*

Responsibility for general domestic duties	Respondents living in households where			
	man works and woman works full-time (%)	man works and woman works part-time (%)	man works and woman does not work (%)	other households (%)
Mainly woman	67	83	89	66
Shared	24	13	6	21

Source: Kiernan 1992b.

equally between them. Men were more likely to say that duties were shared equally (20 per cent), compared with 12 per cent of women. The responses according to employment status are shown in table 2.6.

Households where both partners work full-time are relatively more likely to share responsibility for domestic tasks, but the situation could hardly be construed as egalitarian, when only one in four of such households share such duties. As would be expected, women who work part-time are more likely to be mainly responsible for domestic duties than their full-time counterparts and somewhat less likely than those who do not work. Partnerships where neither work, many of whom are retired couples, are as likely to share as full-time working partners.

The limited data and the growing literature (for example, Hochschild 1989, Ve 1989) on the division of labour in the home, measured according to type and number of tasks or time budgets, suggests that husbands of wives who work outside the home do not share equally in child-care and housework tasks. Wives' employment as yet would seem to have a modest effect on the household division of labour. Wives typically have responsibility for the daily organization of the household and for household work, and do most of the routine tasks such as meals, cleaning, and laundry. Wives who work outside the home, particularly those who work full-time, tend to receive more help from husbands than do wives who are not employed outside the home. Looking after children appears to be a more popular activity among fathers than the more routine housekeeping tasks. More men, on average, may be taking a more active role in the domestic arena than was the case in the past, but this is typically likely to be a *helping role*; few as yet are *sharing* domestic responsibilities and tasks. There may be pressure for men to take their fair share of caring and domestic tasks but the pace of change to date can at best be described as leisurely.

Recent changes in the lives of European men and women have occurred in a social context in which there have been marked changes in norms regarding the equality of women, men's responsibilities in the family, changing economic pressures, and expectations regarding living standards. As with other changes, attitudes and behaviour are not necessarily consistent and are highly variable across countries. There is the continuing dilemma, more prevalent in some countries than others, as to whether policies should recognize the different structures of men's and women's lives. Should women have a choice about whether or not to contribute to the financial support of the family? Should men have a choice about being the primary breadwinner and secondary carer? Or should policies aim at reducing the differences between the lives of men and women?

Until recently, economic changes have not really been required to challenge or make the relations between the sexes a priority. This may be less the case in the future and although the economic changes are largely progressive, they are only a step, albeit an essential step, in the process of achieving equity. As yet, we have seen limited change in the domestic domain where it is a matter of private relations and negotiation between men and women. The Swedes have been bold enough to tackle this issue more directly. The 1987 Swedish Marriage Act has among its general provisions, 'Spouses shall share expenditure and practical responsibilities with one another' and 'They shall jointly take care of their home and children and in consultation promote the best interests of the family'. The wording of these provisions is not quite as explicit as that mooted by the Working Party for the Role of the Male (1986): 'spouses shall share the expenses and discharge of household duties'.

Changes in legislation, increased participation in the labour market, commitment to equal opportunity, and action programmes give the impression that considerable progress has been made in the pursuit of independence and equality for women. Undoubtedly, the trend is towards greater equality and independence between men and women, and away from relationships of asymmetry and dependence. However, there may well be a gap between the reality and the perception of women's independence and equality. The width of this gap may vary considerably across countries and the speed with which the gaps shrink is also likely to vary. Behaviour can often lag behind general norms or opinion formers' views of the world.

2.14 Conclusion

The roles of men and women and the relations between the sexes are changing. There is variability across European countries in the extent to which such changes have taken hold. Paralleling these developments are substantial demographic changes. Men and women are cohabiting more, marrying later, becoming parents at older ages, and having fewer children, as well as terminating their marriages more frequently than was common in the recent past. In addition, men and women are living longer.

Across Europe the automatic nature of marriage and parenthood has been increasingly questioned; they are no longer inevitabilities but are considered as choices. Increasingly, paid work plays a central role in the lives of both men and women. However, if societies are to continue they will require children, and they need them to be well cared for and effectively socialized if they are to function as productive and creative adults and in turn nurture the next generation. Some form of partnership between men and women has previously been required and will probably continue to be required to sustain society.

NOTES

This work was supported under grant number R000 23 2161 from the Economic and Social Science Research Council of the UK. This chapter draws on the following papers: Kiernan 1992a, and Kiernan 1993. Comparative analyses present a range of problems. Standardized information across a range of countries is not plentiful and typically encompasses the more basic measures with all their attendant drawbacks. Here we make use of information collected for the countries that are members of the Council of Europe and the EC.

REFERENCES

ALABERT, A., CABRE, A., DOMINGO, A., FABRE, A., and STLOCKE, V. (1988), 'Changing patterns in household formation in Barcelona and Madrid, 1985', in H. Moors and J. Schoorl (eds.), *Lifestyles, Contraception and Parenthood*, The Hague/Brussels: NIDI.

COUNCIL OF EUROPE (1992), *Recent Demographic Developments in Europe*, Strasburg: Council of Europe.

EC COMMISSION (1987), *Women of Europe Supplement*, No. 26, Luxemburg: Office for Official Publications of the European Communities.

——(1989), *Women of Europe Supplement*, No. 30, Luxemburg: Office for Official Publications of the European Communities.

——(1991), *Employment in Europe, 1990*, ch. 6. 'Employment for Women: Is access to jobs easier or not?', Luxemburg: Office for Official Publications of the European Communities.

EUROSTAT (1993), *Labour Force Survey, Results 1991*, Luxemburg: Office for Official Publications of the European Communities.

HASKEY, J. (1993), 'Formation and dissolution of unions in the different countries of Europe', in A. Blum and J.-L. Rallu (eds.), *European Population*, vol. ii, *Demographic Dynamics*, Paris: John Libbey, Eurotext.

——and Kiernan, K. E. (1989), 'Cohabitation in Great Britain: characteristics and estimated numbers of cohabiting partners', *Population Trends*, 53.

HAUSER, R., and FISCHER, I. (1990), 'Economic well-being among one-parent families', in T. M. Smeeding, M. O'Higgins, and L. Rainwater (eds.), *Poverty, Inequality and Income Distribution in Comparative Perspective*, Brighton: Harvester Wheatsheaf.

HOCHSCHILD, A. (1989), *The Second Shift: Working Parents and the Revolution at Home*, London: Piatkus.

HÖHN, C. (1991), 'Germany', in J.-L. Rallu and A. Blum (eds.), *European Population*, vol. i, *Country Analysis*, Paris: John Libbey.

HOPFLINGER, F. (1990), 'The future of household and family structures in Europe', Paper presented to Council of Europe, Seminar on present demographic trends and lifestyles in Europe.

JORGENSEN, P. S. (1991), 'The family with dependent children in Denmark', in G. Kiely and V. Richardson (eds.), *Family Policy in*

European Perspectives, Dublin: Family Studies Centre.

KEMPENEERS, M., and LELIÈVRE, E. (1992), 'Employment and Family', in EC Commission, *Eurobarometer*, 34, 1990.

KIERNAN, K. E. (1992a), 'The respective roles of men and women in tomorrow's Europe', in *Proceedings of Eurostat Conference on Human Resources in Europe: at the Dawn of the 21st Century*, Luxemburg: Eurostat.

——(1992b), 'Men and women at work and home', in R. Jowell, L. Brook, and G. Prior (eds.), *The British Social Attitudes Survey, 9th Report*, Aldershot: Dartmouth Press.

——(1993), 'The future of partnership and fertility in Europe', in R. Cliquet (ed.), *The Future of Europe's Population*, Strasburg: Council of Europe.

——and ESTAUGH, V. (1993), *Cohabitation, Extra-Marital Childbearing and Social Policy*, London: Family Policy Studies Centre.

LAPINCH, A. (1991), 'Changes in the process of family formation in Baltic countries and Sovereign Republics of the Soviet Union', Workshop, European University Institute, Florence, November 1991.

LERIDON, H. (1990), 'Cohabitation, marriage and separation: an analysis of life histories of French cohorts from 1968 to 1985', *Population Studies*, 44, 127–144.

RALLU, J. R., and BLUM, A. (eds.) (1991), *European Population: a synthesis of European Population*, vol. i, European Population Conference. Paris: John Libbey Eurotext.

ROLL, J. (1992), 'Lone Parent Families in the European Community—A report to the European Commission'. London: Family Policy Studies Centre.

SORENSEN, A. (1990), 'Single mothers, low income and women's economic risks. The cases of Sweden, West Germany and the United States', *Luxembourg Income Study, Working Paper* No. 60.

VE, H. (1989), 'The male gender role and responsibility for childcare', in K. Boh *et al.* (eds.), *Changing Patterns of European Family Life: A Comparative Analysis of 14 European Countries*, London: Routledge.

WORKING PARTY FOR THE ROLE OF THE MALE (1986), *The Changing Role of the Male*, cited p. 310, in L. Segal (1990), *Slow motion, changing masculinities, changing man*, London: Virago.

3
Migration Pressures on Western Europe

JOHN SALT

3.1 Introduction

The chapter begins by demonstrating that immigration pressures on Western Europe continue to grow. It then reviews the demographic and economic backgrounds to emigration from the east and south, together with some of the main characteristics of the movement that occurs. Finally, it reviews briefly some of the main features of the migration of skills.

We currently have only a vague idea of total stocks and flows of international migrants. This is for a variety of reasons, among which inadequate statistical systems and the immense complexity of definitions are among the most important. In 1989 the UN estimated that about 50 million people lived in a country other than their own; for 1992 the World Bank estimated 100 million, including 17 million refugees.

3.2 Recent Trends in the Foreign Population in Western Europe

Stocks

There seems little doubt that in Western Europe as a whole, stocks of foreign population have increased considerably in recent years. Table 3.1 suggests that in 1992 or thereabouts (using the latest date for which statistics are available—see table 3.1) there were around 18.27 million foreign nationals legally resident in Western Europe, with perhaps a further one-third of a million in Eastern Europe.

In 1988, or thereabouts (1990 for France, 1987 for Greece), the foreign national stock figure stood at about 14.85 million. Hence, from 1988 to 1992 total foreign national stocks in Western Europe, for the countries listed, increased by about 3.42 million (a 23 per cent increase). However, a majority of this increase—58 per cent (about two million people)—occurred in Germany, emphasizing the extent to which the rise in immigration in Western Europe in the last few years is predominantly a German problem.

Increased stocks of foreign population seem, therefore, to have become a widespread phenomenon in Western Europe during the 1980s and 1990s. In relative terms the largest increases in foreign population stocks were in countries that have traditionally been considered ones of emigration. In four countries the foreign population more than doubled: Finland (up 218.8 per cent to 1992), Italy (161.5 per cent), Portugal (131.2 per cent) and Spain (124 per cent). It must be noted, however, that 'foreign' populations may be depleted by naturalization: this has particularly been the case in France.

Inflows of foreign population

The data in table 3.2 are from a variety of national sources, and at the time of writing they represent the best estimates of migration flows for European states. Statistics are available for some countries for 1993, for most for 1992. Gaps in the table mean that data for those years are not (yet) available.

For all of the countries listed, the total recorded inflow of foreign population in 1992 (or the latest year, where no 1992 figure was available) was 1,894,300 (excluding *Aussiedler*, see below). It is immediately apparent that Germany plays the dominant role: it received 63.7 per cent of all immigrants to these Western European countries (a gross inflow of 1,207,600). These German data to not include the immigration of ethnic Germans (*Aussiedler*), mainly from Eastern Europe and the former Soviet Union (FSU), who are not treated statistically as foreigners. The next most important country, the United Kingdom, had less than a tenth of the German inflow (6.1 per cent), followed by France (4.2 per cent), the Netherlands (4.4 per cent), Switzerland (5.9 per cent), and (in 1990) Italy (5.1 per cent).

Assessing the trend in gross inflows is not easy, given the vari-

TABLE 3.1. *Stock of foreign population in European countries, 1980–1993 (1).*

(a) Thousands

	1980	1981	1982	1983	1984	1985	1986	1987	1988	1989	1990	1991	1992	1993
Austria	282.7	299.2	302.9	275.0	268.8	271.7	275.7	283.0	298.7	322.6	413.4	512.2	561.8	
Belgium (2)		885.7	891.2	890.9	897.6	846.6	853.2	882.6	888.8	880.8	904.5	909.9	915.9	
Bulgaria (3)													28.0	30.7
Czech Republic (4)											35.1	37.7	41.2	110.0
Denmark (5)	101.6	101.9	103.1	104.1	107.7	117.0	128.3	136.2	142.0	150.6	160.6	169.5		
Finland (6)	12.8	13.7	14.3	15.7	16.8	17.0	17.3	17.7	18.7	21.2	26.3	35.8	40.8	52.8
France			3,714.2			3,752.2					3,607.6			
Germany (7)	4,453.3	4,629.8	4,888.9	4,534.9	4,363.7	4,378.9	4,512.7	4,630.2	4,489.1	4,845.9	5,241.8	5,882.3	6,495.8	
Greece							195.0	193.4			229.0			
Hungary (18)												73.9	88.2	
Ireland (9, 17)										26.0	27.6	29.3		
Italy (10)	298.7	331.7	358.9	381.3	403.9	423.0	450.2	572.1	645.4	490.4	781.1	896.8	923.6	953.1
Liechtenstein	9.3										10.9	11.4		
Luxemburg	94.3	95.4	95.6	96.2	96.9	98.0	96.8	98.6	100.9	104.0	110.0	114.7	119.7	
Netherlands	520.9	537.6	546.5	552.4	558.7	552.5	588	591.8	623.7	641.9	692.4	732.9	757.4	
Norway (11)	82.6	86.5	90.6	94.7	97.8	101.5	109.3	123.7	135.9	140.3	143.3	147.8	154.0	
Poland (12)												20.0–180.0		
Portugal (13, 17)	49.3	53.6	57.7	65.9	72.6	80.0	87.0	89.8	94.7	107.0	107.8	114.0	121.5	
Romania (19)													3.2	
Spain (17)	182.0	197.9	200.9	210.4	226.5	241.9	293.2	334.9	360.0	398.1	407.7	360.7	393.1	
Sweden (14)	421.7	414.0	405.5	397.1	390.6	388.6	390.8	401.0	421.0	456.0	483.7	493.8	499.1	
Switzerland (15)	892.8	909.9	925.8	925.6	932.4	939.7	956.0	978.7	1,006.5	1,040.3	1,100.3	1,163.2	1,213.5	1,228.3
United Kingdom (16)					1,601.0	1,731.0	1,820.0	1,839.0	1,821.0	1,949.0	1,875.0	1,791.0	1,985.0	

(b) Percentages

	1980	1981	1982	1983	1984	1985	1986	1987	1988	1989	1990	1991	1992	1993
Austria	3.7	3.9	4.0	3.6	3.6	3.6	3.6	3.7	3.9	4.2	6.3	6.6	7.1	
Belgium		9.0	9.0	9.0	9.1	8.6	8.6	8.7	8.8	8.9	9.1	9.2	9.0	
Bulgaria														0.3
Czech Republic											0.3	0.4	0.4	1.1
Denmark	2.0	2.0	2.0	2.0	2.1	2.3	2.6	2.7	2.8	2.9	3.1	3.3		
Finland	0.3	0.3	0.3	0.3	0.3	0.4	0.4	0.4	0.4	0.4	0.6	0.7	0.8	1.0
France			6.8								6.4			

Country														
Germany	7.2	7.5	7.5	7.4	7.1	7.2	7.4	7.6	7.3	7.7	8.2	7.3	8.0	
Greece							2.0	1.9			2.2	0.7	0.9	
Hungary												0.8	0.7	
Ireland									0.9		1.4	1.5	1.6	1.6
Italy	0.5	0.6	0.6	0.7	0.7	0.7	0.8	1.0	1.1	0.7	0.8			
Liechtenstein	36.9										37.6		38.1	
Luxemburg	25.8	26.1	26.2	26.3	26.5	26.7	26.2	26.5	26.9	27.5	28.6	29.4	30.3	
Netherlands	3.7	3.8	3.8	3.8	3.9	3.8	3.9	4.0	4.2	4.3	4.6	4.8	5.0	
Norway	2.0	2.1	2.2	2.3	2.4	2.4	2.6	2.9	3.2	3.3	3.4	3.5	3.6	
Poland									0.05–0.5					
Portugal	0.5	0.5	0.5	0.6	0.7	0.8	0.8	0.9	0.9	1.0	1.0	1.1	1.3	
Spain	0.5	0.5	0.5	0.6	0.6	0.6	0.8	0.9	0.9	1.0	1.1	0.9	1.0	
Sweden	5.1	5	4.9	4.8	4.7	4.6	4.7	4.8	5.0	5.3	5.6	5.7	6.7	
Switzerland	14.1	14.3	14.4	14.4	14.4	14.5	14.7	14.9	15.2	15.6	16.3	16.9	17.6	17.8
United Kingdom					2.8	3.1	3.2	3.2	3.2	3.4	3.3	3.2	3.6	

Notes:

1. Data as of 31 Dec. of year indicated extracted, except for France, UK, and otherwise indicated, from population registers.
2. In 1985, as a consequence of a modification of the nationality code, some persons who formerly would have been counted as foreigners were included as nationals. This led to a marked decrease in the foreign population.
3. Permanently resident foreigners, Ministry of Interior.
4. Data derived from Ministries of Labour and Interior, and include only those holding permanent and long-term residence permits.
5. Data from 1991 refer to 1 Jan. 1991 (*source:* Eurostat).
6. Population censuses on 4 Mar. 1982 and 6 Mar. 1990. The figure for the census of 20 Feb. 1975 is 3,442.4.
7. Data as of 30 Oct. up to 1984 and in 1990 and as of 31 Dec. for all other years. Except for 1991 and 1992, refers to FRG (pre-1990 boundaries). FSO.
8. Estimate, SOPEMI 1992 (includes residence permit holders, illegal stayers, work permit holders, asylum seekers).
9. Department of Justice, annual returns (excludes UK citizens).
10. Data are adjusted to take account of the regularizations which occurred in 1987–8 and 1990. The fall in numbers for 1989 results from a review of the foreigners' register (removing duplicate registrations, accounting for returns).
11. From 1987, asylum seekers whose requests are being processed are included. Numbers for earlier years were fairly small.
12. Numbers of permanent residence permit holders.
13. Servicio de Estrangerios e Fronteiras.
14. Some foreigners' permits of short duration are not counted (mainly citizens of other Nordic countries).
15. Numbers of foreigners with annual residence permits (including, up to 31 Dec. 1982, holders of permits of durations below 12 months) and holders of settlement permits (permanent permits). Seasonal and frontier workers are excluded. Data for 1993 are April.
16. Numbers estimated from the annual labour force survey.
17. Percentage figure derived using 1990 stock figure from Eurostat 1992.
18. Temporary residence permit holders only.
19. 1992 census.

TABLE 3.2. *Inflows of foreign population in Western Europe, 1980–1992 ('000s)*[a]

	1980	1981	1982	1983	1984	1985	1986	1987	1988	1989	1990	1991	1992	1993
Belgium	48.8	41.3	36.2	34.3	37.2	37.5	39.3	40.1	38.2	43.5	52.3	54.1	55.1	
Denmark	15.8	13.4	13.0	11.8	13.3	20.2	22.5	20.1	18.4	19.2	19.7	22.1	21.5	20.5
Finland	1.9	2.3	2.4	2.8	2.7	2.6	2.7	2.8	3.2	4.2	6.5	13.2	10.4	
France[b]	59.4	75	144.4	84.2	51.4	43.4	38.3	39.0	44.0	53.2	63.1	65.3	78.8	
Germany	523.6	451.7	275.5	253.5	295.8	324.4	378.6	414.9	545.4	649.5	770.8	820.5	1207.6	
Greece						27.3	25.4	29.1	30.2	28.0	25.0	13.4		
Iceland	0.4	0.5	0.5	0.6	0.5	0.5	0.7	1.0	1.8	1.0	1.1	1.7		
Italy[c]	88.3	91.5	100.1	98.3	86.9	82.2	75.7	104.5	85.8	81.2	96.7			1.3
Luxembourg	7.4	6.9	6.4	6.2	6.0	6.6	7.4	7.2	8.2	8.4	9.3	10.0	9.8	
Netherlands	79.8	50.4	40.9	36.4	37.3	46.2	52.8	60.9	58.3	65.4	81.3	84.3	83.0	87.4
Norway[d]	11.8	13.1	14.0	13.1	12.8	15.0	16.8	23.8	23.2	18.5	15.7	16.1	17.2	
Portugal													13.7	
Spain[e]						6.2	4.3	5.3	9.7	14.4	13.7	13.7	18.2	
Sweden[f]	34.40	27.40	25.10	18.3	26.1	27.9	34.0	37.1	44.5	58.9	53.2	43.9	39.5	34.2
Switzerland[g]	70.5	80.3	74.7	58.3	58.6	69.4	66.8	71.5	76.1	80.4	101.4	109.8	112.1	
United Kingdom[h]	107.0	93.0	104.0	108.0	106.0	122.0	130.0	113.0	127.0	146.0	161.0	150.0	116.0	

Notes:

[a] Asylum seekers are excluded, unless otherwise indicated.

[b] Entries of new foreign workers. Including holders of provisional work permits (APT, autorisation provisoire du travail) and foreigners admitted on family reunification grounds. Does not include residents of EU countries (workers and family members) who have not been processed via the International Migration Office (OMI, Office des Migrations Internationales).

[c] New entries in the population registers.

[d] Entries of foreigners intending to stay longer than six months in Norway.

[e] Instituto Nacional de Estadística (INE).

[f] Some short duration entries are not counted (mainly citizens of other Nordic countries).

[g] Entries of foreigners with annual residence permits, and those with settlement permits (permanent permits) who return to Switzerland after a temporary stay abroad. Includes, up to 31 Dec. 1982, holders of permits of durations below 12 months. Seasonal and frontier workers (including seasonal workers who obtain permanent permits) are excluded. Transformations are excluded.

[h] Data from International Passenger Survey.

ation in numbers of countries for which statistics are available at different dates. For thirteen countries for which data are available throughout the period (see table 3.2), total inflows of foreign immigrants fell during the early 1980s, since when they have risen continuously, the inflow accelerating after 1988. Between 1980 and 1985, numbers fell by 4.9 per cent per annum; from 1985 to 1988 they rose by 12.1 per cent per annum, and by 18 per cent in the years 1988–92.

Two principal conclusions may be drawn from these trends. First, the rise in immigration predated the opening up of Eastern Europe after 1989, and was not instigated by it. Second, the most recent period shows little sign of a diminution of gross inflows; the slowing of the rate of annual increase during 1990–1 was succeeded by a continuation of the acceleration process the following year.

Outflows of foreign population

Because fewer countries have data on emigration, it is not possible to compare directly the aggregate levels of emigration recorded in table 3.3 with those in table 3.2. It is apparent, however, that migration for Western European countries is not one way. The eleven countries for which data are available recorded 872,000 emigrants in 1992. Germany was again dominant, the origin of 70.6 per cent of the emigrants, followed by the United Kingdom (10.8 per cent) and Switzerland (9.2 per cent). However, some of the major immigration countries, especially France and Italy, effectively have no emigration data.

The trend in outflows can be followed for ten countries (listed in table 3.3) for which data are available from 1980. Between 1980 and 1985 outflow fell (as did inflow) by 2.2 per cent per year; between 1985 and 1988 it rose by 1 per cent per year, but rose by 11.2 per cent per year from 1988 to 1992. This follows a similar pattern to that of the thirteen immigration countries. Like inflows, outflows have grown rapidly from 1987. Again, the role of Germany is salient, although in the absence of some of the larger immigration countries its position is exaggerated.

Net population flows of foreigners

The interplay of in- and outflows has resulted in substantial net immigration. For the countries listed in table 3.4, net immigration

TABLE 3.3. *Outflows of foreign population in Western Europe, 1980–1992 ('000s)*

	1980	1981	1982	1983	1984	1985	1986	1987	1988	1989	1990	1991	1992	1993
Belgium[a]	41.3	39.9	40.4	40.2	35.9	33.5	32.7	34.8	32.3	27.5	28	35.3	20.9	
Denmark[a]	11.9	11.1	10.3	9.2	8.2	9.1	9.3	10.1	10.7	9.5	8.6	10.5	9.4	10.0
Finland[a]	0.8	1.0	0.9	1.0	0.9	1.0	1.2	1.2	1.1	0.9	0.9	1.1	1.5	
Germany[b]	385.8	415.5	433.3	424.9	545.1	366.7	347.8	334.0	359.1	438.3	466.4	497.5	814.7	
Iceland													1.5	
Italy[a]											7.1			1.0
Luxemburg	6.0	6.5	6.7	6.2	5.5	5.8	5.5	5.0	5.3	5.5	5.5	5.9	5.6	
Netherlands	23.6	25.0	28.1	28.0	27.0	24.2	23.6	20.9	21.4	21.5	20.6	21.3	22.7	22.2
Norway	7.3	7.2	7.2	8.0	7.6	8.5	8.5	8.7	9.5	11.1	9.9	8.4	8.1	
Sweden[c]	20.8	20.8	19.9	17.4	14.6	14.0	15.4	11.6	11.8	13.1	16.2	15.0	13.2	15.0
Switzerland[d]	63.7	64.0	62.6	61.7	55.6	54.3	52.8	53.8	55.8	57.5	59.6	66.4	80.4	
United Kingdom[e]	79.0	69.0	72.0	63.0	61.0	66.0	81.0	80.0	94.0	83.0	96.0	102.0	94.0	

Notes:
[a] Data from Eurostat 1992.
[b] Data includes registered exits of asylum seekers. From 1991 includes former East Germany.
[c] Some foreign citizens (in particular from other Nordic countries) are not included.
[d] Exits of foreigners with annual residence permits (including, up to 31 Dec. 1982, some holders of permits of durations below 12 months) and holders of settlement permits (permanent permits).
[e] Data from international passenger surveys.

TABLE 3.4 *Net population flows to selected European countries, 1981–1992 ('000s)*

	1980	1981	1982	1983	1984	1985	1986	1987	1988	1989	1990	1991	1992	1993	Net total (dates shown)
Belgium	5.5	1.4	-4.2	-5.9	1.3	4.0	6.6	5.3	5.9	16.0	24.3	36.2	34.2		129.6
Denmark	3.9	2.3	2.7	2.6	5.1	11.1	13.2	10.0	7.7	9.7	11.1	11.6			91.0
Finland	1.1	1.3	1.5	1.8	1.8	1.6	1.5	1.6	2.1	3.3	5.6	12.1	8.9		44.2
Germany	137.8	36.2	-167.8	-171.4	-249.3	-42.3	30.9	80.9	186.3	211.2	304.4	423.0	592.0		1,302.0
Iceland													-0.2	0.3	0.1
Luxemburg	1.4	0.4	-0.3	0.0	0.5	0.8	1.9	2.2	2.9	2.9	3.8	4.1	4.2		24.8
Netherlands	56.2	25.4	12.8	8.4	10.3	22.0	29.2	40.0	35.9	43.9	60.7	63.0	60.3	65.2	634.3
Norway	4.6	6.9	6.8	6.1	6.2	6.5	8.3	16.1	13.7	7.4	6.8	7.7	9.1		101.1
Sweden	13.6	6.6	6.2	0.9	11.5	13.9	18.6	25.5	32.7	45.8	37.0	28.9	26.3		266.5
Switzerland	6.8	16.3	12.1	-3.4	3.0	5.1	14.0	17.7	20.3	22.9	41.8	43.4	31.7		231.7
United Kingdom	28.0	29.0	32.0	45.0	45.0	56.0	49.0	33.0	33.0	63.0	65.0	48.0	22.0		548.0
															3,364.1

Source: SOPEMI and national statistics.

for the dates shown has totalled 3,354,100. This undervalues the real total, since it does not include several countries and, as explained above, emigration is usually undercounted in the statistics.

Germany has gained most through net migration, nearly 1.4 million, but substantial gains have also been made by the United Kingdom and the Netherlands (both over half a million), and by Sweden and Switzerland.

Composition of foreign populations

What are the origins of this foreign population? According to statistics compiled by Eurostat from national sources, there were 14.18 million foreign nationals legally resident in EU states at the beginning of 1991 (table 3.5). Almost five million of these (34.95 per cent) were nationals of other member states. A further 3.169 million (22.35 per cent) were from Other Europe (mainly Yugoslavs and Turks). Africans (mostly North Africans) totalled 2.7 million (19.03 per cent), Asians 1.525 million (10.76 per cent). At the beginning of 1991, with democracy and freedom to exit still relatively new in Eastern Europe, and with the Soviet Union still in one piece, there were 618.9 thousand nationals from these regions, less than 5 per cent of all foreign nationals in the EC.

The data in table 3.5 illustrate the considerable diversity of foreign migrant origins that exists in Western Europe. In Luxemburg, Ireland, and Belgium especially, but also in Spain and the United Kingdom to a lesser extent, substantially higher proportions of foreign nationals than average stem from other EU states. These figures reflect various factors, in the case of the United Kingdom, Ireland and Spain proximity to a fellow EU member with a long history of population interchange (although this is not the case for Portugal as a destination). The situation in Belgium and Luxemburg reflects their geographical location, surrounded as they are by larger EU neighbours with open borders.

The significance of other regions as sources of foreign migrants varies with destination country. Africa is a particularly important source region for France and Portugal, and for Italy and Belgium to a lesser extent. America is important for Portugal and Spain (mainly South America), and also for Greece and Italy. Asia is a major source for the United Kingdom, Greece, and Italy, though for different reasons and with emphases on different parts of that

TABLE 3.5. *Foreign population in EC countries at 1 January 1991*

	Belgium	Denmark	France	Germany	Greece	Ireland	Italy	Lux.	Neths.	Port.	Spain	UK	EC Total
(a) Numbers													
EC	551.5	27.8	1,311.8	1,439	54.2	68.5	149.4	102.5	168.5	28.8	272.8	782.0	4,956.9
Other EEA	5.1	23.8	11.7	212.7	5.7	0.4	15.3	1.5	7.2	1.4	20.8	32.0	337.8
C. & E. Europe	6.8	6.6	63	407.7	26.3	0.1	41.1	0.7	7.9	0.5	3.0	65.0	618.9
Other Europe	93.3	40.8	274.8	2,396.5	8.2		61.6	2.9	218.9	0.7	10.0	62.0	3,168.8
Africa	182.3	7.1	1,633.1	198.0	19.1		238.6	1.7	186.2	45.3	39.9	148.0	2,699.2
America	19.3	7.9	72.8	144.6	28.6	7.6	128.4	1.8	42.2	26.4	98.4	221.0	799.1
Asia	22.2	38.2	227.0	613.4	36.1		140.3	1.6	63	4.2	36.4	453.0	1,626.3
Australia & Oceania	0.5	0.8	2.3	7.1	2.1		6.6	0.1	2.4	0.4	1.1	53.0	75.2
Total	881.0	153.0	3,696.5	6,318.1	180.3	76.6	780.2	112.8	686.3	107.7	482.4	1,806.0	1,4181.2
(b) % Columns													
EC	62.60	18.17	35.47	27.06	30.06	89.43	19.16	90.87	24.55	26.74	56.65	43.30	34.95
Other EEA	0.68	15.66	0.33	4.00	3.16	0.52	1.96	1.33	1.05	1.30	4.31	1.77	2.38
C. & E. Europe	0.77	4.31	1.75	7.67	14.59	0.13	5.27	0.62	1.15	0.46	0.62	3.05	4.36
Other Europe	10.69	26.67	7.64	46.05	4.66		7.90	2.57	31.90	0.65	2.07	3.43	22.35
Africa	20.69	4.64	46.41	3.72	10.69		30.68	1.51	27.13	42.06	8.27	8.19	19.03
America	2.19	5.16	2.02	2.72	16.86	9.92	16.46	1.60	6.15	24.51	20.40	12.24	6.03
Asia	2.62	24.97	6.31	9.65	20.02		17.98	1.42	7.72	3.90	7.65	25.08	10.76
Australia & Oceania	0.06	0.52	0.06	0.13	1.16		0.70	0.09	0.35	0.37	0.23	2.93	0.63
Total	100	100	100	100	100	100	100	100	100	100	100	100	100
(c) % Rows													
EC	11.13	0.56	26.46	29.03	1.09	1.38	3.01	2.07	3.40	0.68	5.50	16.78	100
Other EEA	1.51	7.05	3.46	62.97	1.69	0.12	4.63	0.44	2.13	0.41	6.16	9.47	100
C. & E. Europe	1.10	1.07	10.18	65.87	4.25	0.02	6.64	0.11	1.28	0.08	0.48	8.00	100
Other Europe	2.94	1.29	8.67	75.60	0.26		1.94	0.09	6.91	0.02	0.32	1.96	100
Africa	6.75	0.26	60.6	7.34	0.71		8.84	0.06	6.90	1.68	1.48	5.48	100
America	2.42	0.99	9.11	18.10	3.58	0.95	16.07	0.23	5.28	3.30	12.31	27.66	100
Asia	1.46	2.50	14.88	33.66	2.37		9.20	0.10	3.47	0.28	2.39	29.70	100
Australia & Oceania	0.66	1.06	3.06	9.44	2.79		7.31	0.13	3.19	0.53	1.46	70.48	100
Total	6.21	1.08	25.38	37.50	1.27	0.54	5.50	0.80	4.84	0.76	3.40	12.74	100

Note: Stateless/Unknown excluded.
Source: Eurostat 1993.

large and diverse continent. The United Kingdom receives Asian immigrants largely from the Indian sub-continent, largely for settlement purposes. Italy receives mainly from South-East Asia (particularly Filipinas), Greece from proximate countries in the Middle East region.

The dominance of Germany as a destination for foreign nationals from non-EC European countries is also clear: it received 63 per cent of Other European Economic Area (EEA) nationals, 65.9 per cent of those from Central and Eastern Europe (including the FSU), and 75.6 per cent of those from Other Europe (mainly Yugoslavs and Turks). Germany's Asian numbers are enhanced by Vietnamese recruited to the former GDR. However, African nationals in Germany are proportionately few. Despite the links between Spain and Portugal and the Americas, the United Kingdom receives the largest proportion of foreign nationals from that continent (mainly the United States) and, not surprisingly, about seven in ten of those from Australasia and Oceania.

The diversity expressed by table 3.5, in terms of numbers of foreign nationals and their relative importance in different destinations, is a result of the complex history of migration relationships, including new, recent flows. It also illustrates the potential difficulties in establishing harmonious integration and entry control policies, since government and public perceptions of the immigration 'problem', together with inter-state relations between origins and destinations, will vary enormously.

3.3 The Demographic Background to Current Migration Flows

The world's population looks set to continue its rapid growth, rising from around 5.3 billion in 1990 to 8.5 billion in 2025 (UN Population Fund 1993). With this increase in human numbers, further growth in migration will be inevitable. Most of this movement will be internal to individual countries, but the volume of international migration is also likely to grow.

The demographic situation in Europe

Europe's share of the world's population will be increasingly modest, rising from 498 million in 1990 to 515 million in 2025, according to UN estimates. This will reduce its share of the world total from 9.4 to 6.1 per cent. In contrast, the numbers of Africans will rise from 642 million (12.1 per cent) to 1,597 million (18.8 per cent). Hence, the world's most rapidly growing continent is adjacent to that growing most slowly.

Experience is projected to vary between EU states. Belgium, Denmark, Germany, Ireland, and Italy are expected to have net population decline between 1992 and 2025; Luxemburg and Portugal will experience no change; growth is projected for France, Greece, the Netherlands, Spain and the United Kingdom (see Joshi, Chapter 7). EFTA's situation differs slightly from that of the EU. Thanks to relatively high fertility in Sweden and Norway (see Chapter 1), growth from 33.1 to 33.9 million is projected, a rise of 2 per cent, with Finland the only expected net loser. Despite this slow growth, and its associated ageing process, there is little likelihood of immigration being either necessary or acceptable as a demographic palliative.

In these projections, Eastern Europe's population was thought likely to be more buoyant than that of the West. The projected total in 2025, 132.5 million, was 8.3 per cent higher than that for 1992, 122.4 million. Big increases were projected for Albania, Macedonia, Slovenia, Poland, and Serbia. However, since 1989 fertility in all East European states has fallen, markedly in the case of Bulgaria, Romania, and the former East Germany (see Chapter 1). Any projection for parts of former Yugoslavia may now be very dubious. Bulgaria's population was projected to fall.

The inclusion of the FSU changes the overall European picture radically. It results in an extra 82 million people to the projection for 2025. In the FSU, major growth is now only likely in the Central Asian republics where the number of Uzbekis will more than double. According to previous forecasts, Russia was expected to grow rapidly by the standards of the rest of Europe (14.3 per cent); in contrast Ukraine, the other major republic in population size, was projected to have little change. However, as noted in Chapter 1, by 1992 the number of deaths in Russia had already exceeded the falling number of births, so the population may have already begun to decline, even with immigration from elsewhere in the FSU.

The future behaviour of fertility and mortality in the new democracies is difficult to forecast. In the light of the experience of

Western Europe, and local factors, Coleman (1992) has suggested that fertility in Belarus, Russia, and Ukraine will stabilize at around 1.85 in about five years' time, the same as the higher-fertility countries of Western Europe. Life expectancy, well below that in the West, especially for men, may take longer to improve and equalize (see Meslé, Chapter 4). The state of medical services, the effects of widespread pollution, and personal habits (especially smoking) may need decades rather than years to bring lasting improvements. Overall, it seems unlikely that there will be major demographic pushes from the former Warsaw Pact area.

The demographic situation in the South

Any complacency about the lack of strength of demographic pressure to emigrate from the East is not warranted with respect to the South. Rapidly slowing population growth in the countries of the EU and EFTA, but with continuing high rates of increase to the South, has made the Mediterranean basin the steepest demographic gradient in the world. During the 1960s the ratio of population growth between the countries of the southern and eastern rim of the Mediterranean and those of north-west Europe was 3.3 to 1: it will be 17.6 to 1 in the 1990s (Golini *et al.* 1991).

The demographic and economic pressures of the South are by now well known, and need be only briefly rehearsed here. The decade of the 1990s is likely to see the population of the EU increase by just 1.5 per cent and that of EFTA by 0.7 per cent; the combined increase over the ten years will total 5.5 million people. In contrast, for the Mediterranean rim states (excluding EU members), the increase will be 23.6 per cent, or 58 million people (Golini *et al.* 1991).

Demographic pressures from sheer numbers will be compounded by comparative age structures. In most European countries the ageing process is well under way, in sharp contrast to the situation south of the Mediterranean Sea. These differences have implications for both immigration in the North, where there may be some labour shortages, and emigration in the South, where large numbers of children will pass into the labour force and impose enormous demands on job creation. For example, 43 per cent of the population of Algeria, 42 per cent in Morocco, 45 per cent in Tunisia, and 41 per cent in Egypt are currently aged under 15. The longer-term demographic future is even more eye-catching. The population-doubling time around the southern rim of the Mediterranean is about 25 years. At this rate, by 2025 Algeria and Morocco may well have populations larger than the United Kingdom, while Egypt will have broken the 100 million barrier.

In the third world as a whole, about 36 per cent of the population is aged under 15, and during the 1990s this will ensure an annual labour-force increment of 38 million. Over the next twenty years the additions to the labour force in the third world (732 million) will exceed the entire 1990 labour force (686 million) in the industrialized countries (UN 1993).

Rapid urbanization in the southern and eastern rim of the Mediterranean will mean that during the 1990s the combined population of the principal metropolitan areas in each country will rise by 11–12 million people, a growth rate of about 40 per cent. The situation is exacerbated by the poor performance of urban economies in many less developed countries, and a growing number of unemployed and underemployed workers aware of opportunities and lifestyles elsewhere through the global media. Between 1950 and 1990 per capita income tripled in the rich countries, but was much lower in the poor ones.

Since the urban economies of these places are unlikely to be able to provide the numbers and range of jobs necessary, the frustrated expectations of an internally migrant population will inevitably be channelled into a desire to seek fame and fortune overseas. Many of those taking this course will be educated and skilled, better able to perceive and take advantage of opportunities elsewhere. Their emigration is hardly likely to improve their country's economic prospects. For them, and for others, cheap mass transport, and a raft of legal and illegal agencies, provide a ready means of converting thoughts about living and working in another country into reality.

China would seem to be a new, and potentially disturbing, case in point. It is estimated that up to 100 million Chinese constitute a 'floating' population within that country, many of them unemployed. If they are unable to find jobs in their own urban economy, many will be tempted to try their luck abroad. Clearly, the potential for Chinese emigration is enormous, and the globalization of migration indicates that their peregrinations are unlikely to be confined to the South-East Asian region.

Recent reports suggest that Chinese human smuggling now provides annual profits of $3.5 billion, and has replaced drug trafficking as the enterprise for many gangs (*New York Herald Tribune*, 26 May 1994). In testimony to Congress the Central Intelligence Agency has confirmed that some 100,000 Chinese are being smuggled into the United States each year. Large numbers are also being smuggled into Russia and Europe: there are an estimated 50,000 Chinese living illegally in Moscow; about the same number are estimated to have been smuggled into Spain. Fears of mass Chinese immigration into Russia's Far East are stalling plans for greater co-operation across the border. In both Western and Eastern Europe, human smuggling by the Chinese traffickers is thought to represent a threat to internal security, through rising crime.

3.4 The Economic Context for Migration

Economic circumstances in the south

Economic performance also seems likely to push migrants northwards, given the marked differences between EU/EFTA and the eastern and southern Mediterranean rim. During the period 1960–85 growth rates of GDP per head were nearly matched, but major economic disparities clearly remain. Export of labour from south to north is one way of trying to narrow the gap.

The importance of international migration to sending countries is most obviously apparent in the value of official remittance inflows, estimated for the world at $66 billion in 1989 (Russell and Teitelbaum 1992). Even this underestimates the total value, since an unknown but substantial proportion comes through unofficial channels, and other financial transactions, including savings. The total sum compares with official United States development assistance in 1988 of $51 billion and makes labour globally the second most important 'primary commodity' traded after oil.

Among southern-rim sending countries, the percentage share of remittances to GDP has generally fallen since 1980–9, although the reverse holds for Turkey and Tunisia. Even so, the economic value of this source of income is still very important, especially to Egypt, Jordan, and Morocco. Analysis of the value of remittances to import and export bills makes this clear (table 3.6). In several countries between a quarter and a third of the import bill in 1989 was covered by remittances. The ratio of remittances to the rest of exports is even more striking: 94 per cent for Egypt, over half for Jordan and Sudan, and nearly half for Morocco. These countries have a clear interest in promoting the emigration of their citizens in return for remittances and savings. The economic value of remittances to sending countries emphasizes the importance of specific migration links. Sending countries may become vulnerable to the economic performance of those countries in which many of their citizens live and work.

In addition to their disadvantages in demography (growth too fast) and economy (growth too slow) the countries of North Africa are vulnerable environmentally. Droughts in Africa during the 1980s, with large fluctuations from year to year, suggest that emigration of 'environmental refugees' is a distinct possibility. Ultimately, however, the problem goes deeper than such occurrences might suggest. The economic development thought to be required to raise living standards, and thus prevent large-scale emigration, will itself require the mobilization of new freshwater resources. In much of Africa, especially the north, endemic water scarcity is

TABLE 3.6. *Total remittances as a proportion of merchandise exports and imports for selected countries, 1980–1989 (per cent)*

Country	Share of exports		Share of imports	
	1980	1989	1980	1989
Algeria	3.0	4.0	4.2	4.6
Cyprus	19.2	13.0	8.7	4.5
Egypt	70.0	94.1	39.6	30.9
Jordan	138.1	56.2	33.1	33.1
Morocco	54.1	43.9	34.7	29.1
Sudan	36.3	54.7	16.1	28.3
Syria	36.6	12.6	19.3	19.5
Tunisia	14.8	16.6	10.1	11.8
Turkey	71.2	26.0	27.6	19.2

Source: Russell and Teitelbaum 1992.

a major problem, made more acute by continuing population increase.

Lack of data prevents a detailed assessment, but Falkenmark (1989) has produced an index of water scarcity relating water consumption to water availability. Her analysis showed that by the year 2000 about 150 million people will be living in countries with absolute water scarcity, Tunisia being particularly badly affected. By 2025 about 1,100 million people, two-thirds of Africa's population will have entered a critical phase, principally because of population increase. The North African countries, practically all of them dependent on water security for high-level agricultural yields, may have to import food to feed their populations on a subsistence-level basis, and will all have arrived at absolute water scarcity by 2025.

Further south in Africa a bewildering array of international migrations continues, many of them of long standing. For the most part this migratory tradition has been characterized by movement to wherever a slight advantage in standard of living was available. The prognosis for sub-Saharan Africa is for continued pressure to emigrate. In the 1980s, twenty African countries experienced negative economic growth rates; in the light of falls in average income per capita by a quarter during the decade, poverty seems likely to continue to worsen (UNDP 1990). Adepoju (1991) paints a bleak picture of poor prospects for economic recovery, rising unemployment, reduced opportunities for training and education, and the prospect of closing borders within the continent as economic crises take grip. Such circumstances will encourage many to seek solace in Europe.

A problem for Greece particularly is proximity to the less-developed Arab world, together with multiple economic and cultural links between the Arabs and Southern Europe (Fakiolas, 1993). The Arab population is growing rapidly, around 2.3 per cent a year, while employment opportunities have been declining. Falling oil prices, together with the virtual completion of the basic production and social infrastructure in the rich oil-producing Arab countries, have led to fewer employment opportunities there in construction. Heavy Arab investment outside the region, including commitments to purchase defence equipment from the West has compounded this process. Economic co-operation between Arab states has been made more difficult by the Gulf War, while at the same time Asian labour has been substituted for Arab. In consequence, inter-Arab migration has declined (an estimated 2.5 million Arabs work in the rich oil producers compared with three million before the Gulf War). Even so, poor Arabs continue to move to where things seem better, if only marginally, within the Arab region: Egypt hosts about two million Sudanese, most of whom are underemployed or without work at all. In these circumstances it is natural for Arabs to seek employment in Greece and other Southern European countries.

Immigrants into Mediterranean Europe from the South

Western Europe has also been experiencing growing migration pressures from the south, particularly Africa, but also from Asia and Latin America. This immigration has particularly affected the southern members of the EU. Over the last decade Spain, Portugal, Italy, and Greece, together with Turkey, have become important immigration countries, as well as continuing their traditional roles as founts of emigration. Data problems make it difficult to be sure about the size of migrant stocks and flows in the Mediterranean countries. Simon estimated the total number of foreigners living in Italy, Spain, Greece, and Portugal in 1987 at around two million, of whom only 650 thousand were legally resident (Simon 1987). The ISOPLAN study revised this estimate upwards markedly, suggesting that the number of regular migrants was about 1.43 million for 1988–9 (of which 54 per cent came from non-European countries), while there were a further 1.3–1.5 million irregular migrants, mainly from non-European countries. Hence, on this estimate, the total population of foreigners living in the four countries at the end of the 1980s was 2.7–3 million (2.3 per cent of their total population), nearly half of them illegally (EC Commission 1991). More recent statistics for the early 1990s indicate 1.53 million foreigners legally resident in the four countries, with perhaps 900 thousand there illegally (Salt, Singleton, and Hogarth 1994). This growth in immigrant numbers has led to substantial new legislation in these countries, designed to control cross-border flows.

The two main reasons for this immigration are the attractive force of the rapid economic growth in these countries, together with their attendant social security systems, democratic and constitutional structures, and their geographical proximity to sources of supply. There are other reasons too. They have experienced the secondary effects of restrictive measures further north, and been the recipients of 'diverted' flows. They all have rapidly expanding informal economies, able to absorb large numbers of illegal workers. This process has been made easier by loopholes in their laws and entry controls, a consequence of their traditional operation as emigration countries. For example, it was not until 1985 that the first law was passed regulating foreigners' entry, residence, and work in Spain in a structured and systematic manner. Finally, they each have a colonial and cultural past in which people were exported widely, to form colonial and other links with diverse regions of the world.

The structure of their immigration flows reflects these forces. Around half of the foreigners recorded are from countries with higher income levels (other EU, United States, Australia, Canada, etc). Many of these are retirement migrants, especially in Spain. Others are highly skilled workers, their moves responding to economic globalization and the policies of trans-national corporations. Other immigrants are the low-skilled, their moves reflecting the new need for labour market flexibility, including people who will do inferior jobs, often illegally. Some of the inflows are country-specific, normally the consequence of historic cultural links (for example, Iberia with Latin America, Italy with Somalia/Eritrea), or returning colonial settlers (especially to Portugal), or citizens of former colonies (for example, Equatorial Guinea and the Philippines to Spain).

Many immigrants to Mediterranean Europe come from third world countries—Maghreb, Cape Verde, Philippines, Eritrea, Somalia, Jordan, Egypt, Latin America, Gambia, Ghana, and Guinea. A Council of Europe report (1990) estimated that of 1,158,000 registered immigrants to Italy, Spain, Portugal, and Greece, 25 per cent came from third world countries. This percentage may rise to 50 per cent if illegal immigrants are taken into account.

In Italy, for example, about 9 per cent of migrants from third world countries and Eastern Europe are estimated to work in agriculture, 28 per cent in industry, and the rest in the service sector (Montanari and Cortese 1993). Unfortunately accurate data at the national level are lacking, though this sectoral distribution is partly confirmed by the fact that around 80 per cent of these migrants live in urban areas. Surveys conducted at regional level provide more details. In Campania 43 per cent of migrants from these origins were employed in trade, 42 per cent in private services, and 5 per cent in agriculture (Calvanese 1991). Activities vary by nationality: all Senegalese, 80 per cent of Moroccans, and 12 per cent of Tunisians were self-employed, but for other nationalities self-employment was negligible. Calvanese also found that most workers from Cape Verde, the Philippines, and Vietnam worked as domestics or in the hotel and catering sector, most Senegalese in street hawking, Somalis, Sri Lankans,and Ethiopians in private service provision, and Moroccans in trade. Other nationalities were more evenly distributed among various economic sectors, though most had some presence in construction. The picture is clear: most of Italy's new migrants work in a range of service and marginal jobs, sectorally quite different from those occupied by Italians themselves in the north-west of Europe in the 1950s and 1960s.

A similar situation prevails in Spain, both with regard to the general situation, and to the characteristics of those from particular nationalities of origin. A survey of 10,000 immigrants whose situations were regularized in 1991 showed that most entered Spain on tourist visas, were mainly young and single but hoped to bring their families to join them (Pedrero 1993). They had no trouble finding work in the informal economy, but experienced poor working conditions. They were highly mobile sectorally and geographically, with an above-average level of education. Most did not want to return to their country of origin.

Nationals of Latin American countries have long received preferential treatment in the legislation covering their residence in Spain. Recently this treatment has been tightened, but they are still preferentially treated in terms of access to work permits and naturalization. Spain is also developing co-operation grants and assistance with Morocco, while at the same time seeking bilateral co-operation in curbing illegal immigration. Other co-operation agreements are with Algeria, Tunisia, Cape Verde, Equatorial Guinea, and Mozambique. Preferential treatment is also accorded to the Philippines, whose citizens benefit from many of the advantages available to Latin American countries.

Economic pressures for emigration in the East

Several factors suggest that westward emigration pressures will increase, at least in the short and medium term. First, it seems unlikely now that economic and political transition will halt; open borders to emigration will continue. Second, economic restructuring will increase unemployment in the East. Overemployment in agriculture constitutes a third stimulus to migration, with 20–30 per cent of the employed population on the land. This flow may be manifest mainly as internal rural–urban movement, but it may also spill over into international migration. Fourth, ethnic and minority conflicts may erupt, leading to a flight towards stability and safety; such moves are most likely among ethnic groups who have a mother country to return to, and those whose mother countries no longer exist.

Since the process of economic and political reform began, all countries in Central and Eastern Europe have been in the grip of deep recession, though there were some signs of recovery in 1992 (EC Commission 1993). Unemployment is high and the process of economic reconstruction still in its early stages in most countries in the region. These economic problems are reflected in changes in the labour force and in unemployment levels. The size of the labour force seems to have decreased in 1991–2 in Bulgaria, Czechoslovakia, and Hungary, and increased in Poland and Romania, though data problems prevent an accurate assessment. During 1992 employment declined throughout the region, by 5 per cent in Czechoslovakia and Romania, 4 per cent in Hungary, and 1 per cent in Poland. The state sector was particularly severely hit, with new small businesses as yet making little positive contribution to job creation. During the period 1990–2 registered unemployment increased throughout the region, although the data almost certainly underestimate the real situation. During 1992 only in Poland did the rate of increase in unemployment slow. The young are found disproportionately among the unemployed, the rate among the under-25 age group commonly being 20–30 per cent. An increasing proportion have been out of work for long periods; those with low skill levels are particularly hard hit.

In recent years a number of surveys have sought to identify likely levels of emigration from the former Warsaw Pact states by asking citizens there about their migratory intentions. They have resulted in a number of 'headline' estimates which have caught the popular imagination, persuading people that mass migrations were imminent. For the most part the threatened moves have not yet occurred, illustrating that people's stated intentions in interview do not necessarily translate into their subsequent actions. Nevertheless, such surveys do have a value, when used correctly, of identifying those sections of a population most likely to move, and under what circumstances.

One of the most comprehensive studies of the migration potential from Eastern Europe and the FSU was carried out late in 1992 by the International Organisation for Migration (IOM 1993). Around 1,000 people were interviewed in each of Albania, Bulgaria, Russia, and Ukraine, and information sought on their attitudes, perceptions, motives, and sources of information. Table 3.7 summarizes responses to a series of questions about the likelihood of going abroad. Albanians were more likely than others to wish to leave their own country, around a fifth of them permanently. For each of the national groups, a substantial proportion thought it likely they would go abroad to work for either a few months or a few years. There is thus some evidence that pressures to emigrate to the West may exist for some time.

Analysis of the detailed results of this survey identifies the typical potential migrant: male, single, aged 18–34, aiming to work abroad for 3–12 months or for several years. He will be relatively advantaged at home (a good chance of having received higher educa-

TABLE 3.7. *Migration potential in Albania, Bulgaria, Russia, and Ukraine, 1992*

	Albania	Bulgaria	Russia	Ukraine
Likelihood of going to another country (%)				
— Short visit as a tourist	86	50	47	56
— To live/work for a few months	77	28	26	28
— To live/work for a few years	71	20	18	21
— To live permanently	21	6	8	13

Source: IOM 1993.

tion), or will be among the least well-off, probably unemployed. The most popular destinations were stated as Germany and the United States (except for Albanians for whom Italy is the principal destination), then Australia, Canada, France, Scandinavia, and Switzerland. Few expressed an interest in coming to the United Kingdom. Most potential migrants are not well informed about destination, the strongest impact on their actions coming from personal experiences, family, and friends. It is in this context that prior travel abroad becomes important.

The analysis also came up with a series of identifiers of potential migrants: people learning a foreign language; those with higher education and transferable skills; the unemployed and those discharged from military service (thus with experience of living abroad); applicants for tourist and other visas.

So far, the alarming forecasts of mass permanent migration of 1991 have not been transformed into reality. Official statistics suggest emigration may actually be declining, though this trend may be more an artifact of inadequate data sources for some countries than a true reflection of reality. In general, emigration rates from Eastern Europe have been lower than might have been expected, given Western European rates of emigration (Salt, Singleton, and Hogarth 1994). What is emerging, however, is a picture of intensified short-term migratory movements in the region, often resulting in illegal working. This has become the predominant form of employment of migrants from the Soviet successor states, Romania, and Bulgaria, oriented towards the more affluent countries of Eastern Europe and Turkey.

Ethnicity as a major potential cause of migration

Migration within and from Central and Eastern Europe and the FSU is likely to be strongly influenced by ethnicity. One of the concerns of the Eastern European countries is that they may become destinations or staging-posts for CIS citizens moving westwards, or that they may experience a form of return migration by ethnic groups who have been unwilling or unable to move under Communism. Some 1.2 million Poles and 170 thousand Hungarians live in the FSU, for example. There are also ethnic groups living in Eastern Europe, who may wish to return to their homeland in former Soviet territory. Hungarians are another group whose minority situation in neighbouring countries may encourage them to move. A group that is particularly involved in cross-border movements is the gypsies, of whom some three million live in Eastern Europe. Without a homeland base, they tend to suffer discrimination and occasionally migrate between countries in search of more secure living conditions.

Within the FSU, ethnic Russians living outside the Russian Federation (who total about 25 million) are the only group being almost universally affected by the identifiable areas of inter-regional and local conflicts and tensions in the FSU, and already involved in major migratory movements. The number of refugees in Russia was estimated at 400,000 into October 1992 (SWB 1992). Independent sources put the number of returning Russians close to two million people, attributing discrepancies with official data to the fact that government agencies take into account only officially registered refugees (Kennan Institute 1993). The long-term prognosis of migratory movements within the FSU is for the continuing concentration of the nations within their ethnic territories (state entities). The causes of large-scale migrations within the FSU are not limited exclusively to eruptions of violence. Other factors play major roles: infringement of the civil rights of the minority population, as well as cultural alienation, are the most important.

Transit migration in Eastern Europe

Perhaps the most salient migration phenomenon (beyond events in former Yugoslavia) currently affecting Eastern Europe is that of transit migration. This is turning some of the new democracies into substantial immigration countries, although many (possibly most) of the migrants place themselves in an irregular situation.

A series of studies by the IOM has now been published. Among the large number of findings and conclusions, several are of particular importance. The Polish study points to the high level of diversity in the flows, many of which are highly organized, most with the intention of reaching the West. Transit migration is also highly changeable, with new and logistically intricate routes continually opening up.

Origins vary. Poland receives transit migrants especially from the western parts of the CIS. Two main flows affect Bulgaria. The first, towards Germany and Austria, is made up of migrants from the Middle East, formerly went through Yugoslavia, and is now routed through Romania. The second, from the CIS and Romania, crosses Bulgaria *en route* to Greece. The Czech Republic receives fewer from the CIS, but is a conduit for people from the Balkans, and from Asia.

Immigrant employment in Eastern Europe

Although most of the former Communist countries were accustomed to some immigration, organized between 'fraternal' socialist republics within the former Council for Mutual Economic Assistance (CMEA), popularly known as COMECON, they are increasingly finding themselves attractive in labour market terms. For example, the number of work permits issued in Poland doubled in the period 1991–2 to 12,000. Nationals of the FSU received the largest proportion, mainly for work in construction, heavy industry, and agriculture, although there was a significant group of teachers, doctors, and artists. Numbers of legal foreign workers are dwarfed by those, variously estimated at between 40,000 and 200,000, working illegally, mostly in construction, small manufacturing, agriculture, and (for women) domestic service. A similar pattern exists in the Czech Republic.

3.5 Brain Drains, Gains, and Exchanges

The East–West brain drain in Europe

Highly skilled workers are a major element in current European migrations, their relatively small numbers among total migrants belying their economic importance. It is difficult to see anything but a general increase in the migration of high-level skills, as all modern economies engage in 'brain exchanges'.

Although the feared mass westward migration from Eastern Europe has not occurred, concern continues to be expressed in the East about the possibility of brain drain (Rhode 1993a). The rate at which brain drains will continue depends upon factors at both origin and destination. The academic sector in the West seems likely to have little spare capacity to absorb large numbers of new staff; in any case, it is unlikely that the levels of skill and expertise of Eastern Europeans will prove attractive enough, except for a relatively small number. Similarly, Western industry and services demand higher levels of expertise than is generally available in the East. Only after a period of training and career development will most Eastern Europeans acquire the high levels of professional, managerial, and technical skills necessary.

This explains, in part, why the data do not indicate the massive actual and potential brain drain from East to West, with negative impacts upon sending countries, that is sometimes suggested. In fact the East–West brain migration needs to be disaggregated. First, the processes occurring in the FSU seem to differ from those taking place in other countries of Eastern and Central Europe. Second, the impact of the migration upon sending and receiving countries and on the migrants themselves is mediated by a distinction between nationalist, internationalist, and behavioural perspectives; between internal and international brain migration; and between brain drain, brain gain, and brain waste.

Current patterns and processes of East–West brain migration

After the collapse of Communist regimes in the Eastern bloc, their science sectors were relatively overstaffed yet underfinanced. The subsequent reduction of staff in these sectors occurred very quickly, engendering a current East–West brain migration which is quantitatively and qualitatively different from previous East–West brain migrations. We need to make an analytical distinction between brains who migrate because of the collapse of their sectors, and people who migrate for other reasons who are also brains. For the former, the main reasons for migration can be identified as: the economic situation of home scientific sectors; the financial situation of scientists; the environment and equipment of the workplace; and the accessibility of knowledge and information (Hryniewicz *et al.* 1992). For the latter, the main reasons for migration can be identified as ethnic (Rhode 1993a); political (Rhode 1993a), and better socio-economic and living conditions (Kouzminov 1993).

The data also suggest that there is a disparity between the reduction of employment in the scientific sector in countries of the Eastern bloc, and the migration of scientific personnel. This is explained by the fact that the majority of personnel who have left the science sector have remained within their country but sought employment in alternative sectors, usually the private sector. Hryniewicz *et al.* (1992) showed that since 1989 international brain migration has decreased while what they term internal brain migration has increased significantly. Kouzminov (1993) estimated that what he terms intersectoral movement has accounted for as much as 90 per cent of the absorption of the recent unemployed from the science sector. However, although data are scarce, a general trend seems to be that scientific personnel arriving from Eastern Europe and the FSU are usually not being incorporated into such valuable sectors in the receiving countries. There are two main reasons.

The first reason is the phenomenon of brain waste. Hryniewicz *et al.* (1992) found that only 22.7 per cent of the 2,706 migrants (614 persons) who had migrated from their surveyed institutions were still employed in science. The second reason is the quality of the personnel coming from Eastern Europe and the FSU. Rhode (1993b) suggested that the Soviet science system in particular was characterized by low levels of economic efficiency, nepotism, political appointments, and huge and heavy bureaucracies. Furthermore she argued that the inflexibility of the science system, and especially its failure to adapt to new information technologies, can be considered to have contributed to the collapse of the Soviet system (Rhode 1993a). The implication is that personnel from scientific sectors in Eastern Europe and the FSU are often not the most flexible members of society, and do not have a level of ability which enables their integration into high-expertise sectors in receiving countries. Even where they are incorporated, it is sometimes felt that they are not necessarily of equal standard to their colleagues (SEPSU 1993).

A new role for skills from the south?

It was suggested above that migration by the highly skilled will continue to increase for some time. But it is already possible to see the seeds of future decline. One reason is the application of new information technologies. Unlike low-skilled migrant labour, which demands a physical presence in the performance of tasks, the main contribution of the highly skilled is knowledge. Knowledge can be transferred geographically in a number of ways not necessarily requiring a physical presence.

Modern satellite and fibre-optic communications, faxes, e-mail, and the Internet mean that specialists can be in almost instant touch with each other. Teleconferencing can already deal with routine business. The disadvantage of not being in the same room as the person with whom one is conferring is declining all the time, although the ultimate advantage of physical contact will never disappear in those sectors which traditionally place a premium on the quality of people and personality (O'Brien 1992). New information technology, however, enables a multiplication of possible meeting places, depending on the particular circumstances of the moment: to the modern professional, medical, or technical worker, office support and files are only a fax or modem away. It would be surprising if these facilities did not make some inroads into at least the growth of mobility among the highly skilled.

A growing trend, not yet captured statistically, is the use by companies of high-level skills on what is effectively a labour sub-contract basis. The process has recently come under public scrutiny in the United States, and is also appearing in the United Kingdom and elsewhere. In the United Kingdom it seems to occur particularly in computing/systems and banking. It especially affects third world-based companies which are bringing in foreign staff on secondment to install hard- and software systems, often at low salaries which allow them to undercut Western companies when tendering for contracts. A further complication is that, increasingly, installation work can be done via satellite links, with only brief visits being required for checking purposes.

This process of bringing in what are in effect sub-contract staff calls into question current arrangements for the international migration of the highly skilled. Rising education levels and populations in less developed countries will inevitably lead to larger bodies of high-level skills there, with rates of remuneration that will make them increasingly competitive in the provision of expertise—something that hitherto the developed economies could regard as their particular preserve.

3.6 Refugees and Asylum Seeking

The marked escalation in asylum seeking in the 1980s has faced Europe with a new type of refugee problem. In Western Europe alone the inflow of asylum seekers in 1991 was twice as big as the regular admission of foreign labour that year. Aggregate numbers of applications in Europe rose to 3.6 million during the period 1983–92. At the same time rates of recognition of right to asylum have fallen, and now commonly average less than 10 per cent of applications. Recognition varies with origin, however. In the United Kingdom during 1993, the total recognition rate was 7 per cent; for those from the Middle East it was 22 per cent; Europe and the Americas, 15 per cent; Africa, 7 per cent; Asia, 1 per cent.

During the 1980s the greatest percentage of asylum seekers in Austria, Germany, and Switzerland came from the Eastern bloc countries. In Belgium, Sweden, Greece, Switzerland, Germany, France, Norway, United Kingdom, and the Netherlands, significant numbers from third world countries applied. In the United Kingdom in 1992, for example, Europe accounted for only a third of applications (mainly former Yugoslavia), Africa, 31 per cent, and Asia (outside the Middle East), 25 per cent. The main variation in the flow matrix as a whole is in the countries of origin—the pattern is constantly changing. In 1991, total numbers of asylum seekers from European countries of origin were more than double the numbers of those from Africa and Asia. Of these, the top nine European sending countries sent 195,595 asylum seekers, the top seven African countries sent 54,614, and the top six Asian countries 57,316.

By 1991–2 Yugoslavs has come to head the list of asylum seekers, with Romanians, Turks, Sri Lankans, Somalis, Iranians, Zaireans, Iraqis, Bulgarians, Albanians, Nigerians, Lebanese, and Chinese also prominent. Compared with earlier years, the largest fall was of Polish applications. The importance of Yugoslavia as Europe's leading source of asylum seekers is such that if it is excluded from the figures for 1991 and 1992 for Western Europe, the total increase in asylum applications from the rest of the world increased during these years by only 2 per cent.

Total numbers of asylum seekers from Eastern Europe have risen dramatically in the last few years (Table 3.8), though the data for 1992 are heavily distorted by Yugoslavia. In 1984 there were 25,000 applications from the region, rising to 421,000 in 1992. Individual source countries in Eastern Europe do not follow the same patterns as their neighbours, although some similarities may be identified. During the period 1987–91, Yugoslavia and

Romania provided one-third each of the total numbers of East European asylum seekers in the whole of Central, Western, and Southern Europe. Of the remaining third, one-half came from Poland and the rest came in roughly equal numbers from Albania, Bulgaria, Czechoslovakia, and (lesser numbers) USSR and Hungary. Most of the former Warsaw Pact countries now also receive some asylum applications. For example, Czechoslovakia received 1,533 applications for 1990–2, of which 36 per cent were from Romania and 24 per cent were from the former Soviet Union. During 1993 the Czech Republic began to receive asylum claims from Armenia.

The asylum system in most countries has not been used to process many of the large numbers of people from former Yugoslavia who wish to stay only temporarily in receiving countries. Special arrangements have been made which fall outside the asylum system, including the provisions of 'temporary protection status', allowing people to stay as 'refugees' on humanitarian grounds or as tourists, and authorities having turned a blind eye to certain groups staying in private accommodation and with families. Austria, for example, had twice as many people defined as *de facto* refugees from Yugoslavia in 1992 as the total number of asylum applications.

3.7 Conclusions

The evidence from Western Europe up to 1993 suggests that immigration continues to increase, and that inflows may still be accelerating. If this is the case, it suggests that the region has failed to control movement across its borders, since virtually all countries do not wish to see net migration gains of foreigners.

However, increased movement from Eastern Europe is only to be expected, given the constraints on emigration from that region under former political regimes. What evidence is available suggests that levels of East–West movement are still comparatively low, with the major exceptions of certain ethnic groups, and that of former Yugoslavia. Furthermore, the Eastern European states are themselves beginning to receive immigrants.

However, the time for generalization with regard to the former Warsaw Pact countries has passed. A marked division by level of

TABLE 3.8. *Inflows of asylum seekers into selected European countries, 1980–1993 ('000s)*

	1980	1981	1982	1983	1984	1985	1986	1987	1988	1989	1990	1991	1992	1993
Austria	9.3	34.6	6.3	5.9	7.2	6.7	8.6	11.4	15.8	21.9	22.8	27.3	16.2	4.7
Belgium	2.7	2.4	3.1	2.9	3.7	5.3	7.6	6.0	4.5	8.1	13.0	15.2	17.8	26.9
Denmark	0.2	0.3	0.3	0.3	4.3	8.7	9.3	2.7	4.7	4.6	5.3	4.6	13.9	14.3
Finland							0.1	0.1	0.1	0.2	2.5	2.1	3.6	2.0
France	18.8	19.8	22.5	22.3	21.6	28.8	26.2	27.6	34.3	61.4	54.7	46.7	26.8	27.6
Germany	107.8	49.4	37.2	19.7	35.3	73.8	99.7	57.4	103.1	121.3	193.1	256.1	438.2	322.8
Greece				0.5	0.8	1.4	4.3	6.3	9.3	6.5	4.1	2.7	2.0	0.8
Hungary										27.0	18.3	5.5	6.0	0.2
Italy				3.1	4.6	5.4	6.5	11.0	1.4	2.2	4.7	27.0	2.5	1.5
Luxemburg											0.1	0.2		
Netherlands	1.3	0.8	1.2	2.0	2.6	5.6	5.9	13.5	7.5	13.9	21.2	21.6	17.5	35.4
Norway	0.1	0.1	0.1	0.2	0.3	0.8	2.7	8.6	6.6	4.4	4.0	4.6	5.3	12.9
Portugal	1.6	0.6	0.4	0.6	0.4	0.1	0.3	0.5	0.4	0.2	0.1	0.3	0.7	2.1
Spain				1.4	1.1	2.3	2.8	3.7	4.5	4.0	8.6	8.0	11.7	13.8
Sweden				4.0	12.0	14.5	14.6	18.1	19.6	30.0	29.4	26.5	83.2	37.6
Switzerland	6.1	5.2	7.1	7.9	7.4	9.7	8.5	10.9	16.7	24.4	35.8	41.6	18.1	24.7
United Kingdom	9.9	2.9	4.2	4.3	3.9	5.4	4.8	5.2	5.7	16.5	30.0	57.7	24.6	22.4

Note: All figures include dependants. Figures for UK in 1992 and 1993 exclude dependants. 1993 figure for Spain annualized from Jan–June only.
Source: Various Ministries of the Interior, IGC, UNHCR.

economic development and migration experience is already visible. The geographically more western countries in the region (the Czech and Slovak Republics, Hungary, Poland, Slovenia, and to a lesser extent Bulgaria and the Baltic republics) already have relatively low emigration rates of their citizens, and relatively high immigration from further afield. To the east, and especially in the FSU, pressures for emigration are greater.

There is now no doubt that the Eastern European countries are becoming enmeshed in the paraphernalia of border controls set up by the EEA states, the harmonization process driven by the demands of the EU. Combined with the economic development of the eastern countries, and the commitment of their citizens to making the new democracies work, this should ensure that East–West migration takes place in an orderly fashion. The major challenge would be further Yugoslav-style perturbations.

The main problems are likely to stem in the long term from the south. Not only does this region present enormous pressures for emigration, but the solutions adopted in Eastern Europe will not be appropriate. First, the scale of finance needed for economic development is too vast. Second, and more pragmatically, no suitable forum exists for bringing sending countries into a dialogue with European states on migration-control policy.

The prognosis is, therefore, for a pattern of migration exchange to develop between East and West in Europe, ultimately adopting a similar character to that currently existing among the states of Western Europe.

Migrants from the south will continue to find their way into Europe's labour market, at both ends of the spectrum. The process of labour-market deregulation will make this easier for the low-skilled. In the case of high-level expertise, the potentially formidable combination of a large body of highly educated people in third world countries, with new information technologies at their disposal, will revolutionize the international movement of the highest-level skills.

NOTE

Some of the material in this chapter is derived from that previously published in J. Salt, A. Singleton, and J. Hogarth (1994), *Europe's*

International Migrants; data sources, patterns and trends, London: HMSO.

REFERENCES

ADEPOJU, A. (1991), 'South–north migration: the African experience', *International Migration,* 29: 205–22.

CALVANESE, F. (1991), 'Fattori dispirita e progetto migratorio', in —— and E. Pugliese (eds.), *La Presenza Straniera in Italia,* Milan: Angeli: 87–121.

COLEMAN, D. A. (1992), 'Future emigration from the CIS: a view from the West', Colloquium: The Population of the former Soviet Union in the 21st Century, Royal Netherlands Academy of Arts and Sciences, Amsterdam.

—— (1993), 'The world on the move? International migration in 1992', *Proceedings of the European Population Conference, Geneva, March 1993.* Volume I: pp. 281–368. Strasburg Council of Europe Press.

EC COMMISSION (1991), *Social Europe—Immigration of Citizens from Third World Countries into the Southern Member States of the European Community: a Comparative Survey of the Situation in Greece, Italy, Spain and Portugal,* Brussels.

—— (1993), *Employment Trends in Central and Eastern Europe,* Brussels: Employment Observatory 4.

COUNCIL OF EUROPE (1990), *Report on the New Countries of Immigration.* Parliamentary Assembly, April: document 6211.

DOLGIKH, E. (1993), 'Emigration intentions of Russian scientists', Paper presented at International Seminar: Skilled and Highly Skilled Migration, Latina, 28–29 October.

FAKIOLAS, R. (1993), 1993, SOPEMI Report: Migration from and to Greece. Mimeo, available from author.

FALKENMARK, M. (1989), 'The massive water scarcity now threatening Africa—why isn't it being addressed?', *Ambio,* 18(2).

EUROSTAT (1992), 'Demographic Statistics 1992'. Luxemburg: Office for Official Publications. of the European Communities.

GOLINI, A., RIGHI, A., and BONIFAZI, C. (1991), 'Population vitality and decline: the north–south contrast', OECD/Republica Italiana International Conference on Migration, Rome, 13–15 March, OCDE/GD(91)10.

HRYNIEWICZ, J., JALOWIECKI, B., and MYNC, A. (1992), *The brain drain in Poland,* European Institute for Regional and Local Development, Regional and Local Studies 9, Warsaw: University of Warsaw.

INTERNATIONAL ORGANIZATION FOR MIGRATION (1993), *Profiles and Motives of Potential Migrants: an IOM Study Undertaken in Four Countries— Albania, Bulgaria, Russia and Ukraine*, Geneva: IOM.

—— (March, April, May; December 1994), 'Transit Migration in: Bulgaria; Poland; the Czech Republic Ukraine; Russia; Hungary', Migration Information Programme.

KENNAN INSTITUTE (1993), *Russian Refugees, a Blessing in Disguise*, Washington, DC: Woodrow Wilson Centre.

KORCELLI, P. (1992), 'International migration in Europe: Polish perspectives for the 1990s', *International Migration Review*, 26(2): 292–304.

KOUZMINOV, V. (1993), *Brain Drain Issues in Europe: UNESCO Project on Intellectual Migration*. Paris, UNESCO.

LEDENIOVA, L. (1993), 'Attitude to emigration of students from Universities of the former USSR', Paper presented at International Seminar: Skilled and Highly Skilled Migration, Latina, 28–29 October.

MONTANARI, A., and CORTESE, A. (1993), 'Third World immigrants in Italy', in R. King (ed.), *Mass Migration in Europe: the Legacy and the Future*, London: Belhaven: 275–92.

O'BRIEN, R. (1992), *Global Financial Integration: the End of Geography*, London: Pinter for the Royal Institute of International Affairs. (Chatham House papers.)

OKOLSKI, M. (1993), *Poland: SOPEMI 1993*, Warsaw: Warsaw University.

PEDRERO, CHOZAS, J. (1993), 'Migration in Spain: recent developments', Paper presented at the OECD/CANADA/SPAIN Conference 'Migration and International Co-operation: Challenges for OECD Countries', Madrid, 29–31 March, OCDE/GD(93)17.

RHODE, B. (1993a), 'Brain drain, brain gain, brain waste: reflections on the emigration of highly educated and scientific personnel from Eastern Europe', in R. King (ed.), *The New Geography of European Migrations*, London: Belhaven: 228–45.

—— (1993b), 'Patterns of brain drain from the science sectors in Central and Eastern Europe after the collapse', Brussels, Commission of the European Communities, DG XII.

RUSSELL, S. S., and TEITELBAUM, M. S. (1992), *International Migration and International Trade*, Washington, DC: World Bank, Discussion Paper 160.

SALT, J., SINGLETON, A., and HOGARTH, J. (1994), *Europe's International Migrants. Data Sources, Patterns and Trends*, London: HMSO.

SEPSU (SCIENCE AND ENGINEERING POLICY STUDIES UNIT) (1993), 'The migration of scientists and engineers, 1984–1992', Policy Study No. 8.

SIMON, G. (1987), 'Migration in Southern Europe: an overview', in OECD, *The Future of International Migration*, Paris: OECD: 258–91.

SUMMARY OF WORLD BROADCASTS (SWB), 5 October 1992, SU/1503, B/7.

Tikhonov, V. (1993), 'Russia's military-industrial complex: emigration potential', Paper presented at International Seminar: Skilled and Highly Skilled Migration, Latina, 28–29 October.

UNDP (United Nations Development Programme) (1990), *Human Development Report*, New York: United Nations.

United Nations Population Fund (1993), *The State of World Population 1993*, New York: United Nations.

4

Mortality in Eastern and Western Europe: A Widening Gap

FRANCE MESLÉ

Over the last thirty years, mortality trends in Eastern and Western Europe have developed in quite different ways. Figures 4.1 and 4.2 illustrate the changes in the rank order in the European hierarchy of life expectancy over that period.

Just after the Second World War there was a big difference in life expectancy between the more advanced European countries (all located in the north of Europe) and the less advanced European countries (principally southern and eastern countries). Almost twenty years separated the life expectancy in Albania from that in Norway. During the 1950s and 1960s, there was considerable convergence in life expectancy. Progress was substantial in the earlier part of the period. Mortality decreased more rapidly where it was higher, so that the gap between countries declined over time. This movement was amplified in the 1960s, when the most advanced countries seemed to have reached a point of low mortality which was very difficult to surpass, whereas progress continued in the countries which had a lower life expectancy.

In 1970, the convergence was obvious. Less than ten years separated life expectancy in Albania (females) or Portugal (males) from Sweden (both sexes) or Norway (females). Furthermore, the geographical distribution of countries according to the expectation of life had become much more diversified. Northern countries had always constituted the central core among the most advanced countries, but by 1970 they had been joined by some western or southern countries such as Switzerland, France, Greece, and Spain. Although not in the first rank, some Eastern countries had by then achieved a relatively good position—particularly Bulgaria and the former East Germany (GDR).

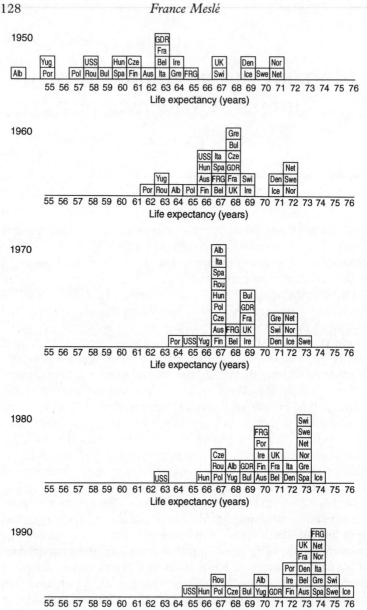

F<small>IG</small>. 4.1. *Life expectancy at birth in European countries from 1950 to 1990, males*

Source: INED (unpublished data). The Institut National d'Études Demographiques in Paris has assembled its own database from which these are figures are derived.

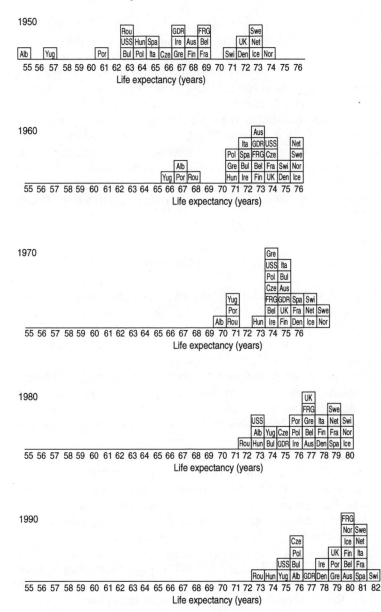

FIG. 4.2. *Life expectancy at birth in European countries from 1950 to 1990, females*

Source: INED (unpublished data). See source to figure 4.1.

Twenty years later, by 1990, the situation has changed again. Most of the Western European countries, have continued to converge on low mortality levels. The countries of Eastern Europe, however, have behaved very differently. They clearly constitute the rearguard of Europe (Bourgeois-Pichat 1985), because of their unfavourable trends in life expectancy in the last two decades.

This chapter describes the main features of mortality trends by age and by cause in Eastern European countries, focusing on the period 1970–90. After giving an overview of the changes in life expectancy at birth, we shall describe more precisely mortality trends in two eastern countries, Bulgaria and Hungary, and compare them with those of two western countries: England and Wales, and France.

4.1 A General Deterioration

Figures 4.1 and 4.2 illustrate the changes in the respective positions of European countries, but they do not adequately describe the trends of life expectancy in each country. In the peculiar case of Eastern Europe, it is interesting to look at these trends from 1960 (figure 4.3).

Data presented as in figure 4.3 show that the group of Eastern European countries was less homogeneous than might have been assumed from the earlier figures. Everywhere, trends in life expectancy were more favourable for women than for men. Except in Yugoslavia for both sexes and in Albania for females, the increase in life expectancy has slowed down everywhere during the last three decades. But timing and intensity differ according to country. Czechoslovakia was the first country to show the new adverse trends. Life expectancy ceased to increase for women, and decreased for men, at the very beginning of the 1960s. During the 1970s and 1980s, there was a slow improvement for women and the decrease stopped for men. For males, the level of life expectancy was lower in 1990 (67.3 years) than it was in 1960 (67.8 years). The case of Hungary is more serious, at least for males. Between 1965 and 1990, Hungarian males lost 1.5 years of life expectancy and there is no visible sign of improvement.

Male mortality trends in Bulgaria, Poland, and Romania show the same pattern: the stagnation or the slight decrease in life

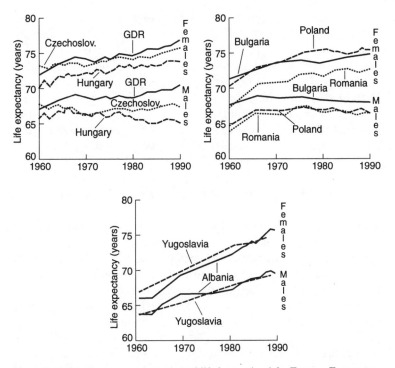

FIG. 4.3. *Trends in the expectation of life by sex in eight Eastern European countries, 1960–1990*

Source: INED (unpublished data). See source to figure 4.1.

expectancy since the middle of the 1960s was slow to end. For women, the situation is even worse than in Hungary: there has been no progress in Poland and Romania since 1980. Only in Bulgaria did female life expectancy improve during the 1980s, but that was following a decrease which took place around 1975. In comparison with these unfavourable trends, the situation of the former East Germany, Albania, and Yugoslavia looked much better up to 1990.

Among the most favoured Eastern European countries at the beginning of the 1960s, the German Democratic Republic (GDR; East Germany) suffered a less acute crisis, and progress in life expectancy resumed very clearly in the 1980s. At the other end of the scale, Albania and Yugoslavia, where improvement in mortality had been slow, have rejoined the eastern group by means of a

subsequently more rapid rate of progress. As we have already
noted, the slowing down of the improvement in health was general
in Europe during the 1960s. But it is only in the Eastern European
countries that this slowing down and in some cases regression has
continued. The phenomenon is particularly acute in Hungary and
in Bulgaria. In the following pages, we shall take these two countries as examples and compare them to two western countries
(England and Wales, and France) to describe more precisely why
there has been such a divergence over two decades.

4.2 The Scope of the Life Expectancy Crisis

The life expectancy crisis affects principally males and specifically
those in the economically active age-groups.

Life expectancy at birth is a synthetic indicator. To understand
the crisis better, it is necessary to look at age-specific death rates.
Figures 4.4 and 4.5 illustrate the change in these rates since 1970
in the four selected countries. For each five-year age group,
we have calculated the ratios of the probabilities of dying from
two life tables (one around 1980 and one around 1990) to the
probability of dying from a life table around 1970. This ratio is
presented graphically in figures 4.4 (males) and 4.5 (females).
In the figures, the probability of dying in each age-group in the
1970 life table is set at 100, represented by a solid straight line.
Death rates which have become smaller by 1980 or 1990 will
therefore lie below the line; death rates which have increased will
lie above it.

For men, in Hungary and in Bulgaria, the problem appears to be
concentrated in the economically active age-groups between 20
and 65. At these ages mortality has increased continuously since
1970. At about the age of 40, the risk of dying in 1990 was 60
per cent higher in Hungary and 40 per cent higher in Bulgaria
than it was in 1970. The increase in mortality at these ages is
partly compensated by the reduction in mortality before the age of
20 and particularly by the fall in infant mortality. For the elderly,
there was no change in the level of mortality rates during the
period. By contrast, in France, and in England and Wales, mortality decreased at almost every age. Except for infant mortality,
the most important reduction in mortality between 1970 and

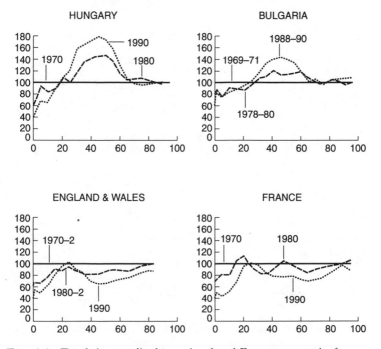

FIG. 4.4. *Trends in mortality by age in selected European countries from 1970 to 1990, males*

Note: Mortality rates around 1970 are set at 100 in each case. Rates for other years are expressed as a ratio to the 1970 rates.

Source: INED (unpublished data). See source to figure 4.1.

1990 occurred at the age of 40 in England and Wales and at the age of 60 in France, while around the age of 25 in both countries there was some stagnation. The reduction in mortality at the older ages explains the continuous increase in life expectancy in these countries. In Hungary, women experienced the same phenomenon of a marked increase in mortality between the ages of 20 and 60, but the movement was less acute. In Bulgaria, mortality more or less stagnated at all ages. The contrast with the experiences of women in the two western countries is nevertheless as obvious as for men because of the particularly favourable trends of mortality in England and Wales and in France.

Another way to estimate the weight of each age to the changes

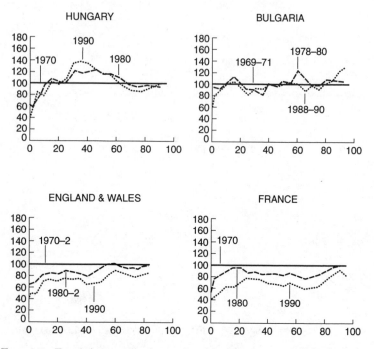

FIG. 4.5. *Trends in mortality by age in selected European countries from 1970 to 1990, females*

Note: Mortality rates around 1970 are set at 100 in each case. Rates for other years are expressed as a ratio to the 1970 rates.

Source: INED (unpublished data). See source to figure 4.1.

in life expectancy is to calculate the contribution of each age group to the change in expectation of life at birth (figure 4.6). This calculation may be made by the application of Pollard's method (Pollard 1990), which divides the total difference in years between two life expectancies into the partial contributions of each age group to the total difference. For example, the method permits the analysis of the change in life expectancy between two periods in terms of the contribution arising from the change in infant mortality and that due to the reduction in mortality at other ages.

For both Eastern European countries, between 1970 and 1980, it is clear that most of the decline in male life expectancy at birth is due to the increase in mortality at ages 30–64. The rise of mortality

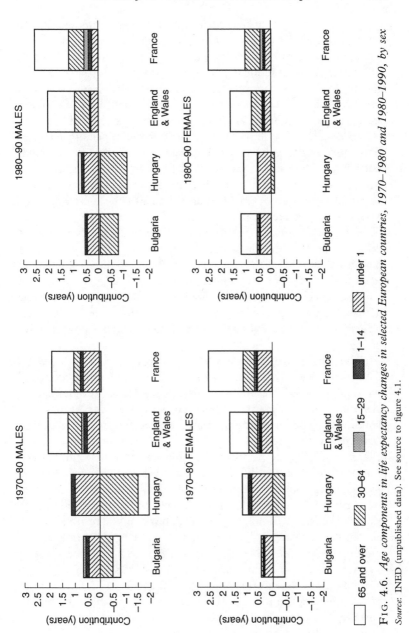

FIG. 4.6. *Age components in life expectancy changes in selected European countries, 1970–1980 and 1980–1990, by sex*

Source: INED (unpublished data). See source to figure 4.1.

at age 65 and over also contributed, but more moderately, to the unfavourable trend. On the other hand the decrease in life expectancy was moderated by the fall in infant mortality, which influenced the level of life expectancy. It was therefore the result of two divergent movements: a decrease in mortality at the youngest ages and a sharp increase at the economically active and the oldest ages. The second influence was greater for males, leading to an overall decline. For females the rise in adult mortality was less sharp and was largely counterbalanced by the decline in infant mortality, leading to a moderate overall rise in life expectancy. The situation was very different in England and Wales and in France, where all ages (except 15–29) contributed to the increase in life expectancy. The decline in mortality at the economically active and the older ages contributed more to the favourable evolution of life expectancy than does the fall in infant mortality because of the rather low level that infant mortality had then reached in these countries. The phenomenon is particularly acute among females, especially in France, where more than 70 per cent of the increase in life expectancy was due to the fall in mortality after the age of 30 and more than 50 per cent to the fall in mortality after the age of 65.

In the most recent decade, the trends and the contrast between eastern and western countries have not fundamentally changed. For England and Wales, and for France, mortality at older ages is now more preponderant. In both countries and for both sexes, around 80 per cent of the increase in expectation of life can be attributed to the progress of adult and elderly mortality while the influence of infant mortality has become very marginal. For eastern countries the situation differs according to sex. For males, there is always a clear opposition between the decline of infant mortality and the increase of mortality at adult ages. In Hungary at least, the amplitude of the variation has reduced, but the final result is always the same: a decline in life expectancy at birth. For females, the situation looks better in this second decade. There is no longer a negative effect (with the exception of a very slight one due to mortality in the age-groups 30–64 in Hungary), and 50 per cent of the improvement in life expectancy is now due to the reduction in mortality at the age of 65 and over.

The role played by mortality at different ages is of course very closely linked to changes in the mortality by cause.

4.3 The Contribution of Cause of Death to Changes in Mortality Levels

It is possible to apportion the differences in life expectancy at two points in time between the different age groups and to study these differences according to the different causes of death. Six major causes of death are distinguished in figure 4.7: infectious and respiratory diseases, neoplasms (cancers), cerebro-vascular disease (stroke), other cardio-vascular diseases (mostly ischaemic heart disease), injury and poisoning, and other diseases.

In Bulgaria and Hungary, between 1970 and 1980, the unfavourable trends in male expectation of life at birth were mostly explained by the rise of cardio-vascular mortality: this includes cerebro-vascular diseases as well as other cardio-vascular diseases (among which ischaemic heart disease is particularly important). Mortality from neoplasms has had a negative effect on Hungarian mortality trends. Its importance grew in the second period, when the increase in the incidence of cancer was mostly responsible for the decrease of life expectancy in Hungary and also began to play a part in Bulgaria. In the latter country, however, other cardio-vascular diseases have always been dominant. On the other hand, between 1980 and 1990, mortality from stroke declined and this development counterbalanced unfavourable trends in cardio-vascular and cancer mortality rates. Here again, trends in western countries are more favourable for all causes (except cancer in France during the 1970s). In both eastern countries, the situation has always been less serious for women. Cerebro-vascular diseases (in the first period in both countries), and other cardio-vascular diseases (in the second period in Bulgaria), have contributed negatively to the change in life expectancy but their effects have been largely counterbalanced by the decreasing trends of infectious mortality in both countries and in both periods. Trends in other cardio-vascular diseases in the 1970s (Hungary) and stroke in the 1980s (both countries) reinforce the positive contribution to life expectancy. However, progress looks very modest in comparison with that occurring in England and Wales and France, where declines in all causes of death contributed substantially to the increase in life expectancy. An analysis of the different trends according to age-groups highlights the very unfavourable position of mortality in the Eastern countries at the economically active

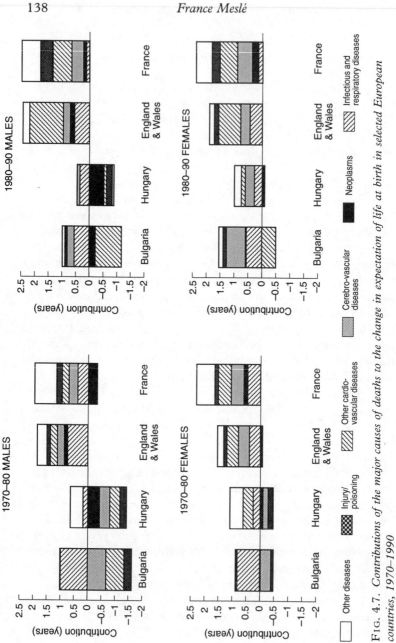

FIG. 4.7. *Contributions of the major causes of deaths to the change in expectation of life at birth in selected European countries, 1970–1990*

Sources: WHO Mortality Data Bank; INED (unpublished data), see source to figure 4.1.

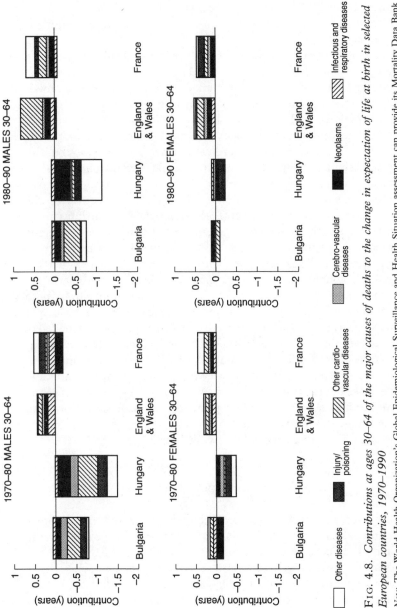

FIG. 4.8. *Contributions at ages 30–64 of the major causes of deaths to the change in expectation of life at birth in selected European countries, 1970–1990*

Note: The World Health Organization's Global Epidemiological Surveillance and Health Situation assessment can provide its Mortality Data Bank on magnetic tape

Sources: WHO Mortality Data Bank; INED (unpublished data), see source to figure 4.1.

ages. Figure 4.8 shows how, between the ages of 30 and 65, different causes of death have contributed to this unfavourable tendency.

Between the ages of 30 and 65, all causes of death contribute to the unfavourable mortality trend in Hungary and Bulgaria, and no one cause is predominant. Infectious and respiratory diseases made a very small contribution to the increase in male life expectancy for both periods in Bulgaria and in the 1980s for Hungary. For all other causes of death, mortality at ages 30–65 has been increasing since 1970. In addition to cardio-vascular mortality, the trend of which almost always makes an unfavourable contribution to the health situation, cancer mortality has also played an important part, especially in the last decade. In the western countries, the situation is again more favourable, although the contributions of these ages to the general changes in life expectancy have been quite moderate: in the 1970s progress was rather limited and even in France an increase in cancer mortality partly counteracted the positive contributions of other causes of death to the rise in life expectancy. Since 1980, trends have clearly improved in both countries. The size of the variation in female mortality (negative or positive) is much smaller. Mortality at these ages has reached very low levels in England and Wales and in France so that even if it were to decrease further it could have no further major influence on life expectancy. We have seen that, for women, it is now the decrease in mortality at older ages which plays the major part in the further improvements in life expectancy. In the Eastern European countries, the mortality level is higher but it appears that among women it has remained relatively unchanged.

4.4 Conclusions

In the 1950s, Eastern European countries benefited, like all other European countries, from substantial progress in health, mainly due to the discovery and the spread of antibiotics. Mortality then decreased dramatically, especially mortality from infectious disease among young children. The decrease of infectious diseases hid the rise of other causes of death, mainly cardio-vascular diseases and neoplasms. During the 1960s, the fall in mortality from infectious causes went on but at so low a level that it could no longer counteract the increasing effects of other causes. All countries then underwent a slowing down of the rate of mortality decline. This trend occurred sooner if infection had been reduced earlier. This pattern was also seen in Eastern European countries (Meslé 1991).

But since 1970, mortality trends in Eastern Europe and those in other countries have diverged sharply. A reduction in mortality levels resumed in Western European countries while the situation continued to worsen in Eastern European countries (Rychtarikova *et al.* 1989). Several explanations can be given for the worsening of the health situation in Eastern Europe (Okolski 1985). From a medical point of view, the fight against chronic diseases required much more advanced medicine than had been needed for the reduction in infectious diseases. Policies of prevention and screening were necessary, which Eastern European health systems were unable to develop. Moreover, the lifestyle in these countries probably exacerbated the problems. Traditional dietary habits based on a heavy consumption of pork and of animal fats, but low in fresh fruit and vegetables, contributed to the increase in heart diseases as well as in neoplasms. Alcohol consumption and cigarette smoking, which increased everywhere, also had a negative influence on the mortality trend. The rise in cigarette smoking is believed by many epidemiologists to be the single most important cause of the failure of overall mortality to improve in the West in the 1960s, primarily through its effect in increasing deaths from lung cancer and from circulatory disease. The decline in smoking in many western countries is likewise believed to be an important factor in the resumption of the mortality decline in the 1980s.

The decline in smoking is not the only factor. The decrease in alcohol consumption, improvements in road safety, better control of hypertension and hypercholesterolaemia, and the development of other new therapies have all had a positive impact upon mortality. More generally, in the 1980s, individuals in Western countries took greater responsibility for their own health. This trend probably did not take place in Eastern Europe. Because of the lack of data, it is difficult to evaluate the impact of these two risk factors on mortality in Eastern Europe. Finally, and more generally, it seems that industrialization has played a very negative part, through the deterioration of working conditions and the spread of pollution. In the Eastern European countries, mortality is generally higher where industrialization is more developed (Nowak 1986, Rychtarykova and Dzurova 1992).

At the time of writing, there is no sign of a real improvement in the situation in the countries which have been hit most severely by the crisis. The available data do not allow us to judge whether the recent political changes which have occurred in these countries will influence mortality trends rapidly. Even if some measures can have a direct impact on mortality, as when a sharp decline in mortality followed Gorbachev's anti-alcohol campaign (Meslé *et al.* 1992), it is likely that a radical change cannot be achieved immediately. Chronic pathology cannot respond quickly to a new health policy. Whether it is possible to enter a new stage in the health of a society, where chronic diseases could be controlled, of course depends on the specific situation of each country. All Eastern European countries are now undergoing radical social, economic, and political changes. It is too early to draw any conclusion as to the impact of these changes on the health situation. The latest figures from most Eastern European countries suggest that mortality has increased from 1990 to 1992. In the republics of the former USSR, the increase was mainly due to an increase in violent deaths (Meslé *et al.* 1994). It is, however, not difficult to imagine that the 'new *Länder*' of Germany (the former GDR), less affected by the crisis than some other Eastern European states, will be able to benefit quickly from the experience of the rest of the country. On the other hand, it is impossible at present to forecast the future of the republics which once comprised Yugoslavia, after the dramatic crisis which they are now undergoing.

REFERENCES

BOURGEOIS-PICHAT, J. (1985), 'Recent changes in mortality in industrialized countries', in J. Vallin and A. Lopez (eds.), *Health Policy, Social Policy and Mortality Prospects*, Liège: IUSSP, Ordina Éditions: 507–39.

MESLÉ, F. (1991), 'La mortalité dans les pays d'Europe de l'Est', *Population*, 46(3): 599–650.

——, SHKOLNIKOV, V., and VALLIN, J. (1992), 'Mortality by cause in the USSR in 1970–1987: the reconstruction of time series', *European Journal of Population*, 8: 281–308.

—— (1994), 'Brusque montée des morts violentes en Russie', *Population* 49(3), 780–90.

NOWAK, L. (1986), 'Territorial distribution of mortality in Poland in the years 1950–1985', in Hungarian Central Statistical Office (CICRED), *Socio-Economic Differential Mortality. Seminar, 9–12 and 13–16 September 1986, Zamardi, Hungary*, No. 5, Budapest: Statistical Publishing House: 148–64.

OKOLSKI, M. (1985), 'The case of Poland', in J. Vallin and A. Lopez (eds.), *Health Policy, Social Policy and Mortality Prospects*, Liège: IUSSP, Ordina Éditions: 445–64.

POLLARD, J. (1990), 'Cause of death and expectation of life: some international comparisons', in J. Vallin, S. D'Souza, and A. Palloni (eds.), *Measurement and Analysis of Mortality: New Approaches*, Liège: IUSSP, and Oxford: Oxford University Press: 291–313.

RYCHTARIKOVA, J., and DZUROVA, D. (1992), 'Les disparités géographiques de la mortalité en Tchécoslovaquie', *Population*, 47(3): 617–44.

RYCHTARIKOVA, J., VALLIN, J., and MESLÉ, F. (1989), 'Comparative study of mortality trends in France and the Czech Republic since 1950', *Population, English selection*, 44(1): 291–321.

5

The Economic Environment for Family Formation

JOHN ERMISCH

The primary thesis of this chapter is that the trends in fertility discussed by Coleman (Chapter 1) can be better understood if they are considered as an integral part of the changes in family structure that have also been taking place in European and other industrialized countries. In particular, marriages are occurring later in people's lives, and in some countries many people will forgo marriage entirely. Figure 5.1 shows the steep decline in first marriage rates in England and Wales (E&W), France, the United States, and Japan. Part of the decline in these countries (other than Japan) reflects the increase in cohabitation without legal marriage, but this is not the entire story. For instance, among British women in their twenties, only about two-fifths of the decline during the 1970s and 1980s in the percentage of those married can be accounted for by increased cohabitation without marriage (Ermisch 1990). Thus, people are waiting longer to enter any cohabiting partnership.

Divorce is also more common, and this has made the main contribution to the growth in one-parent families (see Ermisch 1991). Figure 5.2 illustrates the rise in divorce rates in many European countries. Although no European country has reached the levels of the United States, current divorce rates in England and Wales suggest that about two in five marriages will end in divorce (Haskey 1988). Even in universal marriage countries like Japan, the incidence of divorce has risen to the point where the current rate implies that one in five marriages will end in divorce (Hirosima and Bando 1990).

The proportion of women in paid employment, particularly mothers, has increased dramatically in most industrialized coun-

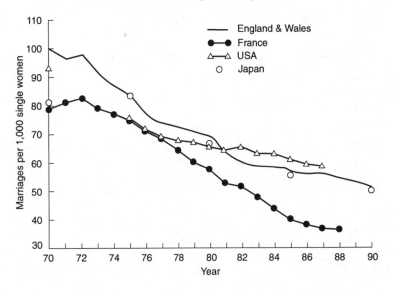

FIG. 5.1. *First marriages per 1,000 single women in selected European countries, 1970–1990*
Source: National statistical abstracts.

tries during the past two decades. This is often linked to the fall in fertility in a simplistic way. This chapter argues that the story is much more complex.

These changes are of one piece. They interact with one another, and will be better understood by considering them together. The following offers an economic perspective on them. Other theoretical approaches, such as that of Lesthaeghe and Moors in Chapter 6, also help us to understand these changes in the family, but here we focus on the contribution of the economic approach. A recent collection of papers (Siegers, de Jong-Gierveld, and van Imhoff 1991) demonstrates that, in understanding fertility and women's participation in paid employment, the different theoretical views, derived from economics, sociology, and psychology, can often complement one another within a rational choice framework, which confronts preferences with restrictions. Economics focuses on the restrictions, examining how changes in the constraints on choice affect behaviour.

The chapter uses the economic analysis of the family to explore the interaction among marriage patterns, divorce, fertility, and

(a) England and Wales, France, USA, and Denmark

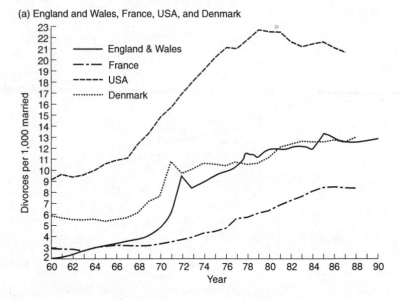

(b) Netherlands, Federal Republic of Germany, and Belgium

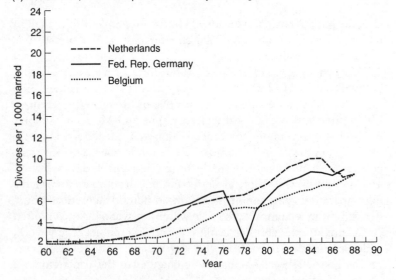

FIG. 5.2. *Divorces per 1,000 existing marriages in selected European countries, 1960–1990*

Source: Eurostat, Demographic Statistics (various years).

women's employment, showing how changes in one of these in-
duce changes in the others. We start with an economist's view of
the family.

5.1 Why Form Households and Families?

We can start by thinking of the household as a little factory,
combining its members' time and purchases of goods and services
from the market to produce 'domestic output'. Its objective would
be to maximize household *production*, and in a one-person household this maximization would be subject to the person's time
constraint and an income constraint. It would entail choosing the
allocation of his or her time between home production and market
work.

The first question we ask is whether multi-person households are
more efficient *producers* than one-person households. Consider two
persons, with one having a higher wage than the second, while the
second has higher non-earned income, such that each produces the
same domestic output. In this situation, the first person would
allocate less of his time to home production than the second, using
more purchased goods and services in home production; that is,
the first person's home production would be less time-intensive
than the second's.

They could do better by collaborating, or 'trading'. If the first
person purchased some of the second's time for household production (that is, bought his or her 'services'), each person's domestic
output would be higher. As the first person has a comparative
advantage in goods, because of his or her earning power (thus
higher cost of time), and the second a comparative advantage in
time, there are gains from trade.

But a combined household could do even better because the
second person would specialize in home production, and the first
person could supply more of his or her higher paid labour to the
market. A merged household always produces at least as much as
the two component households put together, and the gains are
larger, the bigger the difference between the two persons' wage
rates. It also can be shown that *at least one* household member must
specialize *fully* in one of the two activities, market work or home
production (Becker 1981, Cigno 1991).

Innumerable analyses of people's earnings have indicated that employment experience increases earnings. This is consistent with the idea of on-the-job 'investment in human capital', pioneered by Gary Becker. Such 'learning through experience' means that the more time a person allocates to market work, the larger the wage he or she can earn per hour.

When we incorporate this idea into our analysis, even if both persons are equally endowed in initial earning capacity and have the same ability to improve their earning capacity through employment experience, one will usually specialize in home production (Becker 1981, Cigno 1991). That person ends up with a lower wage than she or he would have earned if they had set up a household on their own.

Such complete specialization is likely because of the element of 'increasing returns' created by the accumulation of human capital which is specific to market work, even without any difference in productivity in the home. A slight difference in this regard, say because of women's role in the production of children, could tip the balance firmly in the direction of complete specialization.

So far we have focused on the allocative efficiency gains to be made from forming a two-person household, which arise from the division of labour between household members. There may also be joint consumption economies, because many items of household expenditure have 'public good' characteristics; that is, consumption per head does not decline proportionately with the number of consumers. The most obvious of these is a house, but the concept is also relevant to appliances, furniture and so on. This aspect of cost sharing favours larger households, but the costs of internal transactions and the desire for privacy put limits on household size (Ermisch 1981, Cigno 1991).

These allocative efficiency gains, arising from replacing individual constraints with less restrictive joint constraints, apply to households formed between any two (or more) persons. But most households are formed between two particular people for reasons of love, companionship, and procreation. Such households have larger consumption possibilities, in a broad sense, than two persons taken at random, and they are specific to each particular pair of persons. This forges a link between household formation and fertility.

5.2 Resource Allocation and Distribution within Households

We have demonstrated that consumption possibilities are usually larger in households with more than one person, particularly those containing a couple with emotional ties to one another, which, for convenience, we shall refer to as a married couple, although they may not be legally married. Decisions within households must, however, take into account the individual tastes/preferences of each member. Thus, there is potential for conflict between the partners. Each person has the alternative of not forming the household, which gives each an alternative level of welfare (that is, what they would achieve in a single-person household, or perhaps in forming a household with someone else). There is a range of co-operative solutions for the household, each of which entails different distributions of the gains in welfare from forming the household. The range reflects the fact that each partner must do at least as well within the household as his or her alternative. Some sort of bargaining process would determine the outcome.

Such processes generally have the property that if one partner's welfare outside the household rises relative to the other's, there is a tendency for the bargaining outcome to favour her or him (see, for example, Manser and Brown 1980 or Ott 1992). Thus, factors like opportunities in the marriage market or welfare benefit payments that are available to single but not married mothers, which raise the welfare available outside the household, also affect allocation and distribution within the household. Also, if these raised welfare to a sufficiently high level, the gains from forming the household could disappear.

5.3 Household and Marriage Dissolution

We have so far ignored uncertainty, but the gains from forming a household and their distribution are likely to be very uncertain. Indeed, in our framework, the reasons that households and marriages dissolve is because the gains from household co-operation are revealed to be less than anticipated, or disappear over time because of new developments and information. As long as gains from co-operation exist, one partner can always compensate the other to remain in the marriage; that is, a bargaining solution exists that makes both parties better off within marriage. We would expect that the larger the *ex ante* expected gains, the less likely that they will disappear in the future.

As has been discussed above, in order to benefit from the 'increasing returns' created by the accumulation of human capital which is specific to market work, one of the partners will usually specialize in home production. But that person ends up with a lower wage than he or she would have earned if they had set up a household on their own. It is clearly only worth making this sacrifice in earning power if the household does not dissolve. Thus, there will be more of an incentive to specialize in this way in marriages with larger expected gains from household co-operation.

Recent research by Ogawa and Ermisch (1994) provides support for this hypothesis. In a study of Japanese married women's participation in paid employment in 1988, they find that, after controlling for the usual factors known to affect women's employment decisions (such as woman's potential wage and husband's income), women who said that they had contemplated divorcing their husband are more likely to participate in full-time paid employment. If, as is plausible, women who have contemplated divorce are in marriages with small gains from co-operation, then this finding suggests that such women perceive a lower incentive to specialize in home production because of a higher risk that their marriage will dissolve. To the degree possible with their data, the authors find evidence that this relationship does not merely reflect causation in the other direction, although they also find that working women are more likely to consider divorce.

Furthermore, exogenous factors which reduce the incentives to specialize increase the risk of dissolution by reducing the gains from household co-operation. Let us, for example, consider an exogenous increase in women's earning capacities relative to men's, say because of equal pay legislation. This would raise women's welfare in one-person households relative to men's and also reduce the benefits from the household division of labour, for the reasons discussed earlier. These changes suggest a reduction in the gains from household co-operation, along with an increase in married women's participation in paid employment. We would, therefore, expect that, as a consequence, people would be less willing to marry and more likely to divorce.

Thus, factors which reduce the expected gains from household co-operation not only increase the risk that the household will dissolve, but also reduce specialization in the household division of labour, which in turn reduces further the gains from household formation and discourages specialization. This interaction suggests that women's participation in paid employment and divorce should exhibit a positive association. Despite the fact that there are many other factors affecting divorce and women's employment, figure 5.3 supports such an association across industrialized countries in about 1990. The simple correlation coefficient is 0.86 (statistically significant at the 0.01 level), and its associated regression line is shown in the figure. The Spearman's rank correlation coefficient is also strongly significant, with a value of 0.88. The exclusion of Ireland, where divorce is not available,

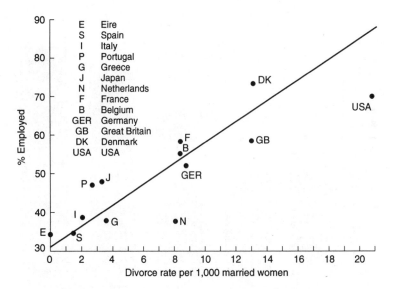

FIG. 5.3. *Divorce rate and percentage of women employed in selected European countries, c.1990*

Note: The women surveyed are those aged 22–60 and in employment.
Sources: Divorce: Eurostat, *Demographic Statistics* (various years). Employment: Kempeneers and Lelièvre 1991: table 6.

does not alter these conclusions (the correlation coefficient is 0.84 without Ireland). Confining the analysis to Europe also produces similar conclusions.

We must, of course, be cautious of simple correlations across countries. But a more detailed analysis of divorce in Great Britain also supports a positive association between divorce and women's employment. Ermisch (1991) estimated the monthly probability of divorce for British mothers as a function of a number of characteristics of a woman and her family (for example, age at marriage, family size), including the proportion of months she has spent in paid employment since becoming a mother. Figure 5.4 shows the strong positive association between this proportion and the risk of divorce, holding other relevant characteristics constant. For instance, mothers who have been employed for 80 per cent of the time since giving birth have roughly double the probability of divorcing of a mother who did not work after childbirth.

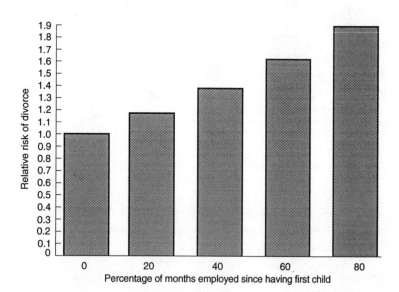

FIG. 5.4. *Mother's employment and divorce risk*

Note: Risk for never-employed mothers = 1.0.
Source: Ermisch 1991.

5.4 Interactions with Fertility

Bringing up children on one's own is very difficult, and it is generally associated with a low standard of living. Furthermore, the absent parent has reduced contact with his children. This suggests that a higher risk of divorce in society will discourage childbearing (and marriage), resulting in a fall in fertility when divorce rates increase.

At the same time, an important source of the gains from co-operation within marriage is the production and nurture of children. Thus, having fewer children and having them later in one's life suggests a tendency for the expected gains from marriage co-operation to decline. This suggests that a fall in fertility will increase divorce rates and reduce marriage rates. Lower fertility also tends to raise women's participation in paid employment.

In sum, the interaction among women's employment, divorce, and fertility reinforces the fall in marriage and fertility rates and the rise in divorce and women's employment. For example, if some outside factor raised divorce rates (such as the liberalization of divorce laws), the higher divorce risk engendered would tend to reduce marriage and fertility rates and raise women's participation in paid employment. Or if some factor raised women's participation (such as equal opportunity legislation), this would tend to increase divorce and reduce marriage and fertility rates. Such an interactive process appears to have played an important role in the trends in fertility, marriage, divorce, and women's employment discussed at the beginning of this chapter.

5.5 Altruism and Fertility

We now consider more direct economic influences on fertility. In current economic parlance, a person is altruistic toward another if the utility of the other person enters his utility function. Altruism is what we would call, in everyday language, 'caring' or 'love'. There are larger gains to be made from the formation of a household by people altruistic toward one another. But our main concern with altruistic behaviour concerns altruism toward children and its relation to the economic analysis of fertility.

In order to simplify matters, we consider a limited form of

altruism: that parents care about the earning capacity of their children when they become adults, a capacity which depends on the child's human capital. It is well known that a child's development and acquisition of skills for his adult life are affected in an important way by the time that parents spend with their children and expenditures on them. In economic jargon, parents 'produce' their children's human capital by combining parental time and goods and services purchased from the market. In other words, parents can increase each child's human capital by increasing the time and money devoted to a child, and a given level of human capital can be obtained with different combinations of time and goods.

Parents' welfare is assumed to depend on their own consumption, the number of children they have, and the human capital of each child (to focus on the fertility decision, we assume parental consensus and that each child is treated in the same way). The parents' lifetime budget constraint is that expenditures on their own consumption plus expenditures on the children's human capital acquisition equals their wealth, and they maximize their welfare subject to this constraint. Human capital 'expenditure' is the product of the number of children, the human capital investment per child, and the full cost per unit of human capital, to which we return in a moment.

This product in the budget constraint implies that the 'shadow price' of an additional child is proportional to the amount of human capital investment per child, and the 'shadow price' of children's human capital is proportional to the number of children the parents have. As a consequence, there is an important interaction between family size and human capital investment in children (Becker 1981). Suppose, for example, that there is an exogenous increase in parents' desired level of human capital per child, say because the types of jobs that are being created require more education. This raises the shadow price of children, which lowers family size, which in turn lowers the shadow price of human capital, which in turn raises human capital investment per child and the shadow price of children further. Thus, a cumulative process favouring human capital investment and reducing fertility ensues.

This interaction between fertility and human capital investment does not derive from assuming that they are close substitutes.

Indeed, just the opposite must be the case, since if both fertility and human capital investment are to be non-zero, which must be the case, then they cannot be close substitutes. Nevertheless, the interaction is stronger when they are better substitutes.

There are a number of important implications of this interaction. First, as we have seen, a *small* exogenous increase in desired human capital investment per child could produce a *large* decrease in family size and a much larger increase in human capital investment. Similarly, a *small* exogenous decrease in fertility, say because of lower contraception costs, can produce *large* increases in human capital investment per child and further large declines in fertility. Thus, family size can be highly responsive to changes in prices and incomes, even though children have no close substitutes.

Another consequence of this interaction is that it may appear that the income elasticity of fertility (the responsiveness of fertility to income changes) is negative, even though children are normal goods, in the sense that we want more of them when parental income increases. The reason is that the true income elasticity is defined with prices constant, but, because of the interaction, we cannot hold the shadow prices of an additional child and of human capital investment per child constant when we measure the elasticity. The measured income elasticity is more likely to be negative (even though the true elasticity is positive), the more responsive is human capital investment to changes in income relative to the responsiveness of fertility, and the better substitute is family size for human capital investment or parental consumption.

With regard to the fertility trends, parents' desire to invest more resources in each child, because they care about their future, is also likely to have an important role to play in the fertility decline in industrialized and newly industrializing countries. As parental income has increased and jobs have shifted in the direction of requiring more education and training, parents have tended to invest more in each child. Through the interaction described above, this contributes to a fall in fertility.

5.6 The Cost of Children and Fertility

We now consider what determines the full cost per unit of human capital. As the two inputs to its production are parental time and purchased goods and services, it is the cost of these inputs that determines the cost of children's human capital. Parental time is primarily the mother's time, and the rearing of children is time-intensive relative to other home production and consumption activities. Thus, the unit cost of children's human capital relative to the cost of parental consumption is directly related to the cost of the mother's time, and if she has ever been in paid employment (as most mothers have), the cost of her time is the wage she could earn in employment (that is, her forgone earnings). It follows that if women's real wages increase, the cost of both additional children and additional human capital investment per child increases.

The economic analysis of fertility suggests, therefore, that men's and women's wages should have important effects on fertility. Higher real wages mean higher real income, thus a couple can afford more children and to have them sooner. The latter would be particularly important if there are constraints on borrowing against future income. But they also mean more income lost by those caring for additional children. Since most child-rearing is done by the mother, higher women's wages raise the cost of a child. Third, the higher income that higher real wages entail means that parents want to invest more human capital in each child, but this means that each child costs more (as discussed above). Thus, with mothers doing most of the child-rearing, higher men's wages mainly affect childbearing through their effect on a couple's income, while higher women's wages increase the opportunity cost of children as well as affecting income.

This line of argument leads us to expect that fertility will be inversely related to women's wages relative to men's. Figure 5.5, which plots, from 1952 to 1985, the first birth rate of women aged 25–29 and women's relative earnings (defined net of taxes: women's average net (after tax and national insurance) hourly wage divided by men's average net weekly earnings), suggests that this has been the case in Britain, and detailed econometric analysis of British birth order and age-specific birth rates since 1952 supports this hypothesis (Ermisch 1988). At almost every age and birth order, higher women's net relative wages reduce the likelihood of birth. As this tax-adjusted measure of women's relative earnings rises from the mid-1960s to a peak in 1975, while the conditional birth rates peak in the mid-1960s and reach a trough in

F I G. 5.5. *First birth rate and relative pay, women aged 25–29 in England and Wales, 1952–1985*

Note: Relative pay is women's average hourly wage divided by men's (index numbers).
Source: Ermisch 1988.

1977, it is not surprising that the measured impact of women's relative earnings on fertility is negative.

Relative generation size and real house prices also appear to be important influences on fertility in the British case, and other variables may be important in other countries. As we would expect from Easterlin (1980), women from larger generations tend to have lower fertility, and higher house prices tend to reduce fertility, particularly first birth rates (see Ermisch 1988).

This analysis suggests that increases in women's relative pay were primarily responsible for the decline in British fertility between 1952 and 1985. The model can also be used to simulate the distribution of family size that would be produced by cohorts of women who experience different levels of particular economic variables throughout their reproductive period. Such analysis shows that if women's pay relative to men's were 10 per cent higher, then average family size would be about 0.1 children lower.

Analysis of variation in family size after fifteen years of marriage among British women supports the finding from the time series analysis (Ermisch 1989). It finds that women with larger earning capacity at marriage have smaller families (holding husband's income constant), and those with higher earning husbands have larger families (given their own earning capacity).

Recent analysis by Ermisch and Ogawa (1994) also suggests that rises in women's relative earning power have contributed to the steep fall in fertility in Japan since the early 1970s. Figure 5.6 illustrates the simple inverse relationship between first birth rates of childless women aged 25–29 and their pay relative to men's (aged 30–34), and this is confirmed by more sophisticated econometric analysis. Analysis of patterns of age at motherhood and educational attainments among individual Japanese women supports the time series relationship, and indicates that lower first birth rates have primarily come about through later marriage.

Econometric analysis of Swedish women's birth order specific fertility by Heckman and Walker (1990) provides further evidence of the depressive effect of women's relative pay on their fertility. They find that higher women's relative wages play an important role in postponing first births and in reducing third births. They find that these wage effects weaken for more recent cohorts of women, which they interpret as evidence consistent with the intro- duction of progressively more pro-natal policies, one of which is subsidized child-care.

When we incorporate into the analysis the possibility of substi- tuting purchased child-care for some of the mother's time, then the negative relationship between women's earning capacity and fertil-

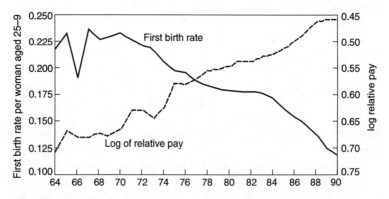

FIG. 5.6. *First birth rate and relative pay, women aged 25–29, Japan 1964–1990*

Note: Relative pay is women's average wage divided by men's (absolute numbers).
Source: Ermisch and Ogawa 1994.

ity need not always hold (Ermisch 1989). Women with high wages would tend to purchase a much larger proportion of child-care time, thereby weakening the link between a woman's wage and the cost of children. For such women, higher wages could raise fertility by raising income while having little effect on the cost of children. Similarly, in countries like Sweden, with heavily subsidized child-care, women would contribute much less of child-care time themselves, making it more likely that women earning higher pay would have larger families.

Nevertheless, when examining changes over time, one finds that the cost of purchased child-care and women's real wages tend to move together, because women's labour is such an important input to the provision of child-care services. Thus, over time we would still expect women's pay relative to men's and fertility to be negatively related, as higher women's pay raises the cost of children. As women's relative pay has risen in most industrialized countries, it probably played a role in their fertility declines.

Considerable attention has been paid to the association between women's participation in paid employment and fertility, while here we have focused on women's relative pay and fertility. That is because the economic analysis of the family indicates that fertility and women's employment participation are jointly determined variables: neither one causes the other, but both respond to changes in the budget constraint faced by couples, particularly spouses' relative pay. Any association between women's employment participation and fertility would be just an association between two mutually dependent variables, as is the case for divorce and employment participation in figure 5.3, and not indicative of any causal relationship.

5.7 European Fertility in the 1990s

In light of the earlier failure by social scientists to predict the 'baby boom' of the 1950s and 1960s in Europe and North America, it would be very brave to offer a firm forecast of fertility during the 1990s. This is particularly the case because the economic perspective cannot tell the whole story. For instance, the arguments concerning the interaction between women's employment, divorce, and fertility certainly would not suggest that the lowest fertility in the world today is in Southern Europe and Japan. Figure 5.3 shows that Spain, Italy, Portugal, Greece, and Japan appear in the bottom left-hand corner, while their total period fertility rates c.1990 (1.30, 1.29, 1.48, 1.43, and 1.54 respectively) are much lower than those of most of the other countries in the figure (Germany's is also very low, at 1.50). In each case, it would be possible to make economic arguments to rationalize their low fertility, for instance, relatively high unemployment rates among young people in Southern Europe or high educational costs in Japan, but many factors play a role in differences in the level of fertility across countries.

Nevertheless, the economic perspective advanced here does suggest the direction of future trends, and on balance it is not upward. First, the nexus between divorce, women's employment, and fertility suggests continued low fertility, as we do not expect either the incidence of divorce or women's paid employment to fall. Second, women's pay relative to men's is likely to increase in the future, both because young women's educational and occupational choices are favouring better paid jobs than in the past and because of a shortage of younger workers, for whom middle-aged women workers have tended to be substitutes. On the positive side, the successively smaller cohorts reaching their prime childbearing years during the 1990s in most European countries may have higher fertility because of better labour market prospects (Easterlin 1980).

Of course, governments may introduce measures which either purposely or inadvertently raise fertility. For instance, subsidies for child-care not only make it easier for women to take paid employment, but would tend to raise fertility. Sweden, which now has one of the highest fertility rates in Europe, may be a case in point. Analyses by Blanchet and Eckert-Jaffé (1994) and Ermisch (1988) suggest child benefits could have a moderate effect on family size. For instance, on the basis of his econometric model for Britain, Ermisch (1988) estimates that doubling child benefit would utimately raise family size by 0.15 children, and the Blanchet and Eckert-Jaffé (1994) analysis, using very different methods and data, comes to a similar conclusion (see also Chapter 9).

On balance, however, the economic perspective on household formation and fertility offered here suggests a continuation of low fertility, accompanied by high divorce and women's participation in paid employment. In some countries, this may entail further falls in fertility and increases in divorce and women's employment, while in others the current situation may be maintained. What is relatively clear, however, is that neither current evidence nor the arguments advanced here suggest a reversal of these trends in industrialized countries.

REFERENCES

BECKER, G. S. (1981), *A Treatise on the Family*, Cambridge, Mass.: Harvard University Press.

—— (1992), 'Fertility and the economy', *Journal of Population Economics*, 5: 185–201.

BLANCHET, D., and EKERT-JAFFÉ, O. (1994), 'The demographic impact of family benefits; evidence from a micro-model and from macro-data', in J. Ermisch and N. Ogawa (eds.) *The Family, the Market and the State in Ageing Societies*, Oxford: Oxford University Press.

CIGNO, A. (1991), *Economics of the Family*, Oxford: Oxford University Press.

EASTERLIN, R. A. (1980), *Birth and Fortune*, London: Grant-McIntyre.

ERMISCH, J. (1981), 'An economic theory of household formation: theory and evidence from the General Household Survey', *Scottish Journal of Political Economy*, 28: 1–9.

—— (1988), 'Economic influences on birth rates', *National Institute Economic Review* (Nov.): 71–81.

—— (1989), 'Purchased child care, optimal family size and mother's employment', *Journal of Population Economics*, 2: 79–102.

—— (1990), *Fewer Babies, Longer Lives*, York: Joseph Rowntree Foundation.

—— (1991), *Lone Parenthood: An Economic Analysis*, Cambridge: Cambridge University Press.

—— and OGAWA, N. (1994), 'Age at motherhood in Japan', *Journal of population Economics*, 7: 393–420.

HASKEY, J. (1988), 'Recent trends in marriage and divorce and cohort analyses of the proportions of marriages ending in divorce', *Population Trends*, 54.

HECKMAN, J. J., and WALKER, J. (1990), 'The third birth in Sweden', *Journal of Population Economics*, 3: 235–75.

HIROSIMA, K., and BANDO, R. (1990), 'Divorce rate of Japan: 1980–88' (in Japanese), *Journal of Population Problems*, 46: 56–64.

KEMPENEERS, M., and LELIÈVRE, E. (1991), *Famille et Emploi dans l'Europe des Douze*, Brussels: Eurostat.

MANSER, M., and BROWN, M. (1980), 'Marriage and household decision-making: a bargaining analysis', *International Economic Review*, 21: 31–44.

OGAWA, N., and ERMISCH, J. F. (1994), 'Women's career development and divorce risk in Japan', *Labour*, 8: 193–219.

OTT, NOTBURGA (1992), *Intrafamily Bargaining and Household Decisions*, Berlin: Springer-Verlag.

SIEGERS, J. J., DE JONG-GIERVELD, J., and VAN IMHOFF, E. (eds.) (1991), *Female Labour Market Behaviour and Fertility*, Berlin: Springer-Verlag.

6

Living Arrangements, Socio-Economic Position, and Values Among Young Adults: A Pattern Description for France, West Germany, Belgium, and the Netherlands, 1990

RON LESTHAEGHE AND GUY MOORS

6.1 Introduction

Since the 1960s life-cycle transitions among young adults have become more complex in virtually all Western countries (see Bumpass 1990; Rindfuss and Vanden Heuvel 1990). New, intermediate states have been added such as sharing or doubling up, premarital cohabitation, or parenthood among cohabitants. The transitions between these states are no longer unidirectional since returns to previous states occur more frequently. Also the states themselves are less clearly defined. For instance, independent living and periodic returns to the parental 'hotel family' are often combined.

One of the main reasons for the emergence of the intermediate states (independent living, sharing, premarital cohabitation) among young adults is clearly prolonged education. We are referring here to the mere mechanistic effect: continued education, say between the ages of 20 and 24, results in complete or partial economic dependence on the family of origin which automatically postpones marriage and parenthood for most young people. Once education is finished and the lag it produced is taken into account, transitions to marriage or cohabitation with parenthood are often accelerated (see Lee *et al.* 1987). However, other theories postulate major additional effects.

According to the neo-classical economic theory (see Becker 1981) cohabitation, later marriage, and later parenthood are essentially the outcome of a general reduction of gains to marriage for women and of a substantial increase in the opportunity costs of motherhood. The latter stem from increased female schooling, greater earning capacity, and therefore from enhanced female economic autonomy. This factor equally accounts for the rise in divorce and the decline of remarriage, both after a divorce or following widowhood.

So far, the explanations are predominantly oriented at those who have enjoyed better education. But the passage through the intermediate states is also found among other segments of the population, despite the fact that, at least in continental Western Europe, the new living arrangements appeared first among the better educated. In Easterlin's theory (Easterlin *et al.* 1990), postponed home-leaving, sharing or doubling up, and cohabitation are not the outcome of the valuation of the female human resource potential, but of the combination of sustained consumption aspirations and deteriorating economic opportunities for new cohorts of young males. The intermediate states between leaving home and marriage are added and the duration of these states is prolonged, not only because of schooling, but also because of unfavourable labour market conditions. The view of Easterlin and colleagues, documented with United States data, is essentially a theory of relative economic deprivation. It is bound to receive a sympathetic hearing in the Mediterranean countries, such as Spain or Italy, where leaving home is postponed to a considerable extent in tandem with unfavourable labour market conditions.

The two economic theories presented above have been criticized on several points. According to Valerie Oppenheimer (1988), the intermediate states stem from marriage market conditions. Higher education for women and concomitant financial independence have increased the quality standards for what constitutes a 'minimally acceptable match'. Prolonged dating and cohabitation reflect a more careful search or a trial run in matching the two utility functions of the partners concerned. In the neo-classical view, diminishing returns to marriage for women results in larger proportions not entering marriage and parenthood. In Oppenheimer's view there is only a postponement effect, not an economically induced 'de-institutionalization'.

The notion of quality is also central in social exchange theory (see Rezsohazy 1991) or economic transaction theory (see England and Farkas 1986). The quality of a relationship can be defined as the degree of satisfaction which partners experience as the result of the incorporation of each other's needs and well-being into their own utility function. We are dealing here with 'giving and taking', mutual trust and respect, fidelity, reciprocated understanding. In surveys probing into the various elements that are needed to constitute a successful partnership or marriage, these items receive the highest scores (see, for example, Harding *et al.* 1986; Lesthaeghe and Moors 1992). Hence, aside from alterations in purely economic living conditions, it is possible that expectations of what partners can get out of a marriage or a union could also have increased.

Support for the latter proposition stems from the rise of Maslow's (1954) theory of 'higher order needs'. In Maslowian needs theory, the 'higher order needs' associated with self-fulfilment, political emancipation, personal recognition, and individual ethical autonomy emerge once the 'lower order needs' associated with basic economic and physical security are satisfied. Inglehart's (1970, 1990) measurement of post-materialism in the economic-political domain shows that the Maslowian 'existential needs' have been accentuated to a higher degree by each successive cohort.

Within the ethical and moral domain, individual autonomy manifests itself in further secularization, the refusal of institutional morality and ethical patronage, the accentuation of freedom of choice, the replacement of conformism by responsibility, and greater tolerance for the choices and lifestyles of others. It was therefore no surprise to find that premarital cohabitation during the late 1960s and 1970s was almost a rite of passage for the 'new left' (Dumon 1977; Lesthaeghe and van de Kaa 1986) in Belgium and the Netherlands. It was a manifestation of a rejection of the conventional 'bourgeois marriage' which was at the time regarded as being hypocritical in the sense that its conformism was more important than the quality of the relationship.

If 'post-materialists' expect more individual recognition and satisfaction in matters related to private life, the evaluation of returns becomes a fundamental issue. If returns are unsatisfactory, reversibility should be an open possibility. Also, positions need to be calibrated repeatedly to work out suitable solutions. Making such positions and opinions overt therefore becomes a basic characteristic of new relationships, especially when two young adults are not only facing strictly domestic issues but also elements of professional lives and their impact on the domestic sphere. This contrasts strongly with the more traditional marriages of their parents based on a relatively clear script, with division of labour and male economic support and companionship being exchanged against female inputs in overall domestic quality.

The economic theories discussed by Ermisch in the previous chapter, which are respectively based on female economic autonomy and on relative economic deprivation among the younger cohorts, obviously chart the passage through the various types of living arrangements to the transitions in socio-economic position. These theories furthermore assume that value orientations are endogenous and equally determined by the socio-economic profiles of individual life courses. In other words, they assume that there is no independent or autonomous additional effect originating in ideational factors. Yet, in Easterlin's version of the economic deprivation theory, ample attention is being paid to consumption aspirations originating during the socialization phase. By the same token, not only consumption aspirations but a wide spectrum of value orientations can be generated during these formative years. Parents, peer groups, and professors all play a major role in the process. Hence, values developed during adolescence may equally direct ambitions, professional options, and ultimately socio-economic positions.

To sum up, monocausal theories cannot do justice to the complexities involved in the emergence of new life-cycle states. In the present chapter, we attempt to provide evidence for the hypotheses that (a) attitudes and values concerning religious, political, and ethical issues are still closely associated with the distribution of individuals over the various forms of living arrangements; and (b) these associations hold for both sexes and irrespective of socio-economic positions.

In short, the basic aim is to show that ideational factors and aspirations regarding the nature of a relationship are necessary complements to the economic theories which have failed so far to incorporate them. In other words, the assumption of the endogeneous origin of these ideational factors found in both the neo-classical theory of G. Becker and the relative deprivation theory of Easterlin constitutes a major weakness of these theories.

6.2 Data and Limitations

The data used here stem from the European Values Surveys (EVS) held in 1990 in a number of Western countries. The main reason for the use of the EVS is its unusually large body of value and attitudinal data, which is ideally suited for an exploratory analysis of this kind. We have used the data for the Netherlands, France, West Germany, and Belgium, largely because these countries exhibit similar developments. There are of course major differences between them, with the Netherlands and France having more young adults than West Germany or Belgium living in premarital cohabitation. Also value-orientations differ, with again the Netherlands and France being more libertarian on moral and sexual issues. However, the data sets for the four countries have been pooled for reasons of sample size. In total, the data pertain to 1,386 persons aged between 20 and 29 years. Once broken down according to living arrangement, the sample sizes obviously decrease, but our aim has been to have about 100 respondents in each category. The resulting sample sizes are shown in table 6.1.

TABLE 6.1. *Sample sizes according to age-group and living arrangements in the weighted pooled EVS data of the Netherlands, Belgium, France, and West Germany, 1990*

Living arrangement	Age		Total
	20–4	25–9	
Single, living with parents	343	85	428
Single, not living with parents	166	146	312
With partner, cohabiting	115	145	260
With partner, married	79	307	386
Total	703	683	1,386

Source: European Values Survey.

Before pooling the four national data sets we inspected the association between the living arrangements and the relevant value characteristics. In almost all instances the national differentials went in the same direction, and differences in orders of magnitude are largely due to the small national sample sizes. It would be interesting to compare the present results with the pooled data for Denmark and Sweden and with those of the United Kingdom (Northern Ireland included) and Ireland. The analysis for Spain, Portugal, and Italy, however, is hampered by the fact that few respondents would be found in the intermediate states ('single, not living with parents' or 'cohabiting') as illustrated in the Appendix (table 6A.1).

From the EVS data it is possible to distinguish between the following living arrangements:

— single, living with parents;
— single, not living with parents (but *without* distinction between living alone or sharing);
— with partner, cohabiting;
— with partner, currently married (divorced omitted from analysis).

Regrettably, no questions were asked about previous states. As a result, no distinction could be made for the currently married between those who had ever cohabited and those who had never done so. Such a distinction would undoubtedly have elucidated differences in value orientations within the category of the currently married respondents.

In pooling the four national data sets a weighting procedure was used so that the proportions of the respective national populations are respected. As a result, the Dutch and Belgian samples contribute considerably less to the weighted pooled sample than the West German and French data sets.

6.3 Values and Living Arrangements: The Problem of Causality

The main problem with the strictly cross-sectional nature of the present data set is that no causal inferences are possible. The value orientations, living arrangements, and socio-economic positions are all measured simultaneously. Hence, it is impossible to break down the overall statistical associations into a *selection effect* and an *affirmation effect* respectively. By the selection effect, we refer to the mechanism whereby individuals select themselves over the various living arrangements depending on their *prior* value orientations. By the affirmation (or negation) effect, we mean the *subsequent* reinforcement (or weakening) of values depending on living arrangements or socio-economic position. The associations measured in this cross-section obviously capture the whole of this recursive process, but not the constituent parts of it.

There are two ways of measuring the selection effect more adequately. First, retrospective questions can be introduced pertaining to earlier positions. In this way a number of authors (for example, Kiernan 1992) have been able to document that the likelihood of earlier home-leaving and subsequent cohabitation increases substantially for persons with divorced or remarried parents. Retrospective questions pertaining to values that were held in the past have highly questionable validity, so that this avenue for research is almost entirely closed for our purposes. In the present data-set, there is only one useful retrospective question that can be used to document the existence of a value-based selection process. This question pertains to whether or not the respondent had received a religious education. We shall therefore devote special attention to this particular item.

The second, and much more promising, way to handle the selection and affirmation issues is provided by a panel design. The respondents in the 1990 round of the EVS can be interviewed again several years later, and changes in living arrangements that have occurred during the interval can then be related to the 1990 value measurements (selection). Conversely, a re-administration of the value questions in the second phase will also allow us to study the affirmation or negation effects, depending on the changes in living arrangements that have been recorded during the interval. We would therefore strongly recommend the addition of a second phase in the near future for the younger respondents in the 1990 round, particularly since these persons are likely to have had more frequent transitions in living arrangements and socio-economic position than the older respondents.

To sum up, except for one particular item, we shall only be able to describe the *overall association* between value orientations, socio-economic position, and living arrangements with the present data-set. In subsequent multivariate analyses involving these three variables, the choice of a dependent variable is totally arbitrary. The reader is therefore strongly urged *not* to give any causal interpretation (either pure selection or pure affirmation) to these associations. On the other hand, the present data are adequate to perform controls for socio-economic position variables. In other words, we can inspect whether or not the association between value orientations and living arrangements continue to emerge once the effect of socio-economic position has been eliminated. The resistance to such a control would strongly suggest that effects of value orientations are not purely endogenous, as the economic theories assume.

6.4 Value Orientations according to Living Arrangements: Overall Results and Controls for Socio-Economic Position

In this section the following domains of value orientations are covered:
(a) religious values (15 items);
(b) political values, including the Inglehart scale (14 items);
(c) political party preference;
(d) factors perceived as contributing to a successful marriage (12 items);
(e) attitudes concerning working women and mothers (6 items);
(f) importance of children, socialization values (15 items);
(g) attitudes concerning public morality (15 items);
(h) attitudes toward sexuality (8 items);
(i) life satisfaction indicators (13 items).

In a first set of tables only the orders of magnitude are described, together with (a) the differences between unmarried respondents living with their parents and those not living at home, and (b) the differences between cohabitants and married respondents. At this point, no significance tests are reported, but differences of 7 percentage points or more are all significant at the 0.05 level.

The second set of tables presents the results of logit regressions performed on a selection of items. The logit regressions are all based on the simple additive model with the effects of living arrangements (four categories) and of socio-economic position (four or five categories depending on sex). These socio-economic categories are:

(a) employed or employers: professionals, senior and middle level white collar;
(b) employed: blue collar and junior white collar workers;
(c) housewives (for women only);
(d) students;
(e) unemployed.

The results in these tables are given in the form of relative risks, by living arrangement (exp. B where B is each regression coefficient derived from the logit regression procedure), controlling for socio-economic position as specified above. The reference category is the group of single respondents still residing with their parents ('home-stayers'). Logit regression is a useful way of estimating the statistical effects of variables such as social groups and categories of living arrangements, where individuals must be placed into one or other category. These distributions can be described by 'odds ratios' which have awkward statistical properties as they have no upper limit. Transformation of the odds ratios to their natural logarithms (logits) resolves these problems.

Religious values

The association between higher degrees of secularization and opting for a period of cohabitation has been a recurrent finding in earlier research. This finding has been reported for the United States (Tanfer 1987, Thornton and Camburn 1987), Canada (Rao 1989), Australia (Khoo 1987), France (Villeneuve-Gokalp 1990), the Netherlands (Liefbroer 1991) and Belgium (Lee *et al.* 1987). The striking feature here is that the association was not only strong in the late 1960s or 1970s when cohabitation was beginning to emerge in these countries, but that it still holds in a virtually unaltered fashion. The data presented in table 6.2 bear witness to this effect, particularly when cohabitants are compared with currently married respondents. Of the fifteen items considered, ten produce differences in excess of 10 percentage points, with the largest being the belief in God (30 percentage points less among cohabitants than married), the non-attendance at religious services (−20 points), the saying of prayers (−18 points), the belief in the notion of sin (−17 points), and the drawing of comfort and

TABLE 6.2. *Indicators of religiosity; according to living arrangements; respondents aged 20–29 in the Netherlands, Belgium, West Germany, and France, 1990 (per cent)*

	Without partner			With partner			Total (N = 1,386)
	Living with parents (1)	Not Living with parents (2)	Difference (2) − (1)	Married (3)	Cohabiting (4)	Difference (4) − (3)	(5)
A. Attends religious service at least once a month[a]	14.7	12.4	−2.3	16.3	5.0	−11.3	12.8
Never or practically never attends a religious service	40.2	44.1	+3.9	41.5	61.9	+20.4	45.5
B. Gets comfort and strength from religion[b]	26.2	24.6	−1.6	35.5	20.9	−14.6	27.2
C. Prays to God outside religious services[c] 'often' and 'sometimes'	28.1	23.0	−5.1	35.1	17.2	−17.9	26.9
D. Believes in: (positive answers)							
— God	57.6	48.9	−8.7	68.6	38.5	−30.1	55.2
— Life after death	41.1	43.9	+2.8	44.4	42.0	−2.4	42.9
— Soul	64.9	66.9	+2.0	55.9	59.0	+3.1	61.8
— Devil	12.2	14.5	+2.3	16.9	14.2	−2.7	14.4
— Hell	10.8	12.9	+2.1	12.3	9.8	−2.5	11.5
— Heaven	27.0	25.1	−1.9	32.8	19.9	−12.9	26.7
— Sin	44.9	39.4	−5.5	47.4	30.6	−16.8	41.5
— Resurrection	28.6	23.7	−4.9	30.1	18.6	−11.5	12.0
— Reincarnation	27.1	29.0	+1.9	19.0	32.9	+13.9	26.4
E. Brought up religiously (positive answers)	61.4	54.4	−7.0	59.4	42.6	−16.8	55.8
F. Considers shared religious belief as very important for a successful marriage[d]	6.9	8.8	+1.9	11.2	1.8	−9.4	7.6

a Excluding weddings, christenings, and funerals.
b Response categories were: yes, no, don't know.
c Response categories were: often, sometimes, hardly ever, only in times of crisis, never, don't know.
d Respondents were to pick up to five qualities in a list of ten.

strength from religion (−15 points). Parental secularity also played a major role in currently being selected into cohabitation since fewer cohabitants (−17 points) than married persons report having been brought up religiously.

By contrast, the differences between cohabitants and married respondents almost vanish for a few items pertaining to particular traditional beliefs, such as life after death (−2 points), the devil (−3 points) and hell (−3 points). The situation is reversed with respect to the belief in the soul, with slightly more cohabitants adhering (+3 points), and particularly with respect to the belief in reincarnation (+14 points). The survey did not probe into other metaphysical and para-psychological beliefs, so that we cannot extrapolate the stronger belief in reincarnation among cohabitants toward the paranormal in general.

The religiosity dimension is, on the other hand, much weaker when single persons residing and not residing with parents are compared. The only major distinctions are a weaker belief in God among the single home-leavers (−9 points) and fewer of them being brought up religiously (−7 points). Also praying and the belief in sin are slightly weaker among them (−5 points). Furthermore, it should be noted that the responses of those without a partner are situated between those of cohabitants and married individuals (results in columns 1 and 2 between those in columns 3 and 4). Hence, it seems that the secularization dimension is particularly operative in the choice of type of union (selection), and/or that the choice of the latter tends to polarize the opinions with respect to religiosity (assertion).

In table 6.3, the control for socio-economic position has been introduced for a selection of these religiosity items. The following contrasts according to living arrangement remain both intact and significant after these controls:

(a) Among both sexes cohabitants have systematically the lowest risks of believing in God or in sin and of having moments of prayer, whereas married persons have the highest relative risks.

(b) The belief in reincarnation is significantly stronger for single male home-leavers and cohabitants, whereas it is significantly lower for married women.

On the whole, these patterns confirm that the zero-order associations documented in table 6.3 are not merely the by-product of differences in socio-economic position.

TABLE 6.3. *Selected religiosity items: likelihood by living arrangements and gender after controlling for socio-economic position; respondents aged 20–29 in Belgium, France, West Germany, and the Netherlands, 1990*

	Men				Women			
	Single, with parents	Single, not with parents	Cohabiting	Married	Single, with parents	Single, not with parents	Cohabiting	Married
Believes in God	1.00	0.75	0.52[a]	1.86[a]	1.00	0.69	0.39[b]	1.54
Believes in sin	1.00	0.82	0.47[b]	1.48	1.00	0.94	0.69	1.35
Prays outside church	1.00	0.75	0.60	1.07	1.00	0.97	0.59	1.85[a]
Believes in reincarnation	1.00	1.89[a]	3.29[b]	1.03	1.00	0.84	0.72	0.35[b]

[a] Significant at 0.05 level.
[b] Significant at 0.01 level.

The selection effect stemming from parental religious orientation, and measured through the item 'having received a religious upbringing', has also been subjected to a similar control. Among men, 39 per cent of the home-leavers have had a religious upbringing against 46 per cent among home-stayers. After controlling for socio-economic position and age (introduced as a set of categorical dummies in order to allow for non-linearity) in an analysis of variance (that is, multiple classification analysis), this 7 percentage point difference becomes an 8 point difference in the same direction. Similarly for women, an original 10 percentage point difference is only reduced to a 7 point difference after these controls. The contrast between cohabiting and married men was slightly larger to start with: 50 per cent of the married men reported a religious upbringing against 41 per cent among cohabiting men. After the controls, the contrast increases to a difference of 11 percentage points. Among women with a partner, the zero-order effect was initially 16 percentage points, with 46 per cent of married women reporting a religious upbringing against only 30 per cent among cohabiting women. This contrast is reduced to a difference of 12 percentage points after controls, but the difference remains highly significant (0.01 level). Hence, these checks strongly suggest that at least a very substantial part of the differences in religiosity according to living arrangement are due to a pure selection effect and are attributable to parental religiosity or secularity. These findings are furthermore perfectly in line with those reported elsewhere for the Netherlands (Liefbroer 1991) and Belgium (Lee *et al.* 1987) using a similar question.

To sum up, home-leavers and especially cohabitants have more commonly received a more secular upbringing and still exhibit, on average, lower degrees of religiosity than the others and particularly the married respondents—irrespective of their current socio-economic position. By contrast, this lower degree of traditional religiosity seems to be associated with a stronger belief in reincarnation, particularly among male home-leavers and cohabitants.

Political attitudes

Differences in political attitudes are studied in this chapter in terms of the approval of emancipation movements (human rights, anti-apartheid, women's liberation) and of the 'green' agenda (ecology, anti-nuclear, and disarmament movements), through the Inglehart 'materialist-postmaterialist' scales, and through preferences for political parties.

Table 6.4 presents attitudes to the various political pressure groups. Again, the proportions expressing approval among the single living with their parents and those living separately fall between the proportions observed among the married and cohabitants. Except with regard to their attitudes towards the human rights and anti-apartheid movements, the differences between single home-stayers and home-leavers are not large. A stronger polarization occurs between cohabitants and married respondents, with cohabitants showing considerably greater support for all pressure groups, and for the women's liberation and anti-apartheid movements in particular. Hence, the responses according to living arrangement in table 6.4 exhibit the same structure as those pertaining to religion in table 6.2, with the stronger contrasts emerging between cohabitants and married couples.

The results for the Inglehart 'materialist' versus 'post-materialist' distinction are reported in table 6.5. Respondents were presented with two sets of views, each of which contained four items, two of which represented a materialist concern with economic and physical security ('maintaining order' and 'fighting rising prices' in set 1 and 'a stable economy' and 'fight against crime' in set 2); the other two represented a postmaterialist concern with grassroots democracy and autonomy ('giving people more say in government' and 'protecting freedom of speech' in set 1, and 'less impersonal and more humane society' and 'society in which ideas count more than money' in set 2). At this point, it is essential to stress that Inglehart's term 'materialist' does *not* refer to high consumption aspirations (for example for luxury goods), a misunderstanding that has frequently been made in the economic literature, but only to *basic* economic and physical security. In each set, respondents were requested to pick two items out of the four presented. 'Materialists' and 'post-materialists' are respectively those respondents who pick the two materialist or post-materialist items in each set. The others constitute the mixed types.

As expected, both home-leavers and cohabitants contain smaller percentages of 'materialists' and higher percentages of 'post-materialists'. The existing contrast between single home-stayers and

TABLE 6.4. *Attitudes toward political pressure groups; according to living arrangements; respondents aged 20–29 in the Netherlands, Belgium, West Germany, and France, 1990 (per cent)*

Approves of	Without partner			With partner			Total (N = 1,339)
	Living with parents (1)	Not living with parents (2)	Difference (2) − (1)	Married (3)	Cohabiting (4)	Difference (4) − (3)	(5)
Human rights movement	58.0	67.1	+9.1	61.4	67.5	+6.1	62.8
Ecology movement	61.0	58.4	−1.6	56.3	63.4	+7.1	59.5
Anti-apartheid movement	50.0	55.7	+5.7	51.0	60.2	+9.2	53.5
Disarmament movement	42.4	44.0	+1.6	40.5	45.6	+5.1	42.9
Anti-nuclear movement	32.8	32.4	−0.4	35.0	38.0	+3.0	34.3
Women's movement	20.9	20.6	−0.3	17.6	27.4	+9.8	21.1

Note: Response categories were 'approve strongly', 'approve somewhat', 'disapprove somewhat', 'disapprove strongly'; the figures above refer to the first two response categories.

TABLE 6.5. *Inglehart 'materialism-post-materialism' scale; according to living arrangements; respondents aged 20–29 in the Netherlands, Belgium, France, and West Germany, 1990 (per cent)*

	Without partner			With partner			Total (N = 1,328)
	Living with parents (1)	Not living with parents (2)	Difference (2) − (1)	Married (3)	Cohabiting (4)	Difference (4) − (3)	(5)
Set 1							
'Materialists' choosing— maintaining order and fighting rising prices	9.4	7.0	−2.4	18.3	11.0	−7.3	11.6
'Post-materialists' choosing— giving people more say in government and protecting freedom of speech	34.8	45.3	+10.5	23.5	45.9	+22.4	36.1
Set 2							
'Materialists' choosing— a stable economy and fight against crime	28.8	13.5	−15.3	32.7	22.3	−10.4	25.2
'Post-materialists' choosing— less impersonal and more humane society and society in which ideas count more than money	19.7	32.9	+23.2	13.4	27.1	+13.7	22.3

home-leavers is maintained, and does not widen for set 2 when cohabitants are compared with married persons. Of all categories, married persons have the lowest proportion of 'post-materialists' and the highest proportion of 'materialists', which is completely consistent with the findings reported for the early 1980s (Lesthaeghe and Meekers 1986).

The distinctions continue to emerge with respect to political party preference. In table 6.6, the results are presented by country to allow for national differences in the political landscape.

The general picture across the countries is that single home-leavers and cohabitants, compared, as usual, to home-stayers and married persons respectively, have a considerably reduced preference for the Christian Democrats or the French Centre, and very pronounced preference for the Green parties instead. The shift in voting intentions among those in the intermediate living arrangements further benefits the Social Democrats in Belgium, the Communists and extreme left in France, and the various Liberal parties in the Netherlands and Germany. Regional parties in Belgium and the extreme right in all countries are less attractive to single home-leavers than home-stayers, but this is not necessarily so among cohabitants compared to married respondents. Finally, the percentages of uncommitted persons among home-leavers and cohabitants is generally smaller in all countries than among home-stayers and married persons respectively.

The relative aversion to the Christian Democrats among those in the intermediate living arrangements obviously stems from the more anti-establishment outlook of home-leavers and cohabitants, and from a reaction against the pro-family and pro-natalist stands of the Christian parties. The large shift towards the Greens is entirely consistent with the more pronounced 'post-materialist' outlook of single home-leavers and cohabitants. The greater attraction of the Liberal parties, particularly in the Netherlands, but to some extent also in Germany and among cohabitants in Belgium, stems from the fact that the economic individualistic outlook, as opposed to welfare state interventionism, does have an appeal to a presumably wealthier segment of those in less conventional living arrangements. In Belgium and France, however, this is more than matched, especially among home-leavers (who are presumably in a more precarious position), by a greater preference for the left.

TABLE 6.6. *Political party preference; according to living arrangements; respondents aged 20–29 in the Netherlands, Belgium, West Germany, and France, 1990 (per cent)*

'If there were a general election tomorrow, which party would you vote for?'	Without partner			With partner			Total
	Living with parents (1)	Not living with parents (2)	Difference (2) − (1)	Married (3)	Cohabiting (4)	Difference (4) − (3)	(5)
Belgium (N = 510)							
Christian democrats (CVP, PSC)	17	6	−11	21	6	−15	16
Social democrats (SP, PS)	10	27	+17	26	36	+10	21
Liberals (PVV, PRL)	25	21	−4	13	19	+6	20
Green parties (AGALEV, ECOLO)	25	39	+14	20	31	+11	25
Regional parties (VU, FDF)	2	0	−2	5	0	−5	3
Extreme right (Vlaams Blok)	3	0	−3	2	0	−2	2
No preference	19	6	−13	13	8	−5	14
Netherlands (N = 225)							
Christian democrats (CDA)	44	13	−31	18	10	−8	22
Social democrats (PvdA)	22	11	−11	32	17	−5	25
Liberals (VVD)	7	11	+4	4	18	+14	9
Progressive Liberals (D66)	13	32	+19	21	28	+7	24

Green party	0	22	+22	5	10	+5	10
Other	6	4	−2	7	3	−4	5
No preference	9	7	−2	13	15	+2	11
Germany (N = 368)							
Christian democrats (CDU, CSU)	32	20	−12	28	20	−8	26
Social democrats (SPD)	38	40	+2	46	44	−2	41
Liberals (FDP)	5	8	+3	8	13	+5	8
Green party	15	23	+8	10	14	+4	15
Extreme right (NDP, Republ.)	2	3	−1	1	2	+1	2
No preference	7	5	−2	7	9	−2	7
France (N = 159)							
Centre (UDF-RPR)	21	18	−3	15	3	−12	15
Socialists	38	39	+1	42	26	−17	37
Communist & extreme left	2	6	+4	8	10	+2	6
Green parties	13	21	+8	17	45	+28	22
Extreme right (Nat. Front)	4	3	−1	0	3	+3	3
No preference	21	12	−9	19	13	−6	17

Note: percentages are rounded.

The attitudes to the various political and emancipation movements are reported in table 6.7 (after controlling for socioeconomic position) in the form of relative risks and their significance. In general, the contrasts relating to single home-stayers are less marked than those in table 6.3 using the religiosity indicators. Nevertheless, the results that are significant operate largely in the expected direction. Cohabitants especially are more likely to approve of these political or emancipation movements. This holds for the female cohabitants with respect to approval of the anti-apartheid movement, and for male cohabitants with regard to the human rights and women's liberation movements. By contrast, married women are significantly less likely to approve of women's liberation movements, even after controlling for the fact that housewives are *over-represented* in the category of married women.

On the whole, we conclude that the living arrangements differentiate in the expected direction, with cohabitants again being the most distinct group. However, the differentiation with respect to the various political dimensions according to living arrangement are generally weaker than those observed for the religiosity/secularization items.

Family, ethical, and social values

This section looks at the perceived prerequisites for a successful marriage, attitudes toward working women, the importance of children, socialization values, attitudes with respect to public morality, and the attitudes toward sexuality.

In table 6.8, the results are presented for the list of characteristics chosen as being important for a successful marriage. The respondents were presented with a list of twelve items and had to indicate their preference on a three-point scale, ranging from 'very important' to 'not very important'. The social exchange theory, as presented in the introduction to this chapter, draws ample support from the results since the items most frequently quoted as being very important are all those that stress reciprocity; mutual respect and appreciation, tolerance and understanding, and faithfulness. Home-leavers and cohabitants score consistently lower on faithfulness than home-stayers and especially married couples, whereas the opposite holds for tolerance and understanding. This indicates

TABLE 6.7. *Selected political items: likelihood by living arrangements and gender after controlling for socio-economic position; respondents aged 20–29 in Belgium, France, West Germany, and the Netherlands, 1990*

Approves of	Men				Women			
	Single, with parents	Single, not with parents	Cohabiting	Married	Single, with parents	Single, not with parents	Cohabiting	Married
Anti-apartheid movement	1.00	1.12	1.05	1.21	1.00	1.53	2.13[b]	1.14
Human rights movement	1.00	1.27	1.61[a]	1.39	1.00	1.84[b]	1.58	1.19
Ecology movement	1.00	0.68	0.79	0.75	1.00	1.28	1.34	0.74
Women's movement	1.00	1.08	2.24[b]	1.37	1.00	0.85	0.80	0.53[a]

[a] Significant at 0.05 level.
[b] Significant at 0.01 level.

TABLE 6.8. Factors perceived as contributing to a successful marriage; according to living arrangements; respondents aged 20–29 in the Netherlands, Belgium, West Germany, and France, 1990 (per cent)

Considers as 'very important' for a successful marriage:[a]	Without partner			With partner			Total (N = 1,385)
	Living with parents (1)	Not living with parents (2)	Difference (2) − (1)	Married (3)	Cohabiting (4)	Difference (4) − (3)	(5)
Mutual respect and appreciation	78.4	85.2	+6.8	83.2	78.2	−5.0	81.2
Tolerance and understanding	75.2	82.2	+7.0	71.8	75.9	+4.1	76.0
Faithfulness	74.3	62.2	−12.1	82.1	66.9	−15.2	72.4
Happy sexual relationship	64.7	64.9	+0.2	68.0	65.1	−2.9	65.7
Children	41.6	31.0	−11.6	64.7	45.0	−19.7	46.4
Sharing household chores	31.0	31.8	+0.8	31.3	37.7	+6.4	32.5
Tastes and interests in common	38.7	35.5	−3.2	37.6	39.7	+2.1	37.9
Adequate income	27.2	22.9	−4.3	31.8	23.7	−8.1	26.9
Good housing	20.8	23.3	+2.5	34.4	23.4	−10.0	25.7
Being of the same social background	12.9	10.4	−2.5	13.6	6.4	−7.2	11.2
Sharing the same religious convictions	6.9	8.8	+1.9	11.2	1.8	−9.4	7.6
Agreement on politics	4.2	5.7	+1.5	2.9	5.9	+3.0	4.5

[a] Response categories were: very important, rather important, not very important.

that those in the intermediate living arrangements wish to maintain some latitude with respect to partner choice and commitment to this partner, and furthermore expect the partner to show tolerance and understanding for this weaker commitment. Home-leavers, furthermore, more frequently think that this can be combined with the maintenance of mutual respect and appreciation, but cohabitants tend to be more realistic in this respect. The latter score lowest on the item 'mutual respect and appreciation' as a consequence.

The item concerning a happy sexual relationship does not provide any major differences according to living arrangement, but the importance of children for a successful marriage exhibits a very strong discriminating power. Single home-leavers stress this item much less than home-stayers (-12 percentage points), and cohabitants much less than married respondents (-20 points). The items of faithfulness and children are consequently the most effective in the entire battery of questions at discriminating between groups defined by residential arrangements.

Further down the ranking according to importance come the items concerning material conditions (adequate income, good housing) and those pertaining to social homogamy. In these respects, the differences between the single respondents according to living arrangement are small, but cohabitants stressed these material items much less than married couples. The same holds for social homogamy with respect to sharing the same social or religious background. But on common tastes and politics, that is, the two non-traditional items, cohabitants score slightly higher than married respondents.

The remaining item, namely, sharing household chores, comes about midway in the overall ranking, but before the items concerning material conditions and social homogamy. As expected, cohabitants attach a greater importance to such symmetry than married respondents.

On the whole, this battery of questions sheds light on the nature of relationships desired by the respondents. It is therefore intimately connected to what the respondents define as 'quality'. The results confirm that cohabitants in particular attach greater value to symmetrical relations. They have weaker commitments in terms of faithfulness, a greater orientation to the adult dyad and less to children, material conditions, or social and religious backgrounds.

In other words, individual autonomy, being less hampered by children and material considerations, continue to be more strongly represented among cohabitants in all four countries. The importance of children is taken up in greater detail in table 6.9. The differences reported here are again very striking and confirm, with three additional items, that home-leavers and cohabitants are far less oriented to having children than are the others. The fourth question, pertaining to abortion where a couple does not want any children, combines the ethical and reproduction issues. This item therefore produces the strongest contrast between those in the intermediate living arrangements and those either at home or already in a marriage.

The opinions about the qualities to be stressed in the education of children, presented in table 6.10, clearly demonstrate the great attachment to individual autonomy and the reduced weight of conformism among those in the intermediate living arrangements. Single home-leavers and cohabitants score much lower on the items concerning good manners, obedience, thrift, hard work, and religious faith than single persons living with parents and married couples. By contrast, the former score higher on items that stress personality development such as independence and imagination. The third group of items in the set pertain to social qualities: responsibility, tolerance, and unselfishness. Since respondents could choose only five items from the entire list (as opposed to Likert-like ratings of each item) and since the conformism-related items were less attractive to those in the intermediate living arrangements, tolerance and unselfishness emerge as more attractive to home-leavers and cohabitants. This is also in agreement with their overall higher tolerance for minorities and for socially more deviant groups. However, home-leavers and cohabitants do not score higher on responsibility, which is correlated with their reduced support for traditional public morality, as we shall now show.

Table 6.11 presents fifteen items pertaining to civic morality. In all instances a 10-point scale has been used, with the score of 1 denoting 'never justified' and 10 meaning 'always justified'. The percentages considering the act as 'never justified' are compared across living arrangements.

The pattern of weakened public morality among those in the intermediate living arrangements holds for virtually all items con-

TABLE 6.9. *Importance of children; according to living arrangements; respondents aged 20–29 in the Netherlands, Belgium, West Germany, and France, 1990 (per cent)*

	Without partner			With partner			Total (N = 1,368)
	Living with parents (1)	Not living with parents (2)	Difference (2) − (1)	Married (3)	Cohabiting (4)	Difference (4) − (3)	(5)
A. Having children is NOT very important for a successful marriage[a]	19.1	27.8	+8.7	8.0	24.6	+16.6	18.9
B. Ideal number of children equals 3 or more	34.6	41.0	+6.4	41.4	35.5	−5.9	38.1
C. A woman needs to have children to be fulfilled[b]	44.7	30.5	−14.2	55.4	41.5	−13.9	43.9
D. Approves of abortion if couple desires no children[c]	34.1	50.4	+16.3	30.7	53.7	+23.0	40.5

[a] Categories were: very important, rather important, not very important.
[b] Categories were: needs children, not necessary, don't know.
[c] Categories were: approve, disapprove.

TABLE 6.10. *Socialization qualities according to living arrangements; respondents aged 20–29 in the Netherlands, Belgium, France, and West Germany, 1990 (per cent)*

Chosen as one of the most important qualities for children to learn at home[a]	Without partner			With partner			Total (N = 1,382)
	Living with parents (1)	Not living with parents (2)	Difference (2) – (1)	Married (3)	Cohabiting (4)	Difference (4) – (3)	(5)
(A) Conformist values							
— good manners	67.1	54.5	−12.6	66.6	55.3	−11.3	61.9
— obedience	27.2	31.5	+4.3	35.4	31.2	−4.2	31.2
— thrift	29.1	17.1	−12.0	38.3	21.7	−16.6	27.6
— hard work	29.1	17.1	−12.0	26.6	22.4	−4.2	24.5
— religious faith	9.4	9.4	0.0	11.6	1.6	−10.0	8.5
(B) Personal development values							
— independence	58.5	62.8	+4.3	52.7	61.6	+8.4	58.4
— imagination	34.7	50.6	+15.9	25.2	46.9	+21.7	37.9
— perseverance, determination	44.2	44.9	+0.7	37.8	42.4	+4.6	42.2
(C) Social values							
— responsibility	81.1	80.7	−0.4	80.6	78.8	−1.8	80.4
— tolerance and respect for others	79.9	85.6	+5.7	74.3	84.1	+9.8	80.4
— unselfishness	15.4	28.5	+13.1	28.4	30.2	+1.8	24.7

[a] Respondents were requested to pick up to five socialization qualities as the more important ones in a list of ten.

TABLE 6.11. *Attitudes concerning public morality; according to living arrangements; respondents aged 20–29 in the Netherlands, Belgium, France, and West Germany, 1990 (per cent)*

Considers as NEVER justified[a]	Without partner			With partner			Total (N = 1,375)
	Living with parents (1)	Not living with parents (2)	Difference (2) − (1)	Married (3)	Cohabiting (4)	Difference (4) − (3)	(5)
Taking drugs: marijuana or hashish	70	50	−20	85	62	−23	68
Buying something you know was stolen	48	41	−7	60	40	−20	49
Cheating on tax if you had a chance	31	20	−11	41	22	−19	31
Avoiding fare on public transport	34	26	−8	48	30	−18	38
Claiming state benefits to which one is not entitled	37	28	−9	46	30	−16	36
Fighting with police	29	17	−12	44	29	−15	31
Keeping found money	17	11	−6	26	14	−12	20
Joyriding	76	76	0	85	73	−12	78
Failing to report damage accidentally done	38	36	−2	60	50	−10	47
Political assassination	70	65	−5	72	62	−10	69
Accepting a bribe in course of duty	45	50	+5	56	51	−5	51
Littering in public place	59	55	−4	65	62	−3	61
Lying in self-interest	13	12	−1	20	18	−2	16
Driving under influence of alcohol	56	54	−2	65	67	+2	60
Threatening workers who refuse to join strike	68	60	−8	67	71	+4	66

[a] Percentage with score = 1 (never justified) on acceptability scale (10 = always justified).

sidered. Single home-leavers score substantially lower than home-stayers (differences in excess of 10 percentage points) on three items, but cohabitants score much lower (same criterion) than married persons on ten items in the battery of fifteen. Moreover, the proportions believing that acts of uncivic behaviour are never justified are consistently lowest among single home-leavers. This holds not only for infringements of a material or economic nature (buying stolen goods, tax cheating, avoiding public transportation fares, claiming social benefits to which one is not entitled) but also for items infringing 'law and order' sanctions (taking drugs, fighting with police, political assassination). Hence, it is necessary to qualify the notion that the replacement of conformism by individual autonomy would also be accompanied by a greater sense of responsibility in public life. Those in intermediate living arrangements may display on average a greater degree of political involvement than the others (see tables 6.4 and 6.6), but this cannot be extended to matters concerning civic morality.

Attitudes concerning the economic and domestic roles of women are presented in table 6.12. The items were presented with response categories varying from 'strongly agree' to 'strongly disagree'. All items that stress domestic duties score much lower among single home-leavers and cohabitants, whereas they favour those that stress female economic autonomy and non-domestic roles. The pattern is also particularly clear when cohabitants and married respondents are compared. Moreover, single home-leavers exhibit the strongest approval of female economic activity and autonomy and are most averse to the restriction of females to domestic roles.

Finally, attitudes concerning sexual permissiveness are considered in table 6.13. Again, the pattern is highly consistent across the various items. There are consistently smaller percentages of home-leavers than home-stayers *never* approving of married persons having an affair, of sexual contact with minors, of homosexuality, and of prostitution. They also have smaller proportions refusing to accept homosexuals and AIDS-carriers as neighbours. More single home-leavers than home-stayers agree with complete sexual freedom and with abortion for non-married women. The contrast between cohabitants and married respondents goes in exactly the same direction, with the former having considerably greater tolerance for sexual permissiveness. The items, extra-marital sex and

TABLE 6.12. *Attitudes concerning working women and mothers; according to living arrangements; respondents aged 20–29 in the Netherlands, Belgium, West Germany, and France, 1990 (per cent)*

'Strongly agrees' or 'agrees' with the following statements[a]	Without partner			With partner			Total (N = 1,330)
	Living with parents (1)	Not living with parents (2)	Difference (2) − (1)	Married (3)	Cohabiting (4)	Difference (4) − (3)	(5)
A. A pre-school child is likely to suffer if his or her mother works	71.8	57.7	−14.1	65.5	55.8	−9.7	63.9
B. Being a housewife is just as fulfilling as working for pay	46.1	35.3	−10.8	61.7	36.5	−25.2	46.7
C. A job is all right, but what most women really want is a home and children	41.6	32.2	−9.4	56.2	45.9	−10.3	44.4
D. A working mother can establish just as warm and secure a relationship with her children as a mother who does not work	59.2	75.3	+16.1	61.3	68.9	7.6	65.3
E. Both husband and wife should contribute to household income	75.2	73.9	−1.3	62.1	75.7	+13.6	71.3
F. Having a job is the best way for a woman to be an independent person	81.9	82.1	+0.2	69.7	79.4	+9.7	78.1

[a] Response categories were: strongly agree, agree, disagree, strongly disagree, don't know.

Ron Lesthaeghe and Guy Moors

TABLE 6.13. *Attitudes toward sexuality; according to living arrangements; respondents aged 20–29 in the Netherlands, Belgium, West Germany, and France, 1990 (per cent)*

	Without partner			With partner			Total (N = 1,386)
	Living with parents (1)	Not living with parents (2)	Difference (2) – (1)	Married (3)	Cohabiting (4)	Difference (4) – (3)	(5)
Never approves of:[a]							
— married women/men having an affair	26.8	16.2	−10.6	43.4	20.5	−22.9	28.1
— sex under the age of consent (18 years)	19.2	15.9	−3.3	32.4	20.7	−11.7	22.4
— homosexuality	22.9	13.0	−9.9	25.8	18.4	−7.4	20.6
— prostitution	27.5	19.4	−8.1	29.3	22.5	−6.8	25.2
Agrees with: 'Individuals should have the chance to enjoy complete sexual freedom, without being restricted'[b]	46.1	52.3	+6.2	35.5	49.1	+13.6	45.2
Would rather *NOT* have as neighbours:[c]							
— homosexuals	24.4	15.9	−8.5	21.1	11.1	−10.0	19.1
— persons with AIDS	15.8	9.7	−6.1	17.1	12.5	−4.6	14.9
Abortion justified if woman is not married[d]	27.0	45.4	18.4	22.5	34.3	+11.8	31.2

[a] Response categories were: 10-point scale from 'never justified' to 'always justified'; percentages above correspond with extreme score 'never justified'.
[b] Response categories were: tends to agree, tends to disagree, neither/it depends, don't know.
[c] Specific groups could be picked as *not* desired as neighbours from a list of 14 groups.
[d] Response categories were: approve, disapprove.

complete sexual freedom, in particular, distinguish cohabitants from married respondents.

The comparison of this large number of items pertaining to a large variety of familial and social values unequivocally show that home-leavers, and cohabitants in particular, compared respectively to home-stayers and married persons, exhibit *on average* more libertarian ideas, and value individual moral and economic autonomy to a significantly greater extent. The patterns across the various domains and measured for a large sample are simply too consistent to be denied. Also, it should be pointed out that for certain dimensions single young adults are less differentiated according to whether they are still residing with parents or not, than those with a partner, depending on whether they are cohabiting or married. However, on a number of moral and economic issues, home-leavers exhibit even more libertarian and autonomy-related attitudes than cohabitants.

The control for social position in the logit regressions barely alters the outcomes with respect to the ethical and civil morality items (see table 6.14). Both married men and married women are the most likely never to accept deviations from standard civil morality, and conversely, the least likely to agree with complete sexual freedom or to accept abortion for single women. The greatest tolerance for deviations or latitude with respect to these ethical issues is found among single home-leavers, followed by cohabitants. Intolerance towards homosexuality and AIDS-patients are issues that produce considerable polarization among female respondents in particular. Again female single home-leavers and cohabitants are the least likely to exhibit such intolerance. The category of women with the highest likelihood is the single home-stayers, not the married women.

The patterning of the socialization values by living arrangement remains much the same after controlling for socio-economic position (see table 6.15). Cohabiting men and single home-leavers are the least likely to choose the conformism items (good manners and thrift) and the most likely to stress the autonomy items (independence and imagination). Very much the same also holds for cohabiting women and female home-leavers. Married persons, on the contrary, show the inverse pattern, but are less often significantly different from the single home-stayers (that is, the reference category). The item 'respect for others' is a correlate of the

TABLE 6.14. *Selected civil morality and ethical items: likelihood by living arrangements and gender after controlling for socio-economic position; respondents aged 20–29 in Belgium, France, the Netherlands, and West Germany, 1990*

	Men				Women			
	Single, with parents	Single, not with parents	Cohabiting	Married	Single, with parents	Single, not with parents	Cohabiting	Married
Never justified:								
— joyriding	1.00	1.45	0.80	1.99[a]	1.00	0.75	0.97	2.51[b]
— use of drugs	1.00	0.37[b]	0.47[b]	1.82[a]	1.00	0.39[b]	0.76	2.10[a]
— tax cheating	1.00	0.75	0.54	1.42	1.00	0.47[b]	0.80	2.14[b]
Agrees with complete sexual freedom	1.00	1.46	1.40	0.53[b]	1.00	1.12	0.95	0.89
Justified: abortion if woman not married	1.00	2.39[b]	2.29[b]	1.02	1.00	2.19[b]	0.91	0.72
Intolerance towards:								
— AIDS-patients	1.00	1.46	1.45	0.81	1.00	0.08[b]	0.31[b]	0.40[b]
— homosexuals	1.00	0.69	0.43[b]	0.69	1.00	0.24[b]	0.22[b]	0.43[b]

[a] Significant at 0.05 level.
[b] Significant at 0.01 level.

TABLE 6.15. *Selected items concerning socialization: relative risks by living arrangements and gender after controlling for socio-economic position; respondents aged 20–29 in Belgium, France, West Germany, and the Netherlands, 1990*

Items stressing	Men				Women			
	Single, with parents	Single, not with parents	Cohabiting	Married	Single, with parents	Single, not with parents	Cohabiting	Married
Good manners	1.00	0.74	0.39[b]	0.77	1.00'	0.41[b]	0.74	1.08
Thrift	1.00	0.57[a]	0.36[b]	1.31	1.00	0.44[b]	0.84	1.44
Independence	1.00	1.09	1.13	0.92	1.00	1.36	0.96	0.55[a]
Imagination	1.00	1.69[a]	1.69[a]	1.15	1.00	2.41[b]	1.99[b]	0.60
Responsibility	1.00	1.00	1.63	1.41	1.00	1.08	0.49[a]	0.88
Respect for others	1.00	1.65	1.73	1.18	1.00	1.82	1.43	0.74

[a] Significant at 0.05 level.
[b] Significant at 0.01 level.

autonomy items, but 'responsibility' is not. Cohabiting men and especially women are much less likely to choose 'responsibility' than any other category, even after controlling for socio-economic position.

Finally, the items pertaining to family issues also continue to exhibit a classic patterning after similar controls have been imposed (see table 6.16). Among both sexes, respondents in the intermediate living arrangements (home-leavers and cohabitants) are the least likely to choose 'faithfulness' as important for a successful partnership or marriage. The items pertaining to the importance of children, either for the success of marriage or as an element for personal life fulfilment, show striking contrasts, with married persons stressing this need much more than any of the others. The notion that a child suffers if the mother works is strongly held by single persons who still reside with their parents. This item differentiates considerably less between respondents who have left the parental home, irrespective of subsequent living arrangements. The emphasis upon female economic autonomy, finally, exhibits the classic negative association with being married, even after allowing for the fact that fewer married women work.

The main conclusion to be drawn from the statistical controls for socio-economic position is that the original associations between living arrangements and the values considered in this section remain virtually intact. Once more we must conclude that selection and/or affirmation processes are operating independently of socio-economic position, and that this holds for both sexes.

Life satisfaction

In this section we hypothesize that non-conformism and individual autonomy with respect to both partner relations and extra-familial relations are associated with increased levels of frustration, uncertainty about the future, and uneasiness with one's actual situation. As a consequence one can expect individuals in the intermediate living arrangements to exhibit *on average* higher degrees of dissatisfaction with life. Striving for 'quality' in relationships combined with similar aspirations in the direction of self-recognition and self-fulfilment seems an ambitious undertaking. Outcomes may not live up to such expectations.

TABLE 6.16. *Selected items pertaining to family values: likelihood by living arrangements and gender after controlling for socio-economic position; respondents aged 20–29 in Belgium, France, West Germany, and the Netherlands, 1990*

	Men				Women			
	Single, with parents	Single, not with parents	Cohabiting	Married	Single, with parents	Single, not with parents	Cohabiting	Married
Important for success of marriage:								
— faithfulness	1.00	0.41[b]	0.67	1.58	1.00	0.59[a]	0.40[a]	0.76
— children	1.00	0.93	1.03	3.54[b]	1.00	0.53[a]	1.41	2.18[b]
— sharing household chores	1.00	0.89	1.50	1.62	1.00	1.37	1.15	0.99
— same tastes & interests	1.00	0.76	1.49	0.72	1.00	1.22	0.96	1.14
Children needed for life fulfilment	1.00	0.72	1.03	1.64[b]	1.00	0.57[a]	1.00	1.82[a]
Child suffers if mother works	1.00	0.58[a]	0.76	0.71	1.00	0.48[b]	0.25[b]	0.36[b]
Job best way of assuring female independence	1.00	0.84	1.05	0.57[a]	1.00	1.71	0.71	0.59

[a] Significant at 0.05 level.
[b] Significant at 0.01 level.

The results for various indicators of life satisfaction, reported in table 6.17, bear this out, particularly if comparisons are made between cohabitants and married individuals, that is, among all those who have a tangible experience of living with a partner. We shall therefore compare these two groups first.

Cohabitants report more frequently than married persons any sentiments associated with restlessness, remoteness from other people or solitude, depression or boredom. They feel less frequently that things are going their way and more rarely have a feeling of exaltation. They also think slightly more often about death and the meaning of life than married respondents. On the other hand, cohabitants take greater pride in accomplishments, thereby signalling their greater need for personal recognition. In terms of an overall life satisfaction rating on a 10-point scale, cohabitants locate themselves more frequently at the dissatisfied end, and considerably less often at the satisfied end of the scale than married respondents.

Among single persons not living with their parents, one could expect that their life satisfaction or lack thereof is related to a greater sense of loneliness, whereas among those still residing with their parents such feelings should be more connected to frustrations with parental interference. The results indeed show that home-leavers suffer more often from loneliness, and this seems to be translated into a slightly more frequent reporting of boredom and depression, more frequent thinking about the meaning of life and about death, and an overall higher dissatisfaction score. Home-stayers, on the other hand, report slightly more frequently that they are upset because of criticism and their greater lack of freedom is reflected in greater temporary restlessness. Their overall satisfaction with life is *on average* greater than that among home-leavers.

Across the entire battery of items collected in table 6.17, the highest frequencies of items that signal dissatisfaction are located either among single home-leavers or among cohabitants. Married persons, on the contrary, consistently have the highest frequencies for positive evaluation and the lowest frequencies for negative evaluation of life satisfaction.

It seems therefore that life in the two intermediate living arrangements does not, *on average*, produce any greater happiness than that in the two conventional states.

TABLE 6.17. *Individual emotions and life satisfaction; according to living arrangements; respondents aged 20–29 in the Netherlands, Belgium, France, and West Germany, 1990 (per cent)*

	Without partner			With partner			Total (N = 1,385)
	Living with parents (1)	Not living with parents (2)	Difference (2) − (1)	Married (3)	Cohabiting (4)	Difference (4) − (3)	(5)
A. During the past few weeks, did you ever feel . . . (positive answers):[a]							
— so restless that you couldn't sit long in a chair?	48.1	42.3	−5.8	35.0	41.5	+6.5	41.9
— very lonely or remote from other people?	27.8	32.7	+4.9	15.8	27.7	+11.9	25.6
— upset because somebody criticized you?	24.1	22.4	−1.7	23.1	26.5	+3.4	23.9
— depressed or very unhappy?	29.4	32.4	+3.0	21.0	29.2	+8.2	27.7
— bored?	32.5	35.9	+3.4	23.6	33.1	+9.5	31.0
— proud because someone had complimented you on something you have done?	65.2	65.1	−0.1	51.6	61.5	+9.9	60.7
— pleased about having accomplished something?	84.1	86.9	+2.8	77.5	77.3	−0.2	81.5
— that things were going your way?	53.9	57.4	+3.5	62.7	55.8	−6.9	57.5
— on top of the world; feeling that life is wonderful?	51.6	47.1	−4.5	54.9	50.8	−4.1	51.3
B. How often, if at all, do you think about . . . :[b]							
— the meaning and purpose of life?	72.6	76.6	+4.0	74.6	77.4	+2.8	74.9
— death?	44.3	50.3	+6.0	46.2	50.4	+4.2	47.4
C. All things considered, how satisfied are you with your life as a whole these days?:[c]							
— not satisfied (scores 1, 2, 3)	3.3	5.4	+2.1	0.5	6.2	+5.7	3.5
— satisfied (scores 8, 9, 10)	50.5	45.2	−5.3	57.3	44.7	−12.6	50.1

[a] Positive answers (yes or no) to the question 'during the past few weeks, did you ever feel . . .?'.
[b] Answers 'sometimes' and 'often' as opposed to 'rarely', 'never', or 'don't know.'
[c] Scores varied on a 10-point scale from 1 (dissatisfied) to 10 (satisfied).

Controls for socio-economic position are necessary before one may formulate final conclusions with respect to life satisfaction, since the unemployed obviously report the lowest satisfaction. Also, life satisfaction tends to increase with socio-economic status. However, several significant differences associated with living arrangement still emerge after this control, as reported in table 6.18.

First and foremost, married persons, and particularly married women, are considerably less likely than others to score at the low end of the overall satisfaction scale, and less likely to report periods of loneliness, depression, or boredom. But they are also less likely to report that they were proud or pleased because of a compliment or achievement. As stated before, this balance seems to be concordant with a more even and settled life.

Women in the intermediate states (single home-leavers and cohabitants) are the least likely to score at the high end of the overall life satisfaction scale, and conversely, they also are the most likely to report recent spells of loneliness, depression or boredom. Men in the intermediate states are relatively the most likely to score at the low end of the overall life satisfaction scale, but this pattern is much less pronounced in the other items. It is very clear that differences between married men and others are weakened when the items become more specific.

On the whole the conclusions tentatively drawn from the results in table 6.17 still hold after controlling for socio-economic position, as can be inferred from the results in table 6.18.

6.5 A Synthesis

In this section we present a synthesis, by reducing the set of items to a number of underlying dimensions, and subsequently by relating these dimensions to gender, socio-economic position, and living arrangement. Again we shall take the value dimensions as a dependent variable, but the reader should bear in mind that we wish merely to *describe associations* rather than to infer causality.

The underlying value dimensions were constructed by means of two successive rounds of principal component analysis (Varimax, orthogonal rotation of factors). In the first round, thirty items were brought together in eleven scales, and in the second round, these

TABLE 6.18. *Selected life satisfaction indicators: likelihood by living arrangements and gender after controlling for socio-economic position; respondents aged 20–29 in Belgium, France, West Germany, and the Netherlands, 1990*

	Men				Women			
	Single, with parents	Single, not with parents	Cohabiting	Married	Single, with parents	Single, not with parents	Cohabiting	Married
Scores on overall life satisfaction:								
— low (1, 2, 3)	1.00	2.90	4.11[a]	0.07[b]	1.00	1.02	0.97	0.07[b]
— high (8, 9, 10)	1.00	0.91	0.66	0.87	1.00	0.61[a]	0.68	1.25
Often/sometimes think about:								
— meaning, purpose of life	1.00	1.43	1.70[a]	1.48	1.00	1.01	0.91	0.88
— death	1.00	1.93[b]	1.57	1.97[b]	1.00	1.17	1.47	0.92
During past few weks, ever felt:								
— lonely	1.00	0.88	0.84	0.40[b]	1.00	2.48[b]	1.52	0.68
— depressed	1.00	0.63	0.68	0.61	1.00	1.76[a]	1.08	0.47[b]
— bored	1.00	0.90	0.88	0.81	1.00	1.74[a]	1.26	0.37[b]
— proud about compliment	1.00	0.89	0.74	0.57[b]	1.00	0.82	0.64	0.39[b]
— pleased about accomplishment	1.00	1.62	1.29	0.96	1.00	1.06	0.32[b]	0.51[b]
— life wonderful	1.00	0.76	1.37	1.64[a]	1.00	1.10	0.76	1.25

[a] Significant at 0.05 level.
[b] Significant at 0.01 level.

scales were reduced to three distinct factors. The results are presented in table 6.19 in the form of the correlations between the
items and the three factors.

The analysis pertains to 1,245 cases. Cases were deleted from
the list if there were more than five items missing, or when all items
were missing for one of the eleven subscales. Otherwise, the remaining occasional missing values were recoded to the gender-
specific mean values of the items.

Factor 1 in table 6.19 clearly describes the dimension characterized by high religiosity and strict ethical morality. Factor 2 corresponds to right-wing political conviction in the sense of favouring
law and order, and having an aversion for emancipation movements and for sexual minorities. Other items, such as the 'law and
order' items in the Inglehart scales and the items pertaining to
intolerance toward racial minorities also correlate strongly with
factor 2 (but are not shown in table 6.19). Factor 3, finally,
describes conservatism with respect to gender roles.

Several items show significant correlations on more than one of
the three factors. The importance of children, for instance, seems
to be upheld by two types of motivations, that is those stemming
respectively from high religiosity and from political right-wing in-
clinations. Conformism in socialization (such as 'good manners') is
equally associated with both high religiosity and a right-wing orientation, whereas the stress on individual autonomy in education (for
example 'imagination' and 'independence') is negatively related to
these two dimensions. The item concerning the fulfilment of
housewives is related to all three factors, and the importance of
transmitting religious faith in socialization is positively correlated
with both high religiosity and preference for inegalitarian gender
roles.

The analysis proceeds by relating the three dimensions to socio-
economic position and type of living arrangement by means of a
Tukey median polish (Tukey 1977). The analysis is done separately by sex. The median polish starts from the average scores for
a particular dimension recorded for the various cells corresponding
to the combinations of socio-economic position and living arrangement. These means are reported in the appendix (table 6A.2),
together with the standard deviations and sample sizes. Obviously,
these three factors have a mean of zero and a standard deviation of
unity.

TABLE 6.19. *Correlation coefficients between thirty indicators and three factors; respondents aged 20–29 in Belgium, France, West Germany, and the Netherlands, 1990*

	Factor 1	*Factor 2*	*Factor 3*
Scale 1: religiosity			
Has moments of prayer outside church	**0.49**	−0.11	0.24
Believes in God	**0.56**	−0.11	0.19
Believes in sin	**0.32**	−0.04 (ns)	0.07 (ns)
Religious faith important in socialization	**0.43**	−0.10	**0.27**
Scale 2: abortion			
Abortion justified if no children desired	**−0.58**	−0.06 (ns)	−0.17
Abortion justified if woman not married	**−0.57**	−0.13	−0.12
Scale 3: requirements for successful marriage			
Faithfulness between partners	**0.49**	0.13	−0.04 (ns)
Having children	**0.54**	0.19	−0.09
Scale 4: civil morality			
Joyriding never justified	**0.41**	−0.09	−0.16
Taking drugs never justified	**0.53**	0.12	−0.07 (ns)
Tax cheating never justified	**0.46**	−0.06 (ns)	−0.11
Scale 5: values stressed in socialization 1			
Good manners	**0.32**	**0.25**	0.00 (ns)
Independence	**−0.29**	**−0.30**	−0.09
Imagination	**−0.32**	**−0.31**	0.01 (ns)
Scale 6: political and emancipation movements			
Approves of human rights movement	0.11	**−0.51**	−0.12
Approves of anti-apartheid movement	0.15	**−0.55**	−0.05 (ns)
Approves of women's movement	0.05 (ns)	**−0.31**	**−0.27**
Approves of ecology movement	0.13	**−0.39**	−0.14
Scale 7: values stressed in socialization 2			
Respect for others	0.03 (ns)	**−0.40**	0.03 (ns)
Responsibility	0.00 (ns)	**−0.26**	0.04 (ns)
Thrift	0.06 (ns)	**0.53**	−0.07 (ns)
Scale 8: intolerance towards sexual minorities			
No AIDS patients as neighbours	0.08 (ns)	**0.41**	−0.07 (ns)
No homosexuals as neighbours	0.09	**0.50**	−0.02 (ns)
Scale 9: traditional female role			
Women need children for life fulfilment	0.23	**0.37**	0.00 (ns)
Housewife has equal fulfilment	**0.24**	**0.35**	0.21
Scale 10: gender equality			
Sharing same tastes & interests important for marriage	0.06 (ns)	−0.05 (ns)	**−0.50**
Approves of complete sexual freedom	−0.17	−0.09	**−0.47**
Sharing household chores important for marriage	0.03 (ns)	−0.14	**−0.54**
Scale 11: female labour-force participation			
Both partners should work	0.01	0.05 (ns)	**−0.55**
Female work needed for independence	−0.06 (ns)	0.01 (ns)	**−0.50**

Notes: Missing values are deleted from list.
ns: not significant at 0.05 level.

A number of cells with small sample sizes, and corresponding to rare combinations of socio-economic position and type of living arrangement, have been dropped from the analysis. For instance, the results for married students or for housewives in parental homes are considered as unknown. Volatile means based on few observations are thereby prevented from distorting the picture.

An example of a median polish is also given in the appendix (table 6A.3). The analysis involves the following steps. First, the overall median value is determined and subtracted from the various cells. Then column medians are determined and subtracted from the results of the first step. Next, the same is done with row medians. The fitted values in a simple additive model are then the sum of the overall median and the corresponding row and column medians. The residuals (observed values minus fitted values) are the values left over after the median extractions.

The results are presented graphically in figures 6.1 to 6.6. As has already been indicated, we have fitted an additive model, which assumes that there are no interaction effects between the 'independent variables'. This means that the effects of each of the socio-economic positions are not allowed to vary according to the particular combination with type of living arrangement (and vice versa). Such an additive fit leads to the rectangular representation in the various figures. These grids show the *fitted values* of a particular value dimension (vertical axes) for each of the combinations of socio-economic position and type of living arrangement, assuming additivity of effects. These fitted values are compared to the observed ones in the figures: the residuals are represented in the form of thin vertical lines.

Better fits can occasionally be obtained by allowing for interactions, but throughout the analysis, the larger residuals are equally associated with the cells having the smaller number of observations. Hence, we refrained from fitting particularities, and preferred to report the deviations from the simple additive model.

The reader should note that the scales on the vertical axes are identical for all six figures.

Religiosity and ethical strictness

Figures 6.1 and 6.2 depict the relationship between the dimension of 'high religiosity and strict morality' and the two 'independent

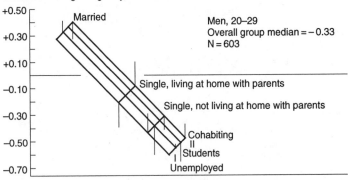

Fig. 6.1. *Scores on religiosity and strict ethics by living arrangements and social position; men aged 20–29 in West Germany, France, Belgium, and the Netherlands, 1990*

Notes: I = employer, managerial, professional, middle white collar.

 II = lower white collar, blue collar.

Source: Median polish fitted values and residuals from the data in Table 6A.2.

variables' for men and women respectively. For men, differences by socio-economic position are very small, with somewhat higher religiosity levels found among junior white collar and blue collar workers, and slightly lower religiosity exhibited by the unemployed. By contrast, the differences in religiosity and ethical strictness by type of living arrangement are very considerable, with married men having much higher values on this dimension than single home-leavers (and cohabiting men in particular). The effects of type of living arrangement among women are of a similar magnitude to those recorded for men, but the effect of socio-economic position is much more pronounced for female respondents. This is partially due to the category of housewives, who have higher scores on religiosity and ethical strictness than employed women. At this point, it is worth mentioning that we were unable to link male socio-economic positions to the position of their partners (employed or not). We would expect that men with partners who are housewives would score higher on dimension 1 than those with employed partners. Most regrettably, the EVS 1990 data do not record employment status of partners.

The residuals are worthy of further comment. First, there are large residuals for female cohabiting students, and similar but

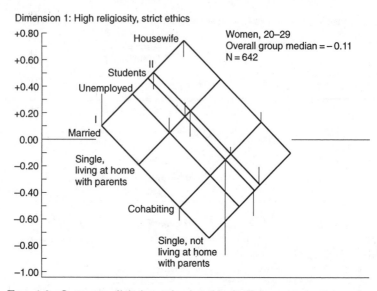

Fɪɢ. 6.2. *Scores on religiosity and strict ethics by living arrangements and social position; women aged 20–29 in West Germany, France, Belgium, and the Netherlands, 1990*

Notes: I = employer, managerial, professional, middle white collar.
 II = lower white collar, blue collar.
Source: Median polish fitted values and residuals from the data in Table 6A.2.

smaller residuals for male cohabiting students and male student home-leavers. In all three instances, these categories have lower average scores on religiosity and ethical strictness than are predicted by the additive model. Second, similar residuals for men and women are also found for the combination of being married and being a junior white collar or blue collar worker. This category scores higher on dimension 1 than predicted. Conversely, married persons with higher-status employment score slightly lower on dimension 1 than could be inferred from the additive model.

Right-wing political convictions and intolerance

The results for right-wing political convictions and intolerance toward minorities are shown in figures 6.3 and 6.4. For men, differences according to both socio-economic position and type of

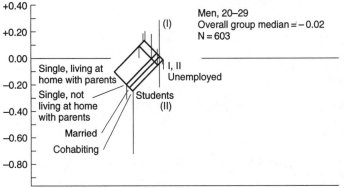

F IG. 6.3. *Scores on political right (law and order, and against minorities) by living arrangements and social position; men aged 20–29 in West Germany, France, Belgium, and the Netherlands, 1990*

Notes: I = employer, managerial, professional, middle white collar.
    II = lower white collar, blue collar.
Source: Median polish fitted values and residuals from the data in Table 6A.2.

living arrangement are small, with only the single home-stayers having slightly higher scores and students having lower scores. The picture for female respondents is very different: both living arrangement and socio-economic position are associated with striking differences for the right-wing political dimension. Married women score *on average* much higher than cohabiting women or female single home-leavers. Unemployed women also show this tendency, in strong contrast to female students. The fact that the average scores for higher-status employed women are lower than those of housewives or lower-status employed women is equally noteworthy. This distinction vanishes, however, for female single home-leavers (see residuals), with higher-status employed women having a slightly higher average score than lower-status employed women.

A second feature of the residuals for both sexes is that the combination of being a student and being either a single home-leaver or a cohabitant leads to average scores on right-wing political orientation that are much lower than are predicted by the additive model. A similar feature was also found for religiosity and moral strictness.

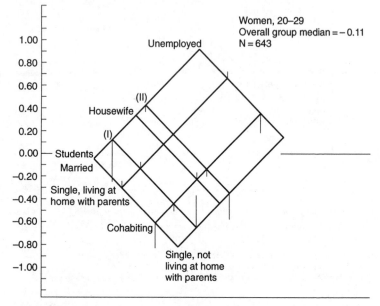

Dimension 2: Political right, law & order, against sexual and ethnic minorities

FIG. 6.4. *Scores on political right (law and order, and against minorities) by living arrangements and social position; women aged 20–29 in West Germany, France, Belgium, and the Netherlands, 1990*

Notes: I = employer, managerial, professional, middle white collar.
     II = lower white collar, blue collar.
Source: Median polish fitted values and residuals from the data in Table 6A.2.

Traditional gender roles

The results for the third dimension, namely, a preference for traditional gender roles, are presented in figures 6.5 and 6.6. For men, the differences according to socio-economic position are again very small, with men employed in junior white collar or blue collar jobs holding *on average* a slightly more conservative position, and those employed in higher social status jobs having a slightly more egalitarian view. The differences according to living arrangement are more pronounced, with averages for married men and cohabiting men being at the more inegalitarian and egalitarian poles respectively. Taking the residuals into account, the differences for married men increase depending on whether they occupy a lower (more inegalitarian than predicted)

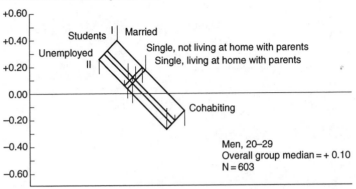

Dimension 3: Traditional gender roles

F IG. 6.5. *Scores on traditional gender roles by living arrangements and social position; men aged 20–29 in West Germany, France, Belgium, and the Netherlands, 1990*

Notes: I = employer, managerial, professional, middle white collar.
II = lower white collar, blue collar.
Source: Median polish fitted values and residuals from the data in Table 6A.2.

or higher (more egalitarian than predicted) socio-economic position. Conversely, the effects of socio-economic position among cohabiting men are the reverse of those implied by the additive model.

The results for female respondents show a somewhat greater contrast depending on employment status: housewives hold on average the most traditional views and employed women or women seeking employment the most egalitarian opinions. The effects of the types of living arrangement distinguish between women with and without a partner. The latter hold on average more egalitarian views. However, there is also a major difference between married and cohabiting women. In this instance, married women have averages indicative of more traditional opinions than cohabitants, as expected.

The most striking feature in figure 6.6 is the existence of considerable residuals. First, cohabiting female students have on average much more egalitarian views than predicted by the model. The same also holds, but to a smaller extent, for cohabiting women employed in blue collar or junior white collar jobs. Second, the differences between married women according to socio-economic

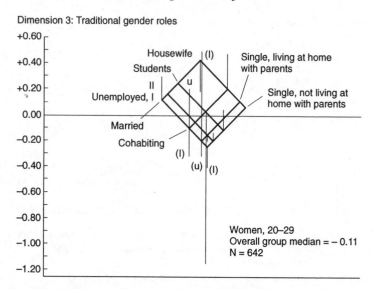

F IG. 6.6. *Scores on traditional gender roles by living arrangements and social position; women aged 20–29 in West Germany, France, Belgium, and the Netherlands, 1990*

Notes: I = employer, managerial, professional, middle white collar.
  II = lower white collar, blue collar.
  u = unemployed.
Source: Median polish fitted values and residuals from the data in Table 6A.2.

position or employment status are smaller than predicted by the additive model, whereas the differences between cohabiting women depending on employment status are larger than predicted. As a result, the few cohabiting women who are housewives (N = 19) are on average more traditional with respect to gender roles than married housewives (N = 110). This interesting interaction may arise from the small sample size of the former category, and needs confirmation by other studies.

Summary

The findings emerging from the preceding analyses can be summarized as follows:
(a) Where there are substantial differences in values among *men*, differences associated with the type of living arrangement are

much more prominent than differences connected with socio-economic position.

(b) The selection and/or subsequent affirmation mechanisms linking values and types of living arrangements for *men* are clearest with respect to the religiosity and ethical dimension and weakest for the right-wing political factor.

(c) The generally weak association with socio-economic position of *men* is subject to a caveat: the employment status of their partners could not be incorporated in the present analysis.

(d) Differences in all three value dimensions by socio-economic position and type of living arrangement are usually much larger for women than for men.

(e) The employment status of *female* respondents not only differentiates with respect to the dimension of traditional gender roles, which is almost a tautological finding, but even more so for both the religiosity or ethical and the political right-wing dimensions.

(f) Housewives score on average highest on the religiosity factor and the traditional gender role factor, but unemployed women score highest on right-wing political convictions and intolerance toward minorities.

(g) *Female* home-leavers and cohabitants are considerably more secular, most averse to right-wing political ideas, and most inclined toward egalitarian gender roles.

(h) These features are enhanced among *women* in these intermediate living arrangements if such states are combined with being a *student*.

(i) Housewives show less variation with respect to the value dimensions depending on living arrangement (married versus cohabiting), but among *working women*, living arrangements are associated with much larger differences in value orientations.

6.6 Conclusions

The main conclusion is that the associations between the various value orientations and the types of living arrangement are either completely or largely resistant to controls for socio-economic position (see also Lesthaeghe and Meekers 1986). This invalidates the common hypothesis made by authors of economic theories which assumes that values and living arrangements are fully co-determined by the economic aspects of the life course.

Second, we have found in this European data-set that single home-leavers and cohabitants resemble each other in terms of the three value dimensions studied. This is completely in line with what Rindfuss and Vanden Heuvel (1990) have reported for the United States. In their study, the gap in value orientations between cohabitants and married persons was also larger than that between cohabitants and single home-leavers.

Third, the present data equally confirm that *parental* religiosity or secularity is a factor involved in the *selections* made by their children. Selection into cohabitation is more likely for persons without a religious upbringing (compare also Liefbroer 1991; Thornton and Camburn 1987). For the other items no such causal conclusions can be drawn and no differences between the selection effect and affirmation effect could be established.

However, American data from the National Longitudinal Study of the High School Class of 1972 show that selection effects are by no means negligible. In this panel study with multiple waves, a dozen questions considered to be of 'life importance' were administered; these touch upon the value of family life, money, success at work, social involvement, activism, and leisure. The analysis recently performed by Clarkberg, Stolzenberg and Waite (1993) indicates that cohabitants were indeed less oriented towards family life to start with, that women stressing careers at the outset also selected themselves disproportionately into cohabitation, but that the same was also true for men with *less* commitment to work and a stronger accentuation of leisure time. Finally, the two 'classic' findings also emerged in the American panel data: namely, that persons with more egalitarian attitudes toward sex roles and with a higher degree of secularization were much more likely to move subsequently into the intermediate cohabitation state.

The opposite influence, that is, that changes in values depend on the stages of the occupational life-cycle, must also play a role. This can be inferred from the fact that the attitudes strongly in favour of more secularism and egalitarian gender roles, and averse to right-wing political ideas, recorded among students living independently in this survey, are no longer necessarily present when the student phase is over. The present data also suggest that these student values are maintained to a higher degree among women if they move into cohabitation and employment. From this cross-section it also appears that socio-economic life-cycle stages play a much smaller part in influencing the value-orientations of men.

Last, important differences in life satisfaction emerged according to living arrangement and controlling for socio-economic position. More stable situations, such as marriage, are more conducive to an increase in life satisfaction. This is probably because individual autonomy and self-fulfilment are less accentuated, thereby facilitating giving and taking within a partnership. More transient states, such as living separately or in cohabitation, are associated with lower self-ratings on the life satisfaction scale and with more frequent feelings of frustration. This seems indicative of a wider gap between aspirations and reality.

APPENDIX

TABLE 6A.1. Sample sizes and percentage distributions by living arrangements in the 1990 EVS data-sets; respondents aged 20–24 and 25–29

	Women, 20–4					Women, 25–9				
	Single, living with parents (%)	Single, not living with parents (%)	Cohabiting (%)	Married or divorced (%)	N	Single, living with parents (%)	Single, not living with parents (%)	Cohabiting (%)	Married or divorced (%)	N
Iceland	22	15	50	13	(40)	5	7	35	53	(43)
Sweden	33	13	36	18	(39)	0	18	21	61	(38)
Denmark	16	45	33	6	(51)	2	18	41	39	(56)
Norway	25	34	31	10	(59)	8	20	27	45	(80)
France	37	20	24	19	(54)	7	10	24	59	(68)
Britain	40	14	24	22	(68)	10	7	15	68	(81)
Netherlands	25	33	23	19	(55)	2	21	14	63	(55)
Belgium	48	7	18	27	(138)	15	6	11	68	(140)
West Germany	46	26	18	10	(104)	10	20	20	50	(99)
Portugal	67	6	7	20	(91)	31	5	0	64	(45)
Ireland	72	15	4	9	(54)	28	14	2	56	(57)
Spain	69	9	3	19	(136)	29	12	3	56	(136)
Italy	78	5	1	16	(100)	44	2	1	50	(108)

	Men, 20–4					Men, 25–9				
	Single, living with parents (%)	Single, not living with parents (%)	Cohabiting (%)	Married or divorced (%)	N	Single, living with parents (%)	Single, not living with parents (%)	Cohabiting (%)	Married or divorced (%)	N
Iceland	45	20	29	6	(51)	14	19	41	26	(57)
Sweden	46	15	32	7	(54)	4	18	42	36	(45)
Denmark	39	34	26	1	(74)	5	32	40	23	(62)
Norway	57	14	21	8	(63)	12	27	29	32	(59)
France	48	25	18	9	(56)	14	30	20	36	(50)
Britain	56	13	16	15	(75)	22	13	12	53	(66)
Netherlands	41	40	12	7	(57)	14	33	20	33	(61)
Belgium	61	15	11	13	(145)	37	13	12	38	(175)
West Germany	68	19	7	6	(115)	14	25	23	38	(103)
Portugal	79	9	0	12	(125)	32	8	1	59	(60)
Ireland	82	16	2	0	(61)	57	8	0	35	(37)
Spain	83	8	3	6	(138)	45	15	2	38	(143)
Italy	90	4	1	5	(104)	64	6	3	27	(112)

Note: All percentages are rounded.
Source: European Values Survey. Kindly made available by L. Halman, Instituut voor Sociaal-wetenschappelijk Onderzoek, Katholieke Universiteit Brabant, Tilburg.

TABLE 6A.2. *Value dimensions: means, standard deviations, and sample sizes by sub-group and sex*

Sub-group			Dimension 1		Dimension 2		Dimension 3		N
			Mean	Std. Dev.	Mean	Std. Dev.	Mean	Std. Dev.	
(a) male									
11	Single, at home with parents	Junior white collar, blue collar	−0.14	0.97	0.02	0.99	−0.07	1.00	603
12		Employer, managerial, senior and middle white collar	0.11	0.86	0.21	0.94	0.03	1.01	101
14		Student	−0.18	0.77	0.20	0.87	−0.37	0.91	17
15		Unemployed	−0.12	0.86	−0.09	0.98	−0.20	1.08	87
21	Single, not at home with parents	Junior white collar, blue collar	−0.39	0.67	−0.03	0.88	0.08	1.00	11
22		Employer, managerial, senior and middle white collar	−0.38	0.99	−0.08	1.19	−0.10	0.95	74
24		Student	−0.61	0.77	0.09	0.87	−0.11	0.90	39
25		Unemployed	−0.33	1.28	−0.30	1.02	−0.06	0.66	31
31	Married	Junior white collar, blue collar	−0.27	0.97	0.19	0.64	−0.22	0.90	13
32		Employer, managerial, senior and middle white collar	0.27	0.91	0.31	1.09	−0.14	1.06	94
34		Student	0.43	1.00	−0.37	0.69	−0.47	0.97	26
35		Unemployed	0.17	0.28	0.57	0.09	0.81	0.12	3
41	Cohabiting	Junior white collar, blue collar	0.41	0.66	−0.67	1.04	−0.10	0.78	4
42		Employer, managerial, senior and middle white collar	−0.36	1.02	−0.06	0.91	0.14	1.15	63
44		Student	−0.52	0.53	−0.02	0.91	0.28	0.78	21
45		Unemployed	−0.65	0.92	−0.71	0.66	0.22	1.03	15
			1.57	1.26	0.13	0.78	0.01	0.88	6

(b) Female									
11	Single, at home with parents	Junior white collar, blue collar	0.08	0.99	-0.06	1.00	0.05	0.99	642
12		Employer, managerial, senior and middle white collar	0.03	1.03	0.14	1.09	0.21	0.96	83
13		Housewife	-0.13	0.82	-0.14	0.36	-0.49	1.29	7
14		Student	0.41	0.00	0.30	0.00	1.51	0.00	1
15		Unemployed	0.26	0.95	-0.29	0.80	0.09	1.00	50
21	Single, not at home with parents	Junior white collar, blue collar	0.15	0.63	0.68	1.20	0.31	1.04	13
22		Employer, managerial, senior and middle white collar	-0.21	1.03	-0.58	0.75	0.13	0.95	64
23		Housewife	-0.75	1.14	-0.38	0.61	0.41	1.04	23
24		Student	-0.63	1.30	-0.98	0.84	-0.09	1.36	2
25		Unemployed	-0.42	0.89	-0.83	0.71	-0.04	0.95	28
31	Married	Junior white collar, blue collar	-0.58	1.26	0.11	1.42	0.25	0.56	11
32		Employer, managerial, senior and middle white collar	0.39	0.73	0.37	1.00	0.20	1.06	76
33		Housewife	0.35	0.95	-0.26	0.71	-0.30	0.78	30
34		Student	0.63	0.83	0.32	0.95	-0.19	0.99	110
35		Unemployed	0.97	0.00	-0.28	0.00	-0.57	0.00	1
41	Cohabiting	Junior white collar, blue collar	0.48	0.63	-0.13	1.01	-0.37	0.76	5
42		Employer, managerial, senior and middle white collar	-0.09	0.97	-0.07	0.99	0.04	0.97	75
43		Housewife	-0.60	0.80	-0.48	1.06	0.29	1.07	26
44		Student	0.20	0.64	-0.21	1.04	-0.47	0.55	19
45		Unemployed	-0.88	0.72	-0.83	0.49	1.15	0.94	9
			-0.29	1.13	0.18	1.05	-0.20	0.91	10

TABLE 6A.3. *Example of a median polish: the effects of socio-economic position and type of living arrangement on the dimension of 'high religiosity and strict morality' for male respondents aged 20–29 in Belgium, France, West Germany, and the Netherlands, 1990*

(a) *Observed mean values*

	Single, living with parents	Single, not living with parents	Cohabiting	Married
I	−0.18	−0.61	−0.52	+0.43
II	+0.11	−0.38	−0.36	+0.27
Student	−0.12	−0.33	−0.65	★
Unemployed	−0.39	−0.27	★	★

Overall median = −0.33.

(b) *Extraction overall median*

	Single, living with parents	Single, not living with parents	Cohabiting	Married
I	0.15	−0.28	−0.19	+0.76
II	+0.44	−0.05	−0.03	+0.60
Student	+0.21	0.00	−0.32	★
Unemployed	−0.06	+0.06	★	★

(c) *Extraction column medians*

	Single, living with parents	Single, not living with parents	Cohabiting	Married
I	−0.03	−0.25	0.00	+0.08
II	+0.26	−0.02	+0.16	−0.08
Student	+0.03	+0.03	−0.13	★
Unemployed	−0.24	+0.09	★	★
Col. median	+0.18	−0.03	−0.19	+0.68

(*d*) *Extraction row medians*

	Single, living with parents	Single, not living with parents	Cohabiting	Married		Row medians
I	−0.01	−0.23	+0.02	+0.10	:	−0.02
II	+0.19	−0.09	+0.09	−0.15	:	+0.07
Student	+0.00	0.00	−0.16	★	:	+0.03
Unemployed	−0.16	+0.17	★	★	:	−0.08

(*e*) *Fitted values (Overall median + Col. median + Row median)*

	Single, living with parents	Single, not living with parents	Cohabiting	Married		Row medians
I	−0.17	−0.38	−0.54	+0.33	:	−0.02
II	−0.08	−0.29	−0.45	+0.42	:	+0.07
Student	−0.12	−0.33	−0.49	★	:	+0.03
Unemployed	−0.23	−0.44	★	★	:	−0.08
Overall median	+0.18	−0.03	−0.19	+0.68		−0.33

Notes: I = Employer, managerial, senior and middle white collar.
II = Junior white collar and blue collar.
★ = Value omitted from analysis.

NOTE

The authors would like to thank the organizers of the European Values Survey for making available the various data sets, and Loek Halman in particular for the first exploratory tabulations.

REFERENCES

AXINN, W., and THORNTON, A. (1992), 'The relationship between cohabitation and divorce: selectivity or causal influence?', *Demography*, 29(3): 357–74.

BECKER, G. (1981), A Treatise on the Family, Cambridge, Mass.: Harvard University Press.

BUMPASS, L. (1990), 'What's happening to the family? Interactions between demographic and institutional changes', *Demography*, 27(4): 483–98.

CLARKBERG, M., STOLZENBERG, R., and WAITE, L. (1993), 'Values and Cohabitation', paper presented at the Annual meetings of the Population Association of America, Cincinnati, April 1993.

DUMON, W. (1977), *Het Gezin in Vlaanderen*, Louvain: Davidsfonds.

EASTERLIN, R., MACDONALD, C., and MACUNOVICH, D. J. (1990), 'How have American baby boomers fared? Earnings and economic well-being of young adults, 1964–1987', *Journal of Population Economics*, 3(4): 277–90.

ENGLAND, P., and FARKAS, G. (1986), *Households, Employment and Gender—A Social, Economic and Demographic View*, New York: Aldine De Gruyter.

HARDING, S., PHILLIPS, D., and FOGARTY, M. (1986), *Contrasting values in Western Europe*, London: Macmillan.

INGLEHART, R. (1970), *The Silent Revolution*, Princeton, NJ: Princeton University Press.

—— (1990), *Culture Shift in Advanced Industrial Society*, Princeton, NJ: Princeton University Press.

KHOO, S. (1987), 'Living together: young couples in de facto relationships', *Australian Institute for Family Studies Working Paper* No. 10, Canberra: Australian National University.

KIERNAN, K. (1992), The impact of family disruption in childhood on transitions made in young adult life', *Population Studies*, 46: 213–34.

LEE, H. Y., RAJULTON, F., and LESTHAEGHE, R. (1987), 'Gezinsvorming in Vlaanderen—Nieuwe vormen, andere timing', *Tijdschrift voor Sociologie*, 8: 35–68.

LESTHAEGHE, R., and MEEKERS, D. (1986), 'Value changes and the dimensions of familism in the European Community', *European Journal of Population*, 2: 225–68.

—— and MOORS, G. (1992), 'De gezinsrelaties—Ontwikkeling en stabilisatie van patronen', in J. Kerkhofs *et al.* (eds.), *De Versnelde Ommekeer*, Tielt: Lannoo: 19–68.

—— and SURKYN, J. (1988), 'Cultural dynamics and economic theories of fertility change', *Population and Development Review*, 14(1): 1–45.

—— and VAN DE·KAA, D. (1986), 'Twee demografische transities?', in R. Lesthaeghe and D. van de Kaa (eds.), *Groei of Krimp?*, Deventer: Van Loghum-Slaterus.

LIEFBROER, A. C. (1991), *Kiezen Tussen Ongehuwd Samenwonen en Trouwen*, Ph.D. dissertation, Vrije University, Amsterdam.

MASLOW, A. (1954), *Motivations and Personality*, New York: Harper & Row.

OPPENHEIMER, V. (1988), 'A theory of marriage timing', *American Journal of Sociology*, 94: 563–91.

RAO, V. K. (1989), 'What is happening to cohabitation in Canada?', Paper presented at the meetings of the Population Association of America, Baltimore, manuscript.

REZSOHAZY, R. (1991), *Les Nouveaux Enfants d'Adam et Eve—Les Formes Actuelles des Couples et des Familles*, Louvain-la-Neuve: Academia.

RINDFUSS, R., and VANDEN HEUVEL, A. (1990), 'Cohabitation: precursor to marriage or alternative to being single?', *Population and Development Review* 16(4): 703–26.

SWEET, J., and BUMPASS, L. (1990), 'Religious differentials in marriage behavior and attitudes', *NSFH Working Paper* No. 15, Center for Demography and Ecology, University of Wisconsin, Madison.

TANFER, K. (1987), 'Patterns of premarital cohabitation among never-married women in the United States', *Journal of Marriage and the Family*, 49: 483–97.

THORNTON, A. (1991), 'Influence of the marital history of parents on the marital and cohabitational experience of children', *American Journal of Sociology* 96(4): 868–94.

—— and CAMBURN, D. (1987), 'Religious commitment and adolescent sexual behavior and attitudes', Institute for Social Research, University of Michigan, manuscript.

TUKEY, J. (1977), *Exploratory Data Analysis*, Reading, Mass.: Addison-Wesley Publishing Co.

VAN RYSSELT, R. (1989), 'Developments in attitudes and value orientations—A comparison between birth cohorts in the Netherlands over the period 1970–85', Paper presented to Symposium on Life Histories and Generations, Netherlands Institute for Advanced Studies, Wassenaar, 22–23 June 1989.

VILLENEUVE-GOKALP, C. (1990), 'Du marriage aux unions sans papiers—Histoire récente des transformations conjugales', *Population*, 45(2): 265–98.

7

Projections of European Population Decline: Serious Demography or False Alarm?

HEATHER JOSHI

No discussion of the trends in the demography of contemporary Europe would be complete without a look into the future, to see where contemporary change appears to be heading. Sub-replacement fertility suggests that Europe's population should be on the decline, though it is still, slowly, growing. The purpose of this chapter is to review some demographic projections of the foreseeable future. It is not to contemplate the social, political, or economic consequences of any population decline. Its purpose is to discuss whether the prospect of decline is likely, not whether it would be alarming if it occurred. It has been argued elsewhere that falling numbers of Europeans might not necessarily be a disaster (Ermisch and Joshi 1987).

Our look into the future is based upon projections made by two international organizations, drawing on data provided by member countries. Population projections, like any other sort of projection, are not forecasts, they are conditional statements of what might be expected if certain assumptions hold. Projections approach being forecasts or predictions when based upon true or most likely assumptions (Pressat 1985). Both sets of projections, by the United Nations and the Statistical Office of the European Communities (Eurostat), make a range of assumptions about fertility, mortality, and migration, and these are coupled with knowledge of the existing size and structure of the population being projected. In other words, our projections have been constructed by the component method (Keilman 1990, Keilman 1991, Keilman and Cruijsen 1992, Land 1986). Such methods also 'walk under the safe future umbrella' of the assumption of no wars or environmental disasters (Cruijsen 1991).

Two definitions of Europe are employed. The wider definition is used by the United Nations (UN). Pan-Europe covers the territory west of the USSR and Turkey. At the time these projections were made, it numbered some twenty-seven countries, a number which has since grown as noted in the introduction to this book. These range, geographically, from Finland and Iceland to Albania and Portugal; in size, from the Federal Republic of Germany (61 million in 1985, before the addition of the new *Länder* then classified in Eastern rather than Western Europe) to the Holy See (population 1,000, total fertility rate, zero). The Europe of the European Community (EC) projections is confined to the twelve member countries making up the EC in 1991.

This chapter looks first at the UN's total population projections for the broadly defined Europe, and the breakdown of these into broad regions. We then turn to the sub-regions covered by the EC and Eurostat's *Two Long-term Population Scenarios* to the year 2020 (Eurostat 1991a). After comparing the two agencies' projections for the same area, we focus further on the EC countries. We review some features of the aggregate projection, in particular, share in world population and age structure. Finally we look at individual countries within the EC, and at the differences among them in terms of the assumptions used in the projections.

7.1 European Population Prospects in Global Perspective

The population future of Europe should be viewed in the perspective of the human race as a whole. The UN's projections for the world population are plotted in figure 7.1 and shown in table 7.1 along with the projections for the population of Europe, broadly defined (United Nations 1991). From a total of 5.3 billion in 1990, the world's population is expected to continue growing. On the 'medium variant' (a central assumption about the future course of fertility) the projection brings the total population of the world up to 8.5 billion by 2025, the end of the period for which these projections are published. The higher fertility scenario, assuming a less rapid fertility decline, would result in perceptibly more people

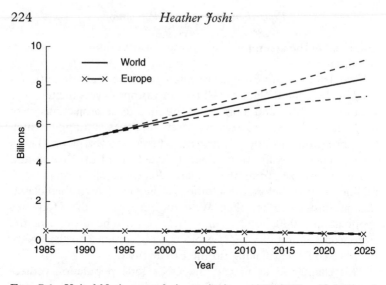

FIG. 7.1. *United Nations population projections, 1985–2025, with high and low fertility variants*
Source: United Nations 1991.

TABLE 7.1. *Population of the world and of Europe, 1985–2025, according to UN projections ('000s)*

Variant	World			Europe		
	Medium	High	Low	Medium	High	Low
1985	4,851,433			492,208		
1990	5,292,195	5,327,388	5,262,013	498,371	499,158	497,369
1995	5,770,286	5,857,008	5,682,499	504,247	507,186	501,169
2000	6,260,800	6,419,673	6,093,224	510,015	516,168	503,822
2005	6,739,230	6,986,014	6,469,169	513,745	523,900	503,458
2010	7,204,343	7,653,541	6,812,985	515,734	530,444	500,602
2015	7,659,858	8,168,517	7,119,697	516,568	536,643	495,829
2020	8,091,628	8,802,293	7,375,582	516,401	543,156	489,319
2025	8,504,223	9,444,224	7,590,613	515,212	549,760	481,187

Source: United Nations 1991.

by 2025, 9.4 billion; and the low variant, with a faster decline in fertility, yields 7.6 billion.

On the scale of figure 7.1, population change in Europe, and variants around its projections, are barely perceptible during this period. The global perspective on Europe's numbers is that they are stagnating, rather than dropping dramatically. Before taking a closer look at the projections up to 2025, we should note that longer-term projections have been made. Further away in time there is more scope for numbers to start falling, though not dramatically even then, on central assumptions. Both the World Bank and the medium variant of the UN's long-range projections have Europe's total population (as then defined) dropping very gently from 0.50 billion in 2000 to 0.49 billion in 2050. Both projections show the gentle decline continuing to 2100, to 0.44 billion in the case of the UN, or to 0.47 billion in the case of the World Bank (United Nations 1992, Bulatao *et al.* 1990, as cited by McNicoll 1992). Of the nine scenarios experimented with in a study by the International Institute for Applied Systems Analysis (IIASA), only one showed substantial population decline, during the second quarter of the twenty-first century (Lutz *et al.* 1991). If the total fertility rate (TFR) of Europe dropped to 1.1 by 2025 and stayed there till 2050, the total population of 'Europe' (including here the USSR) would be 76 per cent of its 1990 level in 2050. By 2020, this scenario puts the total population at more or less the same level as 1990, though decline would be under way outside Eastern Europe, with the population of the remainder of Europe in 2020 set at 96 per cent of the 1990 level. The majority of IIASA's nine scenarios envisage continued population growth in mid-century.

Figure 7.2 focuses the global microscope on the projections for Europe. On this scale, the prospect of population decline becomes perceptible. On the low fertility variant projection, decline starts in the first decade of the twenty-first century, and on the medium variant it starts in the third decade. On the low fertility projection, Europe's population total falls below its current level (492 million in 1985) to 481 million in 2025. On the medium variant the 2025 total would be above that of 1985, 515 million, while on the positive growth path of the high variant it would be, at 550 million, well above the 1985 level.

7.2 Variants on the UN Projections

The only factor which changes between the UN's variants is the trajectory assumed for fertility. Mortality projections change over

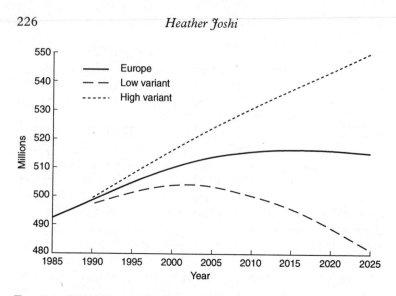

FIG. 7.2. *United Nations European population projections, 1985–2025, with high and low fertility variants*
Source: United Nations 1991.

time, but not across variants. Migration is another matter. On the global level, there is, of course, no coming and going from the outside world. The UN projections avoid the formidable technical and political problems of making assumptions about movements across national boundaries by assuming that no net movement takes place after the year 2000. The only mortality projection made by the UN is one of continued gradual improvements in life expectancy at birth (for Europe as a whole: from 71 years to 76 years for males, from 78 to 82 for females, and from 74 to 79 for both sexes combined).

The medium fertility variant sets total fertility per woman for Pan-Europe at 1.72 over the period 1985–90 and allows for it to remain more or less at this level, rising slightly to 1.85 in 2020–25 (figure 7.3 and table 7.2). The high variant is based on a slightly higher estimate of 1.76 for the period 1985–90, for which not all data were complete, rising steadily to exceed 'replacement' by 2010, reaching 2.16 in 2015–20 and levelling at 2.17 for the last quinquennium of the projection period. The low fertility variant starts with a lower estimate for 1985–90 (1.67), falling further (by less than 1 per cent of a child per year) to reach a 'floor' of 1.52 in

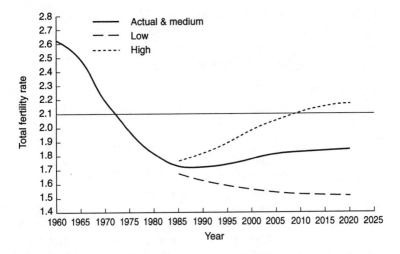

F IG. 7.3. *Total fertility rates, 1960–2025, pan-European projections by the United Nations*

Source: United Nations 1991.

T ABLE 7.2. *Total fertility rate (children per woman), Europe, 1960–2025, actual and projected*

| | Variant | | |
	Medium	High	Low
1960–5	2.63		
1965–	2.50		
1970–	2.19		
1975–	1.98		
1980–	1.81		
1985–	1.72	1.76	1.67
1990–	1.72	1.82	1.62
1995–	1.74	1.90	1.59
2000–	1.78	1.99	1.56
2005–	1.81	2.05	1.54
2010–	1.83	2.11	1.53
2015–	1.84	2.16	1.52
2020–5	1.85	2.17	1.52

Source: United Nations 1991.

2015–20 and 2020–25. This lower limit is still well above levels which have been observed, so far for shorter periods, by some individual countries, and is well above the floor of 1.1 set as a limiting case by IIASA (Lutz *et al.* 1991).

7.3 Regions of the UN's Europe

The breakdown of the UN's projected population into the four broad regions it uses is shown in figure 7.4, and table 7.3. In this instance, as the projections were made before the reunification of Germany, 'Eastern Europe' includes Bulgaria, Czechoslovakia, Hungary, Poland, Romania, and the former German Democratic Republic. Northern Europe includes six Nordic countries and four in the British Isles. Western Europe comprises Austria, Belgium, France, the former Federal Republic of Germany, Liechtenstein, Luxemburg, Monaco, the Netherlands, and Switzerland. The major countries in the Southern region are Italy, Spain, the former Yugoslavia, Portugal, and Greece, along with Albania, Andorra, Malta, San Marino, Gibraltar, and the Vatican. The comparison between this and the current classification is given in table 1.1.

Prospects of decline are stronger, particularly on the low fertility variant, in the Southern and Western regions. All show a similar upward trajectory on the high fertility scenario. On the medium variant, prospects of change in the population total are very modest. Figure 7.5 shows that all regions maintain their relative positions over the projection period, the Western region remaining slightly more populous than the Southern, each well 'ahead' of the smallest, the Northern region, with Eastern Europe in an intermediate position slightly 'gaining ground'.

It was assumed that Eastern Europe would continue showing somewhat higher levels of both mortality and fertility. There is now, however, evidence of falling fertility levels. By 1992, Bulgaria's TFR was down to 1.43, Romania's to 1.51, and Slovenia's to 1.34; Hungary's remains at 1.77 and those of the Czech Republic, Slovakia, and Poland between 1.9 and 2.0 (Council of Europe 1994). For the rest of this chapter we focus on the more narrowly defined set of countries which belong to the EC. These include all the larger countries outside the UN's Eastern region, along with the former East Germany.

TABLE 7.3. *Population of Europe by region, 1985–2025 ('000s), actual and projected*

Variant	1985	1990	1995	2000	2005	2010	2015	2020	2025
Eastern Europe									
Actual/Medium	111,681	113,174	114,820	116,713	118,491	120,018	121,237	122,161	122,904
High		113,424	115,639	118,348	121,179	123,874	126,463	129,030	131,664
Low		112,680	113,970	115,092	115,848	116,182	116,060	115,497	114,578
Northern Europe									
Actual/Medium	83,180	84,233	85,251	86,132	86,724	87,219	87,724	88,144	88,299
High		84,330	85,627	86,992	88,156	89,279	90,575	92,016	93,341
Low		84,111	84,851	85,255	85,215	84,920	84,478	83,764	82,682
Southern Europe									
Actual/Medium	142,362	144,087	145,956	147,811	148,963	149,309	149,073	148,533	147,755
High		144,374	146,797	149,448	151,614	153,200	154,420	155,718	157,083
Low		143,775	145,149	146,245	146,423	145,567	143,893	141,750	139,223
Western Europe									
Actual/Medium	154,985	156,877	158,220	159,359	159,567	159,188	158,534	157,563	156,254
High		157,030	159,123	161,380	162,951	164,091	165,185	166,392	167,672
Low		156,623	157,199	157,230	155,972	153,933	151,398	148,308	144,704

Source: United Nations 1991.

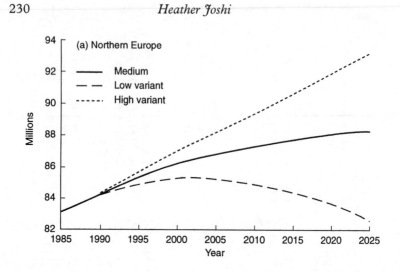

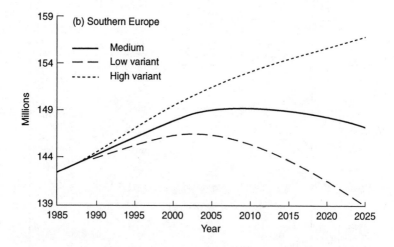

Note: The boundaries of the region are those of the 'old' Europe (see Table P.1).

FIG. 7.4. *Population of Europe by region, United Nations projections, 1985–2025*

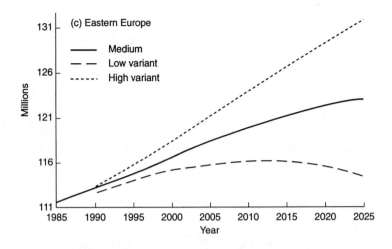

Note: This projection was constructed before the radical reductions
of fertility in many Eastern European countries in the 1990s and it therefore overstates
likely population growth. It is included here as a matter of historical interest.

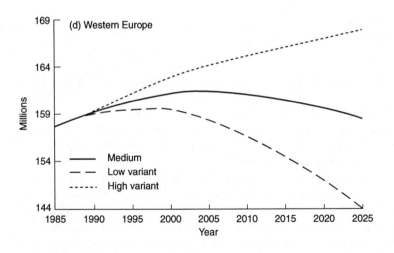

Note: The boundaries of the region are those of the 'old' Europe (see Table P.1).

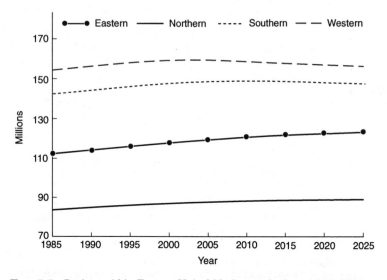

FIG. 7.5. *Regions within Europe: United Nations projections, 1985–2025, medium variant*

Note: The regional boundaries are those of the 'old' Europe (see Table P.1). The Eastern European projections are based on the higher pre-1989 fertility rates.
Source: United Nations 1991.

7.4 The European Community

The United Nations projections for the twelve member states of the EC are plotted in figure 7.6 and reported in table 7.4. The general shape is much the same as for the wider Europe (figure 7.2) or Western Europe (figure 7.3), but around the different level of 0.34 billion as non-EC countries are excluded. The population scenarios envisaged by Eurostat for the same countries up to 2020 are shown in figure 7.7 (Eurostat 1991a). In these there is no central projection, just an upper bound and a lower bound of reasonably plausible scenarios. The shape of the envelope of possibilities is reasonably similar to the UN's. The population trajectories for Europe range somewhere between sustained growth and a mild decline setting in some time after the year 2000. A closer comparison of the two sources is offered by figure 7.8 and table 7.4. The Eurostat projections on the upper bound diverge markedly above those of the UN's high fertility variant, to end with a

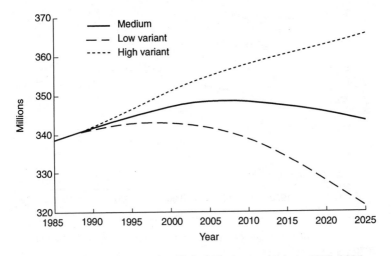

FIG. 7.6. *European Community: United Nations projections, 1985–2025*
Source: United Nations 1991.

TABLE 7.4. *Aggregate projections for the twelve member states of the EC, 1985–2025 ('000s)*

	Eurostat high	UN high	Eurostat low	UN low
1985	338,000	338,673	338,000	338,673
1990	344,000	342,015	344,000	341,030
1995	353,000	346,470	349,000	342,712
2000	363,000	351,377	351,000	343,054
2005	373,000	355,017	351,000	341,971
2010	382,000	355,742	349,000	338,623
2015	390,000	360,205	345,000	339,360
2020	397,000	362,863	339,000	328,060
2025		365,551		321,150

Source: United Nations 1991, Eurostat 1991.

population total of 0.40 billion in 2020 compared to the UN's 0.36 billion in that year. Eurostat's lower bound starts off closer to the UN's medium variant than to its low one though, once decline sets in, the rate of change is about the same in both low projections. The 'low' scenario of Eurostat ends up with 0.34 billion for the EC

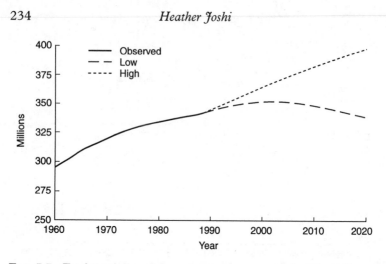

FIG. 7.7. *Total population of the twelve member states of the EC, 1960–2020 (projections)*

Note: EC population here does not include the former East Germany.
Source: Eurostat 1991a.

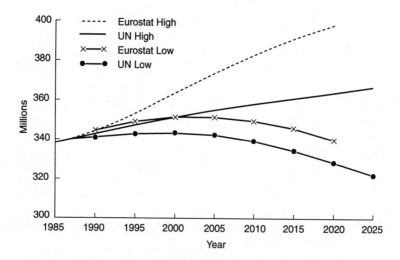

FIG. 7.8. *A comparison of the United Nations and Eurostat projections of the population of the twelve member states of the EC, 1985–2025*

Note: These projections do not include the former East Germany in the EC.
Sources: Eurostat 1991a, United Nations 1991.

countries in 2020 compared to 0.33 billion in the UN's low fertility variant.

These discrepancies have arisen, although both sets of projections use a similar methodology, because they have gone about setting alternative assumptions in rather different ways. Eurostat's variants are not confined simply to fertility, though they present a detailed discussion of the pattern and timing of family formation and its determinants.

7.5 Eurostat's Alternative Scenarios

In Eurostat's low long-term scenario fertility stays around current levels, averaging 1.5 births per woman over her lifetime. In terms of period rates, projected and actual rates are a little above this at the beginning of the 1990s (see table 7.5). The 1.5 cohort fertility results from assuming that 25 per cent of all women remain childless, and that those who do become mothers have an average of 2.0 children. This is described as a likely outcome given European women's improved education and increasing aspirations for a rewarding role in the paid economy, so long as there are no institutional changes which make it easier for women to combine reproduction and production. The 'optimistic' scenario (in the words of Cruijsen, if 'everything goes fine'—Cruijsen 1991:21) would require governments and employers to introduce 'family-friendly' policies, such as support with 'highly individualized childcare', flexible employment practices for male and female partners, and so on, as described in Chapter 9. It is the emergence of such policies, rather than any reversal of existing social trends, that is presented as the condition for a revival of reproduction in the EC. The level of fertility on the upper limit is projected to rise gradually to 2.0 births per woman (10 per cent childlessness, about 2.2 children per mother) (Cruijsen 1991). The range of Eurostat's fertility variants is fractionally smaller than the UN's, but they allow for other sources of growth.

Improvements in mortality are another source of population growth, in each of the projections, but Eurostat allows for possible variation (table 7.6 and figure 7.9). Eurostat's low long-term scenario is pessimistic about any further extension of life expectancy. It assumes that mortality rates might cease to fall after 2000, because

TABLE 7.5. *Total fertility, actual and projected, in the twelve member states of the EC, 1960–2019*

	Total	Belgium	Denmark	Germany	Greece	Spain	France	Ireland	Italy	Luxemburg	Netherlands	Portugal	United Kingdom
Observed													
1960	2.63	2.58	2.54	2.37	2.28	2.86	2.73	3.70	2.41	2.28	3.12	3.01	2.68
1965	2.77	2.61	2.61	2.50	2.30	2.94	2.83	4.03	2.67	2.38	3.04	3.08	2.68
1970	2.45	2.20	1.95	2.03	2.34	2.84	2.48	3.87	2.43	1.97	2.57	2.76	2.44
1975	2.07	1.74	1.92	1.48	2.37	2.79	1.93	3.40	2.21	1.53	1.66	2.52	1.81
1980	1.87	1.67	1.55	1.56	2.23	2.22	1.95	3.23	1.69	1.50	1.60	2.19	1.89
1985	1.62	1.51	1.45	1.37	1.68	1.63	1.82	2.50	1.41	1.38	1.51	1.70	1.80
Projected: Low													
1990	1.54	1.61	1.66	1.45	1.43	1.36	1.79	2.16	1.29	1.59	1.61	1.41	1.78
1995	1.51	1.56	1.63	1.37	1.42	1.32	1.78	1.94	1.34	1.52	1.61	1.36	1.75
2000	1.47	1.53	1.60	1.31	1.45	1.29	1.76	1.81	1.33	1.48	1.6	1.34	1.70
2005	1.47	1.51	1.58	1.29	1.48	1.33	1.73	1.73	1.31	1.45	1.58	1.38	1.66
2010	1.48	1.50	1.55	1.29	1.52	1.37	1.71	1.70	1.30	1.43	1.56	1.44	1.66
2015	1.49	1.50	1.52	1.30	1.56	1.39	1.71	1.70	1.30	1.41	1.52	1.49	1.67
2019	1.50	1.50	1.50	1.30	1.58	1.40	1.70	1.70	1.30	1.40	1.50	1.51	1.69
Projected: High													
1990	1.58	1.63	1.68	1.47	1.48	1.42	1.81	2.21	1.34	1.63	1.63	1.46	1.83
1995	1.72	1.75	1.82	1.59	1.65	1.56	1.99	2.22	1.57	1.73	1.80	1.58	1.96
2000	1.81	1.85	1.91	1.65	1.81	1.64	2.08	2.19	1.68	1.80	1.90	1.67	2.02
2005	1.88	1.92	1.94	1.70	1.93	1.73	2.12	2.17	1.74	1.84	1.95	1.78	2.07
2010	1.94	1.97	1.97	1.76	2.02	1.81	2.15	2.17	1.77	1.87	1.97	1.89	2.12
2015	1.97	1.99	1.98	1.79	2.07	1.87	2.18	2.19	1.79	1.89	1.98	1.98	2.16
2019	2.00	2.00	2.00	1.80	2.09	1.89	2.20	2.19	1.80	1.90	2.00	2.00	2.19

Source: Eurostat 1991a.

TABLE 7.6. *Life expectancy of males and females (years) in the twelve member states of the EC, 1960–2019*

	Total[a]		Belgium		Denmark		Germany		Greece		Spain		France	
	M	F	M	F	M	F	M	F	M	F	M	F	M	F
Observed														
1960–4	67.8	73.0	67.3	73.3	70.4	74.5	67.2	72.6	70.1	73.6	68.0	72.7	67.7	74.6
1965–9	68.3	73.9	67.6	73.9	70.5	75.3	67.8	73.4	70.6	74.5	69.1	74.3	68.1	75.6
1970–4	69.0	75.0	68.2	74.7	70.9	76.4	68.2	74.1	72.0	76.3	70.2	75.7	69.2	77.0
1975–9	69.9	76.3	69.3	75.9	71.5	77.4	68.9	75.4	72.6	77.2	71.1	77.0	70.1	78.3
1980–4	71.1	77.7	70.3	77.1	71.5	77.7	70.2	76.8	73.5	78.1	72.9	79.1	71.2	79.4
Projected: Low														
1990	72.5	78.9	72.5	79.1	72.0	77.7	72.1	78.6	73.6	78.7	73.5	79.9	72.5	80.7
1995	73.0	79.3	73.1	79.7	72.3	77.9	72.3	78.8	13.9	79.2	73.8	80.3	73.1	81.2
2000	73.3	79.6	73.5	80.0	72.5	78.0	72.5	79.0	74.0	79.5	74.0	80.5	73.5	81.5
2005	73.3	79.6	73.5	80.0	72.5	78.0	72.5	79.0	74.0	79.5	74.0	80.5	73.5	81.5
2010	73.3	79.6	73.5	80.0	72.5	78.0	72.5	79.0	74.0	79.5	74.0	80.5	73.5	81.5
2015	73.3	79.6	73.5	80.0	72.5	78.0	72.5	79.0	74.0	79.5	74.0	80.5	73.5	81.5
2019	73.3	79.6	73.5	80.0	72.5	78.0	72.5	79.0	74.0	79.5	74.0	80.5	73.5	81.5
Projected: High														
1990	72.7	79.0	72.6	79.2	72.1	77.9	72.2	78.7	73.8	78.8	73.7	80.1	72.6	20.8
1995	73.7	79.9	73.8	80.2	72.8	78.5	73.3	79.5	74.7	79.7	74.5	80.9	73.7	81.8
2000	74.7	80.9	74.9	81.3	73.5	79.1	74.4	80.6	75.6	80.7	75.3	81.7	74.8	82.8
2005	75.8	81.7	76.0	82.0	74.4	79.9	75.5	81.1	76.5	81.6	76.2	82.5	75.9	83.5
2010	76.7	82.3	76.9	82.5	75.6	80.8	76.6	81.9	77.4	82.3	77.2	83.0	76.8	84.0
2015	77.6	82.8	77.6	82.9	76.7	81.6	77.5	82.6	78.1	82.8	78.0	83.3	77.0	84.4
2019	78.0	83.0	78.0	83.0	77.5	82.0	78.0	83.0	78.5	83.0	78.5	83.5	78.0	84.5

TABLE 7.6. (cont.)

	Ireland		Italy		Luxemburg		Netherlands		Portugal		United Kingdom	
	M	F	M	F	M	F	M	F	M	F	M	F
Observed												
1960–4	68.2	72.0	67.0	72.4	66.4	72.0	71.3	75.9	61.6	67.2	67.9	73.9
1965–9	68.5	72.9	67.8	73.6	66.7	73.2	71.1	76.4	63.0	69.3	68.4	74.7
1970–4	68.7	73.6	69.0	75.1	66.9	74.1	71.1	77.1	64.6	71.0	68.9	75.2
1975–9	69.3	74.6	70.4	76.9	68.2	75.5	71.9	78.5	66.1	73.3	69.7	75.9
1980–4	70.3	76.8	71.5	78.2	69.4	76.2	72.8	79.7	68.7	75.7	71.1	77.1
Projected: Low												
1990	71.8	77.3	73.4	79.9	71.5	78.4	73.7	80.0	71.2	78.1	72.7	78.2
1995	72.1	77.7	74.1	80.6	72.0	79.1	73.9	80.3	71.9	78.7	73.2	78.7
2000	72.5	78.0	74.5	81.0	72.5	79.5	74.0	80.5	72.5	79.0	73.5	79.0
2005	72.5	78.0	74.5	81.0	72.5	79.5	74.0	80.5	72.5	79.0	73.5	79.0
2010	72.5	78.0	74.5	81.0	72.5	79.5	74.0	80.5	72.5	79.0	73.5	79.0
2015	72.5	78.0	74.5	81.0	72.5	79.5	74.0	80.5	72.5	79.0	73.5	79.0
2019	72.5	78.0	74.5	81.0	72.5	79.5	74.0	80.5	72.5	79.0	73.5	79.0
Projected: High												
1990	71.9	77.4	73.5	80.0	71.6	78.6	73.9	80.2	71.2	78.2	72.8	78.3
1995	72.9	78.3	74.7	81.2	72.6	79.6	74.6	80.9	72.5	79.3	73.9	79.3
2000	73.9	79.3	75.9	82.2	73.8	80.7	75.4	81.6	73.9	80.5	75.1	80.3
2005	75.0	80.2	77.0	83.3	75.0	81.6	76.4	82.3	75.1	81.4	76.1	81.2
2010	76.1	81.0	77.9	83.7	76.1	82.3	77.3	82.9	76.2	81.9	77.0	81.7
2015	77.0	81.7	78.6	83.9	77.0	82.8	78.0	83.3	77.1	82.4	77.6	82.3
2019	77.5	82.0	79.0	84.0	77.5	83.0	78.5	83.5	77.5	82.5	78.0	82.5

ᵃ Non-weighted average of the 12 EC member states.
Source: Eurostat 1991a.

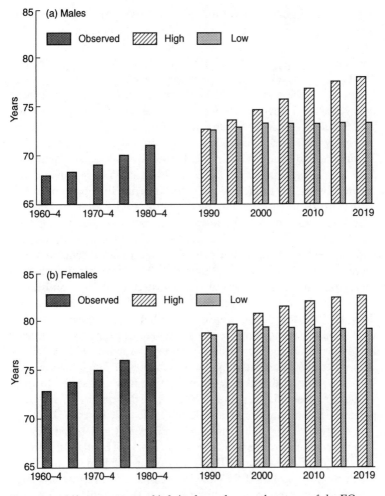

FIG. 7.9. *Life expectancy at birth in the twelve member states of the EC, 1960–2019*

Note: Data for 1985–9 not available.
Source: Eurostat 1991a.

of factors such as the increase in smoking among women and increased environmental pollution. If mortality rates did stop falling, this would stabilize female life expectancy at birth at around 80 and men's at around 73.5. Eurostat's high long-term scenario projects further gains, of four to five years of life expectancy, over the period 1990–2020, raising that of females to 83 years from birth and that of males to 78 years. This scenario envisages further progress with preventive services (like cancer screening), curative care, and the adoption of healthier lifestyles (Lopez and Cruijsen 1991). These levels of life expectancy are close to those projected by the UN for women in 2020 (less than a year more) and around two years more than the UN projects for men in these countries. Nevertheless, these levels are nowhere near bio-medical limits, assuming that such limits exist (Manton 1991, Day 1991). The 'optimistic' mortality scenario adopted by IIASA set male and female life expectancy in 2020 at 90 and 95 respectively. For further discussion of factors likely to influence European mortality in the future see Caselli and Egidi (1992) and Caselli (1993).

Eurostat also makes an allowance for external migration (Muus and Cruijsen 1991). These hazardous extrapolations are concerned with movements from outside the EC, but do not extend to movement between the twelve countries. The current net inflow of about one million per annum is boosted by large numbers of refugees and asylum seekers (640,000 in 1992), but the scenarios do not expect this flow to continue. Actual inflows have risen since then. For these and other reasons, the data for net migration used and projected in the scenarios are modest compared with the actual data up to 1992 presented by Salt in Chapter 3. The low long-term scenario projects that the net immigration flow will settle down to a quarter of a million per annum, the high scenario envisages a figure of three-quarters of a million (table 7.7, figure 7.10). The lower estimates resemble those presented to the 1991 European Population Conference by van de Kaa (1993). The main difference between the Eurostat and UN projections is the fomer's allowance for in migration. The difference between Eurostat's low and high migration assumptions amounts to about seven million additional people in the EC in 2020.

The Eurostat projections tend to label the lower variants of natural sources of population growth as 'pessimistic' and the higher variants of fertility and mortality as 'optimistic'. It is difficult to argue with such use of terminology when it concerns increases in life expectancy, nor with the argument that low fertility represents an undesirable restriction on choices facing potential European parents. The language used by Eurostat in relation to international migration, and to the two population outcomes is more neutral.

TABLE 7.7. *Average annual net migration[a] with the rest of the world in the twelve member states of the EC, 1960–2019 ('000s)*

	Total[a]	Belgium	Denmark	Germany	Greece	Spain	France	Ireland	Italy	Luxemburg	Netherlands	Portugal	United Kingdom
Observed													
1960–4	235	18	1	190	−41	−87	300	−21	−99	2	4	−91	60
1965–9	−26	12	1	221	−36	−50	92	−15	−102	1	10	−116	−45
1970–4	137	15	6	171	−25	−33	112	10	2	4	27	−120	−32
1975–9	286	6	2	15	57	28	34	10	19	1	36	89	−11
1980–4	168	−5	1	24	17	15	33	−8	71	0	14	29	−23
1985–9	482	8	6	330	9	−12	14	−32	74	2	27	14	40
Projected: Low													
1990–4	528	9	5	326	19	16	35	−22	66	1	29	12	31
1995–9	250	9	5	100	15	25	25	−15	30	1	20	15	20
2000–4	250	9	5	100	15	25	25	−15	30	1	20	15	20
2005–9	250	9	5	100	15	25	25	−15	30	1	20	15	20
2010–14	250	9	5	100	15	25	25	−15	30	1	20	15	20
2015–19	250	9	5	100	15	25	25	−15	30	1	20	15	20
Projected: High													
1990–4	986	21	14	574	38	40	66	−12	108	3	50	25	60
1995–9	750	22	15	280	40	70	70	0	100	3	50	40	60
2000–4	750	22	15	280	40	70	70	0	100	3	50	40	60
2005–9	750	22	15	280	40	70	70	0	100	3	50	40	60
2010–14	750	22	15	280	40	70	70	0	100	3	50	40	60
2015–19	750	22	15	280	40	70	70	0	100	3	50	40	60

[a] Including corrections due to population censuses, registration counts, etc., which cannot be classified as births, deaths, or migrations.

Source: Eurostat 1991a.

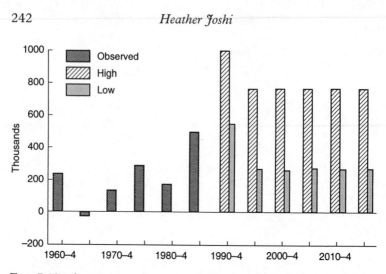

F IG. 7.10. *Average annual net migration in the twelve member states of the EC, 1960–2019*
Source: Eurostat 1991a.

Population decline in the European Community?

Eurostat's population projections show a decline only when all three 'low' variants (fertility, mortality, and migration) are combined. Other projections present different combinations, but in no case which contains a 'high' component is the population in 2020 below that of 1990. It is the fertility variant that makes the most difference to the projections, with 'high' fertility contributing around twenty-five million people to the population by 2020. A 'high' mortality assumption adds twelve million to the 2020 total.

7.6 Some Outcomes of the Eurostat Projections

So far there does not seem much prospect of population decline on a scale sufficient to alarm those who would see population decline as a problem. There are more important, and apparently inevitable features, of these projections which should be noted. The projected share of the EC population in the world seems fairly certain to continue the decline illustrated in figure 7.11 and table 7.8, whichever set of assumptions is adopted. The EC share of the world

TABLE 7.8. *Proportion of total world population living in Europe (per cent), 1960–2020*

	Europe	12 EC states
Observed		
1960	14.1	9.8
1965	13.3	9.3
1970	12.4	8.7
1975	11.6	8.0
1980	10.9	7.5
1985	10.1	7.0
Projected: Low		
1990	9.4	6.5
1995	8.7	6.0
2000	8.1	5.6
2005	7.6	5.2
2010	7.2	4.8
2015	6.7	4.5
2020	6.4	4.2
Projected: High		
1990	9.4	6.5
1995	8.8	6.1
2000	8.3	5.8
2005	7.9	5.5
2010	7.6	5.3
2015	7.3	5.1
2020	7.1	4.9

Source: United Nations 1991.

population, 6.5 per cent in 1990, is set to fall to between 4.9 per cent and 4.2 per cent in 2020. These estimates are based on the UN's 'medium' variant. Even with some positive population growth in Europe, the higher level expected in the rest of the world, illustrated in figure 7.1, means that relative population decline is a near certainty.

A demographic feature of perhaps greater economic and social importance than the population headcount is the age structure, which is discussed further in Chapter 8. As Europe completes the

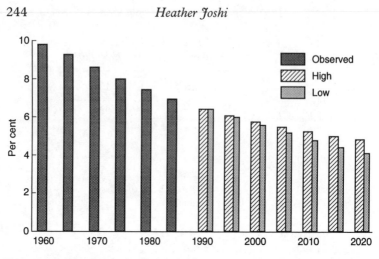

FIG. 7.11. *Proportion of the total world population living in the twelve member states of the EC, 1960–2020*
Source: Eurostat 1991a.

first demographic transition—and whether or not, *pace* van de Kaa (1987), it is going into a second—the history of improving mortality and falling fertility imply a long-term process of population ageing, in which there are relatively more people at the top of what used to be, more accurately, called an age pyramid, fewer at its base (see for example Eurostat 1991b: figure I.1). This process is also known as the rectangularization of the age pyramid. In both sets of projections this process proceeds. Neither of Eurostat's alternative scenarios makes much difference to the projected age structure of the EC, particularly among older people. Figure 7.12 (and table 7.9) show a broad summary of trends in the age structure. The population aged over 60 is set to rise from one in five to one in four in the thirty years between 1990 and 2020—from 20 per cent in 1990 to 26 per cent on the low-growth scenario, or 25 per cent on the high scenario. The proportion of the population aged under 20 is a little more sensitive to the scenario being employed, since this figure has a direct effect on the numbers of children—these might fall from 25 per cent to 24 per cent or 20 per cent of total population.

One reason for the alarm among some observers about the increasing numbers of the elderly is the burden of financing pensions which is often placed on contributors of working age. In this

TABLE 7.9. *Population of the twelve member states of the EC by broad age-group (per cent), 1960–2020*

	0–19	20–59	60+
Observed			
1960	32	52	15
1965	32	52	16
1970	32	50	17
1975	32	50	18
1980	30	52	18
1985	28	54	19
1900	25	55	20
Projected: Low			
1995	24	56	20
2000	23	55	21
2005	22	56	22
2010	21	55	23
2015	20	55	25
2020	20	55	26
Projected: High			
1995	24	56	20
2000	24	54	21
2005	24	54	22
2010	25	52	23
2015	24	52	24
2020	24	51	25

Source: Eurostat 1991a.

context the dependency ratio of old to working-age population is of interest. This is measured in table 7.10 and figure 7.13 as the ratio of persons aged 60 and over to those aged 20–59. In practice, of course, the dividing line between dependency and contribution is much more difficult, if not impossible, to draw (Arber and Ginn 1991). However, on this indicator, there were nearly three non-elderly adults per person over 60 in 1990, reducing to around two in 2020. There is little difference between the scenarios with regard to this ratio as the number of children does not come into the calculation. These projections indicate the

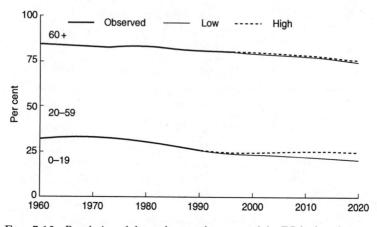

FIG. 7.12. *Population of the twelve member states of the EC by broad age-groups (per cent), 1960–2020*
Source: Eurostat 1991a.

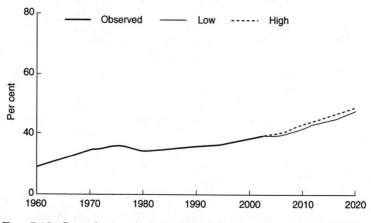

FIG. 7.13. *Dependency ratio of the old, for the twelve member states of the EC, 1960–2020 (per cent)*

Note: Dependency ratio is the population aged 60+ relative to the population aged 20–59.
Source: Eurostat 1991a.

inevitability of an increasing population of elderly Europeans as discussed further in Chapter 8. It seems more useful for plans to be made for this scenario than for a more remote possibility of population decline.

TABLE 7.10. *Dependency ratio of the old[a] in the twelve member states of the EC, 1960–2020 (per cent)*

	Total	Belgium	Denmark	Germany	Greece	Spain	France	Ireland	Italy	Luxemburg	Netherlands	Portugal	United Kingdom
Observed													
1960	29.2	33.0	30.1	31.6	22.2	23.4	32.9	34.9	25.0	28.7	26.7	22.9	31.6
1965	31.8	36.3	32.0	35.4	24.8	24.6	35.9	34.9	27.4	33.1	28.6	24.8	34.0
1970	34.7	37.8	34.0	39.3	31.0	28.1	36.9	35.5	30.6	34.0	29.2	27.6	36.9
1975	36.1	37.8	36.2	40.3	33.8	28.9	36.7	35.2	33.8	36.3	29.6	29.2	39.3
1980	34.3	34.5	37.4	36.3	33.5	29.6	33.1	33.1	32.5	31.9	29.6	29.0	39.6
1985	35.1	36.1	37.6	35.5	33.5	33.0	34.3	31.3	34.1	31.7	30.3	32.8	39.7
1990	35.9	37.3	36.9	35.1	36.0	35.0	35.7	31.6	36.4	32.7	30.3	34.7	38.8
Projected: Low													
1995	36.9	39.1	35.4	36.0	40.5	37.1	36.9	30.6	38.5	35.0	30.6	35.8	37.9
2000	38.7	40.0	35.2	41.1	43.7	37.0	37.4	29.6	41.1	37.0	31.7	36.1	37.8
2005	40.0	39.8	38.1	44.7	43.2	37.3	37.1	29.9	43.3	38.6	33.8	35.8	38.1
2010	42.4	42.5	43.2	44.7	54.3	39.4	41.0	33.3	46.7	41.1	38.9	36.8	40.9
2015	44.8	45.5	45.7	46.8	47.0	41.4	45.0	37.8	48.9	44.3	42.7	38.6	42.0
2020	48.1	50.0	48.0	50.5	48.7	45.1	48.5	42.8	52.0	49.1	47.1	41.7	44.3
Projected: High													
1995	36.9	39.0	35.2	35.7	40.9	37.2	36.9	30.0	38.6	34.2	30.6	35.9	38.0
2000	38.8	40.0	34.9	40.8	44.3	37.2	37.6	28.3	41.3	35.4	31.6	36.1	38.2
2005	40.5	41.1	37.9	44.8	44.0	38.0	37.6	28.1	43.9	36.3	33.7	35.9	39.1
2010	43.5	43.4	43.0	45.5	46.4	40.5	42.2	31.0	48.1	38.2	39.0	37.3	42.6
2015	46.2	46.6	45.5	48.0	48.2	42.8	46.5	34.4	50.6	40.3	42.8	39.1	44.3
2020	49.1	50.6	47.6	51.3	49.1	45.9	49.7	37.4	53.1	43.1	46.5	41.3	46.7

[a] Population aged 60+ relative to population aged 20–59.
Source: Eurostat 1991a.

7.7 Projections for Individual Countries

In practice, many users of demographic projections are more interested in sub-populations by age or geographical breakdowns than in overall totals (Joshi and Diamond 1990). We now turn to the projections for the twelve constituent countries of the EC, which are shown in tables 7.11 and 7.12, according to the UN and Eurostat respectively.

It should be stated at the outset that estimates of the current population made by different agencies are not always identical. Discrepancies may arise at a number of points in the estimation process, but are likely to involve different treatment of uncertain information on temporary or recent migrants.

Population decline is already apparent in the estimates for Germany and Italy made by the UN, but not in those made by Eurostat. The UN's low variant indicates also a possible decline between 1985 and 1990 in Belgium. Declines between 1990 and 2020 are also projected, on all three of the UN's variants, for Germany and Italy, on two variants for Belgium, Luxemburg, and Denmark, and on the low variant only in the United Kingdom and Greece.

On Eurostat's low scenario Germany and Italy are projected to experience the most marked population decline, but on its high scenario no country has a smaller population in 2020 than in 1990. Germany would have the largest European population in 2020 with seventy-three million inhabitants, even if it followed the low scenario and all the others followed the high. The population of France is projected at between sixty and sixty-eight million, that of the United Kingdom at between fifty-seven and sixty-five million, that of Italy at between fifty-four and sixty-three million, and Spain's at between thirty-eight and forty-five million. With the exception of Spain, where Eurostat's projection resembles that of the UN fairly closely, these individual country projections by Eurostat bear the same relationship to the UN's as do the overall projections plotted in figure 7.8—not as low as the UN's low variant, and the upper bound above the UN's. Both sets of projections agree that population growth is least to be expected in Germany and Italy, and proportionally most likely in Ireland. The United Kingdom continues to account for about one in six of the EC's population.

TABLE 7.11. *Population estimates for the twelve member states of the EC, 1985–2025 ('000s)*

Variant	1985	1990	1995	2000	2005	2010	2015	2020	2025
United Germany									
Medium	77,668,000	77,573,000	77,330,000	76,962,000	76,182,000	75,145,000	73,939,000	72,469,000	70,909,000
High		77,650,000	77,906,000	78,162,000	78,087,000	77,837,000	77,476,000	76,976,000	76,566,000
Low		77,442,000	76,851,000	76,011,000	74,592,000	72,827,000	70,833,000	68,523,000	66,062,000
Italy									
Medium	57,141,000	57,061,000	57,114,000	57,195,000	56,889,000	56,199,000	55,248,000	54,138,000	52,964,000
High		57,104,000	57,374,000	57,770,000	57,846,000	57,585,000	57,143,000	56,754,000	56,463,000
Low		57,019,000	56,963,000	56,384,000	56,242,000	55,210,000	53,857,000	52,326,000	50,690,000
Spain									
Medium	38,602,000	39,187,000	39,915,000	40,667,000	41,271,000	41,661,000	41,895,000	42,122,000	42,265,000
High		39,333,000	40,213,000	41,193,000	42,094,000	42,850,000	43,537,000	44,267,000	44,974,000
Low		39,042,000	39,541,000	39,987,000	40,223,000	40,187,000	39,917,000	39,538,000	39,018,000
Belgium									
Medium	9,858,000	9,845,000	9,845,000	9,832,000	9,775,000	9,700,000	9,607,000	9,501,000	9,370,000
High		9,866,000	9,923,000	9,998,000	10,041,000	10,081,000	10,112,000	10,148,000	10,178,000
Low		9,830,000	9,695,000	9,530,000	9,306,000	9,046,000	8,758,000	8,441,000	8,083,000
Luxemburg									
Medium	367,000	373,000	376,000	377,000	375,000	373,000	370,000	366,000	361,000
High		373,000	377,000	380,000	381,000	381,000	382,000	383,000	383,000
Low		372,000	373,000	372,000	368,000	363,000	356,000	349,000	339,000
Denmark									
Medium	5,122,000	5,143,000	5,158,000	5,153,000	5,133,000	5,095,000	5,043,000	4,973,000	4,881,000
High		5,149,000	5,183,000	5,205,000	5,218,000	5,218,000	5,212,000	5,203,000	5,187,000
Low		5,134,000	5,130,000	5,098,000	5,045,000	4,968,000	4,869,000	4,749,000	4,603,000

TABLE 7.11. (*cont.*)

Variant	1985	1990	1995	2000	2005	2010	2015	2020	2025
United Kingdom									
Medium	56,618,000	57,237,000	57,864,000	58,393,000	58,704,000	58,973,000	59,273,000	59,544,000	59,658,000
High		57,279,000	58,055,000	58,886,000	59,532,000	60,172,000	60,975,000	61,924,000	62,806,000
Low		57,173,000	57,630,000	57,858,000	57,759,000	57,479,000	57,102,000	56,543,000	55,763,000
Ireland									
Medium	3,552,000	3,720,000	3,900,000	4,086,000	4,275,000	4,462,000	4,642,000	4,808,000	4,958,000
High		3,733,000	3,934,000	4,151,000	4,381,000	4,612,000	4,840,000	5,061,000	5,277,000
Low		3,707,000	3,865,000	4,020,000	4,168,000	4,312,000	4,445,000	4,559,000	4,650,000
Greece									
Medium	9,934,000	10,047,000	10,124,000	10,193,000	10,247,000	10,249,000	10,201,000	10,139,000	10,080,000
High		10,064,000	10,176,000	10,280,000	10,385,000	10,456,000	10,498,000	10,534,000	10,597,000
Low		10,030,000	10,090,000	10,124,000	10,127,000	10,061,000	9,931,000	9,767,000	9,600,000
Portugal									
Medium	10,157,000	10,285,000	10,429,000	10,587,000	10,718,000	10,810,000	10,876,000	10,917,000	10,941,000
High		10,304,000	10,489,000	10,706,000	10,915,000	11,102,000	11,269,000	11,443,000	11,618,000
Low		10,246,000	10,351,000	10,449,000	10,502,000	10,497,000	10,444,000	10,359,000	10,245,000
France									
Medium	55,170,000	56,138,000	57,138,000	58,145,000	58,856,000	59,404,000	59,828,000	60,169,000	60,372,000
High		56,159,000	57,304,000	58,592,000	59,649,000	60,573,000	61,487,000	62,478,000	63,424,000
Low		56,117,000	56,952,000	57,677,000	57,965,000	57,954,000	57,713,000	57,251,000	56,583,000
Netherlands									
Medium	14,484,000	14,951,000	15,409,000	15,829,000	16,151,000	16,379,000	16,561,000	16,718,000	16,819,000
High		15,001,000	15,536,000	16,054,000	16,488,000	16,875,000	17,274,000	17,692,000	18,078,000
Low		14,918,000	15,271,000	15,544,000	15,674,000	15,719,000	15,711,000	15,655,000	15,514,000

Source: United Nations 1991.

TABLE 7.12. *Population estimates for the twelve member states of the EC, 1985–2020 ('000s)*

	Total	Belgium	Denmark	Germany	Greece	Spain	France	Ireland	Italy	Luxemburg	Netherlands	Portugal	United Kingdom
Observed													
1985	338,199	9,858	5,111	77,720	9,920	38,423	55,063	3,537	57,081	366	14,454	10,129	56,539
1900	343,911	9,948	5,135	79,113	10,204	38,924	56,581	3,508	57,576	378	14,893	10,337	57,313
Projected: Low													
1995	349,021	10,063	51,74	80,566	10,303	39,305	57,865	3,483	57,992	388	15,370	10,467	58,045
2000	351,377	10,120	5,196	80,292	10,352	39,587	58,960	3,466	58,190	394	15,750	10,591	58,480
2005	351,402	10,107	5,191	79,222	10,377	39,688	59,738	3,443	58,013	396	16,012	10,685	58,530
2010	348,950	10,030	5,150	77,576	10,371	39,562	60,114	3,414	57,258	396	16,113	10,735	58,233
2015	344,538	9,908	5,077	75,622	10,312	39,130	60,154	3,368	55,928	394	16,093	10,727	57,826
2020	338,877	9,764	4,990	73,504	10,183	38,416	59,998	3,286	54,255	391	16,007	10,655	57,430
Projected: High													
1995	353,385	10,171	5,243	82,329	10,455	39,683	58,301	3,560	58,559	400	15,554	10,595	58,536
2000	363,275	10,427	5,385	84,245	10,763	40,797	60,357	3,687	59,939	423	16,300	10,998	59,956
2005	373,118	10,680	5,533	85,878	11,130	40,009	62,448	3,846	61,355	445	17,029	11,460	61,305
2010	382,047	10,917	5,667	87,329	11,540	43,167	64,383	4,031	62,415	468	17,658	11,940	62,532
2015	389,888	11,134	5,790	88,763	11,935	44,060	66,137	4,214	62,942	492	18,220	12,388	63,812
2020	397,145	11,344	5,926	90,255	12,269	44,671	67,832	4,370	63,121	517	18,780	12,791	65,270

Note: Germany includes former East Germany, throughout.
Source: Eurostat 1991a.

Projected age structures for the individual countries reflect the general direction of change at the Community level (Table 7.10), with differences partly reflecting different starting points. Ireland and Portugal start out with old-age dependency ratios well below the Community average and end up, on either variant, still with relatively few elderly people. The slow growth of Germany and Italy brings their old-age dependency ratios (35.1 per cent and 36.4 per cent respectively) from close to the Community average of 35.9 per cent in 1990 to levels distinctly above it in 2020—51.3 per cent for Germany and 53.1 per cent for Italy against 49.1 per cent for the Community as a whole, on the high variant. The 'optimistic' assumptions about increases in expectation of life in the high variant help to make the old-age dependency ratio higher than on the low variant. This is true for the Community as a whole, and for most of the individual countries, but not always. In some cases ageing is faster in the low-growth scenario, particularly in Ireland and Luxemburg, given their initial age structure, and the relatively low rate of immigration that is assumed for these countries in the low scenario.

7.8 Mortality and Migration Assumptions by Country

The mortality assumptions used in the Eurostat population scenarios vary very little by country (though more variation is suggested by Caselli and Egidi 1992). Most projections are of life expectancy to be within one year of the Community average (see table 7.6). There are slight exceptions in the higher female life expectancy in France and Italy. The migration assumptions vary considerably across countries (table 7.7, figure 7.14). Even after the anticipated curtailment in migration, discussed above, the largest projected flow by far is into Germany, the country already admitting the most immigrants from outside the Community as already described in Chapter 4. Italy and Germany account for the largest net immigration flows despite, or perhaps because of, their slow to negative population growth. The high variant sets net immigration after 1995 at a higher level than 1985–9 in all countries except Germany. Ireland is the only country set to experience net emigration after 1995, on the low variant. These projected immigration flows tend to dampen inter-country differences in population

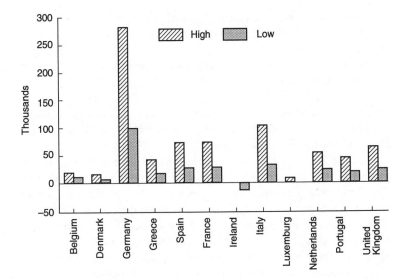

FIG. 7.14. *Projected average annual net migration into the twelve member states of the EC, as from 1995*
Source: Eurostat 1991a.

totals, but they are clearly not the source of the differences. For this we must turn to the fertility record and projections.

7.9 Alternative Projections of Fertility

To arrive at projections of births, the population projections need age-specific fertility rates to apply to the numbers of women at each age-band in each year. Such age-specific fertility rates are often summarized in the total period fertility rates cited above in tables 7.2 and 7.5, and presented as if they represented the average completed fertility of a hypothetical cohort of women who had experienced thirty years of that period's fertility rates. Such fertility rates are arrived at by making assumptions about the childbearing experience of actual cohorts, their ultimate family size, and the rate at which it is reached over the real thirty years in which each cohort passes through childbearing ages. Estimates of ultimate family size for some countries are informed by data from surveys on childbearing intentions, adjusted in various ways for non-response and some degree of overestimation among those who do respond (van de Giessen 1992).

Projections of completed fertility by cohort for the twelve countries as a whole are shown in table 7.13 and figure 7.15. For the cohort of women born in 1945, whose childbearing years can be considered to be finished, completed family size is, on average, 2.2. On either scenario this drops slightly: on the high variant through 1.9 for the cohorts born in the 1960s to recover again to just above 2 for the cohort themselves to be born in 2000. On the low variant, completed fertility follows a downward trend to 1.5. The individual countries show some variation in the position of their 1945 cohorts, ranging from 3.3 in Ireland to 1.8 in Germany. These differences become much more muted in the long term, most countries being projected to converge on the European average by the time the cohort of 2000 has finished reproducing, though Germany and Italy remain a little (0.2 of a child) below most others.

The timing of these fertility histories of the future also affects projected period fertility rates. It is summarized in the cohort's average age at motherhood in table 7.14 and figure 7.16 (mean age at all orders of birth). In all countries and on both variants childbearing is projected to continue starting later, until it con-

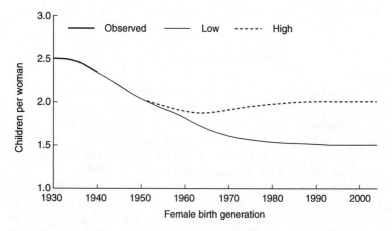

FIG. 7.15. *Completed fertility in the twelve member states of the EC for women born 1930–2000, actual and projected*
Source: Eurostat 1991a.

TABLE 7.13. *Completed fertility (children per woman) for the twelve member states of the EC, actual and projected, women born 1930–2000*

	Total[a]	Belgium	Denmark	Germany	Greece	Spain	France	Ireland	Italy	Luxemburg	Netherlands	Portugal	United Kingdom
Observed													
1930	2.50	2.30	2.36	2.17	2.21	2.59	2.64	3.50	2.29	1.97	2.65	3.00	2.39
1935	2.47	2.27	2.38	2.16	2.02	2.67	2.58	3.44	2.28	2.00	2.50	2.92	2.45
1940	2.34	2.17	2.24	1.98	2.01	2.59	2.42	3.27	2.14	1.95	2.21	2.69	2.40
Projected: Low													
1945	2.20	1.93	2.06	1.79	2.11	2.50	2.22	3.27	2.06	1.82	2.00	2.39	2.23
1950	2.05	1.83	1.90	1.72	2.07	2.20	2.11	3.02	1.88	1.75	1.90	2.12	2.09
1955	1.94	1.81	1.81	1.67	2.02	1.92	2.12	2.63	1.76	1.68	1.87	1.96	2.02
1960	1.82	1.83	1.77	1.63	1.90	1.67	2.06	2.30	1.60	1.60	1.84	1.77	1.92
1965	1.69	1.71	1.70	1.52	1.68	1.50	1.95	2.01	1.50	1.57	1.73	1.59	1.86
1970	1.61	1.63	1.65	1.43	1.60	1.40	1.85	1.89	1.42	1.54	1.65	1.51	1.81
1975	1.57	1.59	1.61	1.38	1.60	1.40	1.78	1.80	1.36	1.50	1.58	1.50	1.77
1980	1.54	1.56	1.57	1.35	1.60	1.40	1.75	1.75	1.33	1.46	1.54	1.50	1.74
1985	1.53	1.52	1.53	1.32	1.60	1.40	1.73	1.72	1.31	1.43	1.51	1.50	1.72
1990	1.51	1.50	1.51	1.30	1.60	1.40	1.71	1.71	1.30	1.41	1.50	1.50	1.71
2000	1.51	1.50	1.50	1.30	1.60	1.40	1.70	1.70	1.30	1.40	1.50	1.50	1.70
Projected: High													
1945	2.20	1.93	2.06	1.79	2.11	2.50	2.22	3.27	2.06	1.82	2.00	2.39	2.23
1950	2.05	1.83	1.90	1.72	2.07	2.21	2.11	3.03	1.89	1.76	1.90	2.12	2.09
1955	1.96	1.82	1.83	1.68	2.04	1.94	2.13	2.66	1.79	1.71	1.88	1.97	2.04
1960	1.90	1.89	1.83	1.70	1.98	1.78	2.12	2.39	1.70	1.66	1.92	1.85	1.99
1965	1.88	1.87	1.85	1.69	1.87	1.73	2.11	2.31	1.72	1.74	1.91	1.77	2.02
1970	1.91	1.91	1.92	1.73	1.90	1.74	2.13	2.25	1.75	1.83	1.93	1.80	2.08
1975	1.95	1.97	1.95	1.76	2.02	1.77	2.15	2.21	1.77	1.87	1.94	1.86	2.13
1980	1.98	2.00	1.97	1.79	2.10	1.80	2.17	2.20	1.79	1.89	1.95	1.90	2.17
1985	2.00	2.00	1.98	1.80	2.10	1.84	2.19	2.20	1.80	1.90	1.97	1.97	2.20
1990	2.00	2.00	1.99	1.80	2.10	1.88	2.20	2.20	1.80	1.90	1.99	2.00	2.20
2000	2.01	2.00	2.00	1.80	2.10	1.90	2.20	2.20	1.80	1.90	2.00	2.00	2.20

[a] Non-weighted average of the 12 EC member states.
Source: Eurostat 1991a.

TABLE 7.14. *Actual and projected average age at first birth (years) for cohorts of women from 1930–2000 for the twelve member states of the EC*

Year of birth of mothers	Total[a]	Belgium	Denmark	Germany	Greece	Spain	France	Ireland	Italy	Luxemburg	Netherlands	Portugal	United Kingdom
Observed													
1930		28.0	26.8	27.5			27.5		29.2	29.2	29.2		28.1
1935		27.2	26.2	26.9			27.1		28.6	28.6	28.1		27.3
1940		26.4	25.8	25.9			26.4		27.8	27.8	27.1		26.3
Projected: Low													
1945	26.7	25.9	25.7	25.3	26.5	28.0	26.0	29.1	27.0	27.5	26.5	27.2	26.0
1950	26.8	26.1	26.2	25.8	26.2	27.4	26.5	28.7	26.8	27.5	27.2	26.8	26.4
1955	27.1	26.6	27.2	26.4	25.8	27.3	26.9	28.4	26.9	27.9	28.2	26.3	27.0
1960	27.5	27.1	28.0	26.9	25.7	27.6	27.3	28.5	27.8	28.2	29.1	26.2	27.5
1965	28.2	27.8	28.5	27.6	26.6	28.7	28.1	29.0	28.9	28.3	29.7	27.0	28.0
1970	28.6	28.3	28.7	27.9	27.6	29.3	28.5	29.2	29.2	28.4	29.9	27.7	28.0
1975	28.9	28.6	28.8	28.3	28.1	29.8	28.7	29.5	29.6	28.6	30.0	28.3	28.2
1980	29.1	28.8	28.9	28.7	28.4	30.0	28.8	29.7	29.8	28.7	30.0	28.7	28.4
1985	29.2	28.9	28.9	28.9	28.7	30.0	28.9	29.9	29.9	28.8	30.0	28.9	28.6
1990	29.3	29.0	29.0	29.0	28.8	30.0	29.0	30.0	30.0	28.9	30.0	29.0	28.8
2000	29.3	29.0	29.0	29.0	29.0	30.0	29.0	30.0	30.0	29.0	30.0	29.0	29.0
Projected: High													
1945	26.7	25.9	25.7	25.3	26.5	28.0	26.0	29.1	27.0	27.5	26.5	27.2	26.0
1950	26.8	26.2	26.2	25.8	26.2	27.4	26.5	28.8	26.8	27.5	27.2	26.8	26.5
1955	27.2	26.7	27.2	26.5	25.9	27.5	27.0	28.5	27.1	27.9	28.3	26.4	27.1
1960	27.8	27.4	28.3	27.2	26.1	28.1	27.6	28.8	28.3	28.4	29.4	26.6	27.8
1965	28.6	28.3	28.9	28.1	27.2	29.3	28.4	29.5	29.4	28.7	30.0	27.6	28.4
1970	29.0	28.7	29.0	28.4	28.1	29.7	28.8	29.6	29.7	28.8	30.2	28.2	28.3
1975	29.1	28.9	29.0	28.7	28.4	30.0	28.9	29.7	29.8	28.8	30.2	28.6	28.5
1980	29.2	29.0	29.0	28.9	28.6	30.1	29.0	29.9	29.9	28.9	30.1	28.6	28.6
1985	29.3	29.0	29.0	29.0	28.8	30.1	29.0	29.9	30.0	28.9	30.1	29.0	28.8
1990	29.3	29.0	29.0	29.0	28.9	30.0	29.0	30.0	30.0	29.0	30.0	29.0	28.9
2000	29.3	29.0	29.0	29.0	29.0	30.0	29.0	30.0	30.0	29.0	30.0	29.0	29.0

[a] Non-weighted average of the 12 EC member states.
Note: Actual data not available for all countries.
Source: Eurostat 1991a.

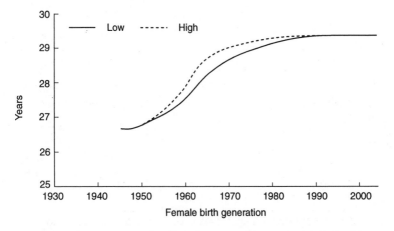

FIG. 7.16. *Average age at first birth for women born 1930–2000, for the twelve member states of the EC (actual and projected)*
Source: Eurostat 1991a.

verges on 29 in most countries, or 30 in those which have traditionally had later childbearing (Ireland, Italy, the Netherlands, and Spain). On the high fertility scenario, childbearing is postponed because time has to be devoted to acquiring career and housing assets before parenthood, in the low fertility scenario the constraints which prevent some people ever becoming parents cause others to delay. According to these projections the postponement effects of prosperity would be greater than the effects of a less supportive social environment.

Some of the ensuing projections of period fertility rates for individual countries are plotted in Figures 7.17 to 7.19, for which the data, for all twelve countries, appear in table 7.5. Two of the countries of Southern Europe which currently have low fertility are shown in figure 7.17, Italy and Spain. The low variant projects that current rates will continue, resulting in 2019 in rates of 1.3 and 1.4 respectively. The high variant allows for some 'catching up', but neither country reaches 'replacement' level TFR by the end of the projection period (1.8 and 1.9 in 2019, respectively). Figure 7.18 compares Germany with its northern neighbour, Denmark. Both trajectories have rather a similar shape—a recent check in a plunge below replacement levels. The continuing low assumption brings Denmark from 1.7 in 1990 to 1.5 in 2019, and Germany from 1.5

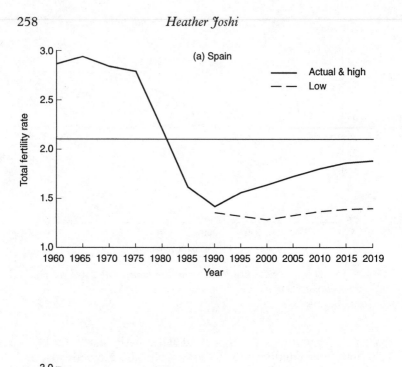

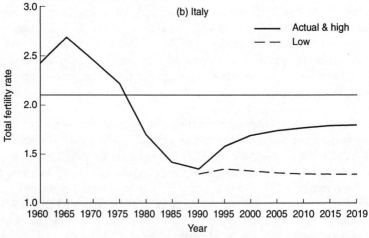

FIG. 7.17. *Actual and projected total fertility rates for Spain and Italy, 1960–2019*

Source: Eurostat 1991a.

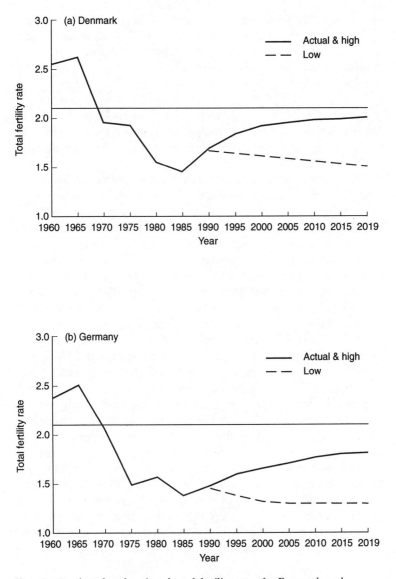

FIG. 7.18. *Actual and projected total fertility rates for Denmark and Germany, 1960–2019*
Source: Eurostat 1991a.

to 1.3. On the high variant, recovery continues, though neither reaches 2.1 within the period. At 2.0 in 2019 Denmark comes closer than Germany (1.8). The final pair of large countries to compare are France and the United Kingdom (figure 7.19). Though divided by the Channel, by their culinary traditions, as well as by a striking contrast in public policy towards parenthood, the graphs for these two countries look remarkably similar. Actual fertility fell less far below 'replacement' there than in the four countries considered above, and could, on the high scenario, rise back above it.

The similarity in fertility performance of these two countries lies a little uneasily with the dissimilarity in public policy, and with Eurostat's assumption that the key to a fertility recovery lies in public policy. Let us briefly trespass on the territory discussed further by Gauthier (Chapter 9) in this volume. Current policies towards the family in all member states of the EC are monitored in great detail by the European National Observatory on Family Policies (see Dumon 1990, 1991, and 1992). The writer Marina Warner (1989) has summarized the inhospitable environment offered to children by the public world in Britain as amounting to the 'privatization of the child'. In contrast French governments have a long history of pro-natal policies, and the institutions exist to give French mothers the opportunity of combining employment with parenthood. The fact that the British continue to have as many children as the French is rather bewildering, and slightly undermines the assumption behind Eurostat's scenarios. The premise is consistent enough with the upturn in fertility in Scandinavia as well as with the relatively high fertility of France, but, if a family-friendly environment is what it takes to raise fertility, why does not the British fertility picture look more like that of Germany than that of France? Warner suggests that an almost perverse underlying philoprogenitiveness keeps up the supply of new Britons. It is anybody's guess whether such forces, whatever they are, will continue to operate into the next century.

7.10 Conclusions

In the range of projections reviewed for Europe as a whole, and for that part of it which belongs to the EC, the population prospects

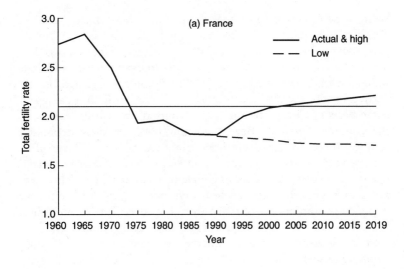

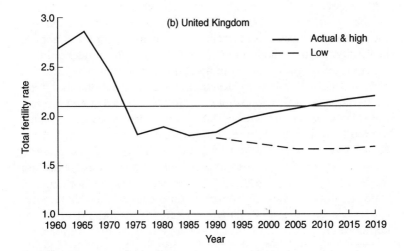

FIG. 7.19. *Actual and projected total fertility rates for France and the United Kingdom, 1960–2019*

Source: Eurostat 1991a.

seem to be of stagnation rather than of imminent drastic decline. Significant population decline due to natural increase is inevitable eventually if fertility remains below replacement for several generations. But in most places this has not happened yet, and it is unlikely to happen much before 2020. Population growth is still carried on the momentum of past population growth, boosted in some parts of Europe by the high fertility of the 1960s. Although the cohorts of women born then may have relatively depressed fertility, there are relatively large numbers of them. Reversal of European population trends is opposed by strong forces of inertia, like those resisting a change of course by a super-tanker. European population growth continues to benefit not only from the effect of population momentum but also from improvements in mortality. It is also likely to gain from immigration, even if more effective controls on this inflow are implemented, and even though some would query the benefits of immigration. While there is some doubt whether the population total will decline, there can be no doubt about population ageing. If the increase in the number of older people is not necessarily alarming, it is certainly challenging, a point developed by Grundy in the next chapter.

The variations in different countries' projected populations over the next thirty years arise largely from existing and past variations in fertility. Neither Eurostat nor the UN makes allowance for intra-Community migration smoothing out the geographical distribution of population. Some such development might reasonably be expected in view of the philosophy of the Single Market and the free movement of labour within the Community although, in fact, migration within the Community declined in the 1980s. Van de Kaa (1993) is sceptical as to whether there will be much intra-Community migration. If local deficits in natural increase are not made up by intra-Community movement, greater immigration from the outside (East or South) is not inconceivable, though not essential according to Coleman (1992). He would prefer to see better development and utilization of Europe's own human resources rather than an influx of the unskilled. In any case, should European governments need to augment the labour supply, we can see from figure 7.1 that there would be no shortage of external candidates, as Salt discussed in detail in Chapter 4.

Unlike some ecologists, who would be delighted to see a bit of depopulation anywhere, pro-natalists apparently want to keep up the supply of home-grown citizens. It is now being suggested, for example by Coleman (1992:457) and in the two Eurostat scenarios, that the way to do this is to make life easier for working mothers, who had earlier been the villains of the pro-natalist piece. There is a danger of confusing objectives. Policies to improve the quality of life should need no other justification. It is ironic that woman-friendly policies are being justified by their supposed positive impact on population totals in Europe, and a supposed negative impact in the third world (Population Crisis Committee 1988, Kabeer 1992). One way of reconciling this paradox could be to say that given more autonomy and choice, individual women will arrive at 'optimal' levels of reproduction desired by themselves and by society at large. This is unlikely to be the whole story, or the complete answer. Women are not the only people concerned in parenthood. I suggest placing more emphasis on the quality of life, for its own sake, of male and female, fathers and mothers, old and young. Population totals may be affected, but this need not be of primary concern, quantity should not be as important as quality. To borrow another slogan from the population politics of the third world, perhaps Europe should take care of the people and let population decline take care of itself.

NOTE

Thanks are due to Chris Shaw and David Coleman for their advice and Adrian Downing for assistance. The author also thanks the Statistical Office of the European Communities for permission to use material from their Report, 'Two Long-term Population Scenarios for the European Community'.

REFERENCES

ARBER, S., and GINN, J. (1991), *Gender and Later Life: a Sociological analysis of Resources and Constraints*, London: Sage.

BULATAO, R. A., BOS, E., STEPHENS, P. W., and VU M. T. (1990), *World Population Projections, 1989–90 Edition: Short- and Long-Term Estimates*,

Baltimore and London: Johns Hopkins University Press for the World Bank.

CASELLI, G. (1993), 'L'evolution à long terme de la mortalité en Europe' in A. Blum and J.-L. Rallu (eds.), *European Population* ii: *Demographic Dynamics*, Paris: John Libbey Eurotext: 111–64.

—— and EGIDI, V. (1992), 'New frontiers in survival—the length and quality of life', *Human Resources in Europe at the Dawn of the 21st Century*, Luxemburg: Eurostat: 91–135.

COLEMAN, D. (1992), 'Does Europe need Immigrants? Population and Workforce Projections', *International Migration Reveiew*, 26(2): 413–61.

COUNCIL OF EUROPE (1994), *Recent Demographic Developments in Europe*, Strasburg: The council.

CRUIJSEN, H. (1991), 'Fertility in the European Community: main trends, recent projections and two future paths', in *Background Papers on Fertility, Mortality, and International Migration under two Long-Term Population Scenarios for the European Community*, International Conference on Human Resources in Europe at the Dawn of the 21st Century, Luxemburg: Eurostat: 1–30.

DAY, L. (1991), 'Upper-Age Longevity in Low-Mortality Countries: a Dissenting View', in W. Lutz (ed.), *Future Demographic Trends in Europe and North America*: *What Can We Assume Today?*, London and San Diego: Academic Press: 117–28.

DUMON, W. (1990), *Families and Policies: Trends and Developments in 1989*, Brussels: European Observatory on National Family Policies and Commission of the European Communities, DG V. Document V/705/91-EN/FR.

—— (1991), *Families and Policies: Evolutions and Trends in 1989–90*, Brussels: European Observatory on National Family Policies and Commission of the European Communities, DG V. Document V/2293/91-EN/FR.

—— (1992), *National Family Policies in EC Countries in 1991*, Brussels: European Observatory on National Family Policies and Commission of the European Communities, DG V. (No Document Number.)

ERMISCH, J. F., and JOSHI, H. E. (1987), 'Demographic Change, Economic Growth and Social Welfare in Europe', in *European Population Conference 1987*: *Plenaries*, 329–86.

EUROSTAT (1991a), *Two Long-term Scenarios for the European Community*, for the International Conference, Human Resources in Europe at the Dawn of the 21st Century, Luxemburg: Eurostat.

—— (1991b) *1991 Demographic Statistics*: 171.

JOSHI, H., and DIAMOND, I. (1990), 'Demographic Projections: who needs to know?, in *Population Projections: Trends, Methods and Uses*, OPCS Occasional Paper 38, London: OPCS: 1–21.

KABEER, N. (1992), 'From Fertility Reduction to Reproductive Choice: Gender Perspectives on Family Planning', Discussion Paper 299, Institute of Development Studies, Brighton.

KEILMAN N. (1990), 'National Population Projections in Industrialized countries: a review of methodology and assumptions', in *Population Projections: Trends, Methods and Uses*, OPCS Occasional Paper 38, London: OPCS: 31–41.

—— (1991), 'National Population Projections Methods in Developed Countries', in W. Lutz (ed.), *Future Demographic Trends in Europe and North America: What Can We Assume Today?*, London and San Diego: Academic Press: 465–86.

—— and CRUISJEN, H. (eds.) (1992), *National Population Forecasting in Industrialised Countries*, Amsterdam: NIDI, and Derwyn, Pa.: Swets and Zeitlinger.

LAND, K. (1986), 'Methods for national population forecasts: a review', *Journal of the American Statistical Association*, 81(396): 888–901.

LOPEZ, A., and CRUIJSEN, H. (1991), 'Mortality in the European Community: Trends and Perspectives' in *Background Papers on Fertility, Mortality and International Migration under two Long-Term Population Scenarios for the European Community*, International Conference on Human Resources in Europe at the Dawn of the 21st Century, Luxemburg: Eurostat: 31–53.

LUTZ, W., PRINZ, C., WILS, A. B., BUTTNER, T., and HELIG, G. (1991), 'Alternative Demographic Scenarios for Europe and North America', in W. Lutz (ed.), *Future Demographic Trends in Europe and North America: What Can We Assume Today?*, London and San Diego: Academic Press: 523–60.

MCNICOLL, G. (1992), 'The United Nations Long Range Population Projections', *Population and Development Review*, 18(2): 333–40.

MANTON, K. (1991), 'New Biotechnologies and the Limits to Life Expectancy', in W. Lutz (ed.), *Future Demographic Trends in Europe and North America: What Can We Assume Today?*, London and San Diego: Academic Press: 97–116.

MUUS, P., and CRUIJSEN, H. (1991), 'International Migration in the European Community: two scenarios', in *Background Papers on Fertility, Mortality and International Migration under two Long Term Population Scenarios for the European Community*, International Conference on Human Resources in Europe at the Dawn of the 21st Century, Luxemburg: Eurostat: 55–73.

POPULATION CRISIS COMMITTEE (1988), 'Poor, powerless and pregnant', *Population Briefing Paper* 20, Washington, DC.

PRESSAT, R. (1985), *The Dictionary of Demography* (ed. C. Wilson), Oxford: Blackwell Reference.

UNITED NATIONS, Department of International Economic and Social Affairs (1991), *World Population Prospects 1990*, New York: United Nations.

—— (1992), *Long-Range World Population Projections: Two Centuries of Population Growth 1950–2150*, New York: United Nations.

VAN DE GIESSEN, H. (1992), 'Using Birth Expectations Information in National Population Forecasts', in N. Keilman and H. Cruijsen (eds.), *National Population Forecasting in Industrialised Countries*, Amsterdam: NIDI, and Derwyn, Pa.: Swets and Zeitlinger.

VAN DE KAA, D. (1987), 'Europe's Second Demographic Transition', *Population Bulletin*, 42(1).

—— (1993), 'European migration at the end of history', in A. Blum and J.-L. Rallu (eds.), *European Population, ii: Demographic Dynamics*, Paris: John Libbey Eurotext: 77–109.

WARNER, M. (1989), *Into the Dangerous World: Some Reflections on Childhood and its Costs*, Counter Blast No. 5, London: Chatto.

8

Population Ageing in Europe

EMILY GRUNDY

8.1 Introduction

To understand the characteristics of today's elderly European populations, it is essential to have an eye to the past. Europe's varying cultural, economic, and political history is evident in contemporary population characteristics. By definition, elderly people have a longer past than the young so this is particularly true of the older population. To take one important example, for at least three centuries before the Second World War, marriage patterns (and consequently fertility patterns) were markedly different (and continue to differ) to the West and East of a line running roughly from St Petersburg to Trieste (Hajnal 1965) and this difference is reflected today in the marital status distributions of Europe's elderly populations. Episodic events, as well as long-term trends, have also left their mark. Many elderly Europeans are the survivors of generations depleted by war; others were among the millions displaced by the aftermath of war. Some may have remained in the same place but have seen their nationality change, while others were born in former colonies.

Major political upheaval is once again a feature of life for many Europeans. Inevitably, statistical systems have not yet caught up with the most recent re-drawing of the European map (see table 1.1). In this chapter we describe the demographic characteristics of the elderly population of most European countries but we have not been able to include some of the newest. Statistically, if not politically, unification is simpler than partition. Where possible we present data for the whole of Germany, but Yugoslavia and Czechoslovakia appear as constituted up to 1989 and 1990. We have drawn predominantly on international compilations of demographic data, respectively, which in turn are largely based on data produced by national statistical offices. It should be noted that such sources do not guarantee freedom from error. Age misreporting, under-enumeration at censuses, and incomplete death registration may all affect some of the data presented. Information derived from mortality data are the most vulnerable to error as the numerators and denominators of death rates are drawn from different sources (death registrations and census-based population estimates respectively). Population projections also obviously rest on assumptions which may prove invalid. Although ageing is a continuous process we have followed conventional practice in adopting 65 as the threshold age of old age.

8.2 The Size and Age Structure of Europe's Elderly Populations

Table 8.1 shows the size of the population aged 65 and over in most countries of Europe in the early 1990s. The proportions of the total population aged 65 and over, 75 and over, and 85 and over are also shown. In general, the proportion of elderly people is higher in Northern and Western than in Southern or Eastern Europe. In Sweden, Norway, the United Kingdom, Denmark, Austria, and Belgium, those aged 65 and over comprise 15 per cent or more of the total, while in Yugoslavia, Romania, and Poland the relative size of the elderly population has not yet reached 10 per cent.

As would be expected, geographical differences in the proportions aged 75 or more or 85 or over are on broadly similar lines; Germany, the Scandinavian countries, and the United Kingdom have the highest proportions of 'older old' and Romania, Yugoslavia, Bulgaria, Iceland, Ireland, and Malta the lowest.

As illustrated in Figure 8.1, in most European countries those aged 65–74 comprise rather more than half of the elderly population, those aged 75–84 about a third and the older old—those aged at least 85—between 5 and 12 per cent.

While, in general, populations with relatively large elderly populations also have relatively old elderly populations, there are some anomalies reflecting the impact of particular historical episodes, notably war. In Germany, for example, the heavy mortality of young men in the Second World War is evident in the relative

TABLE 8.1. *Proportion of the population aged 65 and over, 75 and over, and 85 and over in the countries of Europe, 1991 or 1992*

Country	No. aged 65+ ('000s)	Percentage aged		
		65+	75+	85+
Northern Europe				
Denmark	804	15.6	6.9	1.6
Estonia	183	11.7	5.0	0.9
Finland	673	13.5	5.7	1.0
Iceland	27	10.7	4.6	1.2
Ireland	402	11.3	4.7	0.9
Latvia[a]	315	11.8	5.3	1.0
Lithuania	412	11.0	4.7	1.1
Norway	693	16.3	7.1	1.6
Sweden	1,526	17.8	8.0	1.7
UK	9,036	15.7	6.9	1.5
Southern Europe				
Greece	1,473	14.3	6.3	1.3
Italy	8,558	14.8	6.5	1.2
Malta[b]	37	10.4	3.9	0.7
Portugal	1,317	13.4	5.3	0.9
Spain	5,399	13.8	5.6	1.2
Yugoslavia[b]	2,197	9.3	3.8	0.7
Western Europe				
Austria	1,179	15.1	7.0	1.4
Belgium	1,526	15.2	6.4	1.5
France	8,201	14.3	6.4	1.7
Germany	11,912	14.9	7.1	1.4
Luxemburg	53	13.6	6.0	1.2
Netherlands	1,936	12.8	5.4	1.2
Switzerland	983	14.6	6.7	1.5
Eastern Europe				
Bulgaria[b]	1,167	13.0	4.8	0.7
Czechoslovakia[b]	1,843	11.8	4.9	0.8
Hungary[b]	1,383	13.3	5.5	0.9
Poland[b]	3,833	10.1	4.1	0.7
Romania[b]	2,414	10.4	4.1	0.5
Russian Fed.[b]	14,156	9.6	4.1	0.6
Ukraine[a]	6,023	11.7	5.0	0.8

[a] 1989.
[b] 1990.
Sources: Eurostat 1993, United Nations 1992a.

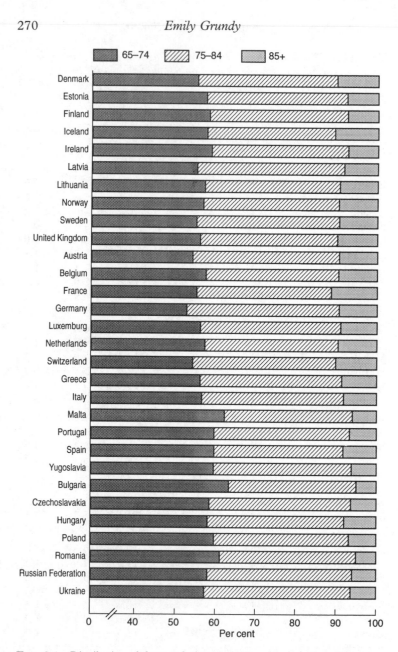

FIG. 8.1. *Distribution of the population aged 65 and over by broad age-group, countries of Europe, late 1980s or early 1990s*
Sources: Eurostat 1993, United Nations 1992a.

under-representation of 65–74 year olds today. The legacy of war-related mortality is also apparent in the very wide variation within Europe in sex ratios at older ages shown in figure 8.2. In parts of the former Soviet Union, Germany, Austria, and Finland, elderly women outnumber elderly men by at least two to one while in Greece there are nearly 80 men per 100 women. These differences also reflect more general variations, particularly between the East and West, in the mortality of men relative to that of women (United Nations Secretariat, 1988).

Changes between 1950/51 and 1990 in the proportion of elderly people in countries now in the European Community are considered in table 8.2. During this period the proportion aged 65 and over more than doubled in Greece but increased by only 6 per cent in Ireland and 19 per cent in France. Increases in the relative size of the population aged 75 or more were greatest (among countries for which data are available) in Greece, Denmark, and Portugal and smallest (although still substantial) in Ireland and France.

Causes of population ageing

In order to understand these differences between European countries in the relative size and sex composition of elderly age groups, it is necessary to have some appreciation of both population dynamics and the effect of particular historical events. The absolute number of elderly people in any population is a simple function of the number of births six or more decades earlier and of subsequent survival, with an addition or subtraction reflecting the balance of past migration patterns. Past fluctuations in the numbers of births in Europe have been substantial. In many countries, for example, birth rates fell in the late 1920s and 1930s and rose in the decades after the Second World War (typically peaking in the mid-1960s). Apart from these secular trends, it should be remembered that wars affect births, as well as deaths. In countries involved in the First World War, the number of births during the operation of hostilities was generally low (particularly in France). Births also fell slightly during the Second World War (although not in Germany). This was followed by an immediate post-war 'reunification' baby boom. These past fluctuations in the numbers of births have had, and continue to have, as impact on the size of elderly age groups. In France today, for example, the number of

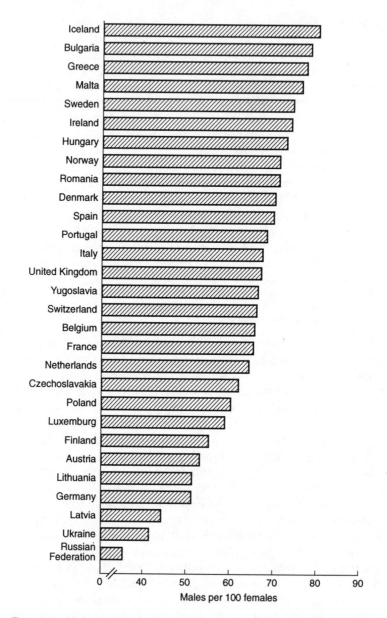

FIG. 8.2. *Males per 100 females among those aged 65+, European countries, early 1990s or late 1980s*
Sources: Eurostat 1993, United Nations 1992a.

TABLE 8.2. *Changes in the proportion of the population aged 65 and over and 75 and over, EC countries, 1950/1–1990*

Country	Aged 65+				Aged 75+			
	1950/1		1970/1	1990	1950/1		1970/1	1990
	Per cent	Index			Per cent	Index		
Belgium	11.2	100	121	132	3.7	100	127	181
Denmark	9.1	100	138	171	2.9	100	155	238
France	11.8	100	114	119	4.1	100	124	166
Greece	6.7	100	166	204ᵃ	2.1	100	181	290
Ireland	10.7	100	104	106	3.7	100	108	122
Italy	8.1	100	132	179				
Luxemburg	10.5ᵇ	100	121	128				
Netherlands	7.9	100	130	162	2.5	100	148	216
Portugal	7.0	100	131	187	2.3	100	126	230
Spain	7.2	100	135	185				
UK	10.9	100	119	143	3.5	100	129	197

Notes: 1950/1 = 100.
  Figures for Germany are not included because of the different geographic composition in 1950/1 and 1990.
[a] 1989.
[b] 1954.
Source: Compiled from *United Nations Demographic Yearbooks* (various years).

those aged 70–75 is low (reflecting the low birth rates of the First World War period). Early in the next century there will be renewed growth in the numbers of 'young' elderly as the 'baby boom' generations reach the age of 65.

While knowing the absolute size of the elderly population is important, the relative size of older age groups is even more so in most contexts. Ageing populations are those in which the proportion, rather than the absolute number, of elderly people is increasing. In most populations, past and current fertility trends are by far the most important determinant age structure of the population and it has been repeatedly demonstrated (see, for example, Carrier 1962) that primary population ageing is the result of sustained downward trends in fertility rates. Historically falls in mortality generally served partially to offset the trend towards an older population, as the young were the chief beneficiaries (Grundy

1991) and the average age of the population would correspondingly fall, not rise, with lower death rates. Population ageing in Europe is chiefly the result of the historical transition from relatively high fertility to the low fertility which all European countries have now experienced. Differences in the timing of this transition, which was set in motion in France in the late eighteenth century, in most of the rest of Western and Northern Europe at the end of the nineteenth century, and more recently in Southern Europe and Ireland (Coale and Watkins 1986), largely account for the differences shown in Tables 8.1 and 8.2.

Although in the past fertility trends have been pre-eminent in shaping the age structures of populations, the situation in many European countries today is rather different. In much of Europe birth and death rates are now low, the proportions of elderly people high, and most deaths occur among those aged 65 or more. In these circumstances trends in mortality, particularly at older ages, become the major determinant of further population ageing, including the ageing of the elderly population itself (Caselli *et al.* 1987; Preston, Himes and Eggers 1989) and now trends to increase, rather than to reduce, the average age of populations. In some European countries recent improvements in later life mortality have been quite substantial. In England and Wales, for example, period life tables indicate that between the early 1970s and the late-1980s the probability of a woman of 65 surviving to the age of 85 increased from 0.33 to 0.42 (OPCS 1979, 1992). Gonnot (1992) has estimated that changes in mortality in the period 1950–80 resulted in decennial increases of 9 or 10 per cent in the number of women aged 80–84 in a number of European countries including France, the Netherlands, Sweden, and the United Kingdom. The extent of these improvements in later life mortality was not generally anticipated, and in many developed countries past projections of the size of the elderly population have proved too low (Murphy 1995; van Poppel and de Beer 1993). This point should be borne in mind when considering projections of the size of the elderly population in the future. Recent improvements in mortality in mid and later life have not, however, been an experience common to the whole of Europe. In some countries, notably in Eastern Europe, there has been a stagnation or even a deterioration in mortality, particularly among males (Velkoff and Kinsella 1993), as Meslé describes in Chapter 3.

8.3 Projected Changes in the Elderly
Populations of Europe

In general those countries with lower proportions of elderly people now are ageing faster than the countries with already 'aged' populations. In these latter countries, however, the proportion and number of *very* old people is increasing. Falls in death rates at older ages are contributing to this increase. In terms of the proportion aged 65 and over, projected increases are greatest in the countries of Eastern and Southern Europe, notably Yugoslavia, Bulgaria, Romania, Italy, and Greece. As figure 8.3 shows, national and projected data indicate a substantial increase in the absolute numbers of younger elderly people (aged 65–74) in most of the former Eastern bloc countries (including Albania and Yugoslavia) during the period 1985–2000. In much of Northern and Western Europe, by contrast, the numbers aged 75 are increasing, but the size of the group aged 65–74 is projected to remain stable or in some cases to fall as the small birth cohorts of the late 1920s and 1930s attain these ages.

These differences in changes in absolute numbers of elderly people reflect, not just the position of countries on the continuum from 'ageing' to 'aged' populations, but also the continuing impact of war-related mortality (and past fluctuations in birth rates). Countries in which the elderly population today includes those from cohorts depleted by war will show larger increases as they are succeeded by generations not so affected. In 1980 the countries with the largest deficits of men aged 55–69 were Germany, Austria, Finland, Yugoslavia, and Poland (Carlson 1990). Elsewhere in Europe, including France and the United Kingdom, the First World War had a greater impact on mortality.

8.4 Expectation of Life at Birth and at Age 65

Figure 8.4 shows average life expectancy at birth and at age 65 for men and women in the countries of Europe. These calculations of life expectancy are based on *current* mortality rates, that is, they show how long the average boy or girl (or man or woman reaching the age of 65) can expect to live, assuming no change in death rates. Differences between European countries on both measures

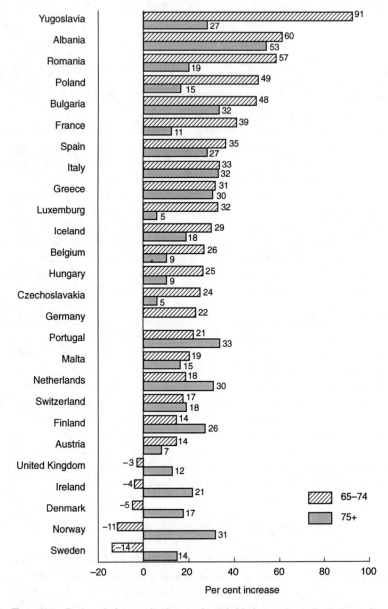

F IG. 8.3. *Projected changes in the number of elderly people aged 65–74 and 75+, 1985–2025, countries of Europe*

Note: Number in 2025 as a percentage increase on the number in 1985.
Source: United Nations 1990.

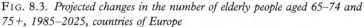

are substantial. In general, life expectancy at birth and at age 65 is highest in Northern and Western Europe and lowest in the East (see Meslé, Chapter 3). Life expectancy for a woman aged 65 is nearly five years longer in Switzerland than in Romania. A boy born in Iceland or Sweden can expect to live nearly ten years longer than a boy born in some former Eastern bloc countries. Differences between East and West, certainly with regard to male mortality, partly reflect a divergence in recent trends. While male mortality rates in mid and later life declined in many Western countries during the 1970s and 1980s, in some Eastern countries they increased.

In all of Europe female life expectancy is greater than male, but there is considerable variation in the extent of this difference. Countries with low mortality generally have larger sex differentials in life expectancies than those with high mortality. This is a reflection of the historical association between falls in mortality and an increasing female advantage (Preston 1976; United Nations Secretariat 1988).

Distinct 'Western' and 'Eastern' patterns of sex differentials in mortality have also been identified (United Nations Secretariat 1988). In most of Europe sex ratios in mortality rise gradually in childhood, reaching a sharp peak in the late teens and early twenties. This is followed by a drop and then a second, less marked 'hump' in late middle age. A number of Eastern countries, however, show a much more gradual decline in sex ratios of mortality rates from age 20–24, with no 'trough' or late middle age hump. In countries displaying this pattern, such as Hungary and Poland, a higher proportion of the sex differential in life expectancy at birth is due to differences in death rates among, for example, those aged 35–44, than is the case in Western countries. As a result of this factor, and age structure differences, in the early 1980s mortality differences between men and women aged 65 and over accounted for only about 25 per cent of the overall difference in life expectancy at birth between the sexes in Romania, and about 30 per cent in Hungary, Bulgaria, and Yugoslavia, whereas they accounted for close to or, in some cases, more than 50 per cent of such differences in the Netherlands, England and Wales, Denmark, Sweden, Norway, and Switzerland (United Nations Secretariat 1988: table 5). As a result, the ranking of European countries according to variations in sex differentials in life expectancy at birth and at age

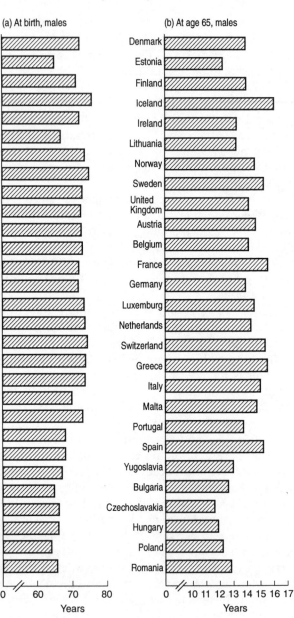

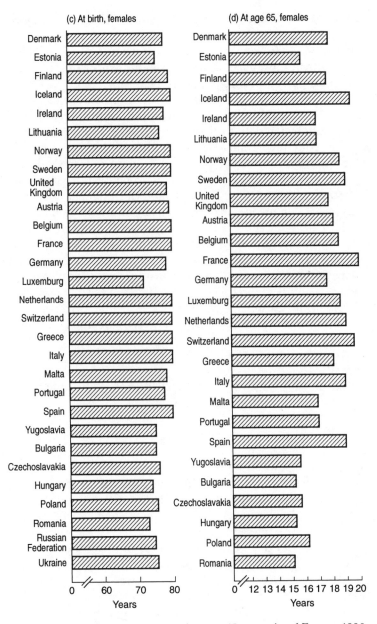

FIG. 8.4. *Life expectancy at birth and at age 65, countries of Europe, 1990*

Note: Data for a few countries are for 1988–9 or 1991. Data on life expectancy at age 65 are not available for the Russian Federation or Ukraine.

Sources: Eurostat 1993, United Nations 1992a.

65 diverges. It should be noted that in some European countries there are signs of recent narrowing of sex differentials in expectation of life. In England and Wales, for example, period life tables show a female advantage of 6.3 years in life expectancy at birth in 1970–2 compared with 5.5 years in 1988–90.

Within Europe sex differentials in life expectancy at birth are greatest in some of the former Eastern bloc countries, particularly the Russian Federation, the new Baltic nations, and Poland. Of the Western countries, France shows the greatest divergence between male and female mortality. Gender differences in lifestyle, including alcohol consumption, are likely to account for some of these differences. In the former Soviet Union, for example, male mortality and sex differences in life expectancy increased from the mid-1960s to the mid-1980s. However, in 1986–7 mortality fell sharply, particularly among men, a decline (unfortunately since reversed) attributed to the effect of measures introduced in May 1985 to reduce alcohol consumption (Virganskaya and Dmitriev 1992; Willekens and Scherbov 1992). At age 65, however, as shown in figure 8.5, the greatest disparity between men and women is observed in the Netherlands and the lowest in Southern European countries.

8.5 The Marital Status Distribution of Europe's Elderly Populations

Sex differentials in mortality, and the common pattern of women marrying men older than themselves, are reflected in the preponderance of widows in all of Europe's elderly populations that is shown in table 8.3. However, differences between countries in the extent of widowhood are substantial. In Switzerland and Malta, 44 per cent of elderly women are widows, compared with 60 per cent in Bulgaria and Hungary. Widowhood is necessarily preceded by marriage, and to some extent differences in the proportions widowed reflect differences in the proportions ever marrying, which are very substantial. In the late 1980s fewer than 2 per cent of elderly men in Bulgaria had never married, compared with nearly a quarter in Ireland. Imbalances between the number of men and women, the result of war-related mortality or differential emigration, affected some of today's elderly Europeans when they were

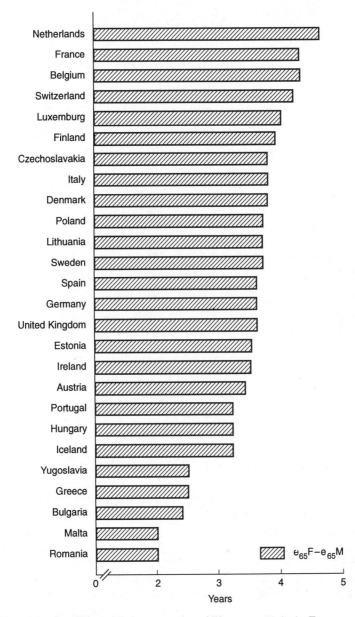

FIG. 8.5. *Sex differentials in expectation of life at age 65 (e_{65}), European countries, 1990*

Note: Data for a few countries are for 1988–9 or 1991. Data on life expectancy at age 65 are not available for the Russian Federation or the Ukraine.

Sources: Eurostat 1993, United Nations 1992a.

TABLE 8.3. *Distribution of population aged 65 and over by marital status, selected countries of Europe, 1988 or 1989 (per cent)*

Country	Marital status							
	Single		Married		Widowed		Divorced/ Separated	
	M	F	M	F	M	F	M	F
Ireland	24.0	20.5	59.2	30.2	16.2	48.7	0.5	0.6
Sweden	11.3	10.1	67.1	39.0	15.0	43.7	6.5	7.3
UK	7.7	9.7	72.1	37.6	17.4	49.5	2.8	3.1
France	7.5	8.4	73.7	36.0	15.9	52.0	2.8	3.7
Netherlands	5.8	9.4	75.5	38.9	15.4	37.7	3.4	4.0
Switzerland	8.3	13.7	74.0	37.4	14.5	44.2	3.2	4.7
Spain[a]	7.4	13.6	75.6	38.0	16.3	47.8	0.7	0.6
Malta[b]	18.2	25.1	60.4	29.8	20.2	44.3	1.1	0.8
Bulgaria[b]	1.6	1.7	74.0	34.4	23.0	62.1	1.4	1.7
Czechoslovakia	4.1	4.9	75.8	31.8	16.8	58.8	3.3	4.6
Hungary	3.5	5.5	72.9	28.9	20.4	60.6	3.1	5.1

[a] 1986.
[b] 1985.
Source: United Nations 1992b.

in the prime marriageable age-groups (Coleman and Salt 1992). However, the major reason for the differences between Northern and Western Europe on the one hand, and Eastern Europe on the other, is the historical difference in marriage patterns referred to earlier. Until relatively recently, the countries of North and West Europe were characterized by high proportions never marrying and a relatively late age at marriage. In Eastern Europe, by contrast, marriage was earlier and more universal (Hajnal 1965).

As yet only small proportions of elderly people in Europe are divorced. Variations in the proportions divorced reflect cultural and religious differences. In most of Southern Europe, as well as in Poland and Bulgaria, only about 1 per cent of elderly people are divorced, compared with 7 per cent in Sweden. In the future these proportions will be substantially higher in a number of European countries. In the short term, however, it is likely that the most important effect of divorce on elderly populations will be an in-direct one, the largely unknown results of divorce and remarriage among younger generations on the ability to provide support for elderly relatives.

Marriage rates rose in much of Europe in the post-war period (although they have declined again for the past quarter century or so; see Chapter 2) and the proportion ever-married is generally higher among those aged 65–74 than among the older old and higher still among those approaching their sixth decade. (Sundström 1994).

Differences in the marital status distributions of Europe's elderly populations are important because the currently married have a source of instrumental and emotional support unavailable to the unmarried. Much of the care needed by disabled elderly people is provided intra- rather than inter-generationally and the currently married make much less use of most formal services, including institutional care, than the unmarried (Cafferata 1987; Grundy 1992a).

8.6 The Availability of Children

Currently, and even more so in the recent past, the elderly populations of some European countries, particularly in Northern and Western Europe, include large proportions who lack living children. In Ireland in the late 1970s, for example, fully one-third of the elderly population were childless, as were a quarter of elderly Swedes and Norwegians in 1987–8 (Sundström 1994). In Britain data from the 1986 British Social Attitudes survey suggest that 17 per cent of the elderly population were childless whereas 23 per cent were estimated as being childless in a 1962 national survey (Shanas *et al.* 1968). Estimates based on the modelling of kin frequencies show a similar downward trend (Timaeus 1986). As figure 8.6 shows, in a number of Western European countries the extent of childlessness was lower among women born in the early 1940s than among those born a decade or so earlier (although there has since been a reversal of this trend, see Chapter 1) so the extent of childlessness in some countries will decline further in the short-term future. In Eastern European countries with historically higher marriage rates the prevalence of childlessness has been, and continues to be lower, as indicated for Hungary in figure 8.6, and shows less fluctuation over time.

This trend towards decreased childlessness in some countries of Europe may at first sight appear paradoxical given the overall downward trend in fertility. However, as has already been noted, above and in Chapter 1, in many countries fertility was higher in the 1950s and 1960s than in the late 1920s and early 1930s. Moreover, reductions in overall fertility and decreases in the proportion of women who have never had a child are not incompatible if lower fertility is achieved through reductions in the number of higher-order births to women who have had at least one child. In Britain, for example, 48 per cent of elderly respondents in the 1962 survey referred to above had three or more children, compared with 38 per cent of elderly respondents in the 1986 British Social Attitudes Survey. The proportion of children surviving to their parents' old age has also increased.

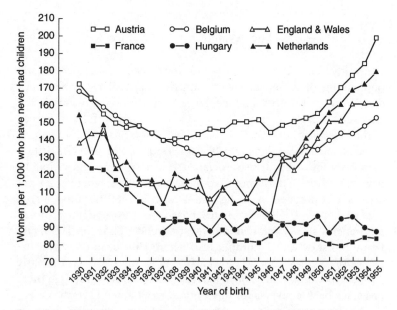

FIG. 8.6. *Proportion of women aged 45–50 never having had children, by year of birth*
Source: Prioux 1993.

In terms of the potential for support for the elderly from their children, clearly the difference between having no children as opposed to one or two is of greater significance than the difference between having two rather than three or four, particularly as numerous studies have shown that the responsibility for providing care to a parent tends to be assumed by one child, rather than shared by siblings (Kendig 1986).

In the short-term future the trends outlined above suggest that a higher proportion of older people in a number of developed countries will have the potential support of children (and also that a higher proportion of middle-aged adults may be called upon to provide support). Increases in the extent of childlessness among post-Second World War birth cohorts, however, suggest a rather different long-term future. Moreover, having children is not of itself an assurance of filial support. Certainly, as the following discussion shows, the extent of inter-generational co-residence has declined markedly in most developed countries.

8.7 The Living Arrangements of Elderly Europeans

The post-war period in many developed countries has been marked by a major shift to smaller, simpler households; this trend includes large increases in the proportions of people living alone (Kobrin 1976; Keilman 1987; Sundström 1994). Changes in the living arrangements of elderly people have played an important part of this change.

In England and Wales and other countries of Northern and Western Europe marriage has been associated with the establishment of a new household since at least pre-industrial times (Smith 1981). While some 'doubling up' of newly married couples with their parents has been a common response to housing shortages (Holmans 1981), co-residence between elderly married couples and their married children seems always to have been unusual (Wall 1990). However, the extent of co-residence between, for example, elderly widows and married daughters or elderly couples and unmarried children was much greater in the past than today. In 1962, for example, 42 per cent of elderly people in Britain lived with one of their children (usually adult) whereas only 14 per cent did so in 1986 (Shanas *et al.* 1968; Jarvis 1993). Historical data from other countries point to a similar decline (Sundström 1994).

The availability of kin is an obvious constraint on living arrangements, particularly in societies in which residence with distant or non-kin is unusual. Reductions in available kin resulting from decreased fertility have been suggested as an important influence on changes in living arrangements (Kobrin 1976). However, as discussed above, the availability of both spouses and at least one child has in some cases increased in the recent past. At least in Britain the proportion of younger elderly people living with a spouse also increased during the 1980s (Murphy and Grundy 1993). However, the proportion of older elderly people living alone continued to grow in this decade and overall the post-war period has been marked by very substantial increases in the extent of residential independence among elderly people. The most usual explanations, apart from demographic ones, offered in explanation of this trend are economic or 'cultural'. Cross-national differences within the developed world point to the latter as an important influence on the living arrangement choices of elderly people.

Table 8.4 shows that in some European countries, such as Italy and Ireland, the proportion of elderly people living with one of their children (usually adult) is still quite high, much higher than in Britain or the Netherlands, for example. As might be expected, where co-residence between elderly parents and children is high, the prevalence of solitary living tends to be relatively low. Long-standing regional and ethnic variations within countries also point to the importance of cultural factors (Bartiaux 1991; van Solinge and Esveldt 1991).

Pampel (1992) has used Eurobarometer data to analyse trends in living alone among elderly people in a number of European countries between 1975 and 1989. He found that in all the countries examined the propensity to live alone increased, but that the rankings between countries remained largely stable. Analyses of differences within each country showed that the measured beliefs and values of individuals in the study had only a weak influence on the propensity to live alone. However, in analyses of differences between countries, aggregate indicators of 'post-materialist' values

TABLE 8.4. *Elderly people living with a child[a] and living alone, selected European countries, 1980s*

Country	Year	Per cent living with child	Per cent living alone	Data source	Analysed by/reported in
Great Britain	1980	16	34	General Household Survey	Dale *et al.* (1987)
Ireland[b]	1979	43	18	Census	Wall (1989)
Italy[c]	1981	35	22	Census sample	Bartiaux (1991)
Netherlands	1986/7	11	34	NCBS Housing Demand Survey	Van Solinge *et al.* (1991)
Poland	1985	35	18	Central Bureau of the Census Survey	Synak (1987)

Notes: [a] Some of the figures given are estimates involving a slight degree of approximation. Percentages refer to all living with a child (or children) of any age or marital status. Either the elderly person or the child may be head of household.
[b] Assumes elderly people in two-family households are living with a child.
[c] Population 60+ (data for other countries relate to population aged 65+).
Source: Compiled from various analyses of census and survey data undertaken by Bartiaux 1991; Dale *et al.* 1987; van Solinge and Esveldt 1991; Synak 1987; Wall 1989, and presented together in Grundy 1992b.

had a greater effect, and these were more consistently associated with propensity to live alone than were aggregate economic indicators.

Commentators on these trends invariably emphasize that these changes in living arrangements do not imply any abandonment of older people by their younger relatives and cite numerous studies showing that elderly people in need of assistance rely heavily on close kin to provide it (Kendig 1986). The preferred model of interaction between generations in many European countries is encapsulated in the term 'intimacy at a distance' and it is argued that economic advances now allow more to realize this.

In this context it should be noted that Eurobarometer data show that the proportion of older people who report often feeling lonely is highest in Portugal and Greece and lowest in Denmark (EC Commission 1991). This finding suggests, if anything, an inverse relationship with the extent of solitary living. Data from the same survey suggest wide variations in the extent of contact with family members, partly reflecting differences in living arrangements. In Ireland half of older people (60+) saw a family member daily and in Greece, Italy, Spain, and Portugal the figure was 60 per cent or more, whereas in the UK, the Netherlands, and Denmark the figure was close to or less than 20 per cent.

8.8 Socio-Demographic Characteristics of Europe's Population

Increases in divorce, lone parenthood, and the participation of married women in the labour market are frequently cited as constraints on the availability of the younger generation to provide support for their elders. Moreover, changes in patterns of family formation and dissolution have been interpreted by some as indicative of a major re-orientation from familial to individual goals and aspirations (van de Kaa 1987; Inglehart 1990). If this is the case, some change in attitudes to inter-generational relationships would also seem highly probable. Table 8.5 shows the proportion of non-marital births and of women in the labour force in European countries. TFRs and an indicator of the extent of lone parenthood are also given. It can be seen that in Austria, Estonia, Norway, and the United Kingdom roughly a quarter or more, and in Denmark and Sweden a half, of all births now occur outside marriage. A large proportion of these are born to couples who have not legally formalized their unions, rather than to single parents, and it is union breakdown, rather than births outside marriage, that is the major cause of lone parenthood (although in many countries births outside marriage are increasing). In much of Northern, Western, and Eastern Europe lon-parent families now constitute 10 per cent or more of all families with children. From a historical perspective this is not unusual (Anderson 1983); what is different is that in

TABLE 8.5. *Selected socio-demographic characteristics of the populations of EC countries, 1980s or 1990s*

Country	1990 or late 1980s			1980s
	Total fertility rate[a]	Births outside marriage	Women in the labour force (%)[a]	Lone-parent families[b]
Austria	1.5	23	54	M
Belgium	1.6	9	52	M
Bulgaria	1.7	12	77	—
Czechoslovakia	2.0	8	74	—
Denmark	1.7	46	77	H
Estonia	2.2	25	—	—
Finland	1.7	19	73	H
France	1.8	28	56	M
Germany	1.5	16	55	M
Greece	1.5	2	44	L
Hungary	1.8	12	62	M
Ireland	2.2	13	38	L
Italy	1.3	6	44	M
Latvia	2.0	16	—	—
Lithuania	2.0	7	—	—
Luxemburg	1.6	13	48	M
Netherlands	1.6	11	51	M
Norway	1.6	34	71	M
Poland	2.0	6	66	H
Portugal	1.4	15	60	L
Romania	2.0	—	68	—
Spain	1.3	8	41	L
Sweden	2.1	52	81	M
Switzerland	1.6	6	59	L
UK	1.8	28	65	H

Notes: [a] As percentage of women aged 15–64 (in nearly all cases).
  [b] Based on estimates of the proportion of all families with children under 18 comprising a parent not living in a couple and one or more children under 18. Because of varying definitions, approximations are involved. H = high: >13%; M = medium: 10 > 13%; L = low: <10%.
Sources: TFRs, births outside marriage, women in the labour force: Population Reference Bureau Inc. 1991 and United Nations 1991; lone-parent families: EC Commission 1989, Council of Europe 1991, Boh, Bak, and Clason 1989.

contemporary developed societies divorce rather than death is the major cause of lone parenthood. As the table shows, in much of Europe over half of all women are now employed outside the home; this too represents a divergence from the recent past (Joshi 1985). These patterns would suggest that women might have less disposable time than in the past to provide support for elderly relatives and, perhaps, less inclination to adopt 'traditional' family-orientated roles.

Evidence on these important issues is unfortunately sparse and in some cases conflicting; moreover most is based on data from the United States rather than Europe. Wolf and Soldo (1988) found that working daughters in the United States were less likely to live with an unmarried elderly mother than daughters not in the labour force. Brody and Schoonover (1986) reported from another United States study of daughters assisting disabled mothers that those who were not in the labour force provided more intensive care than those who were working outside the home. However, studies in a number of European and other developed countries have failed to find a strong negative relationship between women's work and fulfilment of caring obligations (for a review see Sundström 1994). Grundy and Harrop (1992), for example, found no significant association between the labour-force participation of middle-aged women and co-residence with an elderly parent. Grundy and Harrop (1992) also reported that in England and Wales the divorced, including single parents, were more likely to co-reside with an elderly parent than their married peers. These findings point to the important, but sometimes overlooked, role of elderly people as providers rather than recipients of support. Divorced sons and daughters, lone parents, and working mothers may themselves have support needs which are met by their own parents; working mothers in France and Britain, for example, rely heavily on their own mothers for help with child-care (Toulemon and Villeneuve-Gokalp 1988; Martin and Roberts 1984). In at least some cases recent trends in family organization and labour-market participation may thus, perhaps paradoxically, lead to a strengthening of inter-generational ties. However, the ability, and willingness, of grandmothers to provide support to younger kin may itself be changing as their own involvement in the labour market increases.

8.9 Discussion

Demographic changes in Europe have led to substantial increases in the relative, and absolute, size of their elderly populations. In many of these societies the ageing of these elderly populations is currently the major concern (particularly with regard to health-care expenditures which are strongly age related (Grundy 1992c)). Early in the next century when the 'baby boom' generations reach later life the funding of pension schemes is likely to become a predominant issue. This is because nearly all national pension schemes are funded on a 'pay as you go' basis, that is, through the contributions of the *current* work-force rather than through any accumulated reserve of previous contributions. A fall in the ratio of workers to pensioners thus implies either a reduction in the value of pensions or an increase in transfer payments (taxes), or some combination of the two (Johnson 1994).

It should be noted that increases in expenditure on both health care and pensions cannot be attributed to population ageing alone. Advances in medical technology, for example, have exerted a marked effect on health-care expenditures (Robins and Wittenberg 1992), while decreases in the economic participation of older adults have had a major influence on the 'worker'/'pensioner' ratio (Guilmot 1978; Johnson 1994).

While population ageing is largely the result of trends in fertility (recently heightened by changes in mortality), in the short term these changes do not necessarily imply any increase in the proportion of old people who lack close kin. On the contrary, in some countries, those now attaining older ages include larger proportions who have had children, larger proportions not yet widowed, and smaller proportions who have never married. As yet the proportions of elderly people who are divorced is small, but these proportions are rapidly increasing. Cohorts born since the mid-1950s, however, have shown different patterns of family formation and dissolution, and longer-term prospects for the familial support of old people are therefore likely to be less favourable.

These recent changes in family patterns and other, related, changes in, for example, household characteristics may, it is suggested, indicate a 'cultural shift' with far-reaching implications (Inglehart 1990). Despite marked decreases in the extent of inter-generational co-residence, however, numerous studies from developed countries show that younger relatives play a major part in providing assistance to older people who need it. Nevertheless, it is possible that the attitudes of people towards *receiving* care from relatives may be changing. Data from Norway, for example, suggest that there has been a marked shift in the past three decades in preferred sources of support—away from kin towards formally provided services (Daatland 1990).

Finally the very considerable diversity within Europe in, for example, marital status distributions, life expectancy at the age of 65, and the extent of inter-generational co-residence should be stressed. This diversity indicates the important influence of particular historical and cultural contexts on demographic characteristics and patterns of inter-generational interaction.

NOTE

This chapter represents an expanded and updated version of a chapter prepared with Anne Harrop and previously published in R. Anderson *et al.* (1992) *The Coming of Age in Europe*, London: Age Concern England.

REFERENCES

ANDERSON, M. (1983), 'What is new about the modern family: an historical perspective', *BSPS Conference Proceedings 1983*, OPCS Occasional Paper No. 31, London: OPCS.

BARTIAUX, F. (1991), 'La composition des mènages des personnes âgées en Italie (1981)', *European Journal of Population*, 7: 59–98.

BOH, R., BAK, M., and CLASON, C. (1989), *Changing Patterns of European Family Life*, London: Routledge & Kegan Paul.

BRODY, E., and SCHOONOVER, C. (1986), 'Patterns of parent care when adult daughters work and when they do not', *The Gerontologist*, 26: 372–81.

CAFFERATA, G. L. (1987), 'Marital Status, living arrangements and the use of health services by elderly persons', *Journal of Gerontology*, 42: 613–18.

CARLSON, E. (1990), 'European contrasts in sex ratios: implications for living arrangements in old age', *European Journal of Population*, 6: 117–41.

CARRIER, N. (1962), 'Demographic aspects of the ageing of the population', in A. T. Welford (ed.), *Society, Problems and Methods of Study*, London: Routledge & Kegan Paul.

CASELLI, G., VALLIN, J., VAUPEL, J., and YAHSIN, A. (1987), 'Age Specific Mortality Trends in France and Italy since 1990; period and cohort effects', *European Journal of Population* 3: 33–60.

Centre for Policy on Ageing/Family Policy Studies Centre (CPA/FPSC) (1993) *Older People in the European Community*, London.

COALE, A. J., and WATKINS, S. C. (1986), *The Decline of Fertility in Europe*, Princeton: Princeton University Press.

COLEMAN, D., and SALT, J. (1992), *The British Population: Patterns, Trends, and Processes*, Oxford: Oxford University Press.

COUNCIL OF EUROPE (1991), *Seminar on Present Demographic Trends and Lifestyles in Europe*, Strasburg, 18–20 September 1990, Strasburg: Council of Europe.

DAATLAND, S. (1990), 'What are families for? on family solidarity and preference for help', *Ageing and Society*, 10: 1–15.

DALE, A., EVANDROU, M., and ARBER, S. (1987), 'The household structure of the elderly population in Britain', *Ageing and Society*, 7:37–56.

EC COMMISSION (1989), *Lone Parent Families in the European Community: Final Report*. Directorate-General, Employment, Industrial Relations and Social Affairs, V/S45/89-EN, Brussels.

—— (1991), *Age and Attitudes: Main Results from a Eurobarometer Survey*, Directorate-General V, Employment, Industrial Relations and Social Affairs, Brussels.

EUROSTAT (1993), *Demographic Statistics 1993*, Luxemburg: Office for Official Publications of the European Communities.

GONNOT, P. (1992), 'Some selected aspects of mortality in the ECE Region', in G. J. Stolnitz (ed.), *Demographic Causes and Economic Consequences of Population Aging, Europe and North America*, New York: United Nations.

GRUNDY, E. (1991), 'Ageing: age-related change in later life', in M. Murphy and J. Hobcraft (eds.), *Population Research in Britain*, supplement to *Population Studies*, 45: 133–56.

—— (1992a), 'Socio-demographic variations in rates of movement into institutions among elderly people in England and Wales: an analysis of linked census and mortality data', *Population Studies*, 46: 65–84.

—— (1992b), 'The living arrangements of elderly people', *Reviews in Clinical Gerontology*, 2: 353–61.

—— (1992c), 'The epidemiology of aging', in J. C. Brocklehurst,

R. Tallis, and H. Fillit (eds.), *Textbook of Geriatric Medicine and Gerontology*, 4th ed. Edinburgh: Churchill Livingstone: 1–20.

—— and HARROP, A. (1992), 'Co-residence between adult children and their elderly parents in England and Wales', *Journal of Social Policy*, 21: 325–48.

GUILMOT, P. (1978), 'The demographic background', in Council of Europe, *Population Decline in Europe: Implications of a Declining or Stationary Population*, London: Edward Arnold.

HAJNAL, J. (1965), 'European marriage patterns in perspective', in D. V. Glass and D. E. Eversley (eds.), *Population in History*, London: Edward Arnold.

HOLMANS, A. (1981), 'Housing careers of newly married couples', *Population Trends*, 24: 10–14.

INGLEHART, R. (1990), *Culture Shift in Advanced Industrial Society*, Princeton: Princeton University Press.

JARVIS, C. (1993), 'Family and friends in old age, and the implications for informal support: evidence from the British Social Attitudes Survey of 1986', London: Joseph Rowntree Foundation. *Age Concern Institute of Gerontology, Working Paper* No. 6, King's College, London.

Johnson, P. (1994), 'Retirement: evolution and macro-economic implications', *Reviews in Clinical Gerontology*, 4, 161–7.

JOSHI, H. (1985), 'Motherhood and employment: change and continuity in post war Britain', in *Measuring Socio-Demographic Change*, OPCS Occasional Paper No. 34, London: OPCS.

KEILMAN, N. (1987), 'Recent trends in family and household composition in Europe', *European Journal of Population*, 3: 297–325.

KENDIG, H. (1986), 'Intergenerational exchange', in H. Kendig (ed.), *Ageing and Families: A Support Networks Perspective*, Sydney: Allen and Unwin.

KOBRIN, F. E. (1976), 'The primary individual and the family: changes in living arrangements in the United States since 1940', *Journal of Marriage and the Family*, 38: 233–38.

MARTIN, J., and ROBERTS, C. (1984), *Women and Employment*, London: HMSO.

MURPHY, M. J. (1995), 'Methods of forecasting mortality and their performance', *Reviews in Clinical Gerontology*, 5, 217–27.

—— and GRUNDY, E. (1993), 'Co-residence of generations and household structure in Britain, aspects of change in the 1980s', in H.A. Becker and P.L.S. Hermkens (eds.), *Solidarity of Generations: Demographic, Economic and Social Change, and its Consequences*, vol. 2. Amsterdam: Thesis Publishers.

OFFICE OF POPULATION CENSUSES and SURVEYS (OPCS) (1979), *Life Tables 1970–72*, Series DS No. 2, London: HMSO.

—— (1992), 1990 *Mortality Statistics*, Series DH7 No. 23, London: HMSO.

PAMPEL, F. C. (1983), 'Changes in the propensity to live alone: evidence from consecutive cross sectional surveys, 1960–76', *Demography*, 20: 433–7.

—— (1992), 'Trends in living alone among the elderly in Europe', in A. Rogers (ed.), *Elderly Migration and Population Redistribution: a Comparative Study*, London: Belhaven: 97–117.

POPULATION REFERENCE BUREAU INC. (1991), *Europe: Population Data Sheet 1991*, New York: Population Reference Bureau Inc. (Market: Europe).

PRESTON, S. H. (1976), *Mortality in National Populations with Special Reference to Recorded Causes of Death*, London: Academic Press.

—— HIMES, C., and EGGERS, M. (1989), 'Demographic conditions responsible for population aging', *Demography* 26: 691–704.

PRIOUX F. (1993), 'L'infécondité en Europe', in A. Blum and J.-L. Rallu (eds.), *European Population*, Vol. 2: *Demographic Dynamics*, Paris: John Libbey Eurotext.

ROBINS, A., and WITTENBERG, R. (1992), 'The health of elderly people: economic aspects', in Central Health Monitoring Unit, *The Health of Elderly People, an Epidemiological Overview*, Vol. 2, Companion Papers, London: HMSO.

SHANAS, E., *et al.* (1968), *Old People in Three Industrial Societies*, London: Routledge & Kegan Paul.

SMITH, R. M. (1981), 'Fertility, economy and household formation in England over three centuries', *Population and Development Review*, 7: 595–623.

SUNDSTRÖM, G. (1994), 'Care by families: an overview of trends', in OECD, *Caring for Frail Elderly People*, Paris: OECD.

SYNAK, B. (1987), 'The elderly in Poland: an overview of selected problems and changes', in S. di Gregorio (ed.), *Social Gerontology: New Directions*, Beckenham: Croom Helm.

TIMAEUS, I. (1986), 'Families and households of the elderly population: prospects for those approaching old age', *Ageing and Society* 6: 271–93.

TOULEMON, L., and VILLENEUVE-GOKALP, C. (1988), 'Les Vacances des enfants', *Population*, 43: 1065–88.

UNITED NATIONS (1991), *The Sex and Age of Populations. The 1990 Revision of the United Nations Global Estimates and Projections*, Geneva: United Nations.

—— (1992a), *Demographic Yearbook 1991*. New York: United Nations.

—— (1992b), *Demographic Yearbook 1990*, New York: United Nations.

UNITED NATIONS SECRETARIAT (1988), 'Sex differentials in life expectancy and mortality in developed countries: an analysis by age groups and causes of death from recent and historical data', *Population Bulletin of the United Nations*, No. 25, Geneva: United Nations.

VAN DE KAA, D. J. (1987), *Europe's Second Demographic Transition*, Population Bulletin No. 42, Washington, DC: Population Reference Bureau Inc.

VAN POPPEL, F., and DE BEER, J. (1993), 'Evaluation of mortality projections for the elderly: national populations projections in industrialized countries', in G. Caselli and A. Lopez (eds.), *Health and Mortality Among Elderly Populations*. Oxford: Clarendon Press.

VAN SOLINGE, H., and ESVELDT, I. (1991), 'Living Arrangements of the Dutch Elderly (1956–1986), Paper presented at the European Population Conference, Paris, 21–25 October 1991, The Hague: Netherlands Interdisciplinary Demographic Institute.

VELKOFF, V., and KINSELLA, K. (1993), *Aging in Eastern Europe and the Former Soviet Union*, Washington, DC: US Bureau of Census.

VIRGANSKAYA, I. M., and DMITRIEV, V. I. (1992), 'Some problems of medicodemographic development in the former USSR', in World Health Organization, *Demographic Trends, Aging and Non Communicable Diseases, World Health Statistics Quarterly*, 45(1): 4–14 (Geneva).

WALL, R. (1989), 'The residence patterns of the elderly in Europe in the 1980s', in E. Grebenik, C. Höhn, and R. Mackensen (eds.), *Later Phases of the Family Cycle: Demographic Aspects*, Oxford: Clarendon Press.

—— (1990), 'Intergenerational relations in the European past', Paper presented to the British Sociological Association Annual Conference, Guildford, 2–5 April.

WILLEKENS, F., and SCHERBOV, S. (1992), 'Analysis of mortality data from the former USSR: age-period-cohort analysis', in World Health Organization, *Demographic Trends, Aging and Non Communicable Diseases, World Health Statistics Quarterly*, 45(1): 29–49 (Geneva).

WOLF, D., and SOLDO, B. (1988), 'Household composition choices of older unmarried women', *Demography*, 25: 387–403.

9

The Measured and Unmeasured Effects of Welfare Benefits on Families: Implications for Europe's Demographic Trends

ANNE HÉLÈNE GAUTHIER

9.1 Introduction

The transformations undergone by the family since the 1960s have attracted much attention in both academic and non-academic circles. The decline in fertility, the instability of unions, the development of non-marital cohabitation, and the participation of women in the labour force have all become subjects of particular concern. Not only have scholars expressed interest in learning about the extent, causes, and consequences of these changes, as previous chapters have pointed out, but governments have also increasingly done so. The questions of what is happening to the family, what should be the role of the state, and what forms of support should be provided, have indeed been given an increasing priority in Europe, as well as in other industrialized or newly industrialized countries. But, although these academic and governmental queries have led to a multiplication of studies and surveys about the family, an area which remains particularly obscure is that of the effects of welfare benefits on families.

It is this whole question of the effects of welfare benefits on families which this chapter examines. This question is particularly important for the Europe of the 1990s where issues of persistent low levels of fertility and increasing instability of families have received a lot of attention, and have been raised in parallel to the issue of state support for families. Questions such as the extent to

which policies more friendly towards children and parents can lead
to higher fertility levels, and the extent to which some of the
targeted welfare benefits have undesirable effects in encouraging
the breakdown of families, have been at the centre of serious
political and academic debate. These questions are indeed important. If welfare benefits and state support for families do have an
effect on demographic behaviour, then it follows that the future
course of demographic trends in Europe may partly be dependent
on governments' actions and interventions in this field. But, as
pointed out above, knowledge about the effects of welfare benefits
is still limited. It is therefore hoped that this chapter will shed some
light on the subject.

The chapter has two objectives: (a) to review the assumptions
which underlie the theoretical relationships between welfare benefits and demographic behaviour, and (b) to examine the empirical
studies which have addressed this question. In particular, a large
part of the chapter will be devoted to a discussion of the methodological and substantive limitations of studies on the effects of
welfare benefits; limitations which, I will argue, have so far led to
inconclusive findings. More precisely, I will argue that empirical
analyses carried out so far have failed to acknowledge the
heterogeneity among the population in terms of entitlement to, and
actual receipt of, welfare benefits. To carry out this task, the
chapter is divided into five sections. In the first section (9.2), I
discuss the *a priori* interpretations and assumptions which have
surrounded the question of the effects of welfare benefits on families. In section 9.3, I then further examine some of these assumptions by referring to the economic theory. In section 9.4, I present
some data on state support for families for various countries, and
point out the main sources of heterogeneity which have tended to
be overlooked in the literature. A review of empirical studies on the
effects of family benefits on demographic behaviour follows.
Finally, I conclude by suggesting some guidelines for further
research.

This chapter does not present new evidence concerning the
effects of family benefits on demographic behaviour. Instead, it
should be seen as an account of the current 'state of the art', and
as a step towards further analyses. The question addressed here is
complex and it would obviously be impossible to exhaust it completely. Furthermore, for reasons of space, the analysis presented

here will be restricted to particular types of welfare benefits, and will focus only on some of their potential intended and unintended effects. More precisely, I will here leave aside the whole question of the effects of welfare benefits on poverty and income distribution, and will concentrate on the effects of benefits on three specific spheres: fertility, female employment, and family structure.

9.2 The Assumed Effects of Family Benefits

The intervention of governments into family life, through specific legislation and the provision of services and benefits, has a long history. It is however only from the immediate post-Second World War period that the right of families to state support became enshrined in international treaties. For instance, the United Nations Declaration of Human Rights (1948) acknowledges the right of the family to be protected by the society and the state (Article 16), and the right to social security (Article 22). The post-war development of the welfare state was indeed to lead to a multiplication of benefits in cash and in kind, many of which were directed at families. It was the so-called golden age of the welfare state; a period which saw not only an increase in the material well-being of families, but also a growing role of the state as regulator and welfare provider. This rapid expansion of state support for families was, however, halted or at least seriously questioned for several reasons from the 1970s. First, the development of welfare benefits had grown unchecked and had resulted in a complex and expensive package. Second, the transformations undergone by the family were forcing governments to re-evaluate their support for families. Third, the rediscovery of poverty in the 1960s, along with the emergence of new categories of welfare beneficiaries in the 1970s–80s (for example, lone parents and the long-term unemployed) were revealing the inadequacy of the current systems. It is in this context that the question of the effects of welfare benefits on families was to receive increasing attention. More precisely, at least three main questions were to follow.

There was first the question of the effect of family benefits on fertility. In a context of rapidly declining fertility from the mid-1960s, and the reach of below-replacement fertility levels, the potential pro-natalist effects of welfare benefits received increasing attention. It was in France, with its long tradition of pro-natalism, that this question was given most prominence, but from a very distinct angle. While in most countries the potential effect of pro-natalist policies was questioned, and also their legitimacy, in France these two aspects were not questioned. On the contrary, it was instead generally acknowledged that a higher level of state support for families could encourage childbearing, and moreover, that it was the government's responsibility to make such pro-natalist intervention. In France, the question, 'Can welfare benefits encourage childbearing?' tended to be answered positively, and instead replaced by the question, 'What types of benefits may best encourage childbearing?' This near consensus on the pro-natalist effects of benefits, or the *a priori* belief in their efficacy, places France in a very special category; one shared with very few other countries or provinces (Luxemburg, Belgium, Quebec).

The second question which has been raised since the 1970s is of a completely different nature, being concerned not with the potentially pro-natalist effects of benefits, but conversely with their potentially perverse effects in undermining the traditional family. This time the question has received most attention in Britain and the United States where it was feared that state support for families was unintentionally encouraging lone parenthood, marital instability, and welfare dependency. The initial debate on the question was launched in the late 1960s as part of the American government's war on poverty. Welfare benefits, it was argued, were encouraging husbands to desert their wives and were encouraging pregnant mothers to remain unmarried (Berkowitz 1991:123–4). In recent years, the unintended consequences of state support were again stressed, especially by authors such as Murray (1984) who have been advocating substantial cuts in welfare programmes, even their complete abolition. This whole argument has not been confined to the unintended effect of targeted and means-tested benefits. Some scholars have argued that general welfare measures, and especially a high level of welfare support, can also undermine the family. This last argument has been presented most forcefully by Popenoe (1988, 1991) who, referring to the Swedish case, has argued that the high level of welfare provided by the government has led to the decline of the family. Not surprisingly, this attack on the Swedish welfare state has provoked a real controversy, with scholars counter-arguing that, not only was there no evidence of family decline, but, furthermore, that families were instead 'thriving' under the Swedish welfare regime (Sandqvist and Andersson 1992).

Finally, the third question which has been raised in recent years concerns not so much the potential effects of welfare benefits, but more its forms and legitimacy. This question has been addressed more specifically with regard to the participation of women in the labour force, the query being whether the state should discourage women (especially those with small children) from joining the labour force, should stay neutral, or should encourage women to work. At this level, the responses of governments have varied widely, ranging from a high support to working mothers in Sweden to a level of minimal support in the United Kingdom, where the issue is not considered to be a state responsibility. It is not possible here to expand this point further. Instead, in the next section I examine the theoretical arguments which underpin the assumed effects of welfare benefits on families.

9.3 The Theoretical Effects

Most of these theoretical arguments have been derived from the economic theory of fertility, in its New Home Economics version, and are centred around the concept of the cost of children (see Chapter 5 by Ermisch). The argument is in essence simple: the higher the cost of children, the lower the demand for them. And thus, by extension, the higher are the levels of cash benefits or maternity benefits, the higher will be the demand for children since these benefits reduce respectively the direct and opportunity cost of children. The French pro-natalist hypothesis reviewed above, as well as the American 'unintended consequence' hypothesis, are both based on this cost-benefit argument. This theory has its shortcomings. First, it has been argued forcefully by some authors that children are not consumer goods and that it cannot be assumed that a higher income, or a lower cost of children, will result in a higher demand for children (see Blake 1968). Second, it has also been argued that there might be a potential trade-off between the quality and quantity of children and that higher benefits, or a higher income, can lead to children of higher quality (cost) rather than to a higher number of children. This last shortcoming is now widely acknowledged and makes it more difficult to assume, *a priori*, that welfare benefits will encourage childbearing.

Although the New Home Economics theory has been applied mainly to fertility, it can easily be extended to the analysis of family structure. The argument here becomes that the presence of differential cash benefits according to family type (for example, higher benefits for lone-parent families) may encourage individuals to opt for this type of family because it is perceived as financially rewarding. This is essentially the logic behind the American right-wing interpretation: higher benefits for lone-parent families involuntarily encourage the entry into lone parenthood, and involuntarily prolong its duration, by making (re)marriage less attractive. I am generally favourable to this economic theory, but with two major qualifications. First, economic considerations linked with the cost of children are only some of a much larger number of other economic, social, and normative factors influencing decisions with regard to fertility and family structure. It would therefore be difficult to expect family benefits to have major effects. And second, in view of the very high cost of children, as compared to the relatively low levels of family benefits, it follows that the effect of benefits, if any, can only be of a very small magnitude. Bearing in mind these two qualifications, let me introduce a third point. The effects of welfare benefits on fertility or family structure are likely to vary across different sub-groups of the population for economic, social, and normative reasons. In particular, the effects are likely to vary because sub-groups differ in their entitlement to benefits, and in their actual receipt. The relative value of benefits (as a percentage of income) also differs across sub-groups, thus adding to this heterogeneity. This further refinement of the economic theory is important, as the failure explicitly to acknowledge heterogeneity across sub-groups of the population may have partly obscured findings from previous studies.

Let me here comment further on three main sources of heterogeneity which have tended to be overlooked in the literature. First, as discussed in the next section, there are wide disparities within countries with regard to the entitlement to state benefits, their actual take-up, and the entitlement to additional private benefits or benefits provided by employers. This means that the actual amount of benefits received by each family (from both public and private sources) varies substantially, and thus may generate effects of different magnitude. In addition, even if families were to receive the same level of benefits, the relative value of these benefits would vary widely, as they would represent a larger, or smaller, fraction of the household budget. According to the economic theory reviewed above, it may therefore be expected that family benefits may have a larger effect on low-income families than on high-income ones. It should be stressed that the economic theory is formulated in terms of absolute cost of children and absolute level of income and benefits, rather than in terms of relative levels. The further refinement suggested here is, however, only an extension of this theory.

The second source of heterogeneity concerns the variation among women according to their entitlement to maternity benefits and their respective opportunity cost of childbearing. The argument here is that women in low-paid and precarious jobs are likely to be entitled to less generous maternity leave benefits than women in high-paid and more steady jobs, and thus may face higher net opportunity cost of childbearing. The distinction between gross and net opportunity cost is important. If withdrawal from the labour market means smaller loss of income for women in low-paid jobs, compared to women in high-paid jobs (that is, a lower gross opportunity cost), the inequality may be reversed when maternity leave benefits are taken into account (that is, a higher net opportunity cost). In particular, women in low-paid and precarious jobs may be ineligible for public maternity benefits, because they do not meet the appropriate criteria, and they may furthermore be less likely to be entitled to private (occupational) benefits. Conversely, women with better jobs, by being entitled to more generous benefits, may face fewer obstacles to childbearing as well as enjoying the privilege of a more continuous work pattern. As a result, and in terms of net opportunity cost, women in low-paid jobs may face greater obstacles to childbearing than women with better jobs.

There are two further points to consider here. First, in addition to facing a higher net opportunity cost of children, women with poorly paid jobs may also be making a substantial contribution to family income. As argued below, one cannot ignore the household situation and the relative importance of the woman's earning contribution in assessing the effects of welfare benefits. Second, beyond the immediate financial side of the opportunity cost of children, there are also other costs associated with childbearing. For example, a woman who withdraws from the labour market for childbearing, even temporarily, may miss some opportunities for promotion and training, and may also face some psychological costs such as dissatisfaction at being at home or subsequent lower job satisfaction associated with a prolonged absence from work. (For an estimate of the total financial opportunity cost of childbearing, see Joshi 1987. References to the psychological cost of childbearing and the loss of satisfaction towards work can be found in Moen 1989 and Haas 1990.) Maternity benefits, however, cover only the strict immediate financial cost of childbearing, thus forcing women to assume the other costs privately. Assuming that career-oriented women may value these other forms of opportunity cost more highly than do women who are less career oriented, it follows that the former may be less willing to withdraw from work for childbearing than the latter, regardless of the level of maternity benefits. The relationships between women's participation in the labour force, entitlement to maternity benefits, and childbearing are therefore likely to reveal much differentiation and heterogeneity.

Finally, the third source of heterogeneity concerns the variation in the population with regard to the earnings of husbands and wives. The argument here is that low-income families may be more heavily dependent on women's earnings than other families, and may therefore be less able to give up this source of income for the purpose of childbearing. This aspect is important as it suggests not only that the husband's and wife's respective earnings have a separate effect on fertility, as assumed by the economic theory, but that there is also a joint effect. The effects of benefits on families may consequently vary according to the woman's earnings, relative to those of her husband. On the other hand, it can be argued that higher-income families may also be highly dependent on women's earnings, especially if they face high mortgages and other payments. They may be equally unable (or even less able) to afford the loss of one earning.

These three sources of heterogeneity illustrate well the complexity of the potential relationships between welfare benefits and demographic behaviour. In fact, as will be argued in section 9.5, the empirical analyses carried out so far have failed to take this complexity into account. Before examining these analyses, I present in the next section cross-national data on family benefits and further emphasize these sources of heterogeneity.

9.4 Heterogeneity in State Support for Families

As pointed out in section 9.2, since the Second World War, state support for families has grown into a multitude of forms, including cash and in-kind benefits, as well as direct and indirect benefits. For the purpose of this analysis, I focus, however, only on a fraction of the total state support for families. More precisely, three main forms of benefits will be analysed here: cash benefits, maternity/parental leave benefits, and child-care facilities. For each of these, I point out how the conventional comparison between countries has failed to highlight both heterogeneity between and within countries.

Let me begin with cash benefits. Data on family allowances are now routinely published for a large number of countries, and allow inter-country comparison in terms of their absolute or relative value. Such data, as of 1989, are presented in table 9.1, and reveal strong disparities between countries. Focusing on the first column, which gives the amount received by a two-child family (in US dollars), benefits vary between high levels in Norway, Austria, and Belgium, and low levels in Italy, Japan, and Spain.

This ranking is, however, limited on several grounds. First, it hides the fact that in some countries the allowances are not universal but subject to an income test, especially in Australia, Germany, Italy, and Canada (since 1992, when the Canadian government decided to abolish the universal family allowances and to replace them by a means-tested tax-related benefit.) It therefore follows that in these countries, the amount of benefit received by each family varies according to its income and, in Italy, its composition. Second, this ranking of countries is also highly dependent on the index used. For instance, a slightly different ranking is obtained when the benefits are expressed in relative terms, as a percentage of the average male wages in manufacturing, or when the benefits are expressed by reference to a three-child family. In particular, it should be noted that in countries, such as France, where a clear preference is given to the third child, the ranking is substantially improved when the index used refers to a three- rather than a two-

TABLE 9.1. *Family allowances in selected countries, 1989*[a]

	Two-child family				Three-child family			
	US$	Rank	Per cent	Rank	US$	Rank	Per cent	Rank
Australia[b]	48.3	(14)	3.2	(15)	72.5	(15)	4.9	(15)
Austria	146.3	(2)	10.3	(2)	219.5	(4)	15.4	(4)
Belgium[c]	141.9	(3)	12.5	(1)	279.4	(2)	24.6	(1)
Canada	51.6	(13)	2.9	(16)	77.3	(14)	4.3	(16)
Denmark	88.4	(8)	6.7	(8)	132.6	(10)	10.0	(9)
Finland[c]	70.8	(11)	7.3	(6)	119.8	(12)	12.4	(6)
France[c]	76.7	(10)	7.4	(5)	175.0	(6)	16.9	(3)
Germany (West)[cd]	62.2	(12)	4.3	(13)	153.5	(8)	10.5	(8)
Greece[c]	33.8	(16)	3.7	(14)	91.1	(13)	10.0	(11)
Ireland	39.8	(15)	2.8	(17)	59.6	(16)	4.2	(17)
Italy[ce]	13.5	(19)	1.0	(19)	53.9	(17)	4.0	(18)
Japan[c]	12.3	(20)	0.6	(20)	36.8	(20)	1.8	(20)
Luxemburg[c]	29.7	(4)	8.0	(4)	285.3	(1)	17.7	(2)
Netherlands[c]	101.3	(6)	6.2	(10)	162.9	(7)	10.0	(10)
New Zealand	28.7	(17)	2.2	(18)	43.1	(18)	3.2	(19)
Norway[c]	151.2	(1)	8.7	(3)	242.3	(3)	14.0	(5)
Portugal	27.8	(18)	5.6	(11)	41.7	(19)	8.4	(13)
Spain	4.5	(21)	0.4	(21)	6.7	(21)	0.6	(21)
Sweden[c]	104.8	(5)	6.9	(7)	183.9	(5)	12.1	(7)
Switzerland[c]	77.9	(9)	4.8	(12)	120.9	(11)	7.4	(14)
United Kingdom	100.7	(7)	6.3	(9)	151.1	(9)	9.5	(12)
United States	—		—		—		—	

Notes:

[a] Values in US dollars have been calculated on the basis of parity purchasing power indices; values in percentage terms have been calculated by reference to the average male wages in manufacturing.

[b] The amount indicated is that received by a family whose income does not exceed the eligibility threshold (above which no allowance is paid).

[c] In these countries, family allowance rates vary according to the birth order of the child.

[d] The amount indicated is the maximum received by a family whose income does not exceed the threshold (above this threshold the allowances paid are gradually reduced).

[e] Data used here refer to the amount received by a family with an income equal to that of an average worker in manufacturing (family allowance for first child = 0; second child = 20,000 Lire/month; third child = 60,000 Lire/month).

Sources: The following official sources were used, as well as information provided by relevant authorities in each country: EC Commission various years; Council of Europe various years; and United States various years.

child family. Third, data are also limited by the fact that they are restricted to family allowances and exclude other direct (for example, birth grant) and indirect cash benefits (such as tax-related benefits), as well as other means-tested benefits and those targeted at specific families (such as single-parent families). In some countries, these other benefits may in fact exceed the universal ones. A clear example is provided by the United States where there is no universal family allowance but where state support is provided through other forms such as the tax reduction for dependent children, and the means-tested Aid to Families with Dependent Children (AFDC). Finally, the ranking shown in the table is also limited since it is restricted to benefits provided by the central government, and ignores benefits provided by regional governments (as in Germany, Canada, and Switzerland).

As a result of these limitations, a study which focuses only on family allowances, or on AFDC benefits, to evaluate the effects of welfare benefits on families, would introduce a major bias. In particular, it would ignore the fact that families with different incomes, and with different numbers of children (of different ages), are entitled to variable levels of cash benefits. This source of heterogeneity is illustrated well in the study of Bradshaw and Piachaud (1980) which, in addition to incorporating a large number of benefits, also reveals considerable variations by family type in the value of benefits. However, as section 9.5 shows the empirical studies on the effects of welfare benefits have often ignored this source of heterogeneity.

The second type of state support considered here refers to maternity and parental leave benefits. Again, data on these benefits are now routinely published, and reveal the differences between countries in terms of duration of the leave, and in terms of the pay received during this period. Table 9.2 presents such data as of 1990 and clearly shows the leading position of the Nordic countries, which leave countries such as the United Kingdom, Switzerland, and Greece far behind. Moreover, the United States and Australia have still not adopted any national legislation concerning maternity leave. However, in the United States, legislation was adopted in 1992 giving parents the right to twelve weeks' leave for sickness-related reasons, including the birth of a child (Family and Medical Leave Act). The leave is unpaid. Previously, the situation varied widely between States. As of 1990, thirty States

TABLE 9.2. *Maternity leave benefits in selected countries, 1990*

	No. of weeks	As percentage of wages[a]	Index[b]
Australia	—	—	—
Austria	16	100	16.0
Belgium[c]	14	80	11.1
Canada[c]	15	60	9.0
Denmark[c]	28	90	25.2
Finland	44	80	35.2
France[cd]	16	84	13.4
Germany (West)[c]	14	100	14.0
Greece[c]	15	50	7.5
Ireland[ce]	14	70	9.8
Italy	22	80	17.6
Japan	14	60	8.4
Luxemburg[c]	16	100	16.0
Netherlands	16	100	16.0
New Zealand[f]	35	96	33.6
Norway[g]	28	100	28.0
Portugal[c]	18	100	18.0
Spain[c]	16	75	12.0
Sweden[ch]	65	74	48.1
Switzerland[ci]	8	100	8.0
United Kingdom[cj]	18	45	8.1

Notes:

[a] Corresponds to the amount of benefits as a percentage of regular wages.

[b] Index of maternity leave benefit, resulting from the multiplication of the number of weeks of leave by the wage replacement rate.

[c] In these countries, eligibility to maternity benefits is conditional on the employment status and/or the previous social insurance contribution of the woman.

[d] Since 1980 the duration of the maternity leave for the third and subsequent children is 26 weeks, instead of 16 weeks for the first two children.

[e] From 1981 to 1991, an additional (general) scheme was in force which provided women with flat-rate benefits during 12 weeks' leave.

[f] Under the Maternity Leave and Employment Protection Act of 1987, women are entitled to 12 months' leave, including two weeks during which they receive cash benefits.

[g] Women are entitled to between 28 weeks' leave payable at 100% of their regular wages, and 7 weeks' leave payable at 80% of their regular wages.

[h] Parents are entitled to 12 months' leave during which the parent on leave receives benefits equal to 90% of her/his previous earnings. A flat-rate benefit is paid during the following 3 months, and represents around 10% of female wages in manufacturing. Overall, this is equivalent to 15 months' leave at 74% of previous earnings.

[i] By legislation there is a compulsory 8-week leave after confinement. There is no national regulation concerning the pay during this leave. Depending on the collective agreement, benefits are paid for between 3 and 8 weeks at full wage. Mothers insured under a health insurance scheme are entitled to sick pay for a total of 10 weeks. For the purpose of this study, it was assumed that women are entitled to 8 weeks of leave during which they receive 100% of their previous earnings.

[j] The value of maternity benefits paid varies according to the duration of employment and number of hours worked. Data used here refer to a woman having worked full-time at least two years in the same employment. The benefits paid for the first six weeks are equal to 90% of her previous earnings, while the following 12 weeks are paid at a flat rate representing around 25% of the female wages in manufacturing. Overall, this is equivalent to 18 weeks paid at 45% of previous earnings. Changes to the scheme were announced following the 1992 EC directive on maternity.

Sources: The following official sources were used, as well as information provided by relevant authorities in each country: EC Commission various years; Council of Europe various years.

had adopted legislation concerning the duration of unpaid leave, while five had introduced some form of cash benefits (United States 1990). Taking into account these public schemes, as well as those sponsored by employers Kamerman and Kahn (1987: 56) have estimated that 'fewer than 40 percent of working women have income protection at the time of maternity that will permit them a six-week leave without severe financial penalty'. In Australia, since 1979 maternity leave benefits have been widely available through federal and state awards. It is estimated that 94 per cent of female wage and salary earners are covered by a paid or unpaid scheme (Glezer 1988: 15).

But again, this inter-country comparison is seriously limited, in four ways. First, it ignores differences between countries in the coverage of benefits. Strict eligibility criteria, in terms of duration of employment, number of hours of work, and category of employment, mean that in some countries a fraction of women are not covered by any form of maternity leave. But the legislation in this field is complex and, although information is available on the eligibility rules, few data are available on the actual proportion of women not covered by the schemes. In some cases, the proportion can be considerable. For example, in Britain, a study conducted on women having had a baby in 1987–8 revealed that as many as 20 per cent of women in employment during pregnancy did not receive any form of maternity pay (McRae 1991). It should however be noted that the maternity directive adopted by the EC in 1992 restricted the eligibility period to a maximum of twelve months immediately before the presumed date of confinement. Within this limit, it is left to national governments to set conditions for eligibility for maternity leave and pay. The directive also required the benefits to be at least equivalent to those paid under the sickness insurance regimes (CREW 1992).

Second, the data presented above ignore the fact that, in some countries, including Belgium, Canada, Denmark, France, Germany, Greece, Ireland, and the Netherlands, ceilings are imposed on maternity leave benefits. As a result, the amount actually received by women may represent a lower proportion of earnings than that shown in table 9.2. For example, estimates for Denmark suggest that benefits actually received during maternity leave represent less than 70 per cent of the average wages of economically active women, as compared to the theoretical wage replacement rate of 90 per cent (Vedel-Petersen 1990). Unfortunately, no comparable data are available on the proportion of women affected by such restrictions.

Third, the data presented above do not reflect the fact that some women are eligible, in addition to the state benefits, to additional benefits provided by their employers. Again little is known about the proportion of women eligible for such occupational benefits. The few studies which have looked at this issue have revealed that this proportion can be considerable. For example, in Britain, McRae's study has revealed that 14 per cent of women received additional occupational benefits. Comparable data for the other countries are unfortunately not readily available.

Finally, the above data are restricted to only one form of work-related benefits and ignore other types of benefits such as flexitime, part-time work opportunities, and sick-child leave. Sweden is exceptional in the degree of flexibility of its parental leave scheme, which can be shared between parents, taken on a part-time or full-time basis, and spread until the child's fourth birthday. Parents in Sweden are also entitled to leave to look after sick children (120 days per year per child), and have been granted the right to part-time work since 1979 (Sundström 1991: 188).

The same limitations apply to benefits provided in the form of extended child-care leave. In recent years, an increasing number of countries have introduced this type of benefit, which gives mothers (and fathers in some cases) the opportunity to take an extended period of leave to look after their small children while retaining job security. In 1990, sixteen countries offered such leave (see table 9.3). Seven offered cash benefits, in the others the leave was unpaid.

Again, the schemes vary widely in terms of pay and duration. The information reported here can however be misleading to a certain extent since, as a result of strict eligibility criteria, only a fraction of women are actually entitled to these schemes, and when they are, only a fraction of them actually take advantage of them. Again, this points to the great heterogeneity among women in terms of entitlement to, and actual receipt of, benefits. For example, in Austria, it has been estimated that only 60 per cent of women are eligible for the extended leave, but that 95 per cent of those eligible actually took it (Badelt 1991: 32). No comparable data for the other countries are available.

TABLE 9.3. *Child-care leave schemes in countries of Europe, 1990*[a]

	Duration (in months)
Paid optional leave	
Finland	36
France[b]	36
Austria	24
Luxemburg	24
Germany (West)[c]	18
Belgium[d]	12[i]
Italy[e]	12
Unpaid optional leave	
Spain	36
Portugal	24
Sweden[f]	18[i]
Norway	12
United Kingdom	10
Greece[g]	6[i]
Netherlands[h]	6[i]
Switzerland	4
Ireland	3.5

Notes:
[a] Refers to the period during which mothers (and fathers in some cases) can be absent from work in connection with childbirth. It includes the period, after childbirth, covered by the paid maternity leave (see exceptions below). During this period, parents are protected against dismissal.
[b] Only women with 3 or more children are entitled to the child-care benefit. But all women are entitled to unpaid leave until the child's third birthday.
[c] Flat-rate benefits are paid to women during the first 6 months of the leave. Thereafter, benefits are means-tested.
[d] The leave is part of the 'interruption of professional career scheme', which can be taken for several reasons including child-care.
[e] Women are entitled to one year's leave. Benefits equivalent to 30% of previous earnings are paid for 6 months.
[f] This leave is under labour law and is independent of the maternity/parental leave scheme. It permits parents to take unpaid leave until the child reaches 18 months. Parents can then decide to prolong this leave with the paid parental leave (which unlike other countries is not tied to the immediate period surrounding childbirth, but can be taken until the child reaches 4 years). Alternatively, they may combine both the paid and unpaid leave until the child reaches 18 months.
[g] The unpaid leave introduced in 1984 entitles each parent to 3 months' leave.
[h] The leave can only be taken on a part-time basis (with a minimum of 20 hours of work per week) before the child reaches 4 years old.
[i] Excludes the period covered by the paid maternity leave.
Sources: The following official sources were used, as well as information provided by relevant authorities in each country: EC Commission various years; Council of Europe various years.

The third form of state support considered here concerns the provision for child-care. Here again, the provision can take several forms: subsidies to child-care institutions, reduced price for parents, direct cash benefits to parents, and so on. Major differences can also be found with regard to the quality and flexibility of the child-care arrangements. Comprehensive cross-national data in this respect are limited. Rough estimates of the public provision for child-care are given in table 9.4 and express the percentage of children enrolled in publicly funded day-care institutions as a

TABLE 9.4. *Public provision of child-care in selected countries, 1988*

	Percentage of all children under school age enrolled in publicly funded day-care institutions	
	Children aged 3 to school age	Children under 3
Belgium	>95	20
France	>95	20
Italy[a]	>85	5
Denmark[c]	85	50
Sweden[b]	80	30
Greece	65	5
Germany[b]	65	5
Spain	65	n.a.
Luxemburg[c]	55	<5
Netherlands	50	<5
Finland[b]	50	20
Norway[b]	50	10
United Kingdom	35	<5
Portugal	35	5
Japan[bd]	20	n.a.
Canada[b]	15	<5
Australia[cd]	5	n.a.

Notes: These figures include both part-time and full-time care, as well as subsidized family home-care, and pre-primary school institutions.
[a] 1986 figures.
[b] 1987 figures.
[c] 1989 figures.
[d] Children aged 0–5.
Sources: Moss 1990, Nordic Council (various years), Yearbook of Nordic Statistics; OECD 1990.

percentage of children of pre-school age. Differences between countries are wide, with Belgium and France offering extensive provision through their networks of crèches and *écoles maternelles*. Differences within countries are also important. For example, some parents will have access to workplace nurseries or to employers' subsidized nurseries, and some parents (for example, low-income or lone-parent families) may be given priority access to public child-care. Moreover, when the provision of child-care is decentralized and in the hands of local authorities, wide variation may also be found in terms of the availability of child-care and its cost. Again, data on these additional sources of heterogeneity are missing.

Thus, to sum up, there are clear differences between countries in the level of state support for families. But, behind these differences, there are also many differences within countries that may have a significant impact on families.

9.5 Empirical Findings

In view of these wide disparities between countries in state support for families, cross-national comparisons may constitute a relatively good research design to assess the effects of welfare benefits on families. In the absence of real experiments, these inter-country differences may be considered as quasi-experiments. However, such a design overlooks the intra-country heterogeneity which was underlined in the previous section. Not surprisingly, among the studies reviewed below, most have not opted for such a research design, and instead have used individual data to assess the effects of welfare benefits. If the use of such data overcomes the problem of intra-country heterogeneity, it is not exempt from other methodological limitations. In particular, a serious limitation arises because most surveys on family and employment histories have failed to collect data concerning the individuals' and families' entitlement to benefits, and their actual receipt of benefits. Because of this deficiency, attempts to assess the effects of welfare benefits on families had to be based on estimated, or imputed, values of welfare benefits, rather than on observed ones. This limitation will be apparent in the studies which are reviewed in this section. In view of the relatively large number of empirical studies on the effects of welfare benefits, this review will be restricted to some of the most recent or most comprehensive studies. Furthermore, because of limited access to the literature, greater prominence will here be given to British and American studies. The over-representation of studies from these two countries also reflects the greater attention that has been given in these countries to the effects of welfare benefits on families. Below, I concentrate on the effects of welfare benefits on three aspects of family life: fertility, family structure, and female employment. For each, I highlight some of the main methodological features of the selected studies, and comment briefly on their findings.

The effects on fertility

I start this review with some of the main studies which have analysed the effects of welfare benefits on fertility. These studies are summarized in table 9.5, and fall into two categories: those based on aggregate data, and those based on individual data. Among the first group, the study of Ekert (1986) exploits the differences between countries in fertility levels and cash benefits in order to assess the effects of benefits on fertility. This study of eight member states of the EC suggested that higher cash benefits have a slightly positive effect on fertility, of the order of 0.2 child per woman for cash benefits equivalent to those provided by the French system.

This result was confirmed in a later paper by Blanchet and Ekert-Jaffé (1988), this time on the basis of eleven EC and Nordic countries. Although these two studies seem to support the pronatalist hypothesis, their conclusions have to be interpreted with great care for at least two reasons. First, the studies take into account only limited forms of welfare benefits (family allowances and some means-tested benefits). Second, being based on aggregate data, they ignore potential inter- and intra-country differences with respect to the effects of benefits. In particular, it is assumed that the same fertility-welfare benefit relationship applies equally to all countries, and to all sub-groups within each country.

In view of these criticisms, the study by Gauthier (1991), of twenty-two industrialized countries, is therefore more satisfactory since (a) it considers not only cash benefits, but also maternity leave benefits and child-care facilities, and (b) it also takes into

TABLE 9.5. *Effects of welfare benefits on fertility: summary of studies*

	Country	Data type[a]	Dependent variable	Independent variables	I/O[b]
Aggregate data					
Ekert (1986)	8 EC	P	Total fertility rate	Cash benefit index	
Blanchet and Ekert-Jaffé (1988)	11 EC & Nordic	P	Total fertility rate	Cash benefit index	
Gauthier (1991)	22 industrialized	P	Total fertility rate	Cash, maternity, child-care[i]	
Ermisch (1988)	UK	TS	Conditional birth rate[g]	Child benefit	
Individual data					
Barmby and Cigno (1988)	UK	LH[c]	Parity-specific birth rate	Child benefit	I
Robins and Blau (1991)	US	LH[d]	Probit presence of children aged 0–5	Cost of child-care Child-care tax credit AFDC benefit	I
Blau and Robins (1989)	US	LH[e]	Hazard rates fertility/ employment[h]	Cost of child-care Child-care tax credit	I
Whittington (1992)	US	LH[f]	Conditional fertility logit[h]	Tax exemption Child-care tax credit	I

Notes:

[a] Types of data: P: Pooled cross-sectional and time-series data; TS: Time-series data; LH: Life-history data.

[b] I/O: Data on welfare benefits either Imputed or Observed.

[c] 1980 Women and Employment Survey (women aged 16–59).

[d] National Longitudinal Survey of Youth (women aged 14–21 in 1979); data used from 1982 to 1986 surveys.

[e] Employment Opportunity Pilot Projects Survey (married women in 1980).

[f] Panel Study of Income Dynamics (married women aged 15–44); data used from 1977 to 1983 surveys.

[g] Parity-specific indices.

[h] These dependent variables are not parity specific.

[i] Indices of cash benefits, maternity leave benefits, and child-care facilities.

account a first level of heterogeneity in showing that the effects of welfare benefits on fertility tend to vary across countries. But, like the other two studies, this one also uses as dependent variable the total period fertility rate—an index highly sensitive to changes in the timing of births. The potential bias here is serious, especially in view of the trend since the 1960s towards increasing age at entry into motherhood. This index may therefore not be appropriate if one expects benefits to have an effect on both the number of births, and their timing, and to have a differential effect by birth order. From this point of view, the study by Ermisch (1988) on fertility in Britain is methodologically and substantively more satisfactory as it uses as dependent variable a parity-specific index. The results confirm the heterogeneity overlooked in the previous studies in suggesting that higher child benefits have an effect on the completed family size, by encouraging the birth of a third and fourth child, and have also an effect on the timing of births, by encouraging early motherhood.

Like previous studies, Ermisch's analysis was conducted at the aggregate level and ignored potential intra-country differences. The other studies reported in table 9.5, carried out on the basis of individual data, consequently represent a further step. They are, however, also limited since, in all cases, data on welfare benefits were imputed rather than observed, and since they have failed to acknowledge the potential differential effects of benefits upon various sub-groups of the population. The first of these studies, that of Barmby and Cigno (1988), uses life-history data from the British 1980 Women and Employment Survey. Data on cash benefits are here imputed and restricted to the universal child benefit. They find, as Ermisch (1988) did, that higher benefits encourage early motherhood. However, their results contradict Ermisch by concluding that benefits lower, rather than raise, completed fertility. Unfortunately, this study does not take into consideration other cash benefits such as tax-related and means-tested benefits, which may also have an effect on fertility.

The other (American) studies reported in table 9.5 are more comprehensive since they include other forms of cash benefits. However, these other benefits were again not directly observed in the surveys, but had instead to be imputed on the basis of the characteristics of the families and their region of residence. Among them, the study of Blau and Robins (1989) carried out on the basis of life-history data of households in twenty geographical areas in the United States, suggested that higher child-care subsidies (through tax credit) have a small, but not significant, positive effect on the probability of having a child while employed, but no effect on non-employed women. Using a similar framework of analysis, but this time nationally representative data from the National Longitudinal Survey of Youth, Robins and Blau (1991) found that child-care tax credit and AFDC benefits both have a statistically significant effect on fertility (measured through the presence of a pre-school-age child). On the other hand, and as expected, higher child-care costs have a negative effect on fertility. A similar conclusion emerges from the study of Whittington (1992) on the basis of data from the Panel Study of Income Dynamics, in which the author finds some evidence that higher tax-related benefits have an effect on both the timing of births and the number of children.

These studies consequently appear partly to support the pro-natalist hypothesis. In view of their methodological limitations, their findings cannot, however, constitute strong evidence. Not only were data on benefits imputed rather than observed, but also these studies have not examined the possibility of differential effects of benefits upon different sub-groups of the population. In particular these studies ignore the potential effect of housing benefits on fertility. This effect has been tested only indirectly through indices such as housing cost (see Ermisch 1988) and housing tenure (see Murphy and Sullivan 1985). These indirect measures suggest that housing has a determinant effect on both fertility and family structure.

Effects on family structure

The second set of studies examined here addressed the question of the effects of welfare benefits on the entry into lone parenthood, for married or never-married women, and on the exit from lone parenthood. Some of these studies are summarized in table 9.6, and once again they vary widely in terms of research design and variables used. The first series is concerned with the entry into lone parenthood, either through a birth outside wedlock, for never-married women, or through divorce, for married women. Among these studies, that of Duncan and Hoffman (1991), based on data

TABLE 9.6. *Effects of welfare benefits on family structure: summary of studies*

	Country	Data type[a]	Dependent variable	Independent variables	I/O[b]
Entry into lone parenthood					
Ermisch (1991)	UK	LH[c]	Hazard rate of pre-marital birth	Supplementary benefits	I
Duncan and Hoffman (1991)	US	LH[d]	Probability of birth out of wedlock	AFDC benefits	I
Bishop (1980)	US	LH[e]	Probability of divorce	Negative income tax	O
Exit from lone parenthood					
Ermisch (1991)	UK	LH[f]	Hazard rate of remarriage	Supplementary benefits	I

Notes:
[a] Types of data: LH: Life-history data.
[b] I/O: Data on welfare benefits either Imputed or Observed.
[c] 1980 Women and Employment Survey.
[d] Panel Study of Income Dynamics (black women aged 25 in 1980–5).
[e] Four Income Maintenance Experiments (Seattle-Denver, Gary, New Jersey, Rural).
[f] 1980 Women and Employment Survey.

from the Panel Study of Income Dynamics, analyses the effect of AFDC benefits on the probability of having a child out of wedlock for black teenage girls. The study, which uses imputed data on welfare benefits, reveals that girls living in States with higher AFDC benefits were more likely to have a child out of wedlock. This effect appeared, however, to be small when other background variables, notably parental income, are taken into account. The probability of having a pre-marital birth was also investigated by Ermisch (1991) on the basis of data from the British Women and Employment Survey. In this study, the author found that welfare benefits (as measured by the imputed value of means-tested supplementary benefits that a mother with one child would receive) have a slight positive effect on the likelihood of a pre-marital birth. This effect was, however, found to be once again small. For example, it was estimated that a 10 per cent increase in welfare benefits raises the percentage of women having a pre-marital birth by less than two percentage points (Ermisch 1991: 79). Having a child out of wedlock is the first point of entry into lone parenthood. The second, through divorce, has also been analysed in several studies. Among them, the evidence reviewed by Bishop (1980) comes from a study of a completely different nature, in which the demographic behaviour of experimental groups, subject to specific benefits, were compared to that of control groups. The whole experiment, known as the Negative Income Tax experiment, was started in the late 1960s at a time when the American government was looking for welfare solutions which would alleviate poverty among families, but without creating welfare dependency. The solution tested consisted of extending welfare benefits (previously restricted to one-parent families) to two-parent families, in addition to providing them with a minimum guaranteed income, above which all earned and unearned income were subject to taxes. Results from this experiment have been highly controversial. especially those from the Seattle-Denver experiment which suggested that the Negative Income Tax increased the likelihood of divorce by as much as 50 per cent (Bishop 1980; Garfinkel and McLanahan 1986: 60). In fact, as reported by Berkowitz (1991: 137), the results generated more confusion than the neat answer politicians were looking for. Not surprisingly, given this confusion, the suggested welfare reform was never extended beyond this experiment.

The second series of studies refer to the effect of welfare benefits on the exit from lone parenthood, through remarriage for once-married women, or through a first marriage for never-married mothers. In particular, it should be remembered that, according to the American right-wing hypothesis, higher welfare benefits are expected to discourage remarriage and discourage pregnant single women from marrying. This hypothesis does not, however, seem to be supported by studies such as that of Ermisch (1991), which found no evidence to support the hypothesis that higher welfare benefits may involuntarily prolong lone parenthood by discouraging remarriage. This result is consistent with other American studies not reported here (see Ermisch 1991: 152). On the other hand, other studies have suggested that the main effect of welfare benefits is not directly on the probability of remarriage, but instead on the living arrangement of the lone mother in allowing her to establish an independent residence rather than having to live with her own parents (see Garfinkel and McLanahan 1986: 58). This last result thus suggests that studies on the effects of welfare benefits should focus not only on the marital status of the mother, but also on her living arrangements. But, here again, considerable heterogeneity could be found, for example, between economically active and economically inactive women, between women who regularly receive maintenance allowance and those who do not, and between women who have easy access to informal (and cheap) child-care arrangements, and those who do not. Unfortunately, the studies reviewed above do not explicitly take into account these sources of heterogeneity.

Effect on female labour-force participation

The third set of studies reviewed here examine the effects of welfare benefits on the probability of women taking up paid employment. Again this question has attracted considerable interest in Britain and the United States as part of the general concern about the work disincentive nature of welfare benefits. Some of these studies are summarized in table 9.7, and have been grouped for the purpose of the analysis into two categories: one concerned with the employment behaviour of married women, the other with that of lone mothers. As with the other studies reviewed above, one of the main limitations of these empirical studies is the use of imputed rather than observed data on welfare benefits. Among the first group of studies, that of Heckman (1974) was one of the first to examine the effects of child-care programmes on women's work. It did so only indirectly, through a derived measure of the cost of child-care. The results confirmed the expected relationship, that higher child-care costs reduce the participation of women in the labour force. By extension, the author concluded that subsidies for child-care should have the opposite effect, and encourage female labour-force participation. This conclusion was partly supported by subsequent studies. For instance, Blau and Robins (1989) also found that higher child-care costs have a negative effect on employment, by encouraging exit from paid employment, and by deterring

TABLE 9.7. *Effects of welfare benefits on female employment: summary of studies*

	Country	Data type[a]	Dependent variable	Independent variables	I/O[b]
Married women					
McRae (1991)	UK	LH[c]	Return to work after childbirth	Maternity pay	O
Robins and Blau (1991)	UK	LH[d]	Probit of employment	Cost of child-care Child-care tax credit AFDC benefit	I
Blau and Robins (1989)	US	LH[e]	Hazard rates fertility/ employment	Cost of child-care Child-care tax credit	I
Robins, Tuma, and Yeager (1980)	US	LH[f]	Probability of being employed	Negative income tax	O
Lone mothers					
Ermisch (1991)	UK	P[g]	Probability of being employed	Supplementary benefits	I
Ermisch and Wright (1991)	UK	LH[h]	Entry/exit from employment	Supplementary benefits Maintenance allowance	I
Jenkins (1992)	UK	LH[i]	Probability of being employed	Housing benefits Maintenance allowance Cost of child-care	I O I

TABLE 9.7. (*cont.*)

	Country	Data type[a]	Dependent variable	Independent variables	I/O[b]
Walker (1990)	UK	P[j]	Probability of being employed	Supplementary benefits	I
				Maintenance allowance Family income supplement &	O
				Housing benefits	I
Blank (1985)	US	CS[k]	Labour-force participation	AFDC benefits	O
Hausman (1980)	US	LH[l]	Labour-force participation	Negative income tax	O
Moffitt (1983)	US	LH[m]	Labour-force participation	AFDC benefits	I

Notes:
[a] Types of data: LH: Life-history data; P: Panel data; CS: Cross-sectional data.
[b] I/O: Data on welfare benefits either Imputed or Observed.
[c] Nationally representative sample of women who had babies Dec. 1987–Jan. 1988.
[d] National Longitudinal Survey of Youth (women aged 14–21 in 1979); data used from 1982 to 1986 surveys.
[e] Employment Opportunity Pilot Projects Survey (married women in 1980).
[f] Seattle–Denver experiment (including both married women and lone mothers).
[g] General Household Survey; data used from 1973 to 1982 surveys (sample restricted to female-headed households).
[h] 1980 Women and Employment Survey.
[i] 1989 Lone Parents Survey.
[j] Family Expenditures Survey; data used from 1979 to 1984 surveys.
[k] Current Population Survey's March Supplement 1979 (sample used restricted to female-headed households).
[l] Gary maintenance income experiment 1971–4 (sample used restricted to black female-headed households).
[m] Panel Study of Income Dynamics (sample used restricted to female-headed households).

entry into it. Furthermore, they also found that subsidies to child-care, in the form of tax credit, have the opposite effect in reducing departure from paid employment. No significant effect was, however, found with respect to the entry into paid employment. In a later study, Robins and Blau (1991) came up with a slightly different set of findings, and concluded that, contrary to expectation, higher child-care costs have no effect on the likelihood of taking up paid employment. Tax credit for child-care was, however, again found to have a positive effect on employment.

Robins and Blau (1991) also addressed the question of the effect of cash transfers on employment. As expected, they found that the means-tested AFDC payments have a disincentive effect on employment. This result confirmed what had emerged from the Negative Income Tax Experiment some years earlier when guaranteed income had been found to have a disincentive effect on employment by increasing the duration of non-employment by 42 per cent for married women, and by 60 per cent for lone mothers (results from the Seattle-Denver experiment, reported by Robins, Tuma, and Yeager 1980).

The previous studies examined the effects of both direct and tax-related cash transfers. None considered the potential effect on employment of maternity-related benefits. The study of McRae (1991) therefore represents a valuable contribution. Based on a survey of women who had a baby in 1987–8, this study examines the employment pattern of women nine months after childbirth. As expected, the receipt of higher maternity leave benefits seems to be associated with a greater propensity to return to work after childbirth. In particular, it was found that women in receipt of contractual maternity pay (occupational benefits) were two and one-half times more likely to return to work after childbirth than women on ordinary public maternity pay (McRae 1991: 232). Although this result is supported by theory, it may however also be a reflection of the nature of these benefits since the obligation to return to work after childbirth is often associated with the receipt of private benefit. On the other hand, this study also found that ineligibility for public maternity benefits, or eligibility only for reduced maternity benefits, had no significant effect on employment.

We turn now to studies of the employment behaviour of lone mothers. The studies by Ermisch (1991), Jenkins (1992), and Walker (1990), based on British data, all found that supplementary benefits, in the form of income support, had a disincentive effect in lowering the probability of employment of lone mothers. On the other hand, Ermisch and Wright (1991), also based on British data, did not find any evidence to support such a conclusion. Other studies on the effect on employment of other types of cash benefits have also found no evidence in support of the disincentive hypothesis. Instead it was found that maintenance allowance (Jenkins 1992; Walker 1990), family income supplement, and housing benefit (Walker 1990) all have a positive effect on employment. These contradictions may be partly explained by the different nature and eligibility rules of cash benefits (e.g. the extent to which they penalize earned and unearned income). In Britain, the three welfare benefit schemes (Family Credit, Income Support, and Housing Benefit) are means-tested and are dependent on the work status of the claimant. Family Credit (which replaced the former Family Income Supplement in April 1988) is payable to parents who work at least sixteen hours per week, while Income Support (which replaced the former Supplementary Benefits in April 1988) is payable to those who work less than sixteen hours per week or who, if unemployed, are available for work (this qualification does not apply to lone parents). Families with savings or assets above £8,000 are not eligible for either benefit. For others, the amount of benefits to which they are entitled is reduced by 70 pence for each £1 of income in excess of £3,000 (savings between £3,000 and £8,000 are treated as if each £250 is equivalent to bringing in an income of £1 per week). The rules governing Housing Benefit are similar, but the amount of benefit, and the tax on excess income, vary according to whether claimants are receiving Income Support or not. It should also be noted that receipt of maintenance allowance is taken into account in the calculation of a claimant's disposable income.

Several of the American studies also highlight the potential disincentive effect of cash benefits on employment. For instance, Blank (1985) concluded that higher AFDC benefits have a deterrent effect in reducing the number of hours of work. Moffitt (1983) reached a similar conclusion, and also pointed out that the disincentive effect of welfare benefits was small in comparison to the effect of other non-benefit variables. Finally, Hausman (1980) also underlined the potential deterrent effect of welfare benefits on employment. His study, based on the Negative Income Tax experiment, suggests that higher marginal tax rate and higher transfer payments both reduce the probability of taking up paid employment.

In general, these studies support the hypothesis that higher cash benefits can have a deterrent effect on employment; a finding with important policy implications. However, several of these studies were based on imputed data of welfare benefits rather than on observed data. Moreover, these studies do not take into account the problem that the take-up of benefit may actually be far from complete—thus introducing a considerable methodological bias. For example, in Britain it is estimated that less than 60 per cent of families eligible to the means-tested Family Credit actually claim it (Department of Social Security (Britain) 1993: 22), while in the United States, a non-take-up rate of 25 per cent with regard to AFDC benefits was found among female-headed households (Moffitt 1983: 1028). The above studies did not examine the potential heterogeneity in the effect of benefits between welfare recipients, eligible persons who did not receive benefits, and ineligible non-recipients. This methodological point, along with others which came to light in the previous review, are summarized in the last section of this chapter. At this point, it should be pointed out that only the study of Moffitt (1983) directly addresses the problem of non-take-up of benefits. It does so through an evaluation of the effect on employment of the stigmatizing aspect of means-tested benefits. The results of this study underline further the heterogeneity bias which was discussed earlier, in suggesting that perceived stigma affects the decision to join a welfare programme, but that once a person becomes a recipient of welfare, benefit levels have no additional behavioural or stigmatizing effects.

9.6 Conclusion: The Way Forward

From the above review, it is possible to make at least four methodological points about ways of assessing the effects of welfare benefits. First, individual rather than aggregate data appear to be essential to capture the heterogeneity among the population in terms of the entitlement to benefits, and the receipt of them. Second, the analysis should cover not only universal benefits, but also means-tested benefits, tax-related benefits, as well as private (occupational) benefits. In addition, the indices of family benefits should also distinguish welfare recipients from eligible and ineligible non-recipients. Third, the analysis should be designed so as to reflect the potentially differential effects of benefits for different sub-groups of the population (for example, low income versus high income). And finally, the analysis should also consider the potentially variable effects of benefits according to the relative value of the wife's earnings as compared with the household total income. Failure to incorporate such points may partly account for the inconclusive findings of several of the empirical studies reviewed in the previous section. But the non-availability of data is obviously the main limitation and still prevents methodologically more satisfactory analyses.

A further point needs to be considered. Both in the theoretical discussion in sections 9.2 and 9.3, and in the empirical review in section 9.5, the effects of welfare benefits on fertility, family structure, and female employment were considered separately. It must be asked whether this is a methodologically sound way of addressing the question of the effects of benefits. It may be more satisfactory to consider these three aspects of family life as the result of a combined household strategy, rather than as the result of separate behaviour. The decision to have, or not to have, a child does not take place in a vacuum, but instead involves other considerations related to fertility (for example, desired family size and timing of birth), and female employment (such as a woman's career prospects and aspirations). This decision may also involve economic considerations, in terms of the family's current and foreseeable financial situation, as well as normative ones. For example, the fertility decision may be partly dependent on whether or not the well-being of the child is believed to depend on whether the mother stays at home during the pre-school years. Alternatively, a woman may consider other options such as returning to work between births, having children within a very short interval so as to minimize the time off work, or returning to work only on a part-time basis. The fertility decision may consequently be closely interlinked with that on female employment. Similar logic may also be applied to lone parents for whom the presence of children, the possibility of (re)marriage, and the take-up of paid employment may all be closely interrelated, and part of a general strategy. This general strategy may be driven by three objectives:

(a) The desire to *maximize the psychological well-being of children,* for example in having few rather than several children, in assuring the presence of a parent at home rather than sending children to a day-care centre from a very young age, or in (re)marrying as rapidly as possible so as to minimize the time spent in lone parenthood.

(b) The desire to *minimize the opportunity cost of children,* or to maximize the woman's career opportunities, for example in remaining childless, in returning to work immediately after childbirth, in sharing parental leave between the mother and the father, or in having children separated by a short or long interval.

(c) The desire to *maximize the family's income and well-being*, for example in remaining childless, in returning to work shortly after childbirth, or in not (re)marrying if it is financially advantageous to remain a lone parent.

These three objectives are not exhaustive, and one may also want to include additional considerations linked with other forms of consumption (such as the desire to acquire a house in relation to other goals), or other forms of contingency (for example, the potential risk of unemployment in relation to future plans). There is no way for a family to maximize all these objectives, and a trade-off becomes necessary, which will be function of a series of economic and normative factors, including the couple's preferences, and the availability of welfare benefits. The methodological implications are that welfare benefits do not influence decisions about fertility, employment, and family structure separately but all together. Among the studies reviewed in the previous section, only those of Blau and Robins (1989) and Robins and Blau (1991) take into account the potential interdependence between fertility and employment decisions. Obviously, the notion of strategy and planning implies a high degree of rationality, and some may argue that it may overestimate the rationality of individuals. However, it may also be argued that in a context of quasi-perfect control of fertility, and of an apparent deliberate trend towards late entry into parenthood, this notion of a global family/employment strategy may provide a useful framework of analysis, in addition to providing better insights on the effects of welfare benefits on families.

Bearing in mind these methodological limitations and considerations, what can we conclude about the effects of state support for families and their implications on Europe's future demographic trends? First, it should be obvious that even if welfare benefits have an effect on demographic behaviour, this effect is likely to be very small as compared to other factors. It is improbable that we would observe a significant increase in fertility as a result of a higher level of state support for families, or that we would observe much less instability among families by eliminating some of the benefits directly targeted at lone-parents. For if the 'pro-natalist' hypothesis and the 'unintended family breakdown' hypothesis are partly supported by empirical evidence, the magnitude of the effect of welfare benefits on demographic behaviour is very small. Second, since other determinants, such as education and income, are likely to have more effect on demographic behaviour than welfare benefits, it follows that any attempt to influence demographic behaviour could be enhanced by combining interventions on welfare benefits with interventions elsewhere, for example on education and unemployment. European governments may therefore want to direct their efforts towards a general family support plan, rather than a strictly defined family policy. The question of legitimacy of state intervention however remains, and with it the question of public/private boundaries of family and demographic behaviour.

REFERENCES

BADELT, C. (1991), 'Austria: Family, work, paid employment, and family policy', in S.B. Kamerman and A. J. Kahn (eds.), *Child Care, Parental Leave, and the Under 3s; Policy Innovations in Europe*, New York: Auburn House.

BARMBY, T., and CIGNO, A. (1988), 'A sequential probability model of fertility patterns', *Discussion Paper* No. 160, Department of Economics and Commerce, University of Hull.

BERKOWITZ, E. D. (1991), *America's Welfare State; From Roosevelt to Reagan*, Baltimore: The Johns Hopkins University Press.

BISHOP, J. H. (1980), 'Jobs, cash transfers and marital instability: a review and synthesis of the evidence', *The Journal of Human Resources*, 15(3): 301–33.

BLAKE, J. (1968), 'Are babies consumer durables? A critique of the economic theory of reproductive motivation', *Population Studies*, 22(1): 5–25.

BLANCHET, D., and EKERT-JAFFÉ, O. (1988), 'The demographic impact of family benefits: evidence from a micromodel and from macro-data', Paper presented at the IUSSP seminar on the family, the market and the state in ageing societies (Japan, August 1988).

BLANK, R. M. (1985), 'The impact of state economic differentials on household welfare and labor force behavior', *Journal of Public Economics*, 28: 25–58.

BLAU, D. M., and ROBINS, P. K. (1989), 'Fertility, employment, and child-care costs', *Demography*, 26(2): 287–300.

BRADSHAW, J., and PIACHAUD, D. (1980), *Child Support in the European Community*, London: Bedford Square Press.

COUNCIL of EUROPE (various years), *Comparative Tables of the Social Security Schemes*. Strasburg: Council of Europe.

CREW (1992), 'Maternity Directive gets last minute go-ahead', *Reports*, 12: 10.

DEPARTMENT OF SOCIAL SECURITY (BRITAIN) (1993), *Income Related Benefits Estimates of Take Up in 1989*, London: DSS.

DUNCAN, G. J., and HOFFMAN, S. D. (1991), 'Teenage underclass behavior and subsequent poverty: Have the rules changed?', in C. Jencks and P. E. Peterson (eds.), *The Urban Underclass*, Washington, DC: The Brookings Institution.

EC COMMISSION (various years). *Comparative Tables of the Social Security Schemes*, Luxemburg: office for the Official Publications of the European Communities.

EKERT, O. (1986), 'Effets et limites des aides financières aux familles: une expérience et un modèle', *Population*, 2: 327–48.

ERMISCH, J. (1988). 'Econometric analysis of birth rate dynamics in Britain', *The Journal of Human Resources*, 23(4): 563–76.

—— (1991), *Lone Parenthood: An Economic Analysis*, Cambridge: Cambridge University Press.

—— and WRIGHT, R. E. (1991), 'Employment dynamics among British single mothers', *Oxford Bulletin of Economics and Statistics*, 53(2): 99–122.

GARFINKEL, I., and MCLANAHAN, S. S. (1986), *Single Mothers and their Children: A New American Dilemma*, Washington, DC: The Urban Institute Press.

GAUTHIER, A. H. (1991), *Family Policies in Comparative Perspective*, Discussion Paper No. 5, Oxford: Centre for European Studies, Nuffield College.

GLEZER, H. (1988), *Maternity Leave in Australia; Employee and Employer Experiences, Report of a Survey*, Melbourne: Australian Institute of Family Studies.

HAAS, L. (1990), 'Gender equality and social policy—Implications of a study of parental leave in Sweden', Paper presented at the Twelfth World Congress of Sociology, Madrid, July 1990.

HAUSMAN, J. A. (1980), 'The effect of wages, taxes, and fixed costs on women's labor force participation', *Journal of Public Economics*, 14: 161–94.

HECKMAN, J. J. (1974), 'Efforts of child-care programs on women's work effort', *Journal of Political Economy*, 82(2) (Suppl.): S136–69.

JENKINS, S. P. (1992), 'Lone mothers' employment and full-time work probabilities', *The Economic Journal*, 102: 310–20.

JOSHI, H. (1987), 'The cash opportunity costs of childbearing: an approach to estimation using British data', *Discussion Paper* No. 208, London: Centre for Economic Policy Research.

KAMERMAN, S. B., and KAHN, A. J. (1987), *The Responsive Workplace; Employers and a Changing Labor Force*, New York: Columbia University Press.

MCRAE, S. (1991), *Maternity Rights in Britain; The Experience of Women and Employers*, London: Policy Studies Institute.

—— (forthcoming), 'Labour supply after childbirth: Do employers' policies' matter?', *Journal of Sociology*.

MOEN, P. (1989), *Working Parents; Transformations in Gender Roles and Public Policies in Sweden*, London: Adamantine Press.

MOFFITT, R. (1983), 'An economic model of welfare stigma', *The American Economic Review*, 73(5): 1023–35.

MOSS, P. (1990), *Childcare in the European Communities 1985–1990*, Luxemburg: EC Commission.

MURPHY, M. J., and SULLIVAN, O. (1985), 'Housing tenure and family formation in contemporary Britain', *European Sociological Review*, 1(3): 230–43.

MURRAY, C. (1984), *Losing Ground: American Social Policy, 1950–1980*, New York: Basic Books.

NORDIC COUNCIL (various years), *Yearbook of Nordic Statistics*.

OECD (1990), 'Child-care in OECD countries', *Employment Outlook*, July: 123–51.

POPENOE, D. (1988), *Disturbing the Nest: Family Change and Decline in Modern Societies*, New York: Aldine de Gruyter.

—— (1991), 'Family decline in the Swedish welfare state', *Public Interest*, Winter.

ROBINS, P., and Blau, D. (1991), 'Child care demand and labor supply of young mothers over time', *Demography*, 28(3): 333–54.

—— Tuma, N. B., and Yeager, K. E. (1980), 'Effects of SIME/DIME on changes in employment status', *The Journal of Human Resources*, 15(4): 545–73.

SANDQVIST, K., and ANDERSSON, B.-E (1992), 'Thriving families in the Swedish welfare state', *Public Interest*, 109 (Fall).

SUNDSTRÖM, M. (1991), 'Sweden: Supporting work, family, and gender equality', in S. B. Kamerman and A. J. Kahn (eds.), *Child care, Parental Leave, and the Under 3s; Policy Innovations in Europe*, New York: Auburn House.

United States (various dates), Social Security Programs Throughout the World, Washington, DC: Department of Social Security Administration.

UNITED STATES. Women's Bureau, Department of Labor (1990), *Facts on Working Women*, 90(1) (June).

VEDEL-PETERSEN, J. (1990), Personal communication.

WALKER, I. (1990), 'The effects of income support measures on the labour market behaviour of lone mothers', *Fiscal Studies*, 11: 55–75.

WHITTINGTON, L. A. (1992), 'Taxes and the family: the impact of the tax exemption for dependants on marital fertility', *Demography*, 29(2): 215–26.

INDEX